Digital Humanities

Digital Humanities

Victoria Rogers
Declan Morrison

Kruger Brentt
Publishers
2026

Kruger Brentt Publishers UK. LTD.
Company Number 9728962

Regd. Office: 68 St Margarets Road, Edgware, Middlesex HA8 9UU

ISBN: 978-1-78715-609-8

For information on all our publications visit our website at http://krugerbrentt.com/

Preface

Digital Humanities is an emerging and rapidly expanding interdisciplinary field that integrates computational methods with the study of arts, culture, history, and society. This book is designed to introduce readers to the core principles, practices, and debates that define digital humanities (DH) as both an academic discipline and a practical approach to cultural inquiry.

The book begins with a historical overview of the development of digital humanities, tracing its roots in humanities computing and its transformation into a diverse field that now encompasses text analysis, digital archives, cultural analytics, visualization, and digital storytelling. It explores how digital technologies not only provide new tools for research but also reshape the questions, methods, and perspectives of traditional humanities disciplines.

Central to this book is the examination of how digital platforms, big data, artificial intelligence, and interactive media have influenced scholarship, pedagogy, and public engagement with culture. Case studies highlight applications in literature, history, linguistics, art history, and cultural heritage, demonstrating how digital humanities projects create new opportunities for discovery, collaboration, and knowledge dissemination.

At the same time, the book engages with critical debates, including issues of accessibility, authorship, digital ethics, open knowledge, and the challenges of long-term digital preservation. By combining theory with practice, Digital Humanities offers a comprehensive introduction to the field, equipping students, researchers, and practitioners with the knowledge to critically engage with digital tools and cultural data.

This volume serves as a bridge between tradition and innovation, showing how digital humanities opens new pathways for understanding human culture in an increasingly interconnected and technologically mediated world.

Victoria Rogers

Declan Morrison

Contents

Preface v

1. Introduction to Digital Humanities 1

1.1 What Are Digital Humanities (DH)? 1

1.2 Historical Evolution of the Field 4

1.3 Key Debates and Definitions 6

1.4 Interdisciplinarity: Where Humanities Meet Technology 8

1.5 The Global Landscape of Digital Humanities 11

2. Foundational Conceptsand Methodologies 15

2.1 Digitization vs. Digital Scholarship 15

2.2 Quantitative and Qualitative Methods in DH 29

2.3 Data, Metadata, and Ontologies in Humanities Research 33

2.4 Annotation, Tagging, and Encoding Standards (TEI, XML, RDF) 36

2.5 Critical Theory in the Digital Age 38

3. Tools and Technologies in DH 43

3.1 Text Analysis and Natural Language Processing 43

3.2 Digital Archives and Repositories 62

3.3 Geographic Information Systems (GIS) for Humanities 65

3.4 Network Analysis and Visualization 74

3.5 3D Modeling and Virtual Reconstruction 82

3.6 Machine Learning and AI in Humanities Research 88

3.7 Digital Storytelling and Interactive Narratives 92

4. Digital Humanities Across Disciplines 97

4.1 Digital History 97

4.2 Digital Literary Studies 110

4.3 Digital Philosophy and Ethics 118

4.4 Digital Art History 125

4.5 Digital Linguistics and Corpus Analysis 141

4.6 Digital Religious Studies and Theology 144

4.7 Classics and Archaeology in the Digital Age 152

5. Pedagogy and Education in Digital Humanities 161

5.1 Teaching with Digital Tools 161

5.2 Digital Literacy in the Humanities Curriculum 166

5.3 Online and Hybrid Humanities Courses 170

5.4 Student-Centered DH Projects and Labs 173

5.5 Gamification and Interactive Learning Environments 180

6. Project Design and Management 185

6.1 Planning and Developing a DH Project 185

6.2 Data Curation and Management 190

6.3 Sustainability and Long-Term Preservation 194

6.4 Collaboration and Crowdsourcing in DH 198

6.5 Project Evaluation and Impact Assessment 205

6.6 Funding and Grant Writing for DH Initiatives 211

7. Publishing and Dissemination in DH 215

7.1 Digital Editions and Scholarly Publishing 215

7.2 Open Access and Licensing 222

7.3 Digital Journals and Online Platforms 225

7.4 Multimedia and Transmedia Storytelling 228

7.5 Podcasts, Blogs, and Public-Facing Scholarship 235

8. Ethics, Inclusion, and Critical DH 239

8.1 Ethics of Data Use and Representation 239

8.2 Algorithmic Bias and Humanities Research 242

8.3 Decolonizing Digital Humanities 242

8.4 Accessibility and Inclusive Design 245

8.5 Feminist and Queer Digital Humanities 247

9. Infrastructures and Institutions 249

9.1 DH Centers and Labs 249

9.2 Libraries, Museums, and Archives as DH Partners 249

9.3 DH Consortia and Professional Networks 250

9.4 Digital Humanities in the Global South 253

9.5 Policy and Institutional Support for DH 254

10. Future Directions in Digital Humanities 255

10.1 Emerging Technologies in DH 255

10.2 The Role of Artificial Intelligence and Large Language Models 258

10.3 Big Data, Small Data, and Thick Data in Humanities 259

10.4 The Post-Digital Turn and Critical Infrastructure Studies 260

10.5 Reimagining Scholarship in a Digital Culture 261

11. Case Studies and Exemplary Projects 263

11.1 Mapping the Republic of Letters 263

11.2 The Rossetti Archive 264

11.3 The Slave Voyages Project 266

11.4 Europeans and Other Large-Scale Cultural Portals 268

11.5 Local DH Projects and Community-Engaged Scholarship 269

12. Appendices 271

12.1 Glossary of Digital Humanities Terms 271

12.2 List of Key Tools and Platforms 279

12.3 Grant Agencies and Funding Opportunities 286

12.4 Recommended Readings and Online Resources 290

References 295

Index 299

CHAPTER 1

Introduction to Digital Humanities

1.1 WHAT ARE DIGITAL HUMANITIES (DH)?

Digital Humanities (DH) is an interdisciplinary field that integrates computational tools and methods with traditional humanities disciplines such as history, literature, philosophy, linguistics, and the arts. At its core, Digital Humanities represents a fusion of humanistic inquiry with the power of digital technology, facilitating new ways to explore, analyze, preserve, and present cultural and historical data. This domain is not merely about digitizing texts or artifacts, but about reimagining how knowledge is produced, accessed, and interpreted through digital means. Digital Humanities represents a transformative shift in the way scholars engage with cultural and historical materials.

By combining the analytical rigor of the humanities with the computational capabilities of digital tools, DH opens up new avenues for research, teaching, and public engagement. While the field faces important challenges, including issues of access, ethics, and disciplinary recognition, its collaborative, interdisciplinary, and innovative spirit holds great promise. As technology continues to reshape society, Digital Humanities provides a critical framework for understanding and interpreting the digital world, ensuring that humanistic inquiry remains vital and relevant in the twenty-first century.

1.1.1 Historical Development and Evolution of DH

The roots of Digital Humanities can be traced back to the 1940s and 1950s, when Father Roberto Busa, an Italian Jesuit priest, collaborated with IBM to create a computer-generated concordance of the works of St. Thomas Aquinas. This early venture demonstrated the potential of computers to assist in scholarly analysis. Over time, DH evolved from basic text processing and concordance generation to complex modeling, visualization, and data mining techniques. In the 1990s and early 2000s, the expansion of the internet and digital archives propelled DH into mainstream academic discussions. Universities began establishing dedicated DH centers, and scholarly associations such as the Alliance of Digital Humanities Organizations (ADHO) were formed. These developments marked the formal institutionalization of Digital Humanities as a recognized academic discipline.

1.1.2 Key Areas of Research and Practice in DH

Digital Humanities encompasses a broad spectrum of research areas and practices. One prominent area is text encoding and analysis, where texts are marked up using standards like the Text Encoding Initiative (TEI) to facilitate detailed examination and retrieval. Another key domain is digital archiving and preservation, which involves the digitization and long-term storage of manuscripts, artworks, and historical documents. Data visualization is also central to DH, enabling researchers to present complex information in accessible and engaging formats such as maps, graphs, and interactive timelines.

Additionally, DH projects often involve geographic information systems (GIS) to study historical geography or spatial narratives. Other research areas include digital storytelling, scholarly digital editions, computational linguistics, and social network analysis. These tools and methods enable scholars to uncover patterns and insights that are not easily discernible through traditional qualitative methods.

1.1.3 Role of Collaboration and Interdisciplinarity

Digital Humanities is inherently collaborative and interdisciplinary, requiring expertise from various fields such as computer science, information science, design, and domain-specific humanities disciplines. Unlike the solitary scholar often associated with traditional humanities research, DH projects typically involve teams of researchers, programmers, designers, and librarians working together. This collaborative model fosters innovation and encourages diverse perspectives in both the formulation of research questions and the interpretation of results. The interdisciplinary nature of DH also allows it to serve as a bridge between the sciences and the humanities, challenging the conventional dichotomy between the two domains. It encourages humanists to adopt quantitative and computational approaches, while prompting technologists to engage with cultural and ethical considerations.

1.1.4 Digital Humanities in Teaching and Learning

In the realm of education, Digital Humanities has transformed teaching and learning practices. DH tools and projects provide students with hands-on experience in using digital technologies to conduct research, interpret data, and create multimedia presentations. For example, students might participate in collaborative projects involving the creation of digital maps of historical events, building online exhibitions, or encoding historical texts for digital publication.

These activities enhance digital literacy and critical thinking, preparing students for the demands of the digital age. Moreover, DH initiatives often embrace open access and public engagement, making academic knowledge accessible to broader audiences. This democratization of knowledge fosters a participatory culture in which learners and the public can contribute to and benefit from scholarly endeavors.

1.1.5 Challenges and Criticisms of DH

Despite its many contributions, Digital Humanities faces several challenges and criticisms. One major concern is the issue of accessibility and the digital divide. Not all institutions or scholars have equal access to the resources and infrastructure required to undertake DH projects, potentially exacerbating existing inequalities within academia. There are also concerns about the dominance of English-language content in digital archives, which can marginalize non-Western perspectives.

Critics have questioned the extent to which DH truly engages with critical theory, arguing that its emphasis on technology may lead to a depoliticized or technocentric view of culture. Additionally, there are debates over the evaluation and recognition of DH work within academic institutions, particularly when it comes to tenure and promotion. The collaborative and often non-traditional outputs of DH, such as websites or databases, may not always align with established norms of scholarly publishing.

1.1.6 Ethics and the Politics of Digital Humanities

Ethical considerations are integral to the practice of Digital Humanities. Issues such as data privacy, copyright, and the representation of marginalized communities must be carefully addressed in DH projects. Scholars must ensure that digital archives and datasets are curated responsibly, with sensitivity to the contexts and identities of the people and materials involved. Furthermore, DH practitioners are increasingly aware of the political implications of digital technologies, including algorithmic bias, surveillance, and platform capitalism. Engaging with these issues requires a critical digital literacy that goes beyond technical skills to include an understanding of the social and political dimensions of digital systems. By foregrounding these concerns, DH can contribute to more equitable and reflective modes of digital scholarship.

1.1.7 Global Perspectives and the Future of DH

The global landscape of Digital Humanities is rapidly expanding, with growing interest and initiatives in regions such as Asia, Africa, Latin America, and the Middle East. These developments highlight the importance of cultural context in shaping DH practices and the need to decolonize the field. Scholars in the Global South are exploring ways to use digital tools to preserve indigenous knowledge, recover suppressed histories, and challenge dominant narratives. The future of DH lies in its ability to embrace diversity, foster inclusive collaborations, and adapt to emerging technologies such as artificial intelligence, machine learning, and immersive media. As DH continues to evolve, it will play a crucial role in shaping the future of humanities scholarship in the digital age.

1.2 HISTORICAL EVOLUTION OF THE FIELD

The historical evolution of Digital Humanities reflects a dynamic interplay between technological innovation and humanistic inquiry. From early computational experiments to contemporary AI-driven research, DH has continually adapted to new possibilities, reshaping how knowledge is produced and disseminated. As the field grows, it will undoubtedly face new challenges and opportunities, but its core mission—enhancing humanistic study through digital means—remains unchanged. By embracing interdisciplinary approaches and ethical considerations, DH will continue to influence academia and public engagement with culture and history in profound ways.

1.2.1 Early Foundations: Pre-Digital Era and Computational Beginnings

The roots of Digital Humanities can be traced back to the mid-20th century when scholars first experimented with computational methods for textual analysis. Father Roberto Busa, an Italian Jesuit priest, is often credited with pioneering DH through his work in the 1940s and 1950s. Collaborating with IBM, Busa used punch cards to create an index of Thomas Aquinas's writings, marking one of the first instances of humanities computing. This early effort demonstrated how technology could assist in large-scale textual analysis, setting a precedent for future developments.

During the 1960s and 1970s, humanities computing gained traction as universities began adopting mainframe computers. Scholars focused on tasks such as concordance generation, stylometric analysis, and statistical linguistics. Projects like the Oxford English Dictionary's digitization and the Thesaurus Linguae Graecae (a digital library of Greek literature) exemplified the growing intersection between computing and classical studies. These initiatives laid the groundwork for more sophisticated digital methodologies in later decades.

1.2.2 Rise of Digital Humanities in the Late 20th Century

The 1980s and 1990s witnessed significant technological advancements that propelled DH forward. The advent of personal computers and the internet revolutionized how researchers accessed and processed data. Hypertext theory, introduced by Ted Nelson and further developed by scholars like George Landow, influenced digital literary studies by exploring non-linear narratives and interactive texts. This period also saw the emergence of foundational DH organizations, such as the Association for Computers and the Humanities (ACH) and the Text Encoding Initiative (TEI), which established standards for digitizing and encoding texts. Digital archives and electronic editions became prominent during this era.

Projects such as the William Blake Archive and the Rossetti Archive demonstrated how digital platforms could enhance the study of art and literature by providing high-resolution images, searchable texts, and multimedia annotations. The shift from print to digital media allowed for greater accessibility and collaborative scholarship, reinforcing DH's role in modern academia.

1.2.3 21st Century: Expansion and Institutionalization

The turn of the century marked a period of rapid growth and institutional recognition for DH. Universities began establishing dedicated DH centers, offering degree programs, and securing funding for large-scale digital projects. The National Endowment for the Humanities (NEH) in the United States and the European Research Council (ERC) played crucial roles in supporting DH initiatives, fostering international collaboration.

Key developments included the rise of data visualization, Geographic Information Systems (GIS), and text mining. Tools like Voyant for text analysis, Omeka for digital exhibitions, and Zotero for citation management became integral to DH research. The field also embraced open-access movements, advocating for freely available scholarly resources. Platforms such as JSTOR and Project MUSE expanded digital archives, while initiatives like Wikipedia demonstrated the potential of crowdsourced knowledge in humanities research.

1.2.4 Contemporary Trends and Future Directions

In recent years, DH has continued to evolve with advancements in artificial intelligence, machine learning, and big data analytics. Natural Language Processing (NLP) techniques enable scholars to analyze vast corpora, uncovering patterns in historical texts and linguistic trends. Projects like Google Ngram Viewer and Word2Vec illustrate how computational models can reveal cultural shifts through language.

Another emerging trend is the application of virtual and augmented reality in humanities research. Digital reconstructions of ancient sites, 3D modeling of artifacts, and immersive storytelling experiences are redefining historical and archaeological studies. Additionally, ethical considerations—such as data privacy, algorithmic bias, and digital preservation—have become central to DH discourse, prompting scholars to critically assess the societal impact of their work.

Looking ahead, DH is poised to further integrate with global digital infrastructures. Interdisciplinary collaborations with computer science, social sciences, and cultural heritage institutions will likely expand the field's scope. As technology continues to advance, DH will remain at the forefront of innovative humanities scholarship, bridging the gap between traditional academic methods and cutting-edge digital tools.

1.3 KEY DEBATES AND DEFINITIONS

1.3.1 Role of Technology in Digital Humanities

Technology plays a central role in the practice of Digital Humanities, serving as both a tool and a subject of study. The advent of powerful computing systems, the internet, and various software applications has enabled scholars to process and analyze large datasets with unprecedented speed and accuracy. For example, natural language processing (NLP) techniques allow researchers to analyze vast collections of texts, identifying patterns and themes that might otherwise go unnoticed. Similarly, Geographic Information Systems (GIS) enable the creation of detailed maps that can reveal spatial relationships and historical movements. These technological advancements have democratized access to information, allowing researchers from diverse backgrounds to contribute to the field.

However, the reliance on technology in DH also raises important ethical and methodological questions. One of the key debates in this area concerns the potential for technological determinism, where the tools and methods of DH are seen as dictating the research questions and outcomes. Critics argue that an over-reliance on technology can lead to a loss of nuance and context, as algorithms and data visualization tools may oversimplify complex human experiences. Additionally, there are concerns about the digital divide, where access to advanced technologies and digital literacy is not evenly distributed, potentially excluding certain groups from participating in DH research. These debates underscore the need for a critical and reflective approach to the use of technology in the humanities, ensuring that it serves as a means to enhance, rather than replace, traditional scholarly practices.

1.3.2 Interdisciplinary Collaboration in Digital Humanities

One of the defining features of Digital Humanities is its interdisciplinary nature, bringing together scholars from various fields such as literature, history, art, computer science, and information studies. This interdisciplinary collaboration is essential for addressing the complex challenges and opportunities presented by digital technologies. For instance, a historian might collaborate with a computer scientist to develop a digital archive of historical documents, while a literary scholar might work with a data visualization expert to create interactive maps of literary landscapes. These collaborations not only enrich the research process but also foster a more inclusive and diverse academic community.

However, interdisciplinary collaboration in DH is not without its challenges. One of the key debates in this area concerns the potential for disciplinary silos, where scholars from different fields may have difficulty communicating and understanding each other's methodologies and perspectives. This can lead to misunderstandings and a lack of integration between different approaches. Additionally, there are concerns about the power dynamics within interdisciplinary teams, where certain disciplines may dominate the research agenda or receive more recognition for their contributions. To address these challenges, it is crucial to promote open communication, mutual respect, and a shared commitment to the goals of DH. This can be achieved through collaborative workshops, joint publications, and the development of interdisciplinary curricula that emphasize the value of diverse perspectives.

1.3.3 Impact of Digital Humanities on Traditional Scholarship

The rise of Digital Humanities has had a profound impact on traditional humanities scholarship, transforming the way research is conducted, disseminated, and evaluated. One of the most significant changes is the shift towards open access and digital publishing, which makes scholarly work more accessible to a wider audience. This democratization of knowledge challenges the traditional gatekeeping roles of academic journals and conferences, allowing for more diverse and inclusive forms of scholarly communication. For example, digital humanities projects often include interactive elements, multimedia content, and community engagement, making the research process more transparent and participatory.

However, this shift towards digital scholarship also raises important questions about the evaluation and recognition of DH work. Traditional academic metrics, such as publication counts and citation indices, may not adequately capture the impact and significance of digital humanities projects. This can lead to a devaluation of DH work within the academic community, where it may be seen as less rigorous or less scholarly than traditional forms of research. To address this issue, it is essential to develop new evaluation criteria that recognize the unique contributions of DH, such as the quality of digital tools, the engagement with diverse audiences, and the potential for long-term impact. This can be achieved through the creation of interdisciplinary review boards, the development of new metrics for evaluating digital scholarship, and the promotion of open and transparent peer-review processes.

1.3.4 Future of Digital Humanities

As Digital Humanities continues to evolve, it faces both opportunities and challenges. One of the key debates in this area concerns the future direction of the field, with some scholars advocating for a more technologically focused approach and others emphasizing the importance of humanistic inquiry. This debate highlights the tension between the need for technical expertise and the desire to maintain the interpretive and creative aspects of humanities scholarship. To navigate this tension, it is crucial to foster a balanced approach that integrates technical skills with humanistic values, ensuring that DH remains a vibrant and inclusive field.

Another important debate concerns the role of DH in addressing contemporary social and political issues. As digital technologies become increasingly integrated into everyday life, there is a growing recognition of the need for DH to engage with issues such as digital inequality, privacy, and surveillance. This can be achieved through the development of digital humanities projects that address these issues, as well as through the promotion of ethical and responsible practices in the use of digital technologies. By doing so, DH can contribute to a more just and equitable digital future, where technology serves the needs of all members of society.

1.4 INTERDISCIPLINARITY: WHERE HUMANITIES MEET TECHNOLOGY

Interdisciplinarity has become an essential approach to addressing complex questions that transcend traditional disciplinary boundaries. One of the most prominent examples of such interdisciplinary engagement is the field of Digital Humanities (DH), which represents the convergence of humanities and technology. Digital Humanities is not merely the application of computers to humanistic inquiry; it is a transformative domain that redefines the very methods, objects, and practices of humanities research by integrating computational tools, digital media, and technological perspectives. This union fosters innovation, collaboration, and a broader understanding of human culture in the digital age.

As the boundaries between disciplines blur, Digital Humanities emerges as a model of how scholars can work across traditional divides to create knowledge that is both technologically informed and deeply humanistic. Digital Humanities exemplifies the power and promise of interdisciplinarity in the twenty-first century. By bringing together the analytical traditions of the humanities with the tools and methods of technology, DH opens new avenues for understanding human culture, history, and expression.

It challenges conventional academic boundaries and fosters a collaborative, inclusive, and forward-looking scholarly community. As technology continues to reshape every aspect of society, the interdisciplinary approach of Digital Humanities provides a critical framework for navigating and interpreting the digital world. Embracing this convergence not only enriches humanistic research but also ensures that the humanities remain relevant and impactful in a rapidly changing world.

1.4.1 Evolution of Humanities in a Digital Framework

The humanities have long focused on understanding human experiences, values, and cultures through disciplines such as history, literature, philosophy, and the arts. Traditionally, these studies relied on textual analysis, archival research, and critical interpretation. However, the rise of digital technology has introduced new possibilities for inquiry and presentation. With the advent of computing, scholars began to explore how digital tools could enhance their work, initially through projects like the indexing and concordance generation of classical texts. Over time, these efforts evolved into sophisticated endeavors involving text encoding, database construction, digital mapping, and data visualization. This evolution marks the shift from analog to digital modes of scholarship, giving rise to Digital Humanities as a field where humanistic questions are explored through technological means.

1.4.2 Collaboration as the Core of Interdisciplinary Practice

A hallmark of Digital Humanities is its reliance on collaboration between experts from diverse fields. Unlike traditional humanities research, which often centers on individual scholars, DH projects typically involve teams comprising historians, literary critics, computer scientists, designers, archivists, and digital librarians. This collaborative model promotes the sharing of knowledge and methodologies, enabling projects to tackle multifaceted problems that require both technical and humanistic expertise. For instance, creating a digital archive of historical documents necessitates not only historical knowledge but also technical skills in metadata standards, digitization, and user interface design. Such collaboration enriches the research process and leads to more comprehensive and accessible scholarly outputs, demonstrating the value of interdisciplinary cooperation.

1.4.3 Technological Tools Transforming Humanities Research

Digital Humanities utilizes a wide array of technological tools that reshape how humanistic data is analyzed, interpreted, and shared. Text mining and natural language processing allow scholars to identify patterns and trends in large corpora of texts, uncovering insights that would be difficult to discern through close reading alone. Geographic Information Systems (GIS) enable the spatial analysis of historical events, revealing the geographic dimensions of cultural and social phenomena. Digital visualization tools help present data in dynamic and engaging ways, such as through interactive timelines, network graphs, or multimedia narratives. Additionally, digital publishing platforms facilitate open access to scholarly works, broadening their reach and impact. These technologies not only enhance the analytical capabilities of researchers but also transform the very nature of humanities scholarship in the digital age.

1.4.4 Pedagogical Innovations in Digital Humanities

Digital Humanities has also revolutionized teaching and learning in the humanities. By integrating digital tools into the classroom, educators can engage students in hands-on, project-based learning that fosters digital literacy and critical thinking. Students might collaborate on creating digital exhibits, encoding texts for online publication, or building interactive maps of historical events. These activities not only teach technical skills but also deepen students' understanding of humanistic content. Furthermore, DH projects often emphasize public engagement, encouraging students to produce work that is accessible and meaningful to wider audiences. This pedagogical approach aligns with the interdisciplinary ethos of DH, emphasizing experiential learning, collaboration, and the application of diverse skill sets.

1.4.5 Challenges of Interdisciplinary Integration

While the intersection of humanities and technology offers significant benefits, it also presents challenges. One of the major difficulties is the need for scholars to acquire technical skills that are not traditionally part of humanities training. Learning programming languages, mastering data visualization software, or understanding metadata schemas requires time and resources, which may not be readily available in all academic settings. Additionally, the collaborative nature of DH can complicate issues of authorship, credit, and evaluation, particularly within academic systems that prioritize individual achievement. There is also the risk of technological determinism, where the tools themselves begin to shape research questions in ways that may overlook or distort humanistic concerns. Addressing these challenges requires thoughtful integration of disciplines, institutional support, and a commitment to preserving the critical and ethical dimensions of humanities research.

1.4.6 Ethics and Equity in Digital Humanities Practice

Ethical considerations are central to the practice of Digital Humanities, especially as technology is increasingly embedded in scholarly work. Issues such as data privacy, consent, representation, and digital accessibility must be carefully navigated. DH practitioners must consider who is included in digital projects, whose voices are amplified, and whose histories are preserved. The field has also been critiqued for replicating existing power structures, particularly in terms of race, gender, and global inequity. For example, many digital archives are dominated by materials from Western institutions, marginalizing non-Western perspectives and knowledge systems. An ethically grounded DH practice must strive for inclusivity, cultural sensitivity, and a decolonized approach to digital scholarship. This requires ongoing reflection and dialogue among scholars from diverse backgrounds and disciplines.

1.4.7 Global Perspectives and Decolonizing Digital Humanities

Digital Humanities is increasingly becoming a global enterprise, with scholars around the world adapting and redefining DH practices to suit their cultural contexts. In regions such as Africa, Asia, and Latin America, DH is being used to recover indigenous knowledge systems, preserve endangered languages, and document community histories. These efforts challenge the dominance of Western epistemologies and technologies, pushing the field toward a more inclusive and pluralistic future. Decolonizing Digital Humanities involves not only diversifying content but also rethinking the frameworks, methodologies, and infrastructures that shape digital scholarship. It requires an acknowledgment of the historical and political dimensions of technology and a commitment to fostering equitable collaborations across borders.

1.4.8 Future of Interdisciplinary Innovation in DH

The future of Digital Humanities lies in its capacity to remain dynamic and responsive to technological advancements and societal needs. As emerging technologies such as artificial intelligence, machine learning, augmented reality, and virtual reality become more prevalent, DH scholars are exploring how these tools can be harnessed to enrich humanistic inquiry.

For instance, AI can assist in the classification and analysis of vast archives, while virtual reality can create immersive experiences of historical environments. However, the integration of such technologies must be approached critically, ensuring that they serve humanistic goals rather than simply showcasing technical novelty. The continued vitality of DH depends on its ability to balance innovation with reflection, interdisciplinarity with depth, and technological advancement with ethical responsibility.

1.5 THE GLOBAL LANDSCAPE OF DIGITAL HUMANITIES

The global landscape of Digital Humanities is a mosaic of diverse approaches, shaped by regional histories, cultural priorities, and technological capacities. While North America and Europe have traditionally dominated the field, Asia, Africa, Latin America, and Oceania are increasingly contributing unique perspectives that challenge and enrich DH methodologies.

As the field continues to evolve, fostering international cooperation, addressing inequities, and centering ethical considerations will be crucial in ensuring that Digital Humanities remains an inclusive and transformative force in global scholarship. By embracing both technological innovation and cultural specificity, DH can bridge divides and create new possibilities for understanding human culture in the digital age.

1.5.1 North America: Institutionalization and Innovation

North America, particularly the United States and Canada, has been a central hub for Digital Humanities since its inception. Early pioneers such as Father Roberto Busa and later scholars at institutions like the University of Virginia and Stanford University laid the groundwork for DH as an academic discipline. The establishment of organizations like the Association for Computers and the Humanities (ACH) and the Alliance of Digital Humanities Organizations (ADHO) helped formalize the field, promoting conferences, journals, and collaborative projects. Major funding bodies, including the National Endowment for the Humanities (NEH) and the Social Sciences and Humanities Research Council (SSHRC) in Canada, have supported large-scale DH initiatives. Projects such as the Digital Public Library of America (DPLA) and Chronicling America exemplify efforts to democratize access to historical archives. Meanwhile, universities have integrated DH into curricula, offering specialized programs that blend computational methods with humanistic inquiry. Despite these advancements, challenges such as uneven institutional support and the digital divide persist, influencing how DH develops across different academic and public sectors.

1.5.2 Europe: Tradition Meets Digital Transformation

Europe's rich cultural heritage and long-standing academic traditions have made it a fertile ground for Digital Humanities. Countries like the United Kingdom, Germany, France, and Italy have been at the forefront of DH research, often supported by government and European Union funding programs. The European Research Council (ERC) and CLARIN (Common Language Resources and Technology Infrastructure) have played pivotal roles in advancing large-scale digital projects, including multilingual text corpora and historical data repositories.

Notable initiatives include Europeana, a digital platform aggregating millions of artifacts from libraries, museums, and archives across the continent. In the UK, the Programming Historian offers open-access tutorials, making DH methodologies accessible to a broader audience. Meanwhile, Eastern European nations are increasingly engaging with DH, though often with fewer resources. The field in Europe is characterized by a strong emphasis on preserving linguistic diversity, digitizing medieval manuscripts, and exploring the intersections between national heritage and digital innovation.

1.5.3 Asia: Rapid Growth and Local Adaptations

Asia presents a dynamic and rapidly evolving landscape for Digital Humanities, with significant contributions from countries such as Japan, China, India, and South Korea. Japan has been a leader in applying computational methods to classical literature, with projects like the Japanese Text Initiative and digital archives of Edo-period texts. China has invested heavily in large-scale digitization efforts, including the China Academic Digital Associative Library (CADAL), while also exploring AI-driven analysis of ancient texts.

In India, DH has gained momentum through initiatives like the Virtual Museum of Images and Texts (VMIT) and digital reconstructions of historical sites. South Korea has integrated DH into cultural preservation, using 3D modeling to document heritage sites and developing NLP tools for classical Korean texts. A key challenge in Asia is balancing Western DH frameworks with local scholarly traditions, leading to innovative hybrid approaches that respect regional academic practices while embracing global digital trends.

1.5.4 Africa: Emerging DH Ecosystems and Decolonial Approaches

Digital Humanities in Africa is an emerging field, shaped by both opportunities and constraints. While infrastructure limitations and funding disparities pose challenges, scholars across the continent are pioneering innovative DH projects that address local needs. South Africa has been a leader in this regard, with institutions like the University of Cape Town and University of the Witwatersrand establishing DH centers focused on postcolonial studies, indigenous knowledge preservation, and multilingual digital archives.

Projects such as Digital Innovation South Africa (DISA) and African Online Digital Library (AODL) aim to make African historical records more accessible. A significant trend in African DH is the emphasis on decolonial methodologies, which critique Eurocentric digital practices and advocate for community-based digitization efforts. Mobile technology has also played a crucial role, as smartphone penetration enables new forms of digital storytelling and oral history preservation. As internet access expands, African DH is poised to grow, offering unique perspectives on how technology can serve marginalized scholarly traditions.

1.5.5 Latin America: Grassroots Movements and Cultural Activism

Latin America's engagement with Digital Humanities is marked by grassroots initiatives and a strong connection to social activism. Countries like Brazil, Mexico, and Argentina have seen a surge in DH projects that intersect with public history, social justice, and indigenous rights. Brazil's Laboratório de Humanidades Digitais (LHuD) and Mexico's Red de Humanidades Digitales (RedHD) are key networks fostering collaboration among scholars, librarians, and technologists.

A defining feature of Latin American DH is its focus on community participation. Projects such as Memoria Abierta in Argentina use digital platforms to document human rights violations, while indigenous groups in Mexico and Peru employ digital mapping to reclaim ancestral lands. Open-access advocacy is another prominent theme, with initiatives like SciELO providing a model for equitable scholarly publishing. Despite financial and political challenges, Latin American DH demonstrates how digital tools can amplify marginalized voices and democratize knowledge production.

1.5.6 Oceania: Indigenous Knowledge and Digital Preservation

In Oceania, Digital Humanities is closely tied to the preservation of indigenous cultures and languages. Australia and New Zealand have been leaders in this area, with projects like Mukurtu, an open-source platform for indigenous digital archiving, and Te Reo Māori language revitalization efforts. The Australian National University and University of Auckland have established DH programs that emphasize collaborative research with indigenous communities.

A major concern in Oceania's DH landscape is ethical data stewardship, ensuring that digitized cultural materials remain under the control of traditional custodians. The field also explores how digital storytelling and virtual reality can transmit oral histories to younger generations. As climate change threatens cultural heritage in the Pacific, DH is increasingly used to document at-risk sites, blending technology with indigenous epistemologies.

1.5.7 Global Challenges and Future Directions

Despite its worldwide expansion, Digital Humanities faces several cross-regional challenges. Unequal access to funding, technology, and training creates disparities between well-resourced institutions and those in developing regions. Language barriers and the dominance of English in DH discourse also limit inclusivity. Additionally, ethical concerns—such as data sovereignty, algorithmic bias, and the environmental impact of digital infrastructures—require ongoing attention.

Looking ahead, the global DH community is moving toward greater collaboration, with networks like GO::DH (Global Outlook::Digital Humanities) promoting equitable partnerships. The rise of citizen humanities, where public contributors assist in transcription and annotation projects, exemplifies how DH can democratize research. As artificial intelligence and machine learning become more integrated into humanities scholarship, global conversations on ethics and accessibility will shape the field's future.

CHAPTER 2

Foundational Concepts and Methodologies

2.1 DIGITIZATION VS. DIGITAL SCHOLARSHIP

2.1.1 Digitization

Digitization is the process of converting information into a digital (i.e. computer-readable) format. The result is the representation of an object, image, sound, document, or signal (usually an analog signal) obtained by generating a series of numbers that describe a discrete set of points or samples.

The result is called digital representation or, more specifically, a digital image, for the object, and digital form, for the signal. In modern practice, the digitized data is in the form of binary numbers, which facilitates processing by digital computers and other operations, but digitizing simply means "the conversion of analog source material into a numerical format"; the decimal or any other number system can be used instead.

Digitization is of crucial importance to data processing, storage, and transmission, because it "allows information of all kinds in all formats to be carried with the same efficiency and also intermingled." Though analog data is typically more stable, digital data has the potential to be more easily shared and accessed and, in theory, can be propagated indefinitely without generation loss, provided it is migrated to new, stable formats as needed. This potential has led to institutional digitization projects designed to improve access and the rapid growth of the digital preservation field.

Sometimes digitization and digital preservation are mistaken for the same thing. They are different, but digitization is often a vital first step in digital preservation. Libraries, archives, museums, and other memory institutions digitize items to preserve fragile materials and create more access points for patrons. Doing this creates challenges for information professionals and solutions can be as varied as the institutions that implement them. Some analog materials, such as audio and video tapes, are nearing the end of their life cycle, and it is important to digitize them before equipment obsolescence and media deterioration makes the data irretrievable.

There are challenges and implications surrounding digitization including time, cost, cultural history concerns, and creating an equitable platform for historically marginalized voices. Many digitizing institutions develop their own solutions to these challenges.

Mass digitization projects have had mixed results over the years, but some institutions have had success even if not in the traditional Google Books model. Although e-books have undermined the sales of their printed counterparts, a study from 2017 indicated that the two cater to different audiences and use-cases.

In a study of over 1400 university students it was found that physical literature is more apt for intense studies while e-books provide a superior experience for leisurely reading. Technological changes can happen often and quickly, so digitization standards are difficult to keep updated. Professionals in the field can attend conferences and join organizations and working groups to keep their knowledge current and add to the conversation.

Process

The term digitization is often used when diverse forms of information, such as an object, text, sound, image, or voice, are converted into a single binary code. The core of the process is the compromise between the capturing device and the player device so that the rendered result represents the original source with the most possible fidelity, and the advantage of digitization is the speed and accuracy in which this form of information can be transmitted with no degradation compared with analog information.

Digital information exists as one of two digits, either 0 or 1. These are known as bits (a contraction of binary digits) and the sequences of 0s and 1s that constitute information are called bytes. Analog signals are continuously variable, both in the number of possible values of the signal at a given time, as well as in the number of points in the signal in a given period of time. However, digital signals are discrete in both of those respects – generally a finite sequence of integers – therefore a digitization can, in practical terms, only ever be an approximation of the signal it represents.

Digitization occurs in two parts:

- **Discretization:** The reading of an analog signal A, and, at regular time intervals (frequency), sampling the value of the signal at the point. Each such reading is called a sample and may be considered to have infinite precision at this stage.
- **Quantization:** Samples are rounded to a fixed set of numbers (such as integers), a process known as quantization.

In general, these can occur at the same time, though they are conceptually distinct. A series of digital integers can be transformed into an analog output that approximates the original analog signal. Such a transformation is called a digital-to-analog conversion. The sampling rate and the number of bits used to represent the integers combine to determine how close such an approximation to the analog signal a digitization will be.

Examples

The term is used to describe, for example, the scanning of analog sources (such as printed photos or taped videos) into computers for editing, 3D scanning that creates 3D modeling of an object's surface, and audio (where sampling rate is often measured in kilohertz) and texture map transformations. In this last case, as in normal photos, the sampling rate refers to the resolution of the image, often measured in pixels per inch.

Digitizing is the primary way of storing images in a form suitable for transmission and computer processing, whether scanned from two-dimensional analog originals or captured using an image sensor-equipped device such as a digital camera, tomographical instrument such as a CAT scanner, or acquiring precise dimensions from a real-world object, such as a car, using a 3D scanning device.

Digitizing is central to making digital representations of geographical features, using raster or vector images, in a geographic information system, i.e., the creation of electronic maps, either from various geographical and satellite imaging (raster) or by digitizing traditional paper maps or graphs (vector).

"Digitization" is also used to describe the process of populating databases with files or data. While this usage is technically inaccurate, it originates with the previously proper use of the term to describe that part of the process involving digitization of analog sources, such as printed pictures and brochures, before uploading to target databases. Digitizing may also be used in the field of apparel, where an image may be recreated with the help of embroidery digitizing software tools and saved as embroidery machine code. This machine code is fed into an embroidery machine and applied to the fabric. The most supported format is DST file. Apparel companies also digitize clothing patterns.

Analog Signals to Digital

Analog signals are continuous electrical signals; digital signals are non-continuous. Analog signals can be converted to digital signals by using an analog-to-digital converter. The process of converting analog to digital consists of two parts: sampling and quantizing. Sampling measures wave amplitudes at regular intervals, splits them along the vertical axis, and assigns them a numerical value, while quantizing looks for measurements that are between binary values and rounds them up or down. Nearly all recorded music has been digitized, and about 12 percent of the 500,000+ movies listed on the Internet Movie Database are digitized and were released on DVD. Digitization of home movies, slides, and photographs is a popular method of preserving and sharing personal multimedia. Slides and photographs may be scanned quickly using an image scanner, but analog video requires a video tape player to be connected to a computer while the item plays in real time.

Slides can be digitized quicker with a slide scanner such as the Nikon Coolscan 5000ED. Another example of digitization is the VisualAudio process developed by the Swiss Fonoteca Nazionale in Lugano, by scanning a high resolution photograph of a record, they are able to extract and reconstruct the sound from the processed image. Digitization of analog tapes before they degrade, or after damage has already occurred, can rescue the only copies of local and traditional cultural music for future generations to study and enjoy.

Analog Texts to Digital

Academic and public libraries, foundations, and private companies like Google are scanning older print books and applying optical character recognition (OCR) technologies so they can be keyword searched, but as of 2006, only about 1 in 20 texts had been digitized. Librarians and archivists are working to increase this statistic and in 2019 began digitizing 480,000 books published between 1923 and 1964 that had entered the public domain.

Unpublished manuscripts and other rare papers and documents housed in special collections are being digitized by libraries and archives, but backlogs often slow this process and keep materials with enduring historical and research value hidden from most users. Digitization has not completely replaced other archival imaging options, such as microfilming which is still used by institutions such as the National Archives and Records Administration (NARA) to provide preservation and access to these resources.

While digital versions of analog texts can potentially be accessed from anywhere in the world, they are not as stable as most print materials or manuscripts and are unlikely to be accessible decades from now without further preservation efforts, while many books manuscripts and scrolls have already been around for centuries. However, for some materials that have been damaged by water, insects, or catastrophes, digitization might be the only option for continued use.

Library Preservation

In the context of libraries, archives, and museums, digitization is a means of creating digital surrogates of analog materials, such as books, newspapers, microfilm and videotapes, offers a variety of benefits, including increasing access, especially for patrons at a distance; contributing to collection development, through collaborative initiatives; enhancing the potential for research and education; and supporting preservation activities. Digitization can provide a means of preserving the content of the materials by creating an accessible facsimile of the object in order to put less strain on already fragile originals.

For sounds, digitization of legacy analog recordings is essential insurance against technological obsolescence. A fundamental aspect of planning digitization projects is to ensure that the digital files themselves are preserved and remain accessible; the term "digital preservation," in its most basic sense, refers to an array of activities undertaken to maintain access to digital materials over time.

The prevalent Brittle Books issue facing libraries across the world is being addressed with a digital solution for long term book preservation. Since the mid-1800s, books were printed on wood-pulp paper, which turns acidic as it decays. Deterioration may advance to a point where a book is completely unusable. In theory, if these widely circulated titles are not treated with de-acidification processes, the materials upon those acid pages will be lost. As digital technology evolves, it is increasingly preferred as a method of preserving these materials, mainly because it can provide easier access points and significantly reduce the need for physical storage space.

Cambridge University Library is working on the Cambridge Digital Library, which will initially contain digitised versions of many of its most important works relating to science and religion. These include examples such as Isaac Newton's personally annotated first edition of his Philosophiæ Naturalis Principia Mathematica as well as college notebooks and other papers, and some Islamic manuscripts such as a Quran from Tipu Sahib's library. Google, Inc. has taken steps towards attempting to digitize every title with "Google Book Search".

While some academic libraries have been contracted by the service, issues of copyright law violations threaten to derail the project. However, it does provide – at the very least – an online consortium for libraries to exchange information and for researchers to search for titles as well as review the materials.

Digitization versus Digital Preservation

Digitizing something is not the same as digitally preserving it. To digitize something is to create a digital surrogate (copy or format) of an existing analog item (book, photograph, or record) and is often described as converting it from analog to digital, however both copies remain. An example would be scanning a photograph and having the original piece in a photo album and a digital copy saved to a computer. This is essentially the first step in digital preservation which is to maintain the digital copy over a long period of time and making sure it remains authentic and accessible. Digitization is done once with the technology currently available, while digital preservation is more complicated because technology changes so quickly that a once popular storage format may become obsolete before it breaks. An example is a 5 1/4" floppy drive, computers are no longer made with them and obtaining the hardware to convert a file stored on 5 1/4" floppy disc can be expensive. To combat this risk, equipment must be upgraded as newer technology becomes affordable (about 2 to 5 years), but before older technology becomes unobtainable (about 5 to 10 years).

Digital preservation can also apply to born-digital material, such as a Microsoft Word document or a social media post. In contrast, digitization only applies exclusively to analog materials. Born-digital materials present a unique challenge to digital preservation not only due to technological obsolescence but also because of the inherently unstable nature of digital storage and maintenance. Most websites last between 2.5 and 5 years, depending on the purpose for which they were designed. The Library of Congress provides numerous resources and tips for individuals looking to practice digitization and digital preservation for their personal collections.

Digital Reformatting

Digital reformatting is the process of converting analog materials into a digital format as a surrogate of the original. The digital surrogates perform a preservation function by reducing or eliminating the use of the original. Digital reformatting is guided by established best practices to ensure that materials are being converted at the highest quality.

Digital Reformatting at the Library of Congress

The Library of Congress has been actively reformatting materials for its American Memory project and developed best standards and practices pertaining to book handling during the digitization process, scanning resolutions, and preferred file formats. Some of these standards are:

- The use of ISO 16067-1 and ISO 16067-2 standards for resolution requirements.
- Recommended 400 ppi resolution for OCR'ed printed text.
- The use of 24-bit color when color is an important attribute of a document.
- The use of the scanning device's maximum resolution for digitally reproducing photographs.
- TIFF as the standard file format.
- Attachment of descriptive, structural, and technical metadata to all digitized documents.

The Library of Congress has constituted a Preservation Digital Reformatting Program. The Three main components of the program include:

- Selection Criteria for digital reformatting.
- Digital reformatting principles and specifications.
- Life cycle management of LC digital data.

Audio Digitization and Reformatting

Audio media offers a rich source of historic ethnographic information, with the earliest forms of recorded sound dating back to 1890. According to the International Association of Sound and Audiovisual Archives (IASA), these sources of audio data, as well as the aging technologies used to play them back, are in imminent danger of permanent loss due to degradation and obsolescence. These primary sources are called "carriers" and exist in a variety of formats, including wax cylinders, magnetic tape, and flat discs of grooved media, among others. Some formats are susceptible to more severe, or quicker, degradation than others. For instance, lacquer discs suffer from delamination. Analog tape may deteriorate due to sticky shed syndrome.

Archival workflow and file standardization have been developed to minimize loss of information from the original carrier to the resulting digital file as digitization is underway. For most at-risk formats (magnetic tape, grooved cylinders, etc.), a similar workflow can be observed. Examination of the source carrier will help determine what, if any, steps need to be taken to repair material prior to transfer. A similar inspection must be undertaken for the playback machines. If satisfactory conditions are met for both carrier and playback machine, the transfer can take place, moderated by an analog-to-digital converter. The digital signal is then represented visually for the transfer engineer by a digital audio workstation, like Audacity, WaveLab, or Pro Tools. Reference access copies can be made at smaller sample rates. For archival purposes, it is standard to transfer at a sample rate of 96 kHz and a bit depth of 24 bits per channel.

Challenges

Many libraries, archives, museums, and other memory institutions, struggle with catching up and staying current regarding digitization and the expectation that everything should already be online. The time spent planning, doing the work, and processing the digital files along with the expense and fragility of some materials are some of the most common.

Time Spent

Digitization is a time-consuming process, even more so when the condition or format of the analog resources requires special handling. Deciding what part of a collection to digitize can sometimes take longer than digitizing it in its entirety. Each digitization project is unique and workflows for one will be different from every other project that goes through the process, so time must be spent thoroughly studying and planning each one to create the best plan for the materials and the intended audience.

Expense

Cost of equipment, staff time, metadata creation, and digital storage media make large scale digitization of collections expensive for all types of cultural institutions.

Ideally, all institutions want their digital copies to have the best image quality so a high-quality copy can be maintained over time. In the mid-long term, digital storage would be regarded as the more expensive part to maintain the digital archives due to the increasing number of scanning requests. However, smaller institutions may not be able to afford such equipment or manpower, which limits how much material can be digitized, so archivists and librarians must know what their patrons need and prioritize digitization of those items. To help the information institutions to better decide the archives worth of digitization, Casablancas and other researchers used a proposed model to investigate the impact of different digitization strategies on the decrease in access requests in the archival and library reading rooms. Often the cost of time and expertise involved with describing materials and adding metadata is more than the digitization process.

Fragility of Materials

Some materials, such as brittle books, are so fragile that undergoing the process of digitization could damage them irreparably. Despite potential damage, one reason for digitizing fragile materials is because they are so heavily used that creating a digital surrogate will help preserve the original copy long past its expected lifetime and increase access to the item.

Copyright

Copyright is not only a problem faced by projects like Google Books, but by institutions that may need to contact private citizens or institutions mentioned in archival documents for permission to scan the items for digital collections. It can be time consuming to make sure all potential copyright holders have given permission, but if copyright cannot be determined or cleared, it may be necessary to restrict even digital materials to in library use.

Solutions

Institutions can make digitization more cost-effective by planning before a project begins, including outlining what they hope to accomplish and the minimum amount of equipment, time, and effort that can meet those goals. If a budget needs more money to cover the cost of equipment or staff, an institution might investigate if grants are available.

Collaboration

Collaborations between institutions have the potential to save money on equipment, staff, and training as individual members share their equipment, manpower, and skills rather than pay outside organizations to provide these services. Collaborations with donors can build long-term support of current and future digitization projects.

Outsourcing

Outsourcing can be an option if an institution does not want to invest in equipment but since most vendors require an inventory and basic metadata for materials, this is not an option for institutions hoping to digitize without processing.

Non-Traditional Staffing

Many institutions have the option of using volunteers, student employees, or temporary employees on projects. While this saves on staffing costs, it can add costs elsewhere such as on training or having to re-scan items due to poor quality.

MPLP

One way to save time and resources is by using the More Product, Less Process (MPLP) method to digitize materials while they are being processed. Since GLAM (Galleries, Libraries, Archives, and Museums) institutions are already committed to preserving analog materials from special collections, digital access copies do not need to be high-resolution preservation copies, just good enough to provide access to rare materials. Sometimes institutions can get by with 300 dpi JPGs rather than a 600 dpi TIFF for images, and a 300 dpi grayscale scan of a document rather than a color one at 600 dpi.

Digitizing Marginalized Voices

Digitization can be used to highlight voices of historically marginalized peoples and add them to the greater body of knowledge. Many projects, some community archives created by members of those groups, are doing this in a way that supports the people, values their input and collaboration, and gives them a sense of ownership of the collection. Examples of projects are Gi-gikinomaage-min and the South Asian American Digital Archive (SAADA).

Gi-Gikinomaage-Min

Gi-gikinomaage-min is Anishinaabemowin for "We are all teachers" and its main purpose is "to document the history of Native Americans in Grand Rapids, Michigan." It combines new audio and video oral histories with digitized flyers, posters, and newsletters from Grand Valley State University's analog collections. Although not entirely a newly digitized project, what was created also added item-level metadata to enhance context. At the start, collaboration between several university departments and the Native American population was deemed important and remained strong throughout the project.

SAADA

The South Asian American Digital Archive (SAADA) has no physical building, is entirely digital and everything is handled by volunteers. This archive was started by Michelle Caswell and Samip Mallick and collects a broad variety of materials "created by or about people residing in the United States who trace their heritage to Bangladesh, Bhutan, India, Maldives, Nepal, Pakistan, Sri Lanka, and the many South Asian diaspora communities across the globe." (Caswell, 2015, 2). The collection of digitized items includes private, government, and university held materials.

Black Campus Movement Collection (BCM)

Kent State University began its BCM collection when it acquired the papers of African American alumnus Lafayette Tolliver, which included about 1,000 photographs that chronicled the black student experience at Kent State from 1968-1971. The collection continues to add materials from the 1960s up to and including the current student body and several oral histories have been added since it debuted. When digitizing the items, it was necessary to work with alumni to create descriptions for the images. This collaboration created changes in local controlled vocabularies the libraries used to create metadata for the images.

Mass Digitization

The expectation that everything should be online has led to mass digitization practices, but it is an ongoing process with obstacles that have led to alternatives. As new technology makes automated scanning of materials safer for materials and decreases need for cropping and de-skewing, mass digitization should be able to increase.

Obstacles

Digitization can be a physically slow process involving selection and preparation of collections that can take years if materials need to be compared for completeness or are vulnerable to damage. Price of specialized equipment, storage costs, website maintenance, quality control, and retrieval system limitations all add to the problems of working on a large scale.

Data Privacy and Security

Digitization presents significant challenges related to data privacy and security.

As organizations increasingly depend on electronic databases and information systems, their vulnerability to security threats also rises. The risk of data loss rises and cyberattacks can result in significant financial losses and damage the company's reputation . Therefore, there is a need for better cybersecurity measures and protection of data security and privacy to decrease the risks associated with digitization.

Successes

- **Digitization on Demand:** Scanning materials as users ask for them, provides copies for others to use and cuts down on repeated copying of popular items. If one part of a folder, document, or book is asked for, scanning the entire object can save time in the future by already having the material access if someone else needs the material. Digitizing on demand can increase volume because time spent on selection and prep has been used on scanning instead.
- **Google Books:** From the start, Google has concentrated on text rather than images or special collections. Although criticized in the past for poor image quality, selection practices, and lacking long-term preservation plans, their focus on quantity over quality has enabled Google to digitize more books than other digitizers.

Standards

Digitization is not a static field and standards change with new technology, so it is up to digitization managers to stay current with new developments. Although each digitization project is different, common standards in formats, metadata, quality, naming, and file storage should be used to give the best chance of interoperability and patron access.

As digitization is often the first step in digital preservation, questions about how to handle digital files should be addressed in institutional standards. A standard for still images adapted from the Smithsonian digitization standards might include the following:

Table: Still Image Digitization Standards

Filename format	Analog Material Type	Color or B&W	Resol-ution of Scan	RGB Setting for Scan	Digital File Format	File Com-press-ion	Metadata
YYYYMMDD_ Collec-tionID#_ Image#	35 mm print	Color	600 ppi	24 bit; 8 bits per color channel	TIFF	None	Follow Local Controlled Vocabularies and LC SH and NAF

YYYYMMDD_ Collec-tionID#_ Image#	35 mm slide	Color	1400 ppi	24 Bit; 8 bits per color channel	TIFF	None	Follow Local Controlled Vocabularies and LC SH and NAF
YYYYMMDD_ Collec-tionID#_ Image#	microform	B&W	300 ppi	24 Bit	TIFF	None	Follow Local Controlled Vocabularies and LC SH and NAF

Implications

Digitization of community archives by indigenous and other marginalized people has led to traditional memory institutions reassessing how they digitize and handle objects in their collections that may have ties to these groups. The topics they are rethinking are varied and include how items are chosen for digitization projects, what metadata to use to convey proper context to be retrievable by the groups they represent, and whether an item should be accessed by the world or just those who the groups originally intended to have access, such as elders. Many navigate these concerns by collaborating with the communities they seek to represent through their digitized collections.

Lean Philosophy

The broad use of internet and the increasing popularity of lean philosophy has also increased the use and meaning of "digitizing" to describe improvements in the efficiency of organizational processes. Lean philosophy refers to the approach which considers any use of time and resources, which does not lead directly to creating a product, as waste and therefore a target for elimination. This will often involve some kind of Lean process in order to simplify process activities, with the aim of implementing new "lean and mean" processes by digitizing data and activities. Digitization can help to eliminate time waste by introducing wider access to data, or by the implementation of enterprise resource planning systems.

2.1.2 Digital Scholarship

Digital scholarship is the use of digital evidence, methods of inquiry, research, publication and preservation to achieve scholarly and research goals. Digital scholarship can encompass both scholarly communication using digital media and research on digital media. An important aspect of digital scholarship is the effort to establish digital media and social media as credible, professional and legitimate means of research and communication. Digital scholarship has a close association with digital humanities, often serving as the umbrella term for discipline-agnostic digital research methods. Digital scholarship may also include born-digital means of scholarly communication that are more traditional, like online journals and databases, e-mail correspondence and the digital or digitized collections of research and academic libraries. Since digital scholarship is often concerned with the production and distribution of digital media, discussions about copyright, fair use and digital rights management (DRM) frequently accompany academic analysis of the topic. Combined with open access, digital scholarship is offered as a more affordable and open model for scholarly communication.

Development of the Concept

The concept of digital scholarship (DS) emerged early in the 21st century. DS is described as "discipline-based scholarship produced with digital tools and presented in digital form". It is also considered a research agenda concerned with the impact of Internet and digital technologies that are transforming scholarly practices. These include social and technological factors.

In the 2010s, research took mainly two approaches to the subject: The impact of digital infrastructures, in particular the internet, on scholarship, where Christine L. Borgman is reference researcher and the role of the academic library has been discussed in particular, and the impact of digital scholarship on the institutions and organization of academia.

According to Ernest L. Boyer in Scholarship Reconsidered, discovery, integration, application, and teaching are the four main aspects of scholarship. The growth of digital media means that the main areas of scholarship can each benefit from expansions in their own way thanks to the infinite sharability of digital content.

In education, the main areas of relevance are science, technology, engineering and math. It is said that students learn best in a classroom when they are actively engaged. The emergence of digital scholarship and digital media allows for another means for students to become engaged. Key areas of academia that digital media is used on are to illustrate concepts, model displays and reinforce 21st century skills.

Critics cite concerns about the legitimacy, accessibility and verifiability of digital scholarship and the erosion of authors' rights as reasons to be concerned about digital scholarship. As scholarly communication evolves, controversy over the definition and value of the term "digital scholarship" is likely to continue.

Digital scholarship must take all of cultural, economic, personal, and institutional responsibilities to take its position as academic scholarship and to realize the core purpose of higher education with the possibilities of our time.

Digital education opens new openings for collaboration between scholars from different fields through digital platforms. This makes it easier to work together on complex exploration questions that might be delicate to attack within traditional academic structures. also, digital education's global reach allows for a different range of voices and perspectives to contribute to academic conversations. For illustration, enterprise like the Digital Gujarat literacy demonstrate how digital tools can grease educational support and collaboration.

Intellectual Property

Concerns with how to regulate digital scholarship have arisen across universities across the world. The explosion in availability and creation of scholarly works has led many universities to adjust their policies on how they will manage scholarship in the future. These universities feel pressured to take action because digital technologies have led to the easy reproduction and commodification of these creations.

Many universities are unclear how to address the copyrighting of online classes and media presentations. Current law does not cover these specific areas of media produced in the academic world. In the past any printed work done by professors was considered their intellectual property, but now the question stands as to who owns these different forms of multimedia. One of the main concerns of faculty is that universities will soon take ownership of this digital media.

Universities have taken a growing interest in creations that have revenue-generating potential, like online classes or lecture slides, while also showing concern for products that may be used by comparable institutions, potentially reducing their competitive advantage. In order to stay on top of others academically, universities have sought to keep the intellectual property created within the university away from others schools. Not only are universities using digital scholarship to make money and stay ahead, but they also have interests in protecting their brand.

While universities attempt to protect digital scholarship, it is in many professors best interests for their creations to be seen by the world as to grow their brand and acclaim as a professor. Laws that may apply to digital scholarship are largely outdated but professors would like to use the argument of faculty ownership of traditional works as historical practice and practice compatible with mission of higher education as a public good.

Professors argue that it took time and serious effort to make the presentations, slides, media. To date professors have been rarely questioned whether they have the right to bring their course outlines, lecture outlines, and lecture notes with them if they decide to leave the university where they created them. Change over the ability of professors to bring digital scholarship with them is expected as universities have begun to take notice and assert copyrights. Professors will argue that since they are the creators and authors of the product they are the owners according to law.

As of now most copyright laws in America indicate that the author or creator holds the copyright, but the same cannot be said for digital scholarship. The law explicitly states that if the work is within the scope of his or her employment then the work is the property of the employer. Since the employer here would be the university, professors are technically creating work for hire. While faculty of universities appear to not be credited for their work, the primary reason for a university to take ownership of a faculty's work is that the member created the work using university funds mostly. Solutions to the lack of clear laws regarding ownership of digital scholarship are not currently being created but many universities have created written contracts with professors over who owns future work or what they can do with previous work.

For example, in the U.S. Supreme Court case Stanford v. Roche, the court decided that Roche, a former Stanford researcher, was a co-owner with Stanford of patents for testing kits to detect HIV. While this case does not deal with digital scholarship directly, it deals with the ownership of intellectual property of university employees when they leave. This case will set a precedent for future decisions with online classes, lecture notes, and outlines.

National Education Association policy

The National Education Association, the largest professional educational association in the United States, updated its policy on digital learning in 2013. The policy stresses that students need to develop "advanced critical thinking and information literacy skills and master new digital tools", as well as "the initiative to become self-directed learners while adapting to the ever-changing digital information landscape".

The National Education Association also believes that digital learning creates an environment in which learning can be more individualized to meet the needs of each student. It mandates that all public schools must do their best to acquire necessary modern technologies and constantly revise teaching plans to incorporate technology where viable to best prepare students for the 21st century. The National Education Association's digital learning policy also states that technology must be used in an adaptive manner as to not become a distraction and to remain a tool, as well as that technology should not become a replacement for instructors, merely a supplement.

2.2 QUANTITATIVE AND QUALITATIVE METHODS IN DH

The integration of quantitative and qualitative methods in Digital Humanities offers a powerful approach to research, combining the strengths of both approaches to create a more comprehensive and nuanced understanding of the research subject. While this integration presents several challenges, it also offers many opportunities for innovation, collaboration, and ethical engagement. As DH continues to evolve, the integration of quantitative and qualitative methods will play an increasingly important role in shaping the field, contributing to a more just, equitable, and innovative academic community. By embracing this integration, DH can address complex humanities questions, engage with contemporary social and political issues, and contribute to a more just and equitable digital future.

2.2.1 Quantitative Methods in Digital Humanities

Quantitative methods in Digital Humanities are increasingly being used to analyze large-scale data, providing insights that were previously inaccessible. One of the most prominent quantitative techniques in DH is text mining, which involves the use of algorithms to analyze and extract information from large text corpora. Text mining can reveal patterns in language use, identify recurring themes, and even predict future trends.

For example, researchers might use text mining to analyze a collection of historical newspapers, identifying shifts in public opinion over time or tracking the evolution of political discourse. Similarly, sentiment analysis can be employed to gauge the emotional tone of a text, providing insights into the attitudes and sentiments expressed within a particular corpus. These quantitative methods are particularly valuable for identifying broad trends and correlations, allowing researchers to make data-driven arguments and hypotheses.

Another key quantitative method in DH is network analysis, which involves the study of relationships and connections within a dataset. Network analysis can be applied to a wide range of humanities data, from social networks and communication patterns to the relationships between literary characters or historical events. For instance, a network analysis of a literary work might reveal the complex web of relationships between characters, shedding light on the narrative structure and thematic concerns of the text. Similarly, a network analysis of historical correspondence might uncover the social and intellectual networks that shaped a particular historical period. Visualization techniques, such as graphs and maps, are often used to represent these networks, making them more accessible and interpretable. These visualizations can highlight key nodes, clusters, and patterns, providing a clearer understanding of the underlying data.

2.2.2 Qualitative Methods in Digital Humanities

While quantitative methods offer powerful tools for analyzing large-scale data, qualitative methods in Digital Humanities are essential for understanding the context, meaning, and significance of that data. Qualitative approaches often involve close reading, discourse analysis, and ethnographic studies, all of which aim to interpret and contextualize the data within its cultural, historical, or social framework. For example, a qualitative study might involve a detailed analysis of a single literary text, examining its themes, symbols, and narrative techniques to uncover its deeper meanings. This close reading can reveal the subtle nuances and complexities of the text, providing insights that quantitative methods alone cannot capture. Similarly, discourse analysis can be used to examine the language and rhetoric used in a particular text or corpus, shedding light on the underlying ideologies, power dynamics, and cultural assumptions.

Ethnographic studies in DH involve the in-depth examination of a particular community or cultural group, often through participant observation, interviews, and focus groups. These studies aim to understand the lived experiences, beliefs, and practices of the community, providing rich, contextual insights that quantitative data alone cannot capture.

For instance, an ethnographic study might involve conducting interviews with members of a particular cultural group, exploring their experiences of migration, identity, and belonging. These qualitative methods are particularly valuable for understanding the human dimensions of digital technologies, examining how they are used, experienced, and interpreted by different communities. By integrating qualitative methods into DH research, scholars can ensure that their findings are grounded in the lived experiences and cultural contexts of the people they study.

2.2.3 Integrating Quantitative and Qualitative Methods

The integration of quantitative and qualitative methods in Digital Humanities offers a powerful approach to research, combining the strengths of both approaches to create a more comprehensive and nuanced understanding of the research subject. This integration can take many forms, from using quantitative methods to identify broad trends and patterns, which are then explored in depth through qualitative analysis, to using qualitative methods to contextualize and interpret quantitative findings.

For example, a researcher might use text mining to identify recurring themes in a large corpus of historical documents, which are then explored in depth through close reading and discourse analysis. Similarly, a researcher might use network analysis to map the relationships between historical figures, which are then interpreted through ethnographic studies of the communities they belonged to.

One of the key benefits of integrating quantitative and qualitative methods in DH is the ability to triangulate findings, ensuring that they are robust, reliable, and valid. Triangulation involves using multiple methods or data sources to corroborate and validate findings, providing a more comprehensive and nuanced understanding of the research subject. For instance, a researcher might use both quantitative and qualitative methods to study the impact of a particular digital technology on a community, using surveys and statistical analysis to identify broad trends and patterns, and interviews and focus groups to explore the lived experiences and perspectives of community members. By triangulating these findings, the researcher can ensure that their conclusions are well-founded and reliable.

2.2.4 Challenges and Opportunities in Integrating Quantitative and Qualitative Methods

While the integration of quantitative and qualitative methods in Digital Humanities offers many benefits, it also presents several challenges. One of the key challenges is the need for interdisciplinary collaboration, as researchers must draw on expertise from both the humanities and the computational sciences. This collaboration can be challenging, as it requires bridging the gap between different disciplinary cultures, methodologies, and epistemologies. For example, humanities scholars might prioritize close reading, contextual analysis, and interpretive methods, while computational scientists might focus on data mining, statistical analysis, and visualization techniques. Bridging this gap requires open communication, mutual respect, and a shared commitment to the goals of the research.

Another challenge in integrating quantitative and qualitative methods in DH is the need for critical reflection on the limitations and biases of both approaches. Quantitative methods, for instance, can be limited by the availability and quality of data, as well as the assumptions and biases embedded in the algorithms and models used for analysis. Similarly, qualitative methods can be subject to the researcher's own biases, assumptions, and interpretations.

To address these challenges, it is essential to adopt a critical and reflexive approach to research, acknowledging the limitations and biases of both quantitative and qualitative methods, and striving for transparency, rigor, and ethical integrity in the research process. This can be achieved through peer review, collaborative research, and the development of interdisciplinary standards and guidelines for DH research.

2.2.5 Future of Quantitative and Qualitative Methods in Digital Humanities

As Digital Humanities continues to evolve, the integration of quantitative and qualitative methods will play an increasingly important role in shaping the field. One of the key trends in this area is the development of new hybrid methods that combine the strengths of both approaches, creating innovative and interdisciplinary research techniques. For example, researchers might develop new algorithms for text mining that incorporate qualitative insights, such as the use of close reading and discourse analysis to refine and validate the findings of quantitative analysis. Similarly, researchers might develop new visualization techniques that integrate qualitative data, such as the use of maps and graphs to represent the lived experiences and perspectives of a particular community.

Another important trend in the future of quantitative and qualitative methods in DH is the increasing emphasis on ethical and responsible research practices. As digital technologies become increasingly integrated into everyday life, there is a growing recognition of the need for DH to engage with issues such as digital inequality, privacy, and surveillance. This can be achieved through the development of ethical guidelines and standards for DH research, as well as through the promotion of open and transparent research practices. By doing so, DH can contribute to a more just and equitable digital future, where technology serves the needs of all members of society.

2.3 DATA, METADATA, AND ONTOLOGIES IN HUMANITIES RESEARCH

The integration of data, metadata, and ontologies into humanities research represents a fundamental shift in how knowledge is produced, organized, and shared. These tools enable scholars to work with complex digital materials in structured and meaningful ways, opening new avenues for discovery and collaboration. At the same time, they require careful design, ethical awareness, and interdisciplinary cooperation. As the field of digital humanities continues to grow, the thoughtful use of data and semantic structures will be essential to ensuring that digital scholarship remains rigorous, inclusive, and relevant to both academic and public audiences. By embracing these tools with critical insight, humanities researchers can contribute to a more connected and reflective digital culture.

2.3.1 Data in the Humanities Context

Data in the humanities takes many forms, ranging from digitized manuscripts and historical records to audio recordings, images, videos, and born-digital content such as blogs or social media posts. Unlike scientific data, which is often numerical and structured, humanities data is frequently qualitative and contextual. This means that humanities scholars must grapple with data that is open to interpretation, incomplete, and deeply embedded in cultural and historical meanings. In this context, data is not simply raw information but is often shaped by human judgment in the processes of selection, digitization, and categorization. The challenge in humanities research is not only to collect data but to understand its provenance, significance, and interpretative implications. Digital tools can assist in managing large data sets, but the humanistic approach ensures that the interpretation of data remains sensitive to context and meaning.

2.3.2 Metadata in the Humanities Context

Metadata, often described as "data about data," plays a crucial role in the organization and retrieval of digital information. In the humanities, metadata allows researchers to describe cultural objects in ways that make them discoverable and useful for further study. Metadata can include information about the creator of a work, its date of creation, physical dimensions, location, language, subject matter, and much more. These descriptions enable researchers to search for, filter, and analyze resources across digital collections and archives. Standardized metadata schemas such as Dublin Core, MARC, and TEI provide frameworks that ensure consistency and interoperability across digital projects and platforms. In practice, metadata is not neutral; it reflects the priorities, assumptions, and decisions of those who create it. Thus, the creation of metadata in humanities research requires critical awareness of issues such as bias, inclusivity, and representation.

2.3.3 Ontologies in the Humanities Context

Ontologies represent a more complex form of data structuring, involving the formal representation of concepts and their relationships within a specific domain. In the humanities, ontologies help scholars define and map the key terms, categories, and entities relevant to a particular field of study. An ontology is more than a taxonomy or controlled vocabulary; it provides a semantic framework that enables machines to understand and reason about human knowledge. For example, an ontology for historical studies might include classes such as "Person," "Event," "Place," and "Artifact," along with properties that specify relationships like "participated in," "occurred at," or "created by." Ontologies facilitate advanced queries, data integration, and automated reasoning, making them indispensable tools for large-scale digital humanities projects. They also foster interoperability, allowing data from different sources to be connected and understood in meaningful ways.

2.3.4 Applications

Numerous digital humanities projects exemplify the integration of data, metadata, and ontologies. For instance, digital archives such as Europeana or the Digital Public Library of America rely on extensive metadata to provide access to millions of cultural heritage items. Projects like the Linked Jazz initiative use ontologies to map relationships between jazz musicians, enabling network analysis and biographical discovery. Historical GIS platforms combine spatial data with metadata about historical events to reconstruct past landscapes and movements. These applications illustrate how the combination of structured data and semantic modeling can open new research pathways, enhance scholarly collaboration, and engage wider audiences. The success of such projects depends on careful data curation, robust metadata standards, and the thoughtful design of ontologies that reflect the complexity of humanistic knowledge.

2.3.5 Challenges

Despite the promise of data-driven humanities research, several challenges remain. One key issue is the difficulty of standardizing metadata across diverse collections and institutions. Differences in metadata practices can hinder interoperability and limit the ability to conduct cross-collection research. Furthermore, humanities data is often heterogeneous, ambiguous, and culturally specific, making it difficult to fit into rigid metadata schemas or ontological frameworks.

There is also the problem of labor: creating and maintaining high-quality metadata and ontologies requires significant time, expertise, and financial resources. Moreover, scholars must be cautious about the assumptions embedded in data models and metadata standards, which may privilege certain perspectives while marginalizing others. Critical engagement with these tools is essential to ensure that digital humanities research remains inclusive, ethical, and historically grounded.

2.3.6 Metadata and Ontologies in Preserving Cultural Memory

Metadata and ontologies play a critical role in the preservation of cultural memory. As more cultural heritage materials are digitized, the ability to catalog, describe, and relate them to broader contexts becomes increasingly important. Metadata ensures that digital artifacts are not lost in vast repositories but are accessible and interpretable for future generations. Ontologies contribute by providing frameworks through which relationships between artifacts, events, people, and places can be established and understood over time.

These systems of organization support not only academic research but also education, public engagement, and the safeguarding of intangible heritage. However, preserving cultural memory in the digital age also requires attention to the sustainability of digital infrastructures and the long-term stewardship of digital content.

2.3.7 Interdisciplinary Collaboration in Data and Metadata Design

The effective use of data, metadata, and ontologies in the humanities necessitates collaboration across disciplines. Scholars must work closely with archivists, librarians, computer scientists, and information specialists to design systems that meet both technical and scholarly requirements. These collaborations often involve negotiation and compromise, as different disciplines bring distinct priorities and methodologies to the table.

Humanists contribute deep contextual knowledge and interpretive skills, while technologists offer expertise in data modeling, system design, and computational analysis. Successful collaboration depends on mutual respect and a shared understanding of the goals and values of digital scholarship. Training programs and workshops in digital humanities play a vital role in building the capacity for interdisciplinary collaboration and fostering a common vocabulary among diverse participants.

2.4 ANNOTATION, TAGGING, AND ENCODING STANDARDS (TEI, XML, RDF)

Annotation, tagging, and encoding standards are more than technical necessities—they are intellectual instruments that shape how humanities research is conducted, shared, and preserved. TEI, XML, and RDF each contribute to this ecosystem, enabling scholars to model complex textual relationships, ensure data longevity, and participate in the broader semantic web. As Digital Humanities continues to evolve, these standards will adapt, incorporating new methodologies while retaining their core mission: to make humanistic inquiry more precise, accessible, and interconnected.

2.4.1 Annotation

Annotation is a critical practice in Digital Humanities, allowing researchers to add explanatory or analytical layers to texts without altering the original content. Digital annotations can include commentary, linguistic analysis, historical context, or cross-references to related materials. Unlike traditional marginalia, digital annotations are often structured using standardized schemas, making them searchable, reusable, and capable of supporting collaborative research.

Platforms such as Hypothes.is and Recogito demonstrate how annotation facilitates scholarly discourse by enabling multiple users to contribute insights to the same document. The use of formal encoding standards ensures that these annotations remain consistent across different systems, enhancing both accessibility and scholarly rigor.

2.4.2 Tagging

Tagging involves attaching descriptive labels to segments of text, images, or other digital objects to categorize and retrieve them efficiently. In humanities research, tagging can identify themes, historical periods, linguistic features, or authorship attributes. Unlike free-form annotations, tags typically follow controlled vocabularies or ontologies to maintain consistency. For example, a researcher studying medieval manuscripts might tag passages by genre, scribal hands, or thematic motifs. Social tagging, where users collaboratively assign keywords, introduces a folksonomic approach, though it risks inconsistency without formal guidelines. Structured tagging systems, often implemented through XML or RDF, mitigate this issue by enforcing predefined schemas that align with disciplinary conventions.

2.4.3 Text Encoding Initiative (TEI)

The Text Encoding Initiative (TEI) is one of the most influential standards in Digital Humanities, providing a comprehensive framework for encoding literary and historical texts in machine-readable form. Developed by an international consortium, TEI offers guidelines for representing textual features such as headings, footnotes, verse structures, and manuscript revisions. Its modular design allows scholars to customize markup for specific research needs while maintaining interoperability. For instance, a TEI-encoded document might distinguish between an author's original text and later editorial emendations, preserving the textual history for future analysis.

TEI is typically implemented using XML, ensuring that documents adhere to a well-defined syntax. A notable example of TEI in practice is the Women Writers Project, which encodes early modern women's texts to facilitate gender-based literary analysis. Despite its robustness, TEI's complexity can pose challenges for beginners, prompting the development of simplified subsets like TEI Lite and user-friendly editing tools such as OxGarage and TEI Publisher.

2.4.4 Extensible Markup Language (XML)

XML serves as the backbone for many text encoding projects in Digital Humanities due to its flexibility, hierarchical structure, and platform independence. Unlike HTML, which focuses on presentation, XML is designed to store and transport data, making it ideal for scholarly projects requiring detailed metadata and semantic markup. In humanities research, XML enables the encoding of complex textual features, from poetic meter to geographic references, in a way that is both human-readable and machine-processable.

A key advantage of XML is its support for custom schemas, allowing disciplines to develop domain-specific tagging systems. For example, linguists might use XML to annotate syntactic trees, while historians could encode biographical data within archival documents. The widespread adoption of XML in DH is evident in projects like the Perseus Digital Library, where XML markup enables advanced search functionalities and textual analysis. However, the manual creation of XML documents can be labor-intensive, leading to the development of specialized editors (e.g., oXygen XML) and automated tools for converting plain text into structured formats.

2.4.5 Resource Description Framework (RDF)

While TEI and XML excel at document-centric markup, the Resource Description Framework (RDF) addresses the need for linking and contextualizing data across disparate sources. RDF is a cornerstone of the Semantic Web, representing information as triples (subject-predicate-object) that define relationships between entities. This approach is particularly valuable in Digital Humanities for integrating heterogeneous datasets, such as connecting literary texts with biographical databases or archival records.

For instance, a research project on Enlightenment-era correspondence might use RDF to link letters with their senders, recipients, and mentioned locations, creating a networked knowledge graph. Tools like OpenRefine and Protege facilitate the creation and querying of RDF datasets, while ontologies such as CIDOC-CRM (for cultural heritage) and FOAF (for personal relationships) provide standardized vocabularies. Despite its power, RDF's steep learning curve and the relative scarcity of humanities-specific ontologies have limited its broader adoption compared to XML-based standards.

2.4.6 Comparative Analysis: TEI, XML, and RDF in Practice

Each of these standards serves distinct yet complementary roles in Digital Humanities. TEI specializes in the detailed markup of textual features, making it indispensable for editions, translations, and archival projects. XML provides the syntactic structure underlying TEI and other domain-specific schemas, offering a balance between expressiveness and readability. RDF, by contrast, excels at interconnecting data across repositories, supporting large-scale semantic queries and linked open data initiatives. A single project might employ all three: for example, a digital critical edition could use TEI for encoding the primary text, XML for storing supplementary materials, and RDF to link the edition with related artworks or historical events. The choice of standard depends on the project's goals—preservation and close reading favor TEI/XML, while data integration and exploratory research benefit from RDF. Hybrid approaches, such as embedding RDFa (RDF in attributes) within XML documents, are increasingly bridging these paradigms.

2.5 CRITICAL THEORY IN THE DIGITAL AGE

2.5.1 Power Dynamics Online

Power dynamics play a crucial role in shaping online interactions. The internet is not a neutral platform; it is shaped by the social, economic, and cultural contexts in which it is embedded. The role of power in online interactions can be understood through the lens of critical theory, which highlights the ways in which power is exercised and maintained through social structures and relationships.

The Role of Power in Shaping Online Interactions

Power dynamics online are influenced by various factors, including:

- **Social Identity**: Online interactions are shaped by social identity categories such as race, gender, class, and sexuality. These categories influence how individuals are perceived and treated online.
- **Algorithmic Bias**: Algorithms used in online platforms can perpetuate existing power dynamics by reinforcing biases and stereotypes.

- **Digital Literacy:** The ability to effectively navigate and utilize digital technologies is a key factor in determining online power dynamics.

The diagram illustrates the complex interplay between these factors:

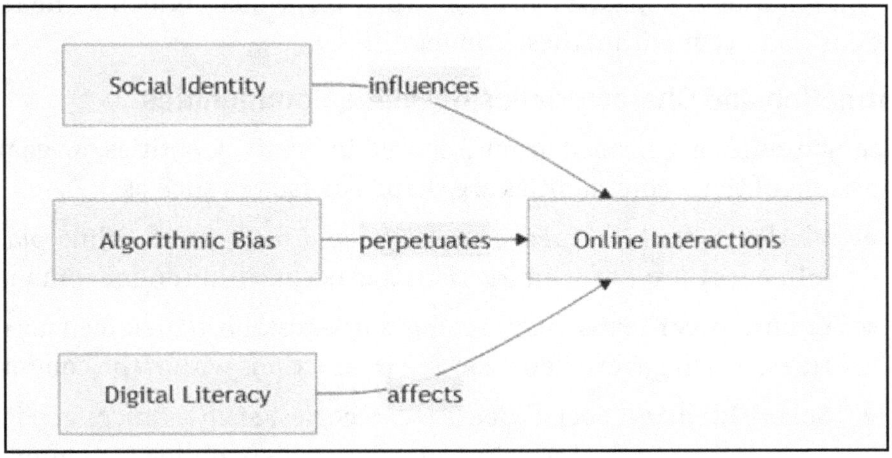

How Social Structures Influence Digital Communication

Social structures, such as economic systems, institutions, and social norms, shape digital communication in various ways. For instance:

- **Economic Systems:** The commercialization of the internet has led to the dominance of corporate interests, influencing the types of content that are promoted and censored online.
- **Institutions:** Online institutions, such as social media platforms and online forums, establish rules and norms that govern online interactions.
- **Social Norms:** Social norms around online behavior, such as trolling and cyberbullying, are shaped by broader cultural attitudes towards communication and interaction.

Examples of Power Dynamics in Internet Culture

Power dynamics are evident in various aspects of internet culture, including:

- **Online Harassment:** Women and minority groups are disproportionately targeted by online harassment, highlighting the ways in which power dynamics shape online interactions.
- **Content Moderation:** The moderation of online content is often influenced by power dynamics, with certain types of content being prioritized or censored based on social and cultural norms.
- **Influencer Culture:** The rise of influencer culture has created new forms of power dynamics online, with influencers wielding significant influence over their followers.

2.5.2 Social Structures and Online Communities

Online communities are a key aspect of internet culture, providing spaces for individuals to connect, share, and interact. The formation and characteristics of online communities are shaped by social structures, which influence the types of interactions that occur within these communities.

The Formation and Characteristics of Online Communities

Online communities are formed around shared interests, identities, or goals. The characteristics of these communities are shaped by factors such as:

- **Platform Architecture:** The design and features of online platforms influence the types of interactions that occur within online communities.
- **Community Norms:** Online communities establish their own norms and rules, which govern behavior and interactions within the community.
- **Social Identity:** Social identity categories, such as race, gender, and class, influence the formation and dynamics of online communities.

The following table summarizes the key factors that shape online communities:

Factor	Description
Platform Architecture	The design and features of online platforms
Community Norms	The rules and norms established by online communities
Social Identity	Social identity categories that influence community dynamics

The Impact of Social Structures on Online Interactions

Social structures have a significant impact on online interactions, shaping the types of content that are shared, the ways in which individuals interact, and the norms that govern online behavior. For instance:

- **Socioeconomic Factors:** Socioeconomic factors, such as access to technology and digital literacy, influence online interactions and shape the types of content that are shared.
- **Cultural Norms:** Cultural norms around communication and interaction influence online behavior, with certain types of content or behavior being deemed acceptable or unacceptable.

Case Studies of Online Communities and their Social Structures

Several case studies illustrate the complex interplay between social structures and online communities. For example:

- **Reddit:** The social news site Reddit is characterized by a complex social structure, with community norms and rules governing behavior within subreddits.

- **Twitter:** Twitter's platform architecture and character limit influence the types of interactions that occur on the platform, with hashtags and trending topics shaping online discourse.
- **4chan:** The anonymous imageboard 4chan is characterized by a distinct culture and set of norms, with users often engaging in trolling and other forms of provocative behavior.

2.5.3 Cultural Norms and Digital Rhetoric

Cultural norms play a significant role in shaping digital communication, influencing the types of content that are created, shared, and consumed online. Digital rhetoric, which refers to the ways in which language and communication are used online, is shaped by cultural norms and social structures.

The Cultural Norms that Shape Digital Communication

Cultural norms around communication and interaction influence digital communication in various ways. For instance:

- **Tone and Language:** The tone and language used online are shaped by cultural norms, with certain types of language or tone being deemed acceptable or unacceptable.
- **Content Creation:** Cultural norms around content creation influence the types of content that are produced and shared online.
- **Engagement:** Cultural norms around engagement and interaction influence the ways in which individuals interact with online content.

How Internet Culture Influences Digital Rhetoric

Internet culture has a significant impact on digital rhetoric, shaping the ways in which language and communication are used online. For instance:

- **Memes and Irony:** Internet culture has given rise to new forms of communication, such as memes and irony, which are used to convey complex ideas and emotions.
- **Hashtags and Trending Topics:** Hashtags and trending topics shape online discourse, influencing the types of content that are shared and discussed.
- **Influencer Culture:** Influencer culture has created new forms of digital rhetoric, with influencers using language and communication to shape their online personas and influence their followers.

The flowchart illustrates the complex interplay between cultural norms, internet culture, and digital rhetoric:

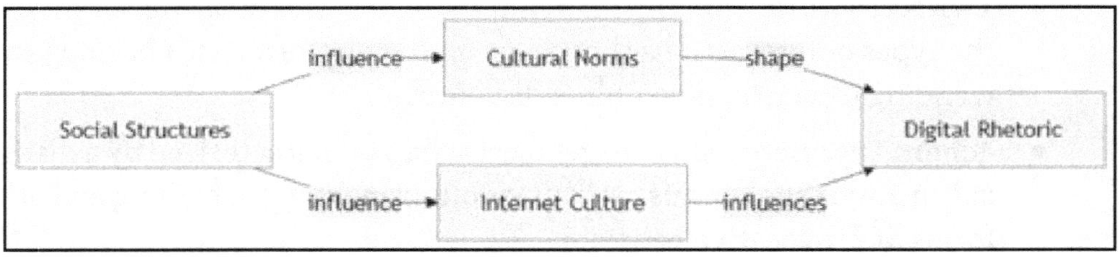

The Implications of Cultural Norms for Online Interactions

Cultural norms have significant implications for online interactions, shaping the types of content that are shared, the ways in which individuals interact, and the norms that govern online behavior. For instance:

- **Online Harassment**: Cultural norms around communication and interaction can contribute to online harassment, with certain types of language or behavior being deemed acceptable or unacceptable.
- **Content Moderation**: Cultural norms influence content moderation practices, with certain types of content being prioritized or censored based on social and cultural norms.
- **Digital Literacy**: Cultural norms around digital literacy influence the ways in which individuals navigate and utilize digital technologies.

CHAPTER

Tools and Technologies in DH

3

3.1 TEXT ANALYSIS AND NATURAL LANGUAGE PROCESSING

3.1.1 Topic Modeling

A topic model is a type of statistical model for discovering the abstract "topics" that occur in a collection of documents. Topic modeling is a frequently used text-mining tool for discovery of hidden semantic structures in a text body. Intuitively, given that a document is about a particular topic, one would expect particular words to appear in the document more or less frequently: "dog" and "bone" will appear more often in documents about dogs, "cat" and "meow" will appear in documents about cats, and "the" and "is" will appear approximately equally in both. A document typically concerns multiple topics in different proportions; thus, in a document that is 10% about cats and 90% about dogs, there would probably be about 9 times more dog words than cat words. The "topics" produced by topic modeling techniques are clusters of similar words. A topic model captures this intuition in a mathematical framework, which allows examining a set of documents and discovering, based on the statistics of the words in each, what the topics might be and what each document's balance of topics is.

Topic models are also referred to as probabilistic topic models, which refers to statistical algorithms for discovering the latent semantic structures of an extensive text body. In the age of information, the amount of the written material we encounter each day is simply beyond our processing capacity. Topic models can help to organize and offer insights for us to understand large collections of unstructured text bodies. Originally developed as a text-mining tool, topic models have been used to detect instructive structures in data such as genetic information, images, and networks. They also have applications in other fields such as bioinformatics and computer vision.

History

An early topic model was described by Papadimitriou, Raghavan, Tamaki and Vempala in 1998. Another one, called probabilistic latent semantic analysis (PLSA), was created by Thomas Hofmann in 1999. Latent Dirichlet allocation

(LDA), perhaps the most common topic model currently in use, is a generalization of PLSA. Developed by David Blei, Andrew Ng, and Michael I. Jordan in 2002, LDA introduces sparse Dirichlet prior distributions over document-topic and topic-word distributions, encoding the intuition that documents cover a small number of topics and that topics often use a small number of words.

Other topic models are generally extensions on LDA, such as Pachinko allocation, which improves on LDA by modeling correlations between topics in addition to the word correlations which constitute topics. Hierarchical latent tree analysis (HLTA) is an alternative to LDA, which models word co-occurrence using a tree of latent variables and the states of the latent variables, which correspond to soft clusters of documents, are interpreted as topics.

Topic Models for Context Information

Approaches for temporal information include Block and Newman's determination of the temporal dynamics of topics in the Pennsylvania Gazette during 1728–1800. Griffiths & Steyvers used topic modeling on abstracts from the journal PNAS to identify topics that rose or fell in popularity from 1991 to 2001 whereas Lamba & Madhusushan used topic modeling on full-text research articles retrieved from DJLIT journal from 1981 to 2018. In the field of library and information science, Lamba & Madhusudhan applied topic modeling on different Indian resources like journal articles and electronic theses and resources (ETDs).

Nelson has been analyzing change in topics over time in the Richmond Times-Dispatch to understand social and political changes and continuities in Richmond during the American Civil War. Yang, Torget and Mihalcea applied topic modeling methods to newspapers from 1829 to 2008. Mimno used topic modelling with 24 journals on classical philology and archaeology spanning 150 years to look at how topics in the journals change over time and how the journals become more different or similar over time.

Yin et al. introduced a topic model for geographically distributed documents, where document positions are explained by latent regions which are detected during inference. Chang and Blei included network information between linked documents in the relational topic model, to model the links between websites. The author-topic model by Rosen-Zvi et al. models the topics associated with authors of documents to improve the topic detection for documents with authorship information.

HLTA was applied to a collection of recent research papers published at major AI and Machine Learning venues. The resulting model is called The AI Tree. The resulting topics are used to index the papers at aipano.cse.ust.hk to help researchers track research trends and identify papers to read, and help conference organizers and journal editors identify reviewers for submissions. To improve the qualitative aspects and coherency of generated topics, some researchers have explored the efficacy of "coherence scores", or otherwise how computer-extracted clusters (i.e. topics) align with a human benchmark. Coherence scores are metrics for optimising the number of topics to extract from a document corpus.

Algorithms

In practice, researchers attempt to fit appropriate model parameters to the data corpus using one of several heuristics for maximum likelihood fit. A survey by D. Blei describes this suite of algorithms. Several groups of researchers starting with Papadimitriou et al. have attempted to design algorithms with provable guarantees. Assuming that the data were actually generated by the model in question, they try to design algorithms that probably find the model that was used to create the data. Techniques used here include singular value decomposition (SVD) and the method of moments. In 2012 an algorithm based upon non-negative matrix factorization (NMF) was introduced that also generalizes to topic models with correlations among topics.

In 2017, neural network has been leveraged in topic modeling to make it faster in inference, which has been extended weakly supervised version. In 2018 a new approach to topic models was proposed: it is based on stochastic block model. Because of the recent development of LLM, topic modeling has leveraged LLM through contextual embedding and fine tuning.

Applications

- **To Quantitative Biomedicine:** Topic models are being used also in other contexts. For examples uses of topic models in biology and bioinformatics research emerged. Recently topic models has been used to extract information from dataset of cancers' genomic samples. In this case topics are biological latent variables to be inferred.
- **To Analysis of Music and Creativity:** Topic models can be used for analysis of continuous signals like music. For instance, they were used to quantify how musical styles change in time, and identify the influence of specific artists on later music creation.

3.1.2 Named Entity Recognition

Named-entity recognition (NER) (also known as (named) entity identification, entity chunking, and entity extraction) is a subtask of information extraction that seeks to locate and classify named entities mentioned in unstructured text into pre-defined categories such as person names (PER), organizations (ORG), locations (LOC), geopolitical entities (GPE), vehicles (VEH), medical codes, time expressions, quantities, monetary values, percentages, etc. Most research on NER/NEE systems has been structured as taking an unannotated block of text, such as transducing:

- Jim bought 300 shares of Acme Corp. in 2006.

Into an annotated block of text that highlights the names of entities:

- $[\text{Jim}]_{\text{Person}}$ bought 300 shares of $[\text{Acme Corp.}]_{\text{Organization}}$ in $[2006]_{\text{Time}}$.

In this example, a person name consisting of one token, a two-token company name and a temporal expression have been detected and classified.

History

Early work in NER systems in the 1990s was aimed primarily at extraction from journalistic articles. Attention then turned to processing of military dispatches and reports. Later stages of the automatic content extraction (ACE) evaluation also included several types of informal text styles, such as weblogs and text transcripts from conversational telephone speech conversations.

Since about 1998, there has been a great deal of interest in entity identification in the molecular biology, bioinformatics, and medical natural language processing communities. The most common entity of interest in that domain has been names of genes and gene products. There has been also considerable interest in the recognition of chemical entities and drugs in the context of the CHEMDNER competition, with 27 teams participating in this task.

- In 2001, research indicated that even state-of-the-art NER systems were brittle, meaning that NER systems developed for one domain did not typically perform well on other domains. Considerable effort is involved in tuning NER systems to perform well in a new domain; this is true for both rule-based and trainable statistical systems.
- As of 2007, state-of-the-art NER systems for English produce near-human performance. For example, the best system entering MUC-7 scored 93.39% of F-measure while human annotators scored 97.60% and 96.95%.

Current Challenges

Despite high F1 numbers reported on the MUC-7 dataset, the problem of named-entity recognition is far from being solved. The main efforts are directed to reducing the annotations labor by employing semi-supervised learning, robust performance across domains and scaling up to fine-grained entity types. In recent years, many projects have turned to crowdsourcing, which is a promising solution to obtain high-quality aggregate human judgments for supervised and semi-supervised machine learning approaches to NER. Another challenging task is devising models to deal with linguistically complex contexts such as Twitter and search queries.

There are some researchers who did some comparisons about the NER performances from different statistical models such as HMM (hidden Markov model), ME (maximum entropy), and CRF (conditional random fields), and feature sets. And some researchers recently proposed graph-based semi-supervised learning model for language specific NER tasks.

A recently emerging task of identifying "important expressions" in text and cross-linking them to Wikipedia can be seen as an instance of extremely fine-grained named-entity recognition, where the types are the actual Wikipedia pages describing the (potentially ambiguous) concepts. Below is an example output of a Wikification system:

> *<ENTITY url="https://en.wikipedia.org/wiki/Michael_I._Jordan"> Michael Jordan </ENTITY> is a professor at <ENTITY url="https://en.wikipedia.org/wiki/University_of_California,_Berkeley"> Berkeley </ENTITY>*

Another field that has seen progress but remains challenging is the application of NER to Twitter and other microblogs, considered "noisy" due to non-standard orthography, shortness and informality of texts. NER challenges in English Tweets have been organized by research communities to compare performances of various approaches, such as bidirectional LSTMs, Learning-to-Search, or CRFs.

Problem

Definition

In the expression named entity, the word named restricts the task to those entities for which one or many strings, such as words or phrases, stand (fairly) consistently for some referent. This is closely related to rigid designators, as defined by Kripke, although in practice NER deals with many names and referents that are not philosophically "rigid". For instance, the automotive company created by Henry Ford in 1903 can be referred to as Ford or Ford Motor Company, although "Ford" can refer to many other entities as well. Rigid designators include proper names as well as terms for certain biological species and substances, but exclude pronouns, descriptions that pick out a referent by its properties and names for kinds of things as opposed to individuals (for example "Bank").

Full named-entity recognition is often broken down, conceptually and possibly also in implementations, as two distinct problems: detection of names, and classification of the names by the type of entity they refer to (e.g. person, organization, or location). The first phase is typically simplified to a segmentation problem: names are defined to be contiguous spans of tokens, with no nesting, so that "Bank of America" is a single name, disregarding the fact that inside this name, the substring "America" is itself a name. This segmentation problem is formally similar to chunking. The second phase requires choosing an ontology by which to organize categories of things. Temporal expressions and some numerical expressions (e.g., money, percentages, etc.) may also be considered as named entities in the context of the NER task. While some instances of these types are good examples of rigid designators (e.g., the year 2001) there are also many invalid ones (e.g., I take my vacations in "June"). In the first case, the year 2001 refers to the 2001st year of the Gregorian calendar. In the second case, the month June may refer to the month of an undefined year (past June, next June, every June, etc.). It is arguable that the definition of named entity is loosened in such cases for practical reasons. The definition of the term named entity is therefore not strict and often has to be explained in the context in which it is used.

Certain hierarchies of named entity types have been proposed in the literature. BBN categories, proposed in 2002, are used for question answering and consists of 29 types and 64 subtypes. Sekine's extended hierarchy, proposed in 2002, is made of 200 subtypes. More recently, in 2011 Ritter used a hierarchy based on common Freebase entity types in ground-breaking experiments on NER over social media text.

Difficulties

- NER involves ambiguities. The same name can refer to different entities of the same type. For example, "JFK" can refer to the former president or his son. This is basically a reference resolution problem.
- The same name can refer to completely different types. "JFK" might refer to the airport in New York. "IRA" can refer to Individual Retirement Account or International Reading Association.
- This can be caused by metonymy. For example, "The White House" can refer to an organization instead of a location.

Formal Evaluation

To evaluate the quality of an NER system's output, several measures have been defined. The usual measures are called precision, recall, and F1 score. However, several issues remain in just how to calculate those values.

These statistical measures work reasonably well for the obvious cases of finding or missing a real entity exactly; and for finding a non-entity. However, NER can fail in many other ways, many of which are arguably "partially correct", and should not be counted as complete success or failures. For example, identifying a real entity:

- With fewer tokens than desired (for example, missing the last token of "John Smith, M.D.").
- With more tokens than desired (for example, including the first word of "The University of MD").

- Partitioning adjacent entities differently (for example, treating "Smith, Jones Robinson" as 2 vs. 3 entities).
- Assigning it a completely wrong type (for example, calling a personal name an organization).
- Assigning it a related but inexact type (for example, "substance" vs. "drug", or "school" vs. "organization").
- Correctly identifying an entity, when what the user wanted was a smaller- or larger-scope entity (for example, identifying "James Madison" as a personal name, when it's part of "James Madison University"). Some NER systems impose the restriction that entities may never overlap or nest, which means that in some cases one must make arbitrary or task-specific choices.

One overly simple method of measuring accuracy is merely to count what fraction of all tokens in the text were correctly or incorrectly identified as part of entity references (or as being entities of the correct type). This suffers from at least two problems: first, the vast majority of tokens in real-world text are not part of entity names, so the baseline accuracy (always predict "not an entity") is extravagantly high, typically >90%; and second, mispredicting the full span of an entity name is not properly penalized (finding only a person's first name when his last name follows might be scored as ½ accuracy).

In academic conferences such as CoNLL, a variant of the F1 score has been defined as follows:

- Precision is the number of predicted entity name spans that line up exactly with spans in the gold standard evaluation data. I.e. when $[_{\text{Person}}$ Hans] $[_{\text{Person}}$ Blick] is predicted but $[_{\text{Person}}$ Hans Blick] was required, precision for the predicted name is zero. Precision is then averaged over all predicted entity names.
- Recall is similarly the number of names in the gold standard that appear at exactly the same location in the predictions.
- F1 score is the harmonic mean of these two.

It follows from the above definition that any prediction that misses a single token, includes a spurious token, or has the wrong class, is a hard error and does not contribute positively to either precision or recall. Thus, this measure may be said to be pessimistic: it can be the case that many "errors" are close to correct, and might be adequate for a given purpose.

For example, one system might always omit titles such as "Ms." or "Ph.D.", but be compared to a system or ground-truth data that expects titles to be included.

In that case, every such name is treated as an error. Because of such issues, it is important actually to examine the kinds of errors, and decide how important they are given one's goals and requirements.

Evaluation models based on a token-by-token matching have been proposed. Such models may be given partial credit for overlapping matches (such as using the Intersection over Union criterion). They allow a finer grained evaluation and comparison of extraction systems.

Approaches

NER systems have been created that use linguistic grammar-based techniques as well as statistical models such as machine learning. State of the art systems may incorporate multiple approaches.

- GATE supports NER across many languages and domains out of the box, usable via a graphical interface and a Java API.
- OpenNLP includes rule-based and statistical named-entity recognition.
- SpaCy features fast statistical NER as well as an open-source named-entity visualizer.

Hand-crafted grammar-based systems typically obtain better precision, but at the cost of lower recall and months of work by experienced computational linguists. Statistical NER systems typically require a large amount of manually annotated training data.

Semisupervised approaches have been suggested to avoid part of the annotation effort. In the statistical learning era, NER was usually performed by learning a simple linear regression model on engineered features, then decoded by a bidirectional Viterbi algorithm. Some commonly used features include:

- **Lexical Items:** The token itself be labeled.
- Stemmed lexical items.
- **Shape:** The orthographic pattern of the target word. For example, all lowercase, all uppercase, initial uppercase, mixed case, uppercase followed by a period (often indicating a middle name), contains hyphen, etc.
- Affixes of the target word and surrounding words.
- Part of speech of the word.
- Whether the word appears in one or more named entity lists (gazetteers).
- Words and/or n-grams occurring in the surrounding context.

A gazetteer is a list of names and their types, such as "General Electric". It can be used to augment any system for NER. They had been often used in the era of statistical machine learning. Many different classifier types have been used to perform machine-learned NER, with conditional random fields being a typical choice. Transformers features token classification using deep learning models.

3.1.3 Sentiment Analysis

Sentiment analysis (also known as opinion mining or emotion AI) is the use of natural language processing, text analysis, computational linguistics, and biometrics to systematically identify, extract, quantify, and study affective states and subjective information.

Sentiment analysis is widely applied to voice of the customer materials such as reviews and survey responses, online and social media, and healthcare materials for applications that range from marketing to customer service to clinical medicine. With the rise of deep language models, such as RoBERTa, also more difficult data domains can be analyzed, e.g., news texts where authors typically express their opinion/sentiment less explicitly.

Simple Cases

- "Coronet has the best lines of all day cruisers."
- "Bertram has a deep V hull and runs easily through seas."
- "Pastel-colored 1980s day cruisers from Florida are ugly."
- "I dislike old cabin cruisers."

More Challenging Examples

- "I do not dislike cabin cruisers." (Negation handling).
- "Disliking watercraft is not really my thing." (Negation, inverted word order).
- "Sometimes I really hate RIBs." (Adverbial modifies the sentiment).
- "I'd really truly love going out in this weather!" (Possibly sarcastic).
- "Chris Craft is better looking than Limestone." (Two brand names, identifying the target of attitude is difficult).
- "Chris Craft is better looking than Limestone, but Limestone projects seaworthiness and reliability." (Two attitudes, two brand names).
- "The movie is surprising, with plenty of unsettling plot twists." (Negative term used in a positive sense in certain domains).
- "You should see their decadent dessert menu." (Attitudinal term has shifted polarity recently in certain domains).

- "I love my mobile but would not recommend it to any of my colleagues." (Qualified positive sentiment, difficult to categorise).
- "Next week's gig will be right koide9!" ("Quoi de neuf?", French for "what's new?". Newly minted terms can be highly attitudinal but volatile in polarity and often out of known vocabulary).

Types

A basic task in sentiment analysis is classifying the polarity of a given text at the document, sentence, or feature/aspect level—whether the expressed opinion in a document, a sentence or an entity feature/aspect is positive, negative, or neutral. Advanced, "beyond polarity" sentiment classification looks, for instance, at emotional states such as enjoyment, anger, disgust, sadness, fear, and surprise.

Precursors to sentimental analysis include the General Inquirer, which provided hints toward quantifying patterns in text and, separately, psychological research that examined a person's psychological state based on analysis of their verbal behavior. Subsequently, the method described in a patent by Volcani and Fogel, looked specifically at sentiment and identified individual words and phrases in text with respect to different emotional scales. A current system based on their work, called EffectCheck, presents synonyms that can be used to increase or decrease the level of evoked emotion in each scale.

Many other subsequent efforts were less sophisticated, using a mere polar view of sentiment, from positive to negative, such as work by Turney, and Pang who applied different methods for detecting the polarity of product reviews and movie reviews respectively. This work is at the document level. One can also classify a document's polarity on a multi-way scale, which was attempted by Pang and Snyder among others: Pang and Lee expanded the basic task of classifying a movie review as either positive or negative to predict star ratings on either a 3- or a 4-star scale, while Snyder performed an in-depth analysis of restaurant reviews, predicting ratings for various aspects of the given restaurant, such as the food and atmosphere (on a five-star scale).

First steps to bringing together various approaches—learning, lexical, knowledge-based, etc.—were taken in the 2004 AAAI Spring Symposium where linguists, computer scientists, and other interested researchers first aligned interests and proposed shared tasks and benchmark data sets for the systematic computational research on affect, appeal, subjectivity, and sentiment in text.

Even though in most statistical classification methods, the neutral class is ignored under the assumption that neutral texts lie near the boundary of the binary classifier, several researchers suggest that, as in every polarity problem, three categories must be identified. Moreover, it can be proven that specific classifiers such as the Max Entropy and SVMs can benefit from the introduction of a neutral class and improve the overall accuracy of the classification. There are in principle two ways for operating with a neutral class. Either, the algorithm proceeds by first identifying the neutral language, filtering it out and then assessing the rest in terms of positive and negative sentiments, or it builds a three-way classification in one step. This second approach often involves estimating a probability distribution over all categories (e.g. naive Bayes classifiers as implemented by the NLTK). Whether and how to use a neutral class depends on the nature of the data: if the data is clearly clustered into neutral, negative and positive language, it makes sense to filter the neutral language out and focus on the polarity between positive and negative sentiments. If, in contrast, the data are mostly neutral with small deviations towards positive and negative affect, this strategy would make it harder to clearly distinguish between the two poles.

A different method for determining sentiment is the use of a scaling system whereby words commonly associated with having a negative, neutral, or positive sentiment are given an associated number on a -10 to +10 scale (most negative up to most positive) or simply from 0 to a positive upper limit such as +4. This makes it possible to adjust the sentiment of a given term relative to its environment (usually on the level of the sentence).

When a piece of unstructured text is analyzed using natural language processing, each concept in the specified environment is given a score based on the way sentiment words relate to the concept and its associated score. This allows movement to a more sophisticated understanding of sentiment, because it is now possible to adjust the sentiment value of a concept relative to modifications that may surround it. Words, for example, that intensify, relax or negate the sentiment expressed by the concept can affect its score.

Alternatively, texts can be given a positive and negative sentiment strength score if the goal is to determine the sentiment in a text rather than the overall polarity and strength of the text. There are various other types of sentiment analysis, such as aspect-based sentiment analysis, grading sentiment analysis (positive, negative, neutral), multilingual sentiment analysis and detection of emotions.

Subjectivity/Objectivity Identification

This task is commonly defined as classifying a given text (usually a sentence) into one of two classes: objective or subjective. This problem can sometimes be more difficult than polarity classification. The subjectivity of words and phrases may depend on their context and an objective document may contain subjective sentences (e.g., a news article quoting people's opinions).

Moreover, as mentioned by Su, results are largely dependent on the definition of subjectivity used when annotating texts. However, Pang showed that removing objective sentences from a document before classifying its polarity helped improve performance. Subjective and objective identification, emerging subtasks of sentiment analysis to use syntactic, semantic features, and machine learning knowledge to identify if a sentence or document contains facts or opinions. Awareness of recognizing factual and opinions is not recent, having possibly first presented by Carbonell at Yale University in 1979. The term objective refers to the incident carrying factual information.

- **Example of an objective sentence:** 'To be elected president of the United States, a candidate must be at least thirty-five years of age.'

The term subjective describes the incident contains non-factual information in various forms, such as personal opinions, judgment, and predictions, also known as 'private states'. In the example down below, it reflects a private states 'We Americans'. Moreover, the target entity commented by the opinions can take several forms from tangible product to intangible topic matters stated in Liu (2010). Furthermore, three types of attitudes were observed by Liu (2010), 1) positive opinions, 2) neutral opinions, and 3) negative opinions.

- **Example of a subjective sentence:** 'We Americans need to elect a president who is mature and who is able to make wise decisions.'

This analysis is a classification problem.

Each class's collections of words or phrase indicators are defined for to locate desirable patterns on unannotated text. For subjective expression, a different word list has been created. Lists of subjective indicators in words or phrases have been developed by multiple researchers in the linguist and natural language processing field states in Riloff et al. (2003). A dictionary of extraction rules has to be created for measuring given expressions.

Over the years, in subjective detection, the features extraction progression from curating features by hand to automated features learning. At the moment, automated learning methods can further separate into supervised and unsupervised machine learning. Patterns extraction with machine learning process annotated and unannotated text have been explored extensively by academic researchers.

However, researchers recognized several challenges in developing fixed sets of rules for expressions respectably. Much of the challenges in rule development stems from the nature of textual information.

- **Metaphorical Expressions:** The text contains metaphoric expression may impact on the performance on the extraction. Besides, metaphors take in different forms, which may have been contributed to the increase in detection.

- **Discrepancies in Writings:** For the text obtained from the Internet, the discrepancies in the writing style of targeted text data involve distinct writing genres and styles.
- **Context-Sensitive:** Classification may vary based on the subjectiveness or objectiveness of previous and following sentences.
- **Time-Sensitive Attribute:** The task is challenged by some textual data's time-sensitive attribute. If a group of researchers wants to confirm a piece of fact in the news, they need a longer time for cross-validation, than the news becomes outdated.
- **Ever-Growing Volume:** The task is also challenged by the sheer volume of textual data. The textual data's ever-growing nature makes the task overwhelmingly difficult for the researchers to complete the task on time.

Previously, the research mainly focused on document level classification. However, classifying a document level suffers less accuracy, as an article may have diverse types of expressions involved. Researching evidence suggests a set of news articles that are expected to dominate by the objective expression, whereas the results show that it consisted of over 40% of subjective expression.

To overcome those challenges, researchers conclude that classifier efficacy depends on the precisions of patterns learner. And the learner feeds with large volumes of annotated training data outperformed those trained on less comprehensive subjective features. However, one of the main obstacles to executing this type of work is to generate a big dataset of annotated sentences manually. The manual annotation method has been less favored than automatic learning for three reasons:

- **Variations in Comprehensions:** In the manual annotation task, disagreement of whether one instance is subjective or objective may occur among annotators because of languages' ambiguity.
- **Human Errors:** Manual annotation task is a meticulous assignment, it require intense concentration to finish.
- **Time-Consuming:** Manual annotation task is an assiduous work. Riloff (1996) show that a 160 texts cost 8 hours for one annotator to finish.

All these mentioned reasons can impact on the efficiency and effectiveness of subjective and objective classification. Accordingly, two bootstrapping methods were designed to learning linguistic patterns from unannotated text data. Both methods are starting with a handful of seed words and unannotated textual data.

- **Meta-Bootstrapping by Riloff and Jones in 1999:** Level One: Generate extraction patterns based on the pre-defined rules and the extracted patterns by the number of seed words each pattern holds. Level Two: Top 5 words will be marked and add to the dictionary. Repeat.

- **Basilisk (Bootstrapping Approach to Semantic Lexicon Induction using Semantic Knowledge) by Thelen and Riloff: Step One:** Generate extraction patterns. Step Two: Move best patterns from Pattern Pool to Candidate Word Pool. Step Three: Top 10 words will be marked and add to the dictionary. Repeat.

Overall, these algorithms highlight the need for automatic pattern recognition and extraction in subjective and objective task. Subjective and object classifier can enhance the several applications of natural language processing. One of the classifier's primary benefits is that it popularized the practice of data-driven decision-making processes in various industries. According to Liu, the applications of subjective and objective identification have been implemented in business, advertising, sports, and social science.

- **Online Review Classification:** In the business industry, the classifier helps the company better understand the feedbacks on product and reasonings behind the reviews.
- **Actionable Insights:** Emotions, sarcasm, tone and other nuances previously difficult to parse via legacy NLP (outside of "positive, "negative" or "neutral"), are more accurately explicated from consumer feedback. This makes the unstructured review data increasingly actionable in terms of customer service, product/service improvements, industry-specific trend identification and competitive analysis.
- **Stock Price Prediction:** In the finance industry, the classifier aids the prediction model by process auxiliary information from social media and other textual information from the Internet. Previous studies on Japanese stock price conducted by Dong et al. indicates that model with subjective and objective module may perform better than those without this part.
- Social media analysis.
- Students' Feedback Classification.
- **Document Summarising:** The classifier can extract target-specified comments and gathering opinions made by one particular entity.
- **Complex Question Answering:** The classifier can dissect the complex questions by classing the language subject or objective and focused target. In the research Yu et al.(2003), the researcher developed a sentence and document level clustered that identity opinion pieces.
- Domain-Specific Applications.

- **Email Analysis:** The subjective and objective classifier detects spam by tracing language patterns with target words.

Feature/Aspect-Based

It refers to determining the opinions or sentiments expressed on different features or aspects of entities, e.g., of a cell phone, a digital camera, or a bank. A feature or aspect is an attribute or component of an entity, e.g., the screen of a cell phone, the service for a restaurant, or the picture quality of a camera. The advantage of feature-based sentiment analysis is the possibility to capture nuances about objects of interest. Different features can generate different sentiment responses, for example a hotel can have a convenient location, but mediocre food. This problem involves several sub-problems, e.g., identifying relevant entities, extracting their features/aspects, and determining whether an opinion expressed on each feature/aspect is positive, negative or neutral. The automatic identification of features can be performed with syntactic methods, with topic modeling, or with deep learning. More detailed discussions about this level of sentiment analysis can be found in Liu's work.

Intensity Ranking

Emotions and sentiments are subjective in nature. The degree of emotions/sentiments expressed in a given text at the document, sentence, or feature/aspect level—to what degree of intensity is expressed in the opinion of a document, a sentence or an entity differs on a case-to-case basis. However, predicting only the emotion and sentiment does not always convey complete information. The degree or level of emotions and sentiments often plays a crucial role in understanding the exact feeling within a single class (e.g., 'good' versus 'awesome'). Some methods leverage a stacked ensemble method for predicting intensity for emotion and sentiment by combining the outputs obtained and using deep learning models based on convolutional neural networks, long short-term memory networks and gated recurrent units.

Methods and Features

Existing approaches to sentiment analysis can be grouped into three main categories: knowledge-based techniques, statistical methods, and hybrid approaches. Knowledge-based techniques classify text by affect categories based on the presence of unambiguous affect words such as happy, sad, afraid, and bored. Some knowledge bases not only list obvious affect words, but also assign arbitrary words a probable "affinity" to particular emotions. Statistical methods leverage elements from machine learning such as latent semantic analysis, support vector machines, "bag of words", "Pointwise Mutual Information" for Semantic Orientation, semantic space models or word embedding models, and deep learning.

More sophisticated methods try to detect the holder of a sentiment (i.e., the person who maintains that affective state) and the target (i.e., the entity about which the affect is felt). To mine the opinion in context and get the feature about which the speaker has opined, the grammatical relationships of words are used. Grammatical dependency relations are obtained by deep parsing of the text. Hybrid approaches leverage both machine learning and elements from knowledge representation such as ontologies and semantic networks in order to detect semantics that are expressed in a subtle manner, e.g., through the analysis of concepts that do not explicitly convey relevant information, but which are implicitly linked to other concepts that do so. Open source software tools as well as range of free and paid sentiment analysis tools deploy machine learning, statistics, and natural language processing techniques to automate sentiment analysis on large collections of texts, including web pages, online news, internet discussion groups, online reviews, web blogs, and social media. Knowledge-based systems, on the other hand, make use of publicly available resources, to extract the semantic and affective information associated with natural language concepts.

The system can help perform affective commonsense reasoning. Sentiment analysis can also be performed on visual content, i.e., images and videos. One of the first approaches in this direction is SentiBank utilizing an adjective noun pair representation of visual content. In addition, the vast majority of sentiment classification approaches rely on the bag-of-words model, which disregards context, grammar and even word order. Approaches that analyses the sentiment based on how words compose the meaning of longer phrases have shown better result, but they incur an additional annotation overhead.

A human analysis component is required in sentiment analysis, as automated systems are not able to analyze historical tendencies of the individual commenter, or the platform and are often classified incorrectly in their expressed sentiment. Automation impacts approximately 23% of comments that are correctly classified by humans. However, humans often disagree, and it is argued that the inter-human agreement provides an upper bound that automated sentiment classifiers can eventually reach.

Evaluation

The accuracy of a sentiment analysis system is, in principle, how well it agrees with human judgments. This is usually measured by variant measures based on precision and recall over the two target categories of negative and positive texts. However, according to research human raters typically only agree about 80% of the time. Thus, a program that achieves 70% accuracy in classifying sentiment is doing nearly as well as humans, even though such accuracy may not sound impressive. If a program were "right" 100% of the time, humans would still disagree with it about

20% of the time, since they disagree that much about any answer. On the other hand, computer systems will make very different errors than human assessors, and thus the figures are not entirely comparable. For instance, a computer system will have trouble with negations, exaggerations, jokes, or sarcasm, which typically are easy to handle for a human reader: some errors a computer system makes will seem overly naive to a human. In general, the utility for practical commercial tasks of sentiment analysis as it is defined in academic research has been called into question, mostly since the simple one-dimensional model of sentiment from negative to positive yields rather little actionable information for a client worrying about the effect of public discourse on e.g. brand or corporate reputation.

To better fit market needs, evaluation of sentiment analysis has moved to more task-based measures, formulated together with representatives from PR agencies and market research professionals. The focus in e.g. the RepLab evaluation data set is less on the content of the text under consideration and more on the effect of the text in question on brand reputation. Because evaluation of sentiment analysis is becoming more and more task based, each implementation needs a separate training model to get a more accurate representation of sentiment for a given data set.

Web 2.0

The rise of social media such as blogs and social networks has fueled interest in sentiment analysis. With the proliferation of reviews, ratings, recommendations and other forms of online expression, online opinion has turned into a kind of virtual currency for businesses looking to market their products, identify new opportunities and manage their reputations.

As businesses look to automate the process of filtering out the noise, understanding the conversations, identifying the relevant content and actioning it appropriately, many are now looking to the field of sentiment analysis. Further complicating the matter, is the rise of anonymous social media platforms such as 4chan and Reddit. If web 2.0 was all about democratizing publishing, then the next stage of the web may well be based on democratizing data mining of all the content that is getting published.

One step towards this aim is accomplished in research. Several research teams in universities around the world currently focus on understanding the dynamics of sentiment in e-communities through sentiment analysis. The problem is that most sentiment analysis algorithms use simple terms to express sentiment about a product or service. However, cultural factors, linguistic nuances, and differing contexts make it extremely difficult to turn a string of written text into a simple pro or con sentiment. The fact that humans often disagree on the sentiment of text illustrates how big a task it is for computers to get this right. The shorter the string of text, the harder it becomes.

Even though short text strings might be a problem, sentiment analysis within microblogging has shown that Twitter can be seen as a valid online indicator of political sentiment. Tweets' political sentiment demonstrates close correspondence to parties' and politicians' political positions, indicating that the content of Twitter messages plausibly reflects the offline political landscape. Furthermore, sentiment analysis on Twitter has also been shown to capture the public mood behind human reproduction cycles globally, as well as other problems of public-health relevance such as adverse drug reactions. While sentiment analysis has been popular for domains where authors express their opinion rather explicitly ("the movie is awesome"), such as social media and product reviews, only recently robust methods were devised for other domains where sentiment is strongly implicit or indirect. For example, in news articles - mostly due to the expected journalistic objectivity - journalists often describe actions or events rather than directly stating the polarity of a piece of information. Earlier approaches using dictionaries or shallow machine learning features were unable to catch the "meaning between the lines", but recently researchers have proposed a deep learning based approach and dataset that is able to analyze sentiment in news articles.

Scholars have utilized sentiment analysis to analyse the construction health and safety Tweets (which is called X now). The research revealed that there is a positive correlation between favorites and retweets in terms of sentiment valence. Others have examined the impact of YouTube on the dissemination of construction health and safety knowledge. They investigated how emotions influence users' behaviors in terms of viewing and commenting through semantic analysis. In another study, positive sentiment accounted for an overwhelming figure of 85% in knowledge sharing of construction safety and health via Instagram.

Application in Recommender Systems

For a recommender system, sentiment analysis has been proven to be a valuable technique. A recommender system aims to predict the preference for an item of a target user. Mainstream recommender systems work on explicit data set. For example, collaborative filtering works on the rating matrix, and content-based filtering works on the meta-data of the items.

In many social networking services or e-commerce websites, users can provide text review, comment or feedback to the items. These user-generated text provide a rich source of user's sentiment opinions about numerous products and items. Potentially, for an item, such text can reveal both the related feature/aspects of the item and the users' sentiments on each feature. The item's feature/aspects described in the text play the same role with the meta-data in content-based filtering, but the former are more valuable for the recommender system. Since these features are broadly mentioned by users in their reviews, they can be seen as the most crucial features that can significantly influence the user's experience on the item, while the meta-data of the item (usually provided by the producers instead of consumers) may ignore features that are concerned by the users. For different items with common features, a user may give different sentiments. Also, a feature of the same item may receive different sentiments from different users. Users' sentiments on the features can be regarded as a multi-dimensional rating score, reflecting their preference on the items.

Based on the feature/aspects and the sentiments extracted from the user-generated text, a hybrid recommender system can be constructed. There are two types of motivation to recommend a candidate item to a user. The first motivation is the candidate item have numerous common features with the user's preferred items, while the second motivation is that the candidate item receives a high sentiment on its features.

For a preferred item, it is reasonable to believe that items with the same features will have a similar function or utility. So, these items will also likely to be preferred by the user. On the other hand, for a shared feature of two candidate items, other users may give positive sentiment to one of them while giving negative sentiment to another. Clearly, the high evaluated item should be recommended to the user. Based on these two motivations, a combination ranking score of similarity and sentiment rating can be constructed for each candidate item.

Except for the difficulty of the sentiment analysis itself, applying sentiment analysis on reviews or feedback also faces the challenge of spam and biased reviews. One direction of work is focused on evaluating the helpfulness of each review. Review or feedback poorly written is hardly helpful for recommender system. Besides, a review can be designed to hinder sales of a target product, thus be harmful to the recommender system even it is well written. Researchers also found that long and short forms of user-generated text should be treated differently. An interesting result shows that short-form reviews are sometimes more helpful than long-form, because it is easier to filter out the noise in a short-form text. For the long-form text, the growing length of the text does not always bring a proportionate increase in the number of features or sentiments in the text.

Lamba & Madhusudhan introduce a nascent way to cater the information needs of today's library users by repackaging the results from sentiment analysis of social media platforms like Twitter and provide it as a consolidated time-based service in different formats. Further, they propose a new way of conducting marketing in libraries using social media mining and sentiment analysis.

Ethical Considerations

Issues such as privacy, consent, and bias are crucial since sentiment analysis regularly analyzes personal data without explicit user consent. The potential for misinterpretation and misuse of sentiment data can significantly impact societal norms. Furthermore, the development of ethical frameworks, as seen in projects like SEWA, where Ethical and Industrial Valorisation Advisory Boards are established, is essential for addressing these challenges. These boards help ensure that sentiment analysis technologies are used responsibly, especially in applications involving the recognition of human emotions and behaviors. Such frameworks are vital for guiding the responsible use of sentiment analysis tools, ensuring they promote equity and respect user autonomy, and effectively address both routine and complex ethical issues.

3.2 Digital Archives and Repositories

In the digital age, the preservation, accessibility, and dissemination of information have taken on new dimensions through the development of digital archives and repositories. These systems have emerged as essential components in the realm of information management, scholarly communication, and cultural preservation. A digital archive is a system or service that stores, preserves, and provides access to digital content, often with a focus on long-term preservation. A digital repository, on the other hand, is typically more focused on collecting, managing, and disseminating digital resources, particularly in academic and research contexts. While these two terms are sometimes used interchangeably, they often differ in purpose and scope. Digital archives and repositories represent a transformative development in the management and dissemination of information in the digital era. They have redefined how knowledge is preserved, accessed, and shared, impacting education, research, and cultural preservation. Despite the challenges they face, the continued evolution of technology and growing global collaboration offer immense potential for their expansion and improvement. As stewards of digital knowledge, archives and repositories are not merely storage systems but dynamic platforms that connect people with information, ideas, and heritage across time and space.

Concept and Purpose

The core objective of digital archives is to preserve digital materials in a manner that ensures their longevity and usability over time. Digital archives are often associated with heritage institutions like libraries, museums, and national archives. These institutions have transitioned from physical to digital formats to maintain and preserve valuable historical documents, photographs, manuscripts, audiovisual materials, and more. Digital archives use sophisticated technology to digitize, catalogue, and maintain metadata about these materials, ensuring their integrity and authenticity over time. They aim to safeguard human knowledge and cultural memory, making it accessible to future generations. In contrast, digital repositories are primarily used by academic and research institutions to manage and disseminate scholarly outputs. They include research articles, theses, dissertations, datasets, conference proceedings, and other academic content. The purpose is not only preservation but also to enhance the visibility and accessibility of scholarly work. Institutional repositories often support open access initiatives, enabling users around the world to access research outputs without subscription barriers. They promote transparency, collaboration, and innovation in research by making information freely available.

Development and Infrastructure

The development of digital archives and repositories has been driven by technological advances, changes in information behavior, and the need for sustainable preservation solutions. These platforms are built upon digital infrastructure that includes storage systems, metadata standards, user interfaces, and security protocols. At the heart of digital repositories and archives is metadata—structured information that describes the content, context, and structure of digital objects. Metadata enables efficient search, retrieval, and management of digital materials. Standards such as Dublin Core, METS (Metadata Encoding and Transmission Standard), and PREMIS (Preservation Metadata: Implementation Strategies) are widely used for creating and maintaining metadata in digital systems.

Digital archives typically require a more rigorous infrastructure for long-term preservation. They use methods such as bitstream preservation, format migration, and emulation to ensure that digital files remain accessible despite changes in technology. Digital repositories, while also concerned with preservation, prioritize ease of access and user-friendly interfaces. They are often built using repository software platforms like DSpace, EPrints, Fedora, and Islandora, which allow institutions to organize, manage, and share their digital collections effectively.

Roles in Research and Academia

Digital repositories have transformed the way scholarly information is disseminated and accessed. They serve as vital tools for academic institutions, enabling them to showcase and manage their intellectual output. By archiving faculty publications, student theses, research data, and institutional reports, repositories help to build the academic reputation of an institution. They also contribute to the global knowledge economy by making academic research accessible to wider audiences beyond traditional journal subscribers.

Open access is a key principle behind many digital repositories. It refers to the practice of providing unrestricted access to scholarly research online. Digital repositories support this movement by offering a platform where researchers can self-archive their work. This improves the visibility and citation of research outputs and fosters an open scientific environment. Moreover, repositories can also serve as teaching resources, offering access to a wide range of materials that educators can use to enrich learning experiences.

Cultural and Historical Preservation

Digital archives play a crucial role in preserving cultural and historical materials. They ensure that fragile, rare, and significant items can be preserved digitally even if their physical counterparts deteriorate or are lost. National libraries and archives around the world have launched major digitization initiatives to create digital surrogates of important heritage materials.

These efforts protect the original documents from damage while making them widely available to researchers, educators, students, and the general public. Projects such as Europeana, the Digital Public Library of America (DPLA), and the National Digital Library of India (NDLI) have demonstrated how digital archives can promote access to cultural heritage on a massive scale.

By aggregating digital collections from various institutions, these platforms create unified portals where users can explore diverse resources, including manuscripts, artworks, photographs, newspapers, and audiovisual materials. This democratization of knowledge helps to bridge the gap between institutions and individuals, bringing heritage closer to people regardless of geographic or economic constraints.

Challenges and Limitations

Despite their numerous benefits, digital archives and repositories face several challenges. One of the primary concerns is digital preservation. Unlike physical materials, digital objects are vulnerable to technological obsolescence, data corruption, and hardware failures. Maintaining the authenticity, integrity, and usability of digital materials over the long term requires continuous monitoring, migration, and technological updates.

This demands significant financial and human resources, which may not be available in all institutions. Another issue is the lack of standardization and interoperability. With various software platforms and metadata standards in use, ensuring seamless integration and exchange of data between different repositories and archives can be difficult. Additionally, legal and ethical issues surrounding copyright, privacy, and data protection present significant hurdles.

Digitizing materials often requires permission from copyright holders, and sharing sensitive or personal data must comply with ethical standards and legal regulations. Furthermore, user engagement and discoverability are ongoing concerns. Many digital archives and repositories suffer from limited visibility due to poor indexing by search engines or ineffective metadata practices. This limits their impact and utility. Institutions must invest in user-centered design, search engine optimization, and outreach efforts to enhance access and engagement with their digital collections.

3.3 GEOGRAPHIC INFORMATION SYSTEMS (GIS) FOR HUMANITIES

3.3.1 Historical Mapping

In recent decades, the intersection of technology and the humanities has given rise to innovative approaches in research and analysis. One of the most transformative tools in this context is Geographic Information Systems (GIS), which has found significant application in historical mapping. Historical mapping using GIS represents a powerful convergence of spatial analysis and historical scholarship. It allows researchers in the humanities to visualize, analyze, and interpret past events, social movements, cultural landscapes, and demographic changes through geographic space and time.

This integration of spatial thinking with historical inquiry not only enhances traditional methods of historical research but also opens new avenues for digital humanities and interdisciplinary collaboration. Historical mapping in Geographic Information Systems has revolutionized the way humanities scholars engage with the past. By integrating spatial analysis with historical research, GIS offers new perspectives, tools, and methodologies that enhance understanding and communication of complex historical processes. Despite challenges, the continued advancement of technology, interdisciplinary collaboration, and a commitment to ethical practices ensure that GIS will remain a vital tool in the humanities for years to come.

Historical mapping in GIS involves the digital representation of past geographies using spatial data tied to specific times and places. This process entails reconstructing historical maps, georeferencing archival materials, digitizing spatial features, and layering temporal data to depict how landscapes and human societies have changed over time.

Unlike conventional historical maps that are static representations, GIS-based historical maps are dynamic, interactive, and capable of incorporating large datasets. Through GIS, historical events can be analyzed within a spatial framework, revealing patterns and relationships that are otherwise difficult to perceive through textual analysis alone. GIS allows scholars to pose spatial questions about the past.

For instance, how did trade routes influence the spread of cultural or religious practices? What geographic factors contributed to the rise and fall of certain empires or cities? How did natural features shape political boundaries or military strategies? By plotting historical data on digital maps, historians can investigate such questions with new clarity and precision. This spatial dimension adds depth to historical narratives, enriching our understanding of complex temporal phenomena.

Applications in Humanities Research

The use of GIS in humanities research is broad and multifaceted. In history, GIS is often used to analyze demographic shifts, urban development, migration patterns, warfare movements, and environmental changes. In archaeology, GIS aids in the spatial analysis of excavation sites, artifact distribution, and ancient settlement patterns. In literature and cultural studies, GIS has been employed to map the geographical contexts of literary works, enabling scholars to study the spatial dynamics of narratives and the influence of place on storytelling.

One significant example is the use of GIS in historical demography. Researchers can map population data from historical censuses, track population growth or decline over decades, and analyze the influence of political, social, or environmental factors on demographic trends. Similarly, GIS has been instrumental in reconstructing historical landscapes that no longer exist. By using old maps, satellite imagery, and topographical data, historians can digitally recreate past environments, such as medieval cities, colonial plantations, or battlefields, to better understand historical developments in their geographic context.

GIS has also become a vital tool in visualizing the spread of ideas, religions, or epidemics across regions. For example, mapping the diffusion of the Black Death in the 14th century Europe or tracing the routes of early Christian missions offers insights into how geography affected human experience and decision-making. These applications underscore the value of GIS not just as a mapping tool but as an analytical framework for exploring the spatial dimensions of human history.

Technological Foundations and Methods

The technological foundation of GIS in historical mapping involves various processes including georeferencing, digitization, data layering, and spatial analysis. Georeferencing is a key step where historical maps are aligned with modern coordinate systems, allowing researchers to overlay old maps on current geographic frameworks. This enables comparisons between past and present landscapes and supports accurate spatial analyses. Digitization follows, where features such as roads, rivers, boundaries, or structures are traced and converted into vector data. These data are then stored in layers, each representing a different type of information, such as political boundaries, demographic data, or natural features.

Temporal information adds complexity to historical GIS projects. Since historical events are bound by time, GIS systems must incorporate temporal data to reflect changes over periods. Temporal GIS allows users to toggle between different time slices, analyze trends over time, and visualize the evolution of geographic phenomena. This capacity for spatio-temporal analysis is crucial for studying dynamic processes such as urbanization, colonization, environmental degradation, and political boundary shifts.

Data sourcing is another important aspect. Historical GIS projects rely on a wide range of sources including historical maps, government records, travel diaries, gazetteers, archival photographs, and literary texts. Extracting spatial data from these sources requires careful interpretation, critical analysis, and sometimes innovative methods of spatial inference. Scholars must deal with inconsistencies in scale, projection, and accuracy, especially when working with historical documents that were not originally intended for GIS use.

Pedagogical and Public Engagement Benefits

Beyond research, GIS-based historical mapping serves as an effective pedagogical tool in the humanities. It encourages spatial literacy, critical thinking, and interdisciplinary learning among students. By engaging with digital maps, students gain a deeper understanding of historical processes and the interconnectedness of geography and human experience. Historical GIS assignments can involve students in collecting data, georeferencing maps, and constructing narratives based on spatial evidence. This hands-on approach fosters engagement and helps bridge the gap between textual analysis and visual interpretation.

Public engagement is another significant dimension of historical mapping in GIS. Interactive web-based platforms enable the public to explore historical content in accessible and visually appealing formats. Digital projects like "Mapping the Republic of Letters" or "The Valley of the Shadow" demonstrate how historical GIS can be used to reach broad audiences, including educators, students, heritage enthusiasts, and policy makers. By making historical data accessible and interactive, these projects enhance public understanding of the past and stimulate interest in historical inquiry.

Such platforms often include search tools, timelines, and interactive layers that allow users to explore specific themes, regions, or time periods. This democratization of historical knowledge not only broadens the audience for humanities scholarship but also promotes transparency and inclusivity in research. Furthermore, crowdsourced GIS projects have emerged, where public users contribute data, photographs, or annotations, adding richness to historical archives and fostering community participation.

Challenges and Ethical Considerations

Despite its advantages, the use of GIS in historical mapping presents several challenges. Data quality and availability are among the foremost issues. Historical data are often incomplete, fragmented, or imprecise, making spatial analysis difficult. Moreover, georeferencing old maps involves estimation and interpretation, which can introduce errors or biases. Scholars must be cautious and transparent in documenting their methods and acknowledging the limitations of their data.

Another challenge lies in the technical skills required. Historical GIS projects demand expertise in GIS software, data management, and spatial analysis—skills that are not traditionally part of humanities training. Bridging this gap requires collaboration between historians, geographers, digital humanists, and computer scientists. Interdisciplinary teams can combine domain knowledge and technical proficiency to create robust and meaningful historical GIS outputs.

Ethical considerations are also important. Mapping sensitive historical data, such as information about indigenous lands, slave trade routes, or wartime atrocities, must be approached with care and respect. The representation of historical events through spatial data should avoid misinterpretation, oversimplification, or appropriation. Ethical historical GIS practice involves engaging with source communities, ensuring accurate representation, and maintaining transparency about data sources and methodologies.

3.3.2 Cultural Landscapes

Cultural landscape is a term used in the fields of geography, ecology, and heritage studies, to describe a symbiosis of human activity and environment. As defined by the World Heritage Committee, it is the "cultural properties [that] represent the combined works of nature and of man" and falls into three main categories:

- "A landscape designed and created intentionally by man".
- An "organically evolved landscape" which may be a "relict (or fossil) landscape" or a "continuing landscape".
- An "associative cultural landscape" which may be valued because of the "religious, artistic or cultural associations of the natural element."

Historical Development

The concept of 'cultural landscapes' can be found in the European tradition of landscape painting. From the 16th century onwards, many European artists painted landscapes in favor of people, diminishing the people in their paintings to figures subsumed within broader, regionally specific landscapes.

The word "landscape" itself combines "land" with a verb of Germanic origin, "scapjan/schaffen" to mean, literally, "shaped lands". Lands were then considered shaped by natural forces, and the unique details of such landshaffen (shaped lands) became themselves the subject of 'landscape' paintings. Geographer Otto Schlüter is credited with having first formally used "cultural landscape" as an academic term in the early 20th century. In 1908, Schlüter argued that by defining geography as a Landschaftskunde (landscape science) this would give geography a logical subject matter shared by no other discipline. He defined two forms of landscape: the Urlandschaft (transl. original landscape) or landscape that existed before major human induced changes and the Kulturlandschaft (transl. 'cultural landscape') a landscape created by human culture. The major task of geography was to trace the changes in these two landscapes.

It was Carl O. Sauer, a human geographer, who was probably the most influential in promoting and developing the idea of cultural landscapes. Sauer was determined to stress the agency of culture as a force in shaping the visible features of the Earth's surface in delimited areas. Within his definition, the physical environment retains a central significance, as the medium with and through which human cultures act. His classic definition of a 'cultural landscape' reads as follows:

- "The cultural landscape is fashioned from a natural landscape by a cultural group. Culture is the agent, the natural area is the medium, the cultural landscape is the result"

Since Schlüter's first formal use of the term, and Sauer's effective promotion of the idea, the concept of 'cultural landscapes has been variously used, applied, debated, developed and refined within academia. In the 1950s, for instance, J.B. Jackson and his publication 'Landscape' influenced a generation of particularly American scholars, including architectural historians Denise Scott Brown, and Gwendolyn Wright.

By 1992, the World Heritage Committee elected to convene a meeting of the 'specialists' to advise and assist redraft the Committee's Operational Guidelines to include 'cultural landscapes' as an option for heritage listing properties that were neither purely natural nor purely cultural in form (i.e. 'mixed' heritage).

Relevance of Concept

The World Heritage Committee's adoption and use of the concept of 'cultural landscapes' has seen multiple specialists around the world, and many nations identifying 'cultural landscapes', assessing 'cultural landscapes', heritage listing 'cultural landscapes', managing 'cultural landscapes', and effectively making 'cultural landscapes' known and visible to the world, with very practical ramifications and challenges.

Multiple specialists around the world, and nations to apply the concept of 'cultural landscapes', observed and concluded that:

- "Although the concept of landscape has been unhooked for some time from its original art associations ... there is still a dominant view of landscapes as an inscribed surface, akin to a map or a text, from which cultural meaning and social forms can simply be read."

Within academia, any system of interaction between human activity and natural habitat is regarded as a cultural landscape. In a sense this understanding is broader than the definition applied within UNESCO, including, as it does, almost the whole of the world's occupied surface, plus almost all the uses, ecologies, interactions, practices, beliefs, concepts, and traditions of people living within cultural landscapes. Following on this, geographer Xoan Paredes defines cultural landscape as:

- "... the environment modified by the human being in the course of time, the long-term combination between anthropic action on this environment and the physical constraints limiting or conditioning human activity. It is a geographical area – including natural and cultural resources – associated to historical evolution, which gives way to a recognizable landscape for a particular human group, up to the point of being identifiable as such by others."

The concept of cultural landscape is useful for the sustainable management and conservation of heritage. Adopting a cultural landscape perspective can interlink individual aspects of cultural heritage, such as historic buildings, regional material resources, and vernacular construction techniques, into a unified notion of identity and place. This can unify tangible and intangible heritage, expose risks within complex system dynamics, and draw the focus of conservation from the protection of past fabric towards the management of future change. It can be a vehicle for people-centric approaches, which support local ownership and participation at cultural heritage sites. This paradigm aligns the management of the historic environment with contemporary attitudes to environmental management in general, which are also influenced by cultural landscape perspectives. Some universities now offer specialist degrees in the study of cultural landscapes, including, for instance, the Universities of Naples, St.-Etienne, and Stuttgart who offer a Master of Cultural Landscapes diploma.

Examples

- **Tongariro National Park, New Zealand (1993):** "In 1993 Tongariro National Park, became the first property to be inscribed on the World Heritage List under the revised criteria describing cultural landscapes. The mountains at the heart of the park have cultural and religious significance for the Maori people and symbolize the spiritual links between this community and its environment. The park has active and extinct volcanoes, a diverse range of ecosystems and some spectacular landscapes."
- **Uluru-Kata Tjuta National Park, Australia (1994):** "This park, formerly called Uluru (Ayers Rock – Mount Olga) National Park, features spectacular geological formations that dominate the vast red sandy plain of central Australia. Uluru, an immense monolith, and Kata Tjuta, the rock domes located west of Uluru, form part of the traditional belief system of one of the oldest human societies in the world. The traditional owners of Uluru-Kata Tjuta are the Anangu Aboriginal people."
- **Rice Terraces of Philippine Cordilleras (1995):** "For 2,000 years, the high rice fields of the Ifugao have followed the contours of the mountains. The fruit of knowledge handed down from one generation to the next, and the expression of sacred traditions and a delicate social balance, they have helped to create a landscape of great beauty that expresses the harmony between humankind and the environment."
- **Cultural Landscape of Sintra, Portugal (1995):** "In the 19th century Sintra became the first centre of European Romantic architecture. Ferdinand II turned a ruined monastery into a castle where this new sensitivity was displayed in the use of Gothic, Egyptian, Moorish and Renaissance elements and in the creation of a park blending local and exotic species of trees. Other fine dwellings, built along the same lines in the surrounding serra, created a unique combination of parks and gardens which influenced the development of landscape architecture throughout Europe".
- **Portovenere, Cinque Terre, and the Islands (Palmaria, Tino and Tinetto), Italy (1997):** "The Ligurian coast between Cinque Terre and Portovenere is a cultural landscape of great scenic and cultural value. The layout and disposition of the small towns and the shaping of the surrounding landscape, overcoming the disadvantages of a steep, uneven terrain, encapsulate the continuous history of human settlement in this region over the past millennium."
- **Hortobagy National Park, Hungary (1999):** Hortobagy National Park is the largest continuous natural grassland in Europe, which means that

it was not formed as a result of deforestation or river control. The first Hungarian national park (established in 1973), it is the country's largest protected area (82 thousand hectares). A significant part of it is Biosphere Reserve and a quarter of its area enjoys international protection under the Ramsar Convention on the conservation of wetlands.

- **Matobo Hills, Zimbabwe (2003):** The Matobo Hills area exhibits a profusion of distinctive rock landforms rising above the granite shield that covers much of Zimbabwe. The large boulders provide abundant natural shelters and have been associated with human occupation from the early Stone Age right through to early historical times, and intermittently since. They also feature an outstanding collection of rock paintings. The Matopo Hills continue to provide a strong focus for the local community, which still uses shrines and sacred places closely linked to traditional, social and economic activities.
- **Royal Botanic Gardens, Kew (2003):** The Royal Botanic Gardens Kew (Kew Gardens), is a historic landscape garden which illustrates significant garden styles from the 18th to 20th centuries. Kew Gardens is home to botanic collections (conserved plants, living plants, and documents) that are of global historical significance and continue to be used today, this includes a herbarium collection with over 8.5 million preserved plant and fungal specimens. The living collections within the gardens cover over 27000 taxa. Since their creation in 1759, the gardens have made a significant and continuous contribution to research into plant diversity and economic botany.
- **Dresden Elbe Valley, Germany (2004):** "The 18th- and 19th-century cultural landscape of Dresden Elbe Valley ... features low meadows, and is crowned by the Pillnitz Palace and the centre of Dresden with its numerous monuments and parks from the 16th to 20th centuries. The landscape also features 19th- and 20th-century suburban villas and gardens and valuable natural features." This landscape was struck from the World Heritage list in 2009, due to the construction of a four lane highway across the Elbe.
- **St Kilda, United Kingdom (2005):** The archipelago of St Kilda in the Outer Hebrides of Scotland was originally inscribed as a natural heritage site in 1986 following recommendation by IUCN, due to its superlative natural features and habitats for rare and endangered species of birds. ICOMOS also recommended in 1986 that the property should be listed for a cultural criterion (relating to traditional human settlement), stating that "the St. Kilda archipelago corresponds perfectly to the

definition of a cultural and natural property whose value should be taken into consideration in an evaluation complementary to that of IUCN", however this was not executed by UNESCO. IUCN commented in their initial evaluation, and the UNESCO committee also stated upon inscription, that the marine environment surrounding the archipelago should be considered for listing and the boundaries extended. The state party had not nominated this in their original application. In response to a report prepared by Greenpeace in 1998 which raised concerns on potential impacts to the site from oil exploration of the surrounding seabed, the boundary was extended in 2004/5 and the property was additionally listed for a further natural criterion (relating to ecological processes). As part of the relisting process, it was re-nominated for two cultural criteria, recommended for listing by ICOMOS, and this time inscribed by UNESCO in 2005 and designated as an 'organically evolved relict cultural landscape'. "Overlaying the spectacular natural landscape and giving scale to it all, is a rich cultural landscape that bears exceptional testimony to millennia of human occupation."

- **Lavaux Vineyard Terraces, Switzerland (2007):** "The Lavaux vineyard landscape demonstrates in a highly visible way its evolution and development over almost a millennium, through the well preserved landscape and buildings that demonstrate a continuation and evolution of longstanding cultural traditions, specific to its locality."
- **Kuk Early Agricultural Site (2008):** Kuk Early Agricultural Site (Kuk Swamp) is located in the western highlands of Papua New Guinea, at 1500m and covering 116ha. Kuk is one of the few places in the world where archaeological evidence suggests independent agricultural development, with the wetlands preserving archaeological evidence of agricultural practices stretch back 10000 years.
- **West Lake Cultural Landscape of Hangzhou, China (2011):** "The West Lake Cultural Landscape of Hangzhou, comprising the West Lake and the hills surrounding its three sides, has inspired famous poets, scholars and artists since the 9th century. It comprises numerous temples, pagodas, pavilions, gardens and ornamental trees, as well as causeways and artificial islands."
- **Qhapaq Ñan (Inca Road System), Northwestern Argentina, South Colombia, Ecuador, Bolivia, Peru, Chile (2014):** Qhapaq Ñan is an extensive Inca communication, trade and defense network of roads covering 30,000 km. Constructed by the Incas over several centuries and partly based on pre-Inca infrastructure, this extraordinary network

through one of the world's most extreme geographical terrains linked the snow-capped peaks of the Andes – at an altitude of more than 6,000 m – to the coast, running through hot rainforests, fertile valleys, and absolute deserts. It reached its maximum expansion in the 15th century when it spread across the length and breadth of the Andes. The Qhapac Ñan, Andean Road System includes 273 component sites spread over more than 6,000 km that were selected to highlight the social, political, architectural and engineering achievements of the network, along with its associated infrastructure for trade, accommodation, and storage, as well as sites of religious significance.

3.3.3 Geohumanities

Geohumanities is an interdisciplinary field that explores the relationship between human beings and the natural and built environment, as well as the cultural, social, and historical aspects of place. It involves the integration of humanities disciplines such as history, literature, philosophy, and art with geography, environmental studies, and other social sciences.

The term "geohumanities" was first coined in the early 2000s, as a way of bringing together scholars from different disciplines to examine how people create, experience, and understand places. Geohumanities seeks to explore the ways in which the cultural, historical, and social dimensions of place are intertwined with the physical and ecological characteristics of landscapes, and how this knowledge can be used to address environmental and social challenges.

Some examples of research in geohumanities include:

- Analyzing literary and artistic representations of landscape to understand how people have imagined and interacted with their environment over time.
- Studying the social and political dimensions of urban space, including issues of segregation, gentrification, and access to public resources.
- Examining the role of place in shaping identity, memory, and cultural practices, particularly in relation to indigenous communities and other marginalized groups.

3.4 NETWORK ANALYSIS AND VISUALIZATION

3.4.1 Social Network Graphs

In the contemporary landscape of humanities research, the intersection of Geographic Information Systems (GIS) and social network analysis has led to the development of powerful tools for understanding human relationships in spatial and temporal contexts. Social network graphs in GIS represent a sophisticated method of mapping and analyzing social interactions, affiliations, and movements of individuals or groups over geographical space and historical time. These graphs help visualize how people, places, and events are connected, revealing hidden patterns and structures within societies, past and present. Within the humanities, such analyses have found applications in history, archaeology, literature, religious studies, political science, and cultural studies, transforming how scholars interpret the spatial dimensions of social life.

Social network graphs are diagrams that illustrate the relationships between nodes, which can represent individuals, groups, institutions, or locations, and edges, which represent the connections or interactions between them. When these graphs are integrated into GIS, they become geographically grounded, allowing researchers to study not only how people are connected but also where those connections occur. This spatial component is critical for humanities research because it links social dynamics with the physical world—enabling scholars to explore how geography shapes and is shaped by human interaction.

In a GIS-enabled environment, nodes in a social network are often geolocated, meaning they have specific coordinates that place them on a map. Edges between nodes can vary in type, such as communication links, kinship ties, trade relationships, or shared participation in events. The spatial analysis of these networks allows for the investigation of questions such as how information or influence spread through historical populations, how migration or travel routes contributed to cultural diffusion, or how certain locations functioned as central hubs within broader social systems.

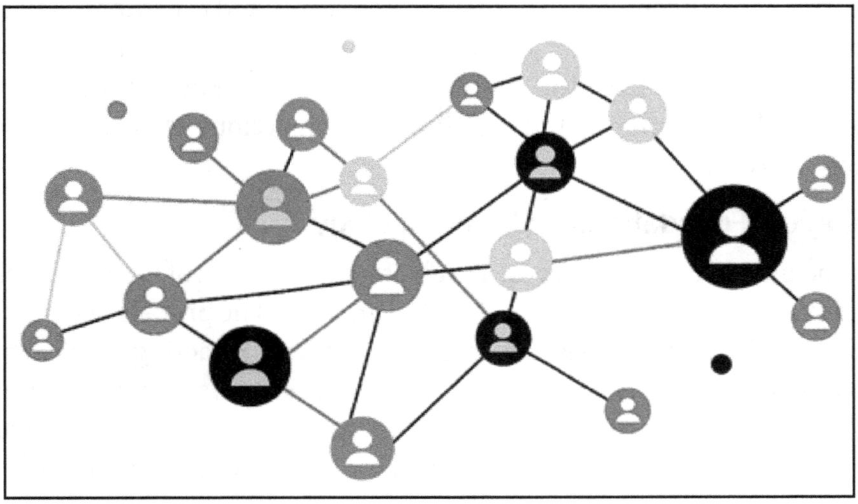

Fig: Social Network Graphs

Applications in Humanities Research

Social network graphs in GIS have enriched many areas of humanities research. In historical studies, they allow scholars to examine the dynamics of power, alliance, and conflict in ancient and medieval societies. For example, by mapping diplomatic correspondence or military alliances in a historical period, researchers can identify key players, influential regions, and the spatial reach of political networks. These insights are invaluable for understanding the mechanisms of historical change, governance, and resistance.

In literary studies, social network graphs are used to analyze relationships between characters in a narrative and to correlate fictional social structures with real-world geographies. When combined with GIS, such analysis can uncover the geographic dimensions of plot development, character mobility, and thematic symbolism. A novel set in multiple cities, for instance, can be studied not only for its literary content but also for the spatial pattern of interactions between its characters. Archaeology also benefits significantly from this integration. Excavations often uncover material evidence of past human interaction, such as trade goods, inscriptions, or settlement patterns. By constructing social network graphs from these findings and mapping them with GIS, archaeologists can reconstruct the social organization of ancient communities and understand how regional or interregional connections influenced cultural development. The distribution of artifacts, for instance, can be visualized as a network of trade relations, helping to illuminate economic systems that traditional methods might overlook.

In religious and cultural studies, mapping the movement of religious figures, pilgrimage routes, and the spread of beliefs or rituals can be effectively done using social network graphs in GIS. These analyses help scholars explore the diffusion of religious practices, the influence of sacred geography, and the interaction between religious institutions and local communities. The spatial mapping of religious networks can highlight both the central nodes—such as key temples or monastic centers—and the peripheral but significant connections that sustain cultural coherence across vast areas.

Technological Foundations and Methodology

Creating social network graphs in GIS involves a combination of tools and techniques drawn from both network science and spatial analysis. The process begins with data collection, which in humanities research may involve extracting names, locations, and relationships from historical documents, literary texts, archival materials, or archaeological databases. These data are structured in terms of nodes and edges, where each entry describes a social entity and the relationship it has with others.

Once the network is constructed, GIS software is used to map the geographic location of the nodes. Tools such as ArcGIS, QGIS, and Gephi can be used in tandem to manage spatial data and visualize complex networks. Advanced platforms also allow for the inclusion of temporal data, creating dynamic visualizations that show how networks evolve over time. For example, a historian studying correspondence during the Enlightenment can map how ideas and letters circulated across Europe, showing the rise and fall of intellectual hubs over decades.

The analysis phase involves examining various metrics such as centrality, density, and clustering to understand the structure of the network. Centrality measures identify the most influential nodes, while clustering can reveal tightly connected communities within the network. When these metrics are considered in spatial terms, they can show, for example, which cities acted as cultural epicenters or how marginalized groups maintained connections despite geographical or political obstacles.

Pedagogical Value and Interdisciplinary Opportunities

The integration of social network graphs in GIS has also created rich opportunities for teaching and interdisciplinary collaboration in the humanities. By engaging students with interactive maps and network visualizations, educators can foster a deeper understanding of historical and cultural phenomena.

Students can work on projects that involve building networks from primary sources, georeferencing historical events, and analyzing spatial patterns using digital tools. This approach not only enhances their technical skills but also sharpens their critical thinking about the relationships between people, places, and ideas.

Interdisciplinary collaboration is essential in this field. Historians may work with computer scientists to develop algorithms for text mining historical archives; archaeologists may partner with geographers to model settlement dynamics; literary scholars may consult with data analysts to interpret narrative networks. These collaborations enrich humanities research by bringing diverse perspectives and methodologies to complex questions, resulting in more nuanced and comprehensive interpretations.

Challenges and Ethical Considerations

Despite its many advantages, the use of social network graphs in GIS for humanities research is not without challenges. One major concern is data reliability. Historical and literary sources often contain incomplete or ambiguous information, making it difficult to establish accurate connections or locations. The process of interpreting relationships from texts requires careful judgment, and the results are often contingent on the assumptions and choices made by the researcher.

Technical challenges also exist, particularly in managing large or complex datasets.

Creating meaningful visualizations that accurately reflect the underlying data while remaining comprehensible to users can be difficult. The spatial resolution of historical data is often imprecise, and representing movement or temporal change within static maps can oversimplify dynamic processes.

Ethical considerations must also be addressed, particularly when dealing with sensitive historical subjects such as colonialism, slavery, or conflict. The visualization of social networks can inadvertently reinforce certain narratives or power structures if not handled carefully.

Researchers must remain vigilant in ensuring that their work is inclusive, transparent, and respectful of the communities and individuals represented in their data. Engaging with source communities, where possible, and maintaining openness about data sources and methodologies are crucial ethical practices in this field.

Future Directions and Innovations

Looking ahead, the future of social network graphs in GIS for the humanities is marked by exciting possibilities. Advances in artificial intelligence and machine learning are making it easier to extract relational data from large textual corpora, enabling researchers to build more comprehensive networks with less manual effort. Natural language processing tools can identify and categorize relationships in historical texts, feeding into network graphs that are then mapped using GIS technologies.

The development of three-dimensional GIS and virtual reality environments opens up new ways of experiencing historical networks. Scholars and the public alike may soon be able to immerse themselves in historical cities or cultural landscapes, exploring networks of people and events in spatially realistic settings. This immersive approach holds great potential for education, public history, and scholarly analysis.

Moreover, as open data initiatives and digital humanities platforms expand, researchers will have greater access to pre-built datasets, collaborative tools, and shared infrastructures. Projects like Pelagios, Linked Places, and Recogito provide frameworks for linking and mapping historical data, encouraging a more connected and collaborative approach to humanities research. These initiatives make it easier for scholars to integrate their work into larger knowledge ecosystems, increasing the impact and accessibility of their research.

3.4.2 Citation Networks

A citation network (or citation graph), in information science and bibliometrics, is a directed graph that describes the citations within a collection of documents.

Each vertex (or node) in the graph represents a document in the collection, and each edge is directed from one document toward another that it cites (or vice versa depending on the specific implementation). Citation graphs have been utilised in various ways, including forms of citation analysis, academic search tools and court judgements. They are predicted to become more relevant and useful in the future as the body of published research grows.

Implementation

There is no standard format for the citations in bibliographies, and the record linkage of citations can be a time-consuming and complicated process. Furthermore, citation errors can occur at any stage of the publishing process. However, there is a long history of creating citation databases, also known as citation indexes, so there is a lot of information about such problems. In principle, each document should have a unique publication date and can only refer to earlier documents. This means that an ideal citation graph is not only directed but acyclic; that is, there are no loops in the graph. This is not always the case in practice, since an academic paper goes through several versions in the publishing process. The timing of asynchronous updates to bibliographies may lead to edges that apparently point backward in time. Such "backward" citations seem to constitute less than 1% of the total number of links.

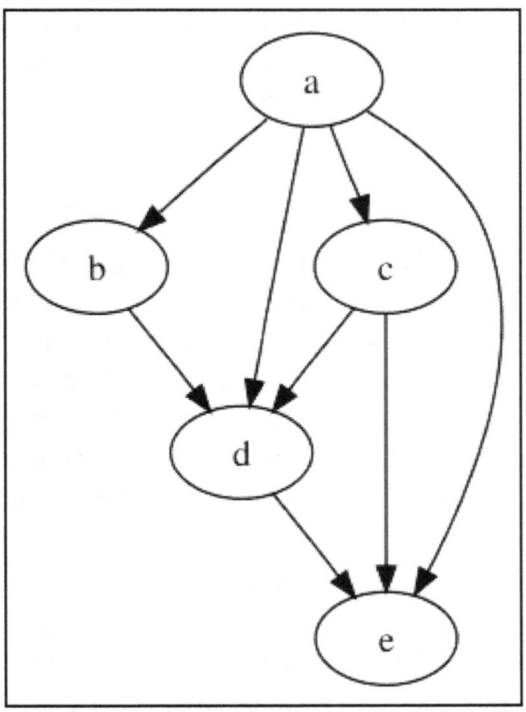

Fig: In this example, document b cites document d, both of which are cited by document a.

As citation links are meant to be permanent, the bulk of a citation graph should be static, and only the leading edge of the graph should change. Exceptions might occur when papers are withdrawn from circulation.

Background and History

A citation is a reference to a published or unpublished source (not always the original source). More precisely, a citation is an abbreviated alphanumeric expression embedded in the body of an intellectual work that denotes an entry in the bibliographic references section of the work. Its purpose is to acknowledge the relevance of the works of others to the topic of discussion at the point where the citation appears. Generally the combination of both the in-body citation and the bibliographic entry constitutes what is commonly thought of as a citation (whereas bibliographic entries by themselves are not). References to single, machine-readable assertions in electronic scientific articles are known as nanopublications, a form of micro attributions.

Citation networks are one kind of social network that has been studied quantitatively almost from the moment citation databases first became available. In 1965, Derek J. de Solla Price described the inherent linking characteristic of the Science Citation Index (SCI) in his paper entitled "Networks of Scientific Papers." The links between citing and cited papers became dynamic when the SCI began to be published online. In 1973, Henry Small published his work on co-citation analysis, which became a self-organizing classification system that led to document clustering experiments and eventually what is called "Research Reviews."

Applications

Citation Analysis

Citation graphs can be applied to measures of scholarly impact, the impact a particular paper has had on the academic world. While a hard value to quantify, scholarly impact is useful, as having a measure of scholarly impact for many papers can aid in identifying important papers. It can also provide a measure of the relevance of a particular academic community. Citation graphs are very useful in measuring this as the number of connections on the citation graph corresponds with the scholarly impact of an article, as this means it has been cited by many other papers.

Similarity analysis is another area of citation analysis which frequently makes uses of citation graphs. The relationship between two papers in the citation graph has been compared to their text-based similarity, and it is found that closeness in the citation graph can predict a level of text-based similarity. Additionally, it has been found that the two methods – citation graph closeness and traditional content-based similarity – work well in conjunction to produce a more accurate result.

Analyses of citation graphs have also led to the proposal of the citation graph as a way to identify different communities and research areas within the academic world. It has been found that analysing the citation graph for groups of documents in conjunction with keywords can provide an accurate way to identify clusters of similar research. In a similar vein, a way of identifying the main "stream" of an area of research, or the progression of a research idea over time can be identified by using depth first search algorithms on the citation graph. Instead of looking at similarity between two nodes, or clusters of many nodes, this method instead goes through the links between nodes to trace a research idea back to its beginning, and so discover its progression through different papers to where its current status is.

Search Tools

The traditional method used by academic search tools is to check for matches between a search term and keywords in papers to return potential matches. While mostly effective, this method can lead to errors where a paper is recommended from a different discipline because of keyword matches even when the two topics actually have little in common. Many have argued that this way of searching for relevant papers could be improved and made more accurate if citation graphs were incorporated into academic paper search tools.

For example, one system was proposed which used both the keyword system and a popularity system based on how many connections a paper had in the citation graph. In this system, more connected papers were considered more popular and therefore given a higher weighting in the paper recommendation system. In more recent years, visual search tools have been developed which use citation graphs to provide a visual representation of the connections between papers. A commercial implementation of this concept is the search tool Connected Papers.

Court Judgements

Citation graphs have a history of being used to aid in organising and mapping citations of legal documents. In a similar way to the aforementioned search tools, constructions of citation graphs specific to the types of citations found in legal documents have been used to allow relevant past legal documents to be found when needed for a court decision. As a way of replacing or improving upon traditional search methods, this citation graph aided way of organising legal documents can provide higher efficiency, accuracy, and organisation.

Related Networks

There are several other types of network graphs that are closely related to citation networks. The co-citation graph is the graph between documents as nodes, where two documents are connected if they share a common citation. Other related networks are formed using other information present in the document.

For instance, in a collaboration graph, known in this context as a co-authorship network, the nodes are the authors of documents, linked if they have co-authored the same document. The link weights between two authors in co-authorship networks can increase over time if they have further collaboration.

Future Developments

While citation graphs have had a noticeable impact on several areas of academia, they are likely to become more relevant in the future. As the body of published research grows, more traditional ways of searching for papers will become less effective in narrowing down relevant papers to a particular topic. For example, text-based similarity can only go so far in selecting which papers are relevant to a topic, whereas the addition of citation graphs could make use of giving higher priority to those papers which have a lot of connections to other papers relevant to the topic. However, developments like this face similar challenges to that of most applications of citation graphs, which is the face that there is no standardized format or way of citing. This makes the construction of these graphs very difficult, since it requires complex software analysis to extract citations from papers. One solution proposed to this problem is to create open databases of citation information in a format which could be used by anyone and easily converted to a different form, for example a citation graph.

3.5 3D MODELING AND VIRTUAL RECONSTRUCTION

3.5.1 Archaeological Sites

An archaeological site is a place (or group of physical sites) in which evidence of past activity is preserved (either prehistoric or historic or contemporary), and which has been, or may be, investigated using the discipline of archaeology and represents a part of the archaeological record. Sites may range from those with few or no remains visible above ground, to buildings and other structures still in use.

Beyond this, the definition and geographical extent of a "site" can vary widely, depending on the period studied and the theoretical approach of the archaeologist.

Geographical Extent

It is almost invariably difficult to delimit a site. It is sometimes taken to indicate a settlement of some sort, although the archaeologist must also define the limits of human activity around the settlement. Any episode of deposition, such as a hoard or burial, can form a site as well. Development-led archaeology undertaken as cultural resources management has the disadvantage (or the benefit) of having its sites defined by the limits of the intended development. Even in this case, however, in describing and interpreting the site, the archaeologist will have to look outside the boundaries of the building site.

According to Jess Beck in "How Do Archaeologists Find Sites?" the areas with numerous artifacts are good targets for future excavation, while areas with a small number of artifacts are thought to reflect a lack of past human activity. Many areas have been discovered by accident. The most common people who have found artifacts are farmers who are plowing their fields or just cleaning them up, and they often find archaeological artifacts. Many people who are out hiking and even pilots find artifacts, and they usually end up reporting them to archaeologists for further investigation. When they find sites, they have to first record the area, and if they have the money and time for the site, they can start digging.

Field Survey

There are many ways to find sites, one example can be through surveys. Surveys involve walking around analyzing the land and looking for artifacts. It can also involve digging, according to the Archaeological Institute of America, "archaeologists actively search areas that were likely to support human populations, or in places where old documents and records indicate people once lived." This helps archaeologists in the future. In case there is no time or money during the site's discovery, archaeologists can come back and visit the site for further digging to find out the extent of the site. Archaeologist can also sample randomly within a given area of land as another form of conducting surveys. Surveys are very useful, according to Jess Beck, "it can tell you where people were living at different points in the past." Geophysics is a branch of survey becoming more and more popular in archaeology, because it uses different types of instruments to investigate features below the ground surface.

It is not as reliable because although they can see what is under the surface of the ground, it does not produce the best picture. Archaeologists still have to dig up the area in order to uncover the truth. There are also two most common types of geophysical survey, which is, magnetometer and ground penetrating radar. Magnetometry is the technique of measuring and mapping patterns of magnetism in the soil. It uses an instrument called a magnetometer, which is required to measure and map traces of soil magnetism. The ground penetrating radar is a method that uses radar pulses to image the subsurface. It uses electromagnetic radiation in the microwave band of the radio spectrum and detects the reflected signals from subsurface structures.

There are many other tools that can be used to find artifacts, but along with finding artifacts, archaeologists have to make maps. They do so by taking data from surveys, or archival research and plugging it into a Geographical Information Systems (GIS) and that will contain both locational information and a combination of various information. This tool is very helpful to archaeologists who want to explore in a different area and want to see if anyone else has done research. They can use this tool to see what has already been discovered. With this information available, archaeologists can expand their research and add more to what has already been found.

Traditionally, sites are distinguished by the presence of both artifacts and features. Common features include the remains of hearths and houses. Ecofacts, biological materials (such as bones, scales, and even feces) that are the result of human activity but are not deliberately modified, are also common at many archaeological sites. In the cases of the Palaeolithic and Mesolithic eras, a mere scatter of flint flakes will also constitute a site worthy of study.

Different archaeologists may see an ancient town, and its nearby cemetery as being two different sites, or as being part of the same wider site. The precepts of landscape archaeology attempt to see each discrete unit of human activity in the context of the wider environment, further distorting the concept of the site as a demarcated area. Furthermore, geoarchaeologists or environmental archaeologists would also consider a sequence of natural geological or organic deposition, in the absence of human activity, to constitute a site worthy of study. Archaeological sites usually form through human-related processes but can be subject to natural, post-depositional factors. Cultural remnants which have been buried by sediments are, in many environments, more likely to be preserved than exposed cultural remnants.

Natural actions resulting in sediment being deposited include alluvial (water-related) or aeolian (wind-related) natural processes. In jungles and other areas of lush plant growth, decomposed vegetative sediment can result in layers of soil deposited over remains. Colluviation, the burial of a site by sediments moved by gravity (called hillwash) can also happen at sites on slopes. Human activities (both deliberate and incidental) also often bury sites. It is common in many cultures for newer structures to be built atop the remains of older ones. Urban archaeology has developed especially to deal with these sorts of site. Many sites are the subject of ongoing excavation or investigation. Note the difference between archaeological sites and archaeological discoveries.

3.5.2 Historical Spaces

The concept of historical spaces plays a vital role in understanding how the past is embedded in physical environments and how those environments, in turn, shape human experiences and collective memory. Historical spaces are not just geographical locations marked by past events; they are dynamic arenas where social, cultural, political, and economic forces intersect and evolve. These spaces may include monuments, cities, battlefields, religious sites, trade routes, or even landscapes shaped by long-term human activity.

In the field of humanities and social sciences, historical spaces are studied not merely as remnants of the past but as active elements in the construction of identity, memory, and historical consciousness. Their meanings are continuously reinterpreted, contested, and redefined, making them central to discussions about heritage, nationalism, urban development, and cultural preservation. Historical spaces are not merely remnants of the past; they are active arenas where history, identity, memory, and power converge. They embody the layered experiences of generations and the struggles over meaning and belonging. In every preserved ruin, contested monument, or forgotten site lies a story waiting to be told—or retold—in light of new perspectives. As societies continue to evolve, the role of historical spaces becomes increasingly significant. They offer opportunities for reflection, dialogue, and reconciliation. Whether through preservation, reinterpretation, or digital innovation, engaging with historical spaces allows communities to reclaim their histories, honor their ancestors, and imagine futures rooted in an awareness of the past.

To understand historical spaces is to recognize the enduring relationship between people and place, memory and materiality, history and meaning. It is through this understanding that we can hope to preserve the richness of human experience and ensure that the voices of the past continue to resonate in the landscapes of the present and the visions of the future.

Defining

Historical spaces are spaces that are invested with historical significance, whether through their association with important events, persons, or cultural practices. These spaces may be recognized formally through heritage designations or may exist informally in the collective memory of communities. They range from monumental structures such as forts, palaces, and religious buildings to everyday settings like markets, villages, or residential neighborhoods that have borne witness to historical processes. Importantly, the significance of a historical space is not solely derived from what happened there but also from how it is remembered, represented, and utilized in the present.

Historians, geographers, and anthropologists study historical spaces to understand how societies anchor their narratives of the past in the physical world. These studies often focus on the materiality of space—its architecture, layout, and physical features—but also examine the symbolic and experiential dimensions. A battlefield, for instance, may be preserved as a museum site, with signs and reconstructions to educate visitors, but it may also hold emotional weight for descendants of those who fought there, functioning as a space of mourning or pride. Similarly, a religious shrine may serve as a site of pilgrimage while simultaneously acting as a repository of regional history and identity.

Memory and the Politics of Space

One of the most compelling aspects of historical spaces is their role in the politics of memory. Collective memory is not merely a record of past events; it is shaped by the power dynamics of who gets to remember, what is remembered, and how it is remembered. Historical spaces often become focal points in this struggle. Monuments and memorials, for example, do not simply commemorate the past but actively construct narratives about national heroes, cultural achievements, or traumas.

Decisions about which events to commemorate, whose statues to erect, and which buildings to preserve are inherently political acts that reflect and reinforce dominant ideologies. Throughout history, regimes and governments have used historical spaces to legitimize their rule or to erase inconvenient truths. The deliberate construction of imperial architecture, the renaming of streets and cities, or the destruction of rival heritage sites are examples of how space can be manipulated to control historical narratives. Conversely, marginalized groups have also reclaimed historical spaces to assert their identity and challenge dominant histories. Protests, heritage walks, and grassroots memorials are ways in which people engage with historical spaces to demand recognition and justice.

The politics of memory can also be seen in post-conflict societies where historical spaces are reimagined to promote reconciliation or to acknowledge past atrocities. Former prison camps, war memorials, and genocide museums are often transformed into sites of education and remembrance. However, these transformations are not always unifying. Disagreements over how to represent the past can lead to controversies and debates about authenticity, representation, and historical accuracy.

Urban Development and the Transformation of Historical Spaces

Urbanization has had a profound impact on historical spaces, often leading to tension between preservation and development. In many cities around the world, historical districts are under constant threat from modernization, commercial interests, and population pressures. Skyscrapers rise beside centuries-old temples, colonial buildings are replaced with shopping complexes, and traditional neighborhoods are gentrified or demolished. These changes can erode the physical and cultural fabric of historical spaces, making it difficult for future generations to connect with their heritage.

However, urban development does not always mean the destruction of historical spaces. In some cases, cities have successfully integrated heritage conservation into their planning strategies. Initiatives to restore old neighborhoods, pedestrianize historic centers, and promote heritage tourism have helped to preserve historical character while meeting contemporary needs. The key challenge is to strike a balance between protecting historical integrity and allowing cities to grow and evolve. This requires thoughtful policies, community engagement, and sustainable tourism practices that prioritize the long-term value of cultural heritage.

Architectural conservation, adaptive reuse of historic buildings, and cultural mapping are some of the tools used by urban planners and heritage professionals to maintain the vitality of historical spaces. By repurposing old structures for new functions—such as converting a colonial-era warehouse into a museum or cultural center—cities can ensure that historical spaces remain relevant and accessible in the modern context.

Cultural Identity and the Role of Historical Spaces

Historical spaces are deeply intertwined with the construction and expression of cultural identity. They serve as tangible links to ancestral roots, religious traditions, and community histories. For indigenous peoples and minority communities, certain landscapes and sacred sites carry meanings that go beyond conventional historical narratives. These spaces often embody cosmologies, oral traditions, and ecological knowledge that are integral to cultural survival.

Recognizing the cultural significance of such spaces requires a broader understanding of heritage that moves beyond monumental architecture and elite histories. Intangible aspects—such as rituals, festivals, language, and storytelling—are often rooted in specific places and landscapes. Preserving these spaces means safeguarding the cultural practices and ways of life that give them meaning. It also involves respecting the rights of communities to manage and interpret their heritage on their own terms.

Cultural identity is also reinforced through communal interactions with historical spaces. Festivals celebrated in town squares, traditional crafts practiced in ancestral homes, or local legends tied to geographical features all contribute to a sense of belonging and historical continuity. These everyday practices keep history alive, not as a static archive but as a lived experience shaped by space and memory.

Digital Humanities and the Reconstruction of Historical Spaces

With advancements in digital technology, scholars and educators are increasingly using digital tools to reconstruct and interpret historical spaces. Virtual reality, 3D modeling, GIS mapping, and augmented reality applications have opened new possibilities for engaging with the past. These tools allow users to experience reconstructed environments, visualize spatial changes over time, and interact with historical content in immersive ways.

Digital reconstructions can bring lost or damaged historical spaces back to life, providing insights into their original appearance and function. For example, digital models of ancient cities or monuments can help researchers understand architectural techniques, urban planning, and cultural symbolism. Interactive maps can show the evolution of cities, trade routes, or religious networks, revealing the spatial dimensions of historical processes.

Digital platforms also democratize access to historical spaces. Online exhibits, virtual tours, and open-access archives enable people around the world to explore and learn about places they may never visit in person. This global accessibility helps to promote cross-cultural understanding and appreciation of shared heritage. However, digital representations must be carefully researched and ethically produced to avoid misinterpretation or cultural appropriation.

3.6 MACHINE LEARNING AND AI IN HUMANITIES RESEARCH

In the 21st century, the integration of machine learning and artificial intelligence (AI) into humanities research has revolutionized traditional methodologies and opened up entirely new avenues of inquiry. While the humanities have long been rooted in critical thinking, textual analysis, and historical interpretation, the emergence of digital technologies has introduced quantitative and algorithmic tools that complement and expand the discipline. Machine learning, a subset of AI that allows systems to learn patterns from data and improve over time without explicit programming, is especially transformative. When applied thoughtfully, it enables humanities scholars to analyze large volumes of complex data, uncover hidden patterns, and generate new interpretations across diverse fields such as literature, history, linguistics, cultural studies, and art history.

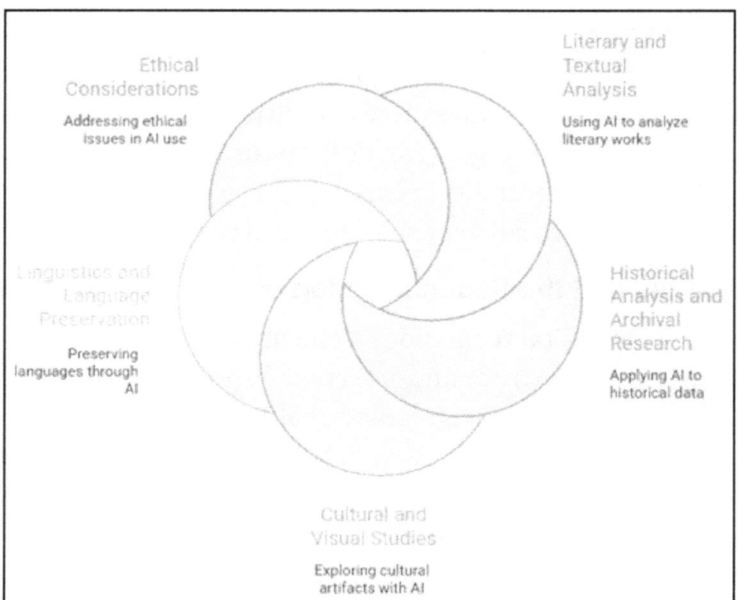

Fig: Expanding Humanities with AI

Machine learning and AI are not replacing humanistic inquiry; rather, they are expanding its horizons by providing new tools to ask old questions and uncover new ones. As the digital transformation continues, humanities scholars have the opportunity to shape the future of AI through critical engagement, ethical practice, and interdisciplinary collaboration. The fusion of humanistic interpretation with computational power promises to deepen our understanding of culture, history, language, and society in ways that were previously unimaginable. It calls for a symbiotic relationship where technology serves human insight, and human values guide the development and application of technological tools. In this evolving landscape, the humanities remain essential, not only in interpreting the past but also in navigating the digital futures that lie ahead.

3.6.1 Redefining the Scope of Humanities through Data

The application of machine learning and AI in the humanities has led to the development of what is commonly referred to as the digital humanities. This interdisciplinary field uses computational methods to explore traditional humanistic questions in innovative ways. One of the most significant changes brought about by AI is the ability to handle vast corpora of text, images, or audio files that were previously unmanageable due to their sheer size. With machine learning algorithms, researchers can now process and analyze millions of documents in multiple languages, spanning centuries of human expression.

This capacity has redefined the scope of what is possible in humanities research. For instance, text mining and natural language processing (NLP) techniques allow scholars to examine patterns in literary styles, rhetorical strategies, or thematic developments across time and authorship. Historical newspapers, legal documents, and letters can be digitized and analyzed to uncover trends in public discourse or shifts in political sentiment. Rather than replacing human interpretation, machine learning enhances it by providing new forms of evidence and pattern recognition that might otherwise remain invisible to the human eye.

3.6.2 Applications in Literary and Textual Analysis

One of the most fruitful areas for the application of machine learning in the humanities is literary and textual analysis. Algorithms can be trained to detect stylistic features such as word frequency, sentence structure, metaphor usage, and sentiment across large bodies of literature. This has allowed researchers to compare different authors or genres, trace the evolution of literary trends, and even attribute anonymous works to specific writers based on linguistic patterns. For example, stylometric analysis using AI has helped scholars resolve long-standing debates about authorship in historical texts.

Machine learning also facilitates topic modeling, a method that groups words into clusters based on their co-occurrence in texts. This helps identify themes and subjects in large corpora, even without prior knowledge of the content. Such techniques have been employed to study the changing representation of race, gender, class, and emotion in literature over centuries. Furthermore, sentiment analysis enables researchers to track the emotional tone of texts, revealing how attitudes toward particular events or characters evolve over time.

In addition to literature, these methods are used in religious studies, philosophy, and classical studies, where ancient texts are analyzed for moral themes, theological concepts, or philosophical debates. Machine learning thus offers new ways to re-examine canonical texts, democratize access to rare materials, and support comparative studies across cultures and languages.

3.6.3 Historical Analysis and Archival Research

Machine learning and AI have made a significant impact on historical research, particularly in dealing with large archival datasets. Digitization efforts by libraries and institutions have resulted in vast online repositories of historical documents, including census records, court proceedings, military reports, and personal diaries. Machine learning tools can process and categorize this data, identify entities such as names, places, and dates, and establish connections between them. This ability to extract structured information from unstructured sources has enabled historians to construct social networks, trace migration patterns, and map historical events with greater precision.

Geographic Information Systems (GIS) integrated with AI tools allow scholars to visualize historical data spatially, making it possible to explore how events unfolded across geographic regions. For example, mapping the spread of revolutions, epidemics, or religious movements can reveal the interconnectedness of local and global histories. Furthermore, AI has been used to predict missing data points in incomplete historical records, offering informed reconstructions that can guide further research. Another promising area is handwriting recognition and Optical Character Recognition (OCR), where AI models are trained to read and transcribe old manuscripts and printed documents. This significantly reduces the time and effort needed to access and analyze archival materials, making historical research more efficient and inclusive.

3.6.4 Cultural and Visual Studies

In the realm of art history and cultural studies, AI and machine learning have opened up new possibilities for image recognition, visual pattern analysis, and the classification of artworks. Deep learning algorithms, especially convolutional neural networks (CNNs), can be trained to identify visual elements in paintings, photographs, or architectural designs. These models can classify artworks by artist, period, style, or region with remarkable accuracy, and can even detect forgeries or unauthorized reproductions by comparing stylistic and material features. Visual AI tools also support the digitization and analysis of film, television, and other media, enabling researchers to study visual culture at scale. Shot detection, facial recognition, and object tracking are now used to analyze patterns in visual storytelling, representation of minorities, or recurring symbols across genres. This assists scholars in evaluating how narratives are constructed visually and how cultural themes are conveyed through imagery. In museum studies and heritage conservation, AI is used to monitor the condition of artifacts, predict deterioration, and simulate restoration techniques. Virtual and augmented reality tools, powered by machine learning, also allow for the recreation of historical spaces and immersive experiences, thus transforming public engagement with cultural heritage.

3.6.5 Linguistics, Language Preservation, and Translation

Machine learning has brought about significant advances in linguistics and language studies, especially in the analysis of endangered and lesser-known languages. AI models trained on multilingual datasets can assist in documenting, translating, and preserving languages that face extinction. Speech recognition, automated transcription, and machine translation tools make it easier to analyze oral traditions and spoken word performances, contributing to the preservation of intangible cultural heritage.

In historical linguistics, machine learning enables the tracing of language evolution, the identification of language families, and the study of how vocabulary and syntax change over time. By analyzing phonetic patterns and grammatical structures across texts, AI helps linguists reconstruct proto-languages and understand the diffusion of linguistic features across regions and communities. Translation technologies powered by neural machine translation have also improved cross-cultural research. Although not perfect, these tools offer scholars the ability to access texts in multiple languages and conduct comparative analyses across cultures, which is especially valuable in postcolonial studies, world literature, and global history.

3.6.6 Ethical Considerations and Critical Engagement

While machine learning and AI offer powerful tools for humanities research, their use also raises important ethical questions. Algorithms reflect the biases present in their training data, and if not critically examined, they can perpetuate historical inequalities or cultural misrepresentations. For example, sentiment analysis models trained on biased corpora may misinterpret texts that deviate from mainstream language norms, especially those from marginalized communities.

The opacity of AI systems, often referred to as the "black box" problem, challenges the transparency and accountability of research. Humanities scholars must engage critically with the assumptions and limitations of AI tools, questioning how models are built, what data they are trained on, and whose perspectives they privilege. Interdisciplinary collaboration is essential in this regard, bringing together technical experts and humanists to ensure that digital methodologies uphold the values of inclusivity, fairness, and interpretative depth. There is also a need to address issues of data privacy, especially when dealing with sensitive historical or contemporary material. Responsible data management, open access policies, and community engagement must guide the ethical use of AI in humanities research.

3.7 DIGITAL STORYTELLING AND INTERACTIVE NARRATIVES

The art of storytelling has undergone a profound transformation in the digital era, evolving from traditional oral and written forms to dynamic, multimedia experiences. Digital storytelling represents the convergence of narrative techniques with digital technologies, enabling creators to craft immersive stories that engage audiences in unprecedented ways. Unlike conventional storytelling, which follows a linear structure, digital storytelling leverages interactive elements, multimedia integration, and user participation to create richer, more engaging experiences. This shift has been driven by advancements in technology, including virtual reality (VR), augmented reality (AR), artificial intelligence (AI), and interactive platforms, which allow for non-linear narratives and personalized story arcs.

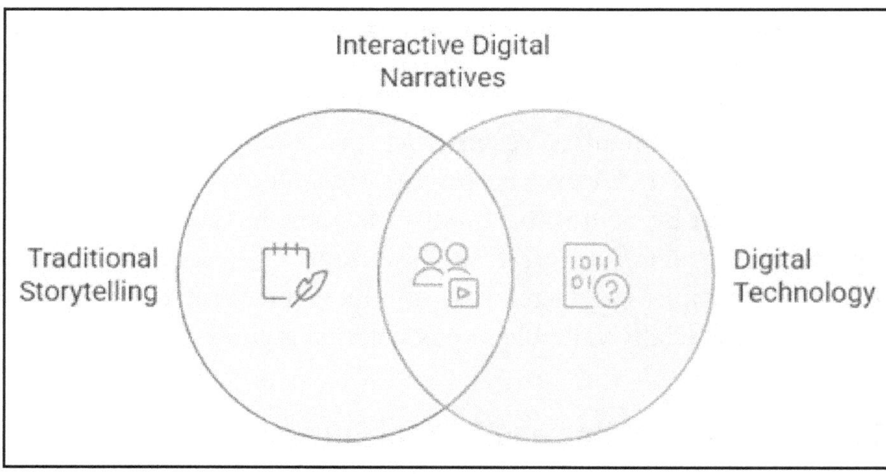

Fig: The Synergy of Storytelling and Technology

Digital storytelling and interactive narratives represent a paradigm shift in how stories are created, shared, and experienced. By blending technology with traditional narrative techniques, these innovations have expanded the possibilities of storytelling across education, marketing, entertainment, and activism. While challenges such as ethical concerns and technological limitations persist, the potential for digital storytelling to foster empathy, engagement, and creativity is undeniable. As emerging technologies like AI, VR, and the metaverse continue to evolve, the future of storytelling will be increasingly participatory, immersive, and boundary-defying. In an age where digital interaction dominates, storytelling remains a fundamental human experience—one that is being reimagined for the digital era in ways that are as transformative as they are timeless.

Foundations of Interactive Narratives

Interactive narratives represent a significant departure from traditional storytelling by placing the audience at the center of the experience. Unlike passive consumption, where the audience follows a predetermined plot, interactive narratives empower users to influence the story's direction through choices, branching paths, and real-time engagement. This form of storytelling draws from video games, hypertext fiction, and transmedia storytelling, where multiple platforms contribute to a cohesive narrative universe. Early examples, such as "Choose Your Own Adventure" books, laid the groundwork for modern interactive storytelling, which now includes complex video games like The Witcher and Detroit: Become Human, where player decisions shape the outcome. The rise of interactive films, such as Netflix's Black Mirror: Bandersnatch, further demonstrates how mainstream media is embracing non-linear storytelling, blurring the lines between viewer and participant.

Technologies Driving Digital Storytelling

The rapid advancement of digital technologies has been instrumental in shaping contemporary storytelling methods. Virtual reality (VR) and augmented reality (AR) have introduced new dimensions to narratives, allowing users to step inside stories and interact with virtual environments. VR experiences like The Invisible Hours and Half-Life: Alyx immerse users in fully realized worlds, while AR applications, such as Pokemon GO and interactive museum exhibits, overlay digital narratives onto the physical world. Artificial intelligence (AI) is also revolutionizing storytelling by enabling dynamic, adaptive narratives that respond to user input in real time. AI-driven chatbots and procedural storytelling algorithms, as seen in games like AI Dungeon, generate unique storylines based on user interactions, offering endless possibilities for personalized narratives. Additionally, social media platforms and user-generated content have democratized storytelling, allowing anyone to create and share interactive stories through tools like Twine, Instagram Stories, and TikTok.

Applications in Education and Learning

Digital storytelling has emerged as a powerful tool in education, enhancing engagement and retention by transforming passive learning into an interactive experience. Educators use multimedia storytelling techniques to present complex subjects in an accessible and compelling manner, incorporating videos, animations, and gamified elements to capture students' attention. Interactive e-books and educational games, such as Prodigy Math and Duolingo, employ storytelling to make learning more intuitive and enjoyable. Furthermore, digital storytelling fosters creativity and critical thinking by encouraging students to create their own narratives using digital tools. In higher education, virtual simulations and scenario-based training leverage interactive storytelling to prepare students for real-world challenges, particularly in fields like medicine, law, and business. By integrating storytelling with digital pedagogy, educators can cater to diverse learning styles and foster a deeper understanding of subject matter.

Role of Digital Storytelling in Marketing and Branding

Brands have increasingly adopted digital storytelling as a strategy to connect with consumers on an emotional level, moving beyond traditional advertising to create compelling narratives that resonate with audiences. Interactive campaigns, such as Coca-Cola's "Share a Coke" and Nike's "Choose Your Own Adventure" ads, invite consumers to participate in the brand's story, fostering a sense of personal connection. Social media platforms have become key venues for digital storytelling, with brands using Instagram Reels, YouTube series, and Twitter threads to craft serialized narratives that build long-term engagement.

User-generated content campaigns, where consumers contribute their own stories, further amplify brand authenticity and community building. Moreover, immersive technologies like VR and AR are being used for experiential marketing, allowing customers to engage with products in narrative-driven virtual environments. By leveraging digital storytelling, brands can differentiate themselves in a crowded market and cultivate lasting customer loyalty.

Interactive Narratives in Entertainment and Gaming

The entertainment industry has fully embraced interactive narratives, revolutionizing how stories are delivered in films, television, and video games. Video games, in particular, have pioneered interactive storytelling, with titles like The Last of Us, Red Dead Redemption 2, and Life is Strange offering emotionally driven narratives where player choices impact the storyline.

The success of interactive films, such as Netflix's Black Mirror: Bandersnatch, has demonstrated that audiences are eager for participatory storytelling experiences beyond gaming. Streaming platforms are experimenting with interactive episodes, allowing viewers to influence plot developments in real time. Additionally, live-action role-playing games (LARPs) and escape rooms incorporate digital elements to create hybrid storytelling experiences that blend physical and virtual interactions. As technology continues to evolve, the line between traditional media and interactive entertainment will further blur, offering audiences unprecedented control over the stories they consume.

Social Impact and Activism through Digital Storytelling

Digital storytelling has become a vital tool for social activism, enabling marginalized voices to share their experiences and advocate for change. Nonprofits and advocacy groups use multimedia storytelling to raise awareness about social issues, combining personal narratives with data visualization and interactive documentaries to engage audiences emotionally and intellectually. Projects like The Guardian's "Firestorm" and The New York Times' "The Displaced" use immersive journalism to bring global crises to life, fostering empathy and driving action. Grassroots movements leverage social media storytelling to mobilize communities, with hashtags like #MeToo and #BlackLivesMatter amplifying personal stories on a global scale. Virtual reality has also been employed in empathy-building campaigns, such as Clouds Over Sidra, which immerses viewers in the life of a Syrian refugee. By harnessing the power of digital storytelling, activists can humanize complex issues and inspire collective action.

Challenges and Ethical Considerations

Despite its transformative potential, digital storytelling presents several challenges and ethical dilemmas. The interactive nature of these narratives raises questions about authorship and creative control, as user input can lead to unintended story outcomes. Ensuring narrative coherence while allowing for meaningful interactivity requires careful design and balancing. Additionally, the use of AI in storytelling introduces concerns about bias, as algorithms may perpetuate stereotypes if not properly regulated. Privacy is another critical issue, particularly in immersive experiences that collect user data to personalize narratives. The potential for deepfake technology to manipulate digital stories further complicates ethical boundaries, necessitating guidelines to prevent misuse. As digital storytelling evolves, creators must address these challenges to maintain integrity and trust in interactive narratives.

CHAPTER

Digital Humanities Across Disciplines 4

4.1 DIGITAL HISTORY

4.1.1 Archives

The preservation of history has undergone a profound transformation with the advent of digital technologies. Traditional archives, once confined to physical repositories of manuscripts, photographs, and artifacts, have expanded into the digital realm, creating unprecedented opportunities for accessibility and analysis. Digital history represents the intersection of historical scholarship and computational methods, enabling historians to collect, preserve, and interpret vast amounts of data with greater efficiency.

The digitization of archives has democratized access to historical materials, allowing researchers, students, and the general public to explore primary sources from anywhere in the world. This shift has not only changed how history is studied but also raised important questions about preservation, authenticity, and the future of historical research in an increasingly digital world. Digital archives have redefined the ways in which history is preserved, accessed, and interpreted, offering both opportunities and challenges for historians and archivists alike.

By bridging the gap between traditional scholarship and technological innovation, digital history has expanded the scope of historical research, making it more inclusive, dynamic, and interconnected. However, the success of digital archives depends on addressing critical issues of preservation, ethics, and accessibility to ensure their longevity and relevance. As we move further into the digital age, archives will continue to evolve as living repositories of collective memory, adapting to new technologies while maintaining their fundamental mission: to safeguard the past for the enlightenment of the future.

Process

Digitizing historical materials involves more than simply scanning documents and uploading them to databases. It requires meticulous planning, specialized equipment, and careful consideration of metadata standards to ensure that digital surrogates remain useful for future research. Archivists and historians must address challenges such as fragile physical conditions of original materials, varying formats, and the need for high-resolution imaging. Optical Character Recognition (OCR) technology has revolutionized the digitization of printed texts, making them searchable and analyzable, while three-dimensional scanning techniques have enabled the preservation of artifacts in digital form. Institutions like the Library of Congress and the British Library have pioneered large-scale digitization projects, setting benchmarks for quality and accessibility. However, the process remains resource-intensive, requiring significant funding and technical expertise to maintain the integrity of historical records in their digital transformations.

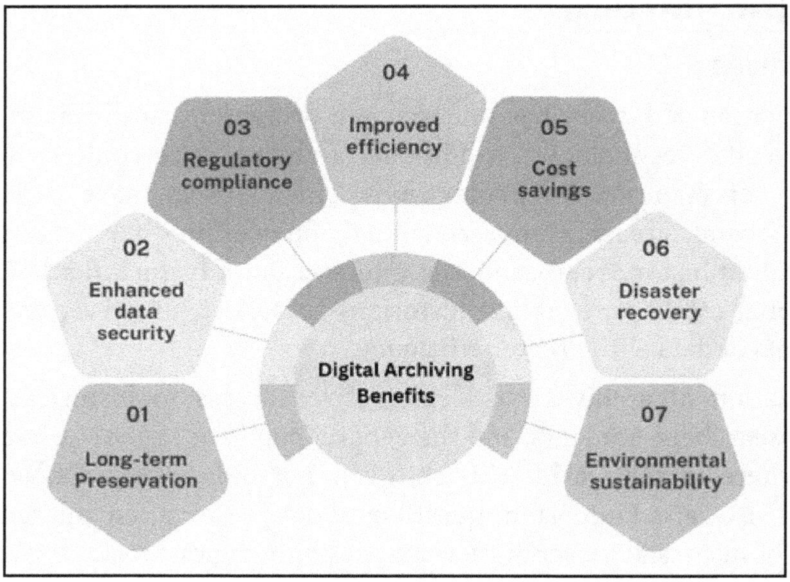

Fig: Digital Archives

Digital Archives and the Democratization of History

One of the most significant impacts of digital archives is the democratization of historical knowledge. Previously, accessing rare manuscripts or specialized collections required physical travel to specific institutions, limiting research opportunities to those with the means to do so. Digital archives have removed many of these barriers, providing open access to primary sources that were once restricted to elite academic circles.

Projects like the Internet Archive, Europeana, and Google Books have made millions of historical texts available to a global audience. Community-based digitization initiatives have also empowered local historians and marginalized groups to preserve and share their own histories, ensuring that diverse narratives are included in the historical record. This shift has fostered a more inclusive approach to history, where multiple voices and perspectives can be explored and analyzed by anyone with an internet connection.

Challenges in Digital Preservation and Data Longevity

While digital archives offer numerous advantages, they also present unique challenges related to preservation and long-term accessibility. Unlike physical documents that can endure for centuries with proper care, digital files are vulnerable to technological obsolescence, data corruption, and format incompatibility. The rapid pace of technological change means that storage media and software used today may become obsolete within decades, risking the loss of valuable historical data.

Institutions must implement robust digital preservation strategies, including regular migration to updated formats, redundancy through multiple backups, and adherence to international standards like the Open Archival Information System (OAIS). Additionally, issues of digital rights management and copyright restrictions complicate the sharing of some materials, creating legal barriers to full accessibility. Addressing these challenges requires ongoing collaboration between archivists, technologists, and policymakers to ensure that digital history remains preserved for future generations.

Computational Methods

The digitization of archives has enabled historians to employ computational methods that were previously unimaginable. Text mining, network analysis, and geographic information systems (GIS) have opened new avenues for analyzing large datasets, revealing patterns and connections that traditional close reading might overlook. Digital tools like Voyant for text analysis and Palladio for network visualization allow researchers to process vast quantities of historical records efficiently.

These methods have proven particularly valuable in fields such as social history, where census data, newspapers, and personal correspondence can be analyzed to uncover trends in migration, labor, and cultural exchange. However, the use of computational techniques also raises methodological questions about the interpretation of data and the potential for algorithmic bias, emphasizing the need for historians to combine digital analysis with critical humanistic inquiry.

Ethical Considerations

The creation and use of digital archives involve significant ethical considerations, particularly concerning privacy, representation, and cultural sensitivity. Many historical records contain personal information about individuals who may not have consented to its public dissemination, raising concerns about the ethics of digitizing sensitive materials. Indigenous communities, for example, have advocated for greater control over how their cultural heritage is digitized and shared, emphasizing the importance of respecting traditional knowledge systems.

Archivists must navigate these ethical dilemmas by developing protocols for community consultation and implementing access restrictions where appropriate. Furthermore, the digitization of colonial archives has sparked debates about restitution and the need to address historical injustices in how materials were acquired. Ethical digital archiving requires a commitment to transparency, accountability, and inclusivity to ensure that the digitization process does not perpetuate existing inequalities.

Role of Artificial Intelligence in Archival Work

Artificial intelligence (AI) is increasingly being integrated into archival practices, offering tools for automating tasks such as transcription, translation, and metadata tagging. Handwritten Text Recognition (HTR) software, like Transkribus, uses machine learning to decipher historical handwriting, significantly reducing the time required to transcribe manuscripts. AI-driven image recognition can also assist in classifying and organizing visual materials, from photographs to maps. While these technologies enhance efficiency, they are not without limitations; accuracy varies depending on the quality of source materials, and human oversight remains essential to correct errors. AI also holds potential for enhancing search capabilities within digital archives, enabling more intuitive and context-aware retrieval of information. As AI continues to evolve, its applications in archival science will likely expand, though its use must be carefully managed to avoid over-reliance on automated systems at the expense of scholarly rigor.

Case Studies of Pioneering Digital Archive Projects

Several groundbreaking digital archive projects illustrate the transformative potential of digital history. The Digital Public Library of America (DPLA) aggregates millions of items from libraries, archives, and museums across the United States, providing a centralized platform for exploring the nation's cultural heritage. The Trans-Atlantic Slave Trade Database offers a comprehensive digital record of slave voyages, enabling researchers and the public to engage with this dark chapter of history through interactive maps and datasets. In Europe, the EHRI Project (European Holocaust Research Infrastructure) has created a virtual archive for Holocaust documentation, integrating dispersed collections into a unified digital resource. These projects demonstrate how digital archives can facilitate new forms of historical inquiry while serving as vital educational tools for confronting complex historical legacies.

4.1.2 Timelines

In the realm of historical research and representation, timelines have long served as fundamental tools for organizing, understanding, and communicating chronological sequences of events. In the digital age, the simple linear timeline has evolved into a dynamic and interactive medium through which history can be explored with greater depth and clarity. Digital timelines are not merely visual aids; they are powerful instruments of analysis, interpretation, and education. They enable historians, educators, students, and the general public to engage with historical narratives in ways that traditional methods could not offer.

Timelines in digital history represent far more than chronological lists of events. They are dynamic tools that combine visual representation, narrative structure, and interactive exploration to deepen historical understanding. By incorporating multimedia, interactivity, and user participation, digital timelines transcend the limitations of traditional historical formats. They serve educational, scholarly, and public purposes, fostering critical engagement with the past and inviting new voices into the conversation.

As technology continues to advance, timelines will become even more integral to how we record, analyze, and communicate history. Yet, their power lies not just in technological sophistication, but in the careful choices scholars and creators make in crafting them. In embracing the potential of digital timelines, historians must remain mindful of their interpretive nature, their cultural assumptions, and their capacity to shape collective memory. Used thoughtfully, timelines offer a path toward a more inclusive, accessible, and insightful understanding of the past.

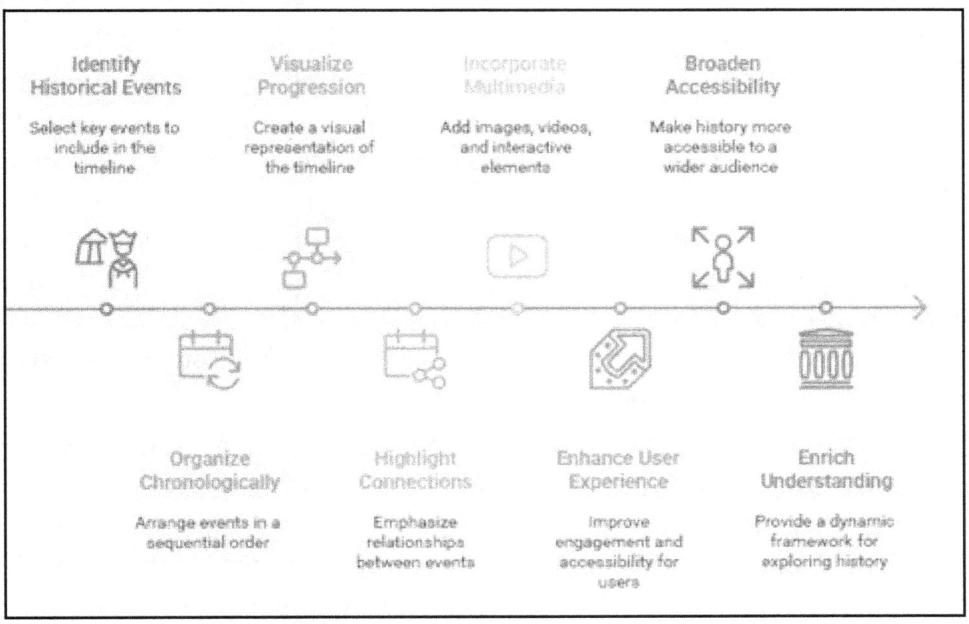

Fig: Digital Timeline Creation and Impact

Nature and Purpose

Timelines in historical study serve the primary function of presenting events in a sequential order, making it easier to understand causality, patterns, and overlaps between historical developments. They allow historians to chart progress, regression, conflict, innovation, and transformation over time. Traditional timelines, found in textbooks or as wall charts, provided limited space and scope. They typically focused on key political events, rulers, wars, or discoveries, often omitting the multifaceted social, cultural, and local narratives that form the foundation of comprehensive history.

The advent of digital tools has changed this limitation by allowing timelines to expand in scope and detail. With interactive digital platforms, it is now possible to include multiple perspectives, layered narratives, multimedia elements, and even hyperlinks that allow users to delve deeper into each event or period. A digital timeline is no longer just a linear progression of events; it becomes a multidimensional space where history is not only represented but also explored critically and collaboratively.

Digital Turn in Historical Timelines

Digital history, as a methodological approach, emphasizes the use of technology to collect, curate, analyze, and present historical data. Digital timelines are one of the most accessible and popular forms of presenting historical research within this paradigm. They offer both visual structure and interactivity, making them ideal tools for public history projects, museum exhibitions, educational resources, and academic research. Unlike static timelines, digital timelines can be updated, modified, and customized according to user needs or scholarly developments.

Various digital tools such as TimelineJS, Tiki-Toki, TimeMapper, and Knight Lab have enabled users with limited technical expertise to create sophisticated timelines that integrate images, videos, maps, and primary source documents. These tools support a user-centered approach, allowing historians to frame historical questions and narratives while enabling viewers to navigate the information at their own pace. The non-linear structure supported by many of these tools challenges the conventional chronological format by allowing events to be grouped thematically or comparatively across regions and cultures.

Furthermore, timelines are now being generated using data from large digital archives and databases, often supported by metadata and machine learning algorithms. This data-driven approach enables the creation of scalable and comprehensive timelines that reflect vast historical trends or focus on highly specialized topics. As such, digital timelines have become research tools as much as they are educational or presentational devices.

Timelines as Pedagogical Tools

One of the most important uses of digital timelines is in the field of education. Digital timelines help students visually contextualize historical events, recognize patterns, and build a deeper understanding of continuity and change over time. In history classrooms, timelines are used to teach chronological thinking, a fundamental skill that enables learners to understand the order and timing of events and their relationships to one another.

Digital timelines promote active learning by encouraging students to engage with historical data directly. When students build their own timelines as part of classroom projects, they engage in historical research, source evaluation, and analytical writing. They also learn to think critically about which events to include, how to categorize them, and what narratives they want their timelines to convey. This process promotes historical literacy and fosters a sense of ownership over knowledge creation.

Moreover, digital timelines support interdisciplinary learning. In subjects such as literature, art, philosophy, and science, timelines are used to map intellectual movements, cultural periods, or technological advancements. By placing developments in broader historical contexts, learners gain a holistic understanding of how ideas and innovations have evolved and intersected over time.

Collaborative and Public History

Digital timelines are especially valuable in collaborative and public history projects, where multiple contributors can work together to produce, edit, and expand a historical narrative. Crowdsourced timelines invite input from communities, allowing local histories, personal stories, and lesser-known events to be included alongside major historical milestones. This democratization of historical knowledge challenges traditional hierarchies of expertise and representation and invites a more inclusive and pluralistic approach to the past.

For example, community history projects often use digital timelines to document shared experiences such as migration, urban development, social movements, or pandemics. These timelines incorporate oral histories, photographs, and local archives, giving voice to individuals and groups who have traditionally been marginalized in historical narratives. By integrating diverse sources and perspectives, digital timelines help create richer and more representative accounts of the past.

Museums and cultural institutions also use digital timelines to enhance visitor experiences. Exhibits that include interactive timelines enable visitors to explore content in personalized ways, deepening engagement and understanding. For digital exhibitions, timelines provide structure and coherence while allowing for exploration and discovery. In online spaces, they function as portals through which users can access a wide array of historical content curated around specific themes or questions.

Timelines, Visualization, and Critical Interpretation

While digital timelines offer many benefits, they also require critical interpretation. The design of a timeline—its structure, the selection of events, the visual emphasis—shapes the viewer's understanding of history. Every timeline reflects the perspective of its creator, and therefore must be understood as an interpretation rather than an objective account. Questions about what is included or omitted, how time is segmented, and how categories are constructed are essential to the ethical use of digital timelines.

The visual representation of time itself can be a subject of critique. Linear timelines imply a progression that may not be accurate for all histories, particularly for cultures that understand time cyclically or relationally. Moreover, the visualization of time often prioritizes Western concepts of periodization, such as the Renaissance or the Industrial Revolution, which may not resonate globally. Scholars working with Indigenous histories, postcolonial narratives, or alternative chronologies must therefore consider how to adapt or challenge conventional timeline formats.

Timelines must also grapple with the complexity of simultaneity and causality. Events do not occur in isolation, and the simplification necessary for visual representation can sometimes obscure interconnectedness. However, digital tools offer possibilities for layered and relational timelines that allow users to see multiple streams of events concurrently or explore causal links between developments in different regions or domains.

4.1.3 Historical Simulations

Historical simulations in digital history represent a cutting-edge approach to understanding and interpreting the past through the use of computational models and digital technologies. Digital history leverages the power of computers, data analysis, and visualization tools to recreate and explore historical events, processes, and phenomena. Historical simulations go beyond traditional narrative-based history by providing interactive and dynamic representations of the past, allowing researchers and the public to engage with history in new and immersive ways. These simulations can range from simple models that illustrate basic historical processes to complex, multi-layered simulations that incorporate vast amounts of data and sophisticated algorithms.

The primary goal of historical simulations in digital history is to create a more comprehensive and nuanced understanding of the past. By using computational models, historians can test hypotheses, explore "what-if" scenarios, and analyze historical data in ways that were previously impossible. For example, a historical simulation might model the spread of a disease during a historical epidemic, allowing researchers to understand the factors that contributed to its spread and the effectiveness of various interventions. Similarly, a simulation of a historical battle might model the movements of troops, the impact of terrain, and the decisions made by commanders, providing insights into the dynamics of the conflict. These simulations can help historians to identify patterns, test theories, and gain new perspectives on historical events.

Historical simulations in digital history represent a powerful and innovative approach to understanding and interpreting the past. By leveraging the power of computational models, data analysis, and visualization tools, historians can create dynamic and interactive representations of historical events, processes, and phenomena. These simulations provide new insights and perspectives on the past, allowing researchers and the public to engage with history in new and immersive ways. From academic research to public education and cultural heritage preservation, historical simulations have a wide range of applications and potential benefits.

The evolution of historical simulations has been driven by advancements in computing power, data availability, and digital technologies. From simple rule-based models to complex, multi-layered simulations, historical simulations have become more sophisticated and nuanced, incorporating a wider range of variables and more complex algorithms. The integration of agent-based modeling, geographic information systems, and spatial analysis has enabled historians to explore the emergent properties of historical systems and the geographical dimensions of historical events and processes.

Despite their potential, historical simulations face several challenges, including the availability and quality of historical data, the complexity of historical processes, and ethical and methodological considerations. To address these challenges, historians use a range of data collection and analysis techniques, modeling techniques, and ethical guidelines to ensure the accuracy, reliability, and ethical integrity of historical simulations. The future of historical simulations lies in the integration of AI and ML, the development of immersive and interactive simulations, and the creation of collaborative and participatory simulations that engage a wider range of stakeholders in the study and interpretation of the past.

As digital history continues to evolve, historical simulations will play an increasingly important role in the study and interpretation of the past. By addressing the challenges and exploring new directions, historians can ensure that historical simulations are accurate, reliable, and ethically sound, providing new insights and perspectives on the past. The principles of historical simulations, with their dynamic and interactive representations of the past, will continue to influence the development of digital history, ensuring that the study of history is engaging, inclusive, and relevant to a wider audience. Through the use of historical simulations, historians can create a more comprehensive and nuanced understanding of the past, providing new insights and perspectives on the events, processes, and phenomena that have shaped our world.

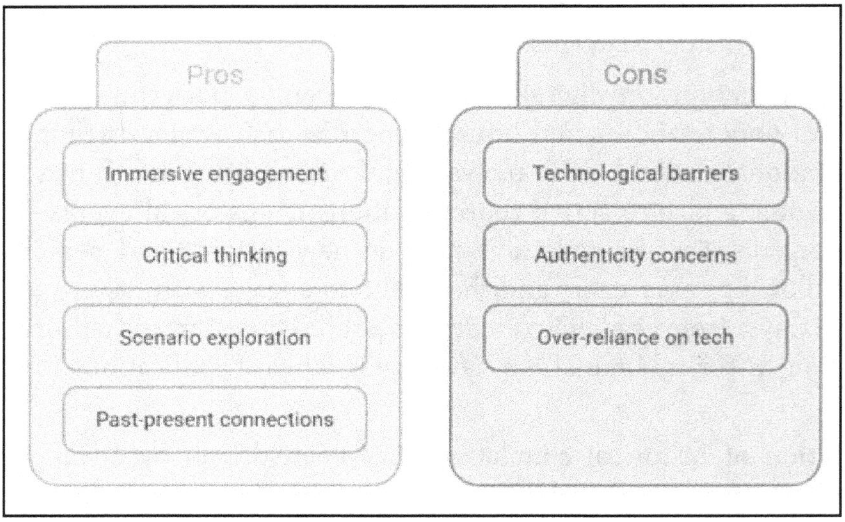

Fig: Historical Simulations: Pros and Cons

Evolution

The use of simulations in historical research has evolved significantly over the past few decades, driven by advancements in computing power, data availability, and digital technologies. Early historical simulations were often simple, rule-based models that focused on specific aspects of historical events.

For example, early simulations of historical battles might model the movements of troops and the impact of terrain, but they would not account for more complex factors such as morale, supply lines, or the decisions made by individual soldiers. As computing power and data availability increased, historical simulations became more sophisticated, incorporating a wider range of variables and more complex algorithms. The advent of agent-based modeling (ABM) has been a significant development in the field of historical simulations.

ABM allows researchers to model the behavior of individual agents, such as people, animals, or even abstract entities, and to observe how their interactions and decisions shape larger historical processes. For example, an ABM of a historical city might model the movements and interactions of individual residents, allowing researchers to understand how social networks, economic activities, and political dynamics shaped the city's development. ABM has enabled historians to explore the emergent properties of historical systems, where complex patterns and behaviors emerge from the interactions of individual agents. Another important development in historical simulations has been the integration of geographic information systems (GIS) and spatial analysis. GIS allows researchers to map and analyze historical data in a spatial context, providing insights into the geographical dimensions of historical events and processes.

For example, a GIS-based simulation of historical migration patterns might model the movements of people across a landscape, allowing researchers to understand the factors that influenced their decisions and the impact of their movements on the environment. Spatial analysis can also be used to model the spread of diseases, the impact of natural disasters, and the dynamics of urban development, providing a more comprehensive understanding of historical processes.

Applications

Historical simulations have a wide range of applications in digital history, from academic research to public education and cultural heritage preservation. In academic research, historical simulations are used to test hypotheses, explore "what-if" scenarios, and analyze historical data.

For example, a historian might use a simulation to model the impact of a specific policy on a historical population, allowing them to understand the factors that contributed to its success or failure. Similarly, a simulation of a historical conflict might model the decisions made by commanders, the movements of troops, and the impact of terrain, providing insights into the dynamics of the conflict.

In public education, historical simulations are used to create interactive and immersive learning experiences that engage students and the public in the study of history. For example, a simulation of a historical battle might allow students to take on the roles of commanders, making decisions and observing the outcomes of their actions.

This hands-on approach to learning can help students to understand the complexities of historical events and the factors that shaped their outcomes. Similarly, a simulation of a historical city might allow students to explore the streets, interact with residents, and observe the dynamics of urban life, providing a more immersive and engaging learning experience.

Historical simulations are also used in cultural heritage preservation, where they are used to recreate and preserve historical sites, artifacts, and cultural practices. For example, a simulation of a historical building might allow researchers to study its architecture, understand its construction techniques, and explore its cultural significance. Similarly, a simulation of a historical event might allow researchers to preserve the memories and experiences of those who participated, providing a more comprehensive and nuanced understanding of the past. Historical simulations can also be used to create virtual museums and exhibitions, allowing the public to explore and interact with cultural heritage in new and immersive ways.

Role of Data

Data plays a crucial role in historical simulations, providing the foundation for computational models and enabling researchers to test hypotheses and explore "what-if" scenarios. Historical simulations rely on a wide range of data sources, including archival documents, oral histories, archaeological findings, and contemporary records. This data is used to create detailed and accurate representations of historical events, processes, and phenomena, allowing researchers to analyze and interpret the past in new and innovative ways. For example, a simulation of a historical epidemic might use data on population demographics, disease transmission rates, and historical interventions to model the spread of the disease and the effectiveness of various responses.

The quality and accuracy of historical simulations depend on the quality and accuracy of the data used to create them. Historical data can be incomplete, biased, or subject to interpretation, which can affect the outcomes of simulations and the insights they provide. To address these challenges, historians use a range of data collection and analysis techniques, including archival research, oral history interviews, and statistical analysis. Additionally, historians use data visualization tools to explore and interpret historical data, providing new insights and perspectives on the past. For example, a visualization of historical migration patterns might use GIS to map the movements of people across a landscape, allowing researchers to understand the factors that influenced their decisions and the impact of their movements on the environment.

Challenges

Despite their potential, historical simulations face several challenges that can limit their effectiveness and accuracy. One of the primary challenges is the availability and quality of historical data. Historical data can be incomplete, biased, or subject to interpretation, which can affect the outcomes of simulations and the insights they provide. For example, a simulation of a historical conflict might rely on incomplete or biased accounts of the events, leading to inaccurate or misleading results. To address these challenges, historians use a range of data collection and analysis techniques, including archival research, oral history interviews, and statistical analysis, to ensure the accuracy and reliability of the data used in simulations.

Another challenge in historical simulations is the complexity of historical processes and the difficulty of modeling them accurately. Historical events and processes are often shaped by a wide range of factors, including social, economic, political, and environmental variables. Modeling these factors accurately can be challenging, as it requires a deep understanding of the historical context and the ability to incorporate a wide range of data and variables into the simulation. To address these challenges, historians use a range of modeling techniques, including agent-based modeling, system dynamics, and spatial analysis, to create detailed and accurate representations of historical events and processes. Historical simulations also face ethical and methodological challenges, particularly in relation to the interpretation and representation of the past. Historical simulations can be subject to bias and interpretation, which can affect the outcomes of the simulation and the insights they provide. For example, a simulation of a historical conflict might be influenced by the historian's own biases and interpretations, leading to a skewed or incomplete representation of the events. To address these challenges, historians use a range of ethical and methodological guidelines, including transparency, peer review, and interdisciplinary collaboration, to ensure the accuracy and reliability of historical simulations.

Ethical Considerations

Ethical considerations are crucial in the development and use of historical simulations, as they involve the interpretation and representation of the past. One of the primary ethical considerations is the potential for bias and misrepresentation in historical simulations. Historical simulations can be influenced by the historian's own biases and interpretations, leading to a skewed or incomplete representation of the events. To address this challenge, historians use a range of ethical guidelines, including transparency, peer review, and interdisciplinary collaboration, to ensure the accuracy and reliability of historical simulations. For example, historians might use peer review to evaluate the assumptions and methods used in a simulation, ensuring that the results are based on sound historical evidence and rigorous analysis.

Another ethical consideration in historical simulations is the potential for misuse or misinterpretation of the results. Historical simulations can be used to support a wide range of interpretations and narratives, some of which may be inaccurate or misleading. To address this challenge, historians use a range of ethical guidelines, including transparency, accountability, and public engagement, to ensure that the results of historical simulations are interpreted and used responsibly. For example, historians might use public engagement to share the results of a simulation with a wider audience, providing context and interpretation to ensure that the results are understood and used appropriately.

Historical simulations also raise ethical considerations related to the representation of marginalized or vulnerable groups. Historical simulations can inadvertently perpetuate stereotypes or misrepresent the experiences of marginalized groups, leading to harm or injustice. To address this challenge, historians use a range of ethical guidelines, including inclusivity, representation, and cultural sensitivity, to ensure that historical simulations are respectful and accurate in their representation of diverse groups. For example, historians might use inclusive data collection and analysis techniques to ensure that the voices and experiences of marginalized groups are represented in the simulation.

4.2 DIGITAL LITERARY STUDIES

4.2.1 Text Mining in Literature

Text mining in literature represents a powerful and innovative approach to analyzing and interpreting literary texts. By leveraging the power of computational models, data analysis, and visualization tools, scholars can uncover patterns, themes, and insights that might not be immediately apparent through traditional close reading. Text mining enables researchers to explore vast corpora of literature efficiently, identifying key themes, motifs, and stylistic features. This method can also help in comparing and contrasting different works, authors, or genres, providing a more comprehensive view of literary trends and influences.

The evolution of text mining in literature has been driven by advancements in computational power, data availability, and digital technologies. From basic statistical analyses to sophisticated machine learning and AI-driven models, text mining has become more nuanced and context-aware, allowing scholars to delve deeper into the complexities of literary texts. The integration of digital corpora and repositories has made it possible for scholars to conduct large-scale text mining analyses, exploring patterns and trends across entire literary periods or genres.

Despite its potential, text mining in literature faces several challenges, including the availability and quality of textual data, the complexity of literary texts, and ethical and methodological considerations. To address these challenges, scholars use a range of data collection and analysis techniques, modeling techniques, and ethical guidelines to ensure the accuracy, reliability, and ethical integrity of text mining analyses. The future of text mining lies in the integration of AI and ML, the development of immersive and interactive text mining tools, and the creation of collaborative and participatory text mining tools that engage a wider range of stakeholders in the analysis and interpretation of literary texts.

As digital literary studies continue to evolve, text mining will play an increasingly important role in the analysis and interpretation of literary texts. By addressing the challenges and exploring new directions, scholars can ensure that text mining analyses are accurate, reliable, and ethically sound, providing new insights and perspectives on literary texts.

The principles of text mining, with their dynamic and interactive representations of literary texts, will continue to influence the development of digital literary studies, ensuring that the study of literature is engaging, inclusive, and relevant to a wider audience. Through the use of text mining, scholars can create a more comprehensive and nuanced understanding of literary texts, providing new insights and perspectives on the themes, motifs, and stylistic features that shape our literary heritage.

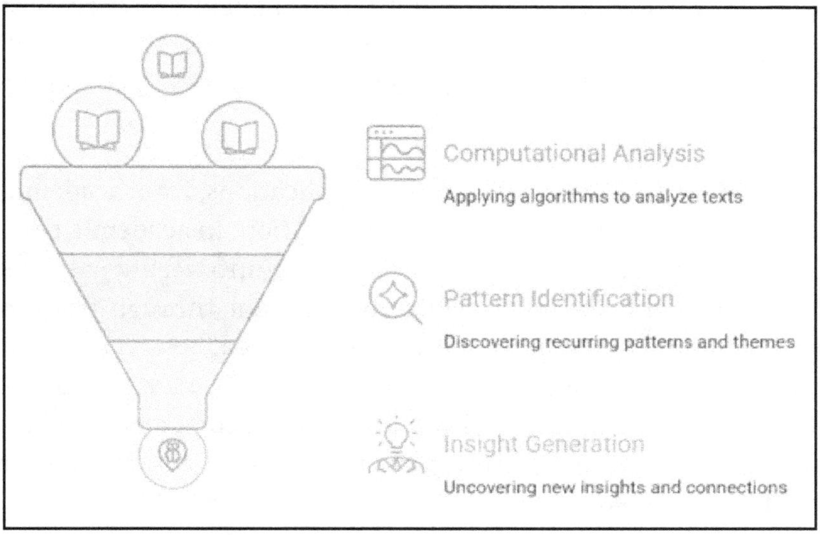

Fig: Text Mining in Literature Process

Evolution

The use of text mining in literature has evolved significantly over the past few decades, driven by advancements in computational power, data availability, and digital technologies. Early efforts in text mining were often limited to basic statistical analyses and keyword searches, which provided a starting point for more in-depth investigations. As computational techniques advanced, so did the sophistication of text mining methods. The development of natural language processing (NLP) and machine learning algorithms has enabled more nuanced and context-aware analyses, allowing scholars to delve deeper into the complexities of literary texts.

One of the key developments in text mining has been the integration of machine learning and artificial intelligence (AI) techniques. These technologies have enabled the creation of more sophisticated models that can analyze and interpret textual data with a high degree of accuracy. For example, machine learning algorithms can be trained to recognize and classify different literary genres, styles, or themes, providing insights into the underlying structures of literary works. AI-driven text mining can also be used to generate predictive models, allowing scholars to anticipate future trends or developments in literature based on historical data.

Another significant advancement in text mining has been the development of digital corpora and repositories, which provide access to vast collections of literary texts. These digital resources have made it possible for scholars to conduct large-scale text mining analyses, exploring patterns and trends across entire literary periods or genres. For example, the Google Books Ngram Viewer allows researchers to analyze the frequency of words and phrases in a corpus of millions of books, providing insights into the evolution of language and literary styles over time. Similarly, the HathiTrust Digital Library offers access to a vast collection of digitized books, enabling scholars to conduct comprehensive text mining analyses.

Applications

Text mining in literature has a wide range of applications, from academic research to public education and cultural heritage preservation. In academic research, text mining is used to explore and analyze literary texts, uncovering patterns, themes, and insights that might not be immediately apparent through traditional close reading. For example, a text mining analysis might reveal how a particular author's use of metaphors evolves over time, or how certain themes are prevalent in a specific literary period. This method can also help in comparing and contrasting different works, authors, or genres, providing a more comprehensive view of literary trends and influences.

In public education, text mining is used to create interactive and immersive learning experiences that engage students and the public in the study of literature. For example, a text mining tool might allow students to explore the themes and motifs in a literary work, providing a more engaging and interactive learning experience. Similarly, a text mining analysis might reveal the evolution of a particular literary style or genre, providing insights into the cultural and historical contexts that shaped it. This approach can help students to understand the complexities of literary texts and the factors that influence their development.

Text mining is also used in cultural heritage preservation, where it is used to analyze and interpret historical and literary texts, providing new insights into the cultural and historical contexts that shaped them. For example, a text mining analysis might reveal the prevalence of certain themes or motifs in a particular literary period, providing insights into the cultural and historical contexts that shaped them. Similarly, a text mining tool might allow researchers to explore the evolution of a particular literary style or genre, providing a more comprehensive view of its development and influence.

Role of Data

Data plays a crucial role in text mining, providing the foundation for computational models and enabling scholars to test hypotheses and explore "what-if" scenarios. Text mining relies on a wide range of data sources, including digitized books, manuscripts, and other textual materials. This data is used to create detailed and accurate representations of literary texts, allowing scholars to analyze and interpret them in new and innovative ways. For example, a text mining analysis might use data on word frequency, phrase usage, and stylistic features to identify patterns and trends in a literary work. The quality and accuracy of text mining analyses depend on the quality and accuracy of the data used. Textual data can be incomplete, biased, or subject to interpretation, which can affect the outcomes of text mining analyses and the insights they provide. To address these challenges, scholars use a range of data collection and analysis techniques, including digitization, transcription, and annotation. Additionally, scholars use data visualization tools to explore and interpret textual data, providing new insights and perspectives on literary texts.

Challenges

Despite its potential, text mining in literature faces several challenges that can limit its effectiveness and accuracy. One of the primary challenges is the availability and quality of textual data. Textual data can be incomplete, biased, or subject to interpretation, which can affect the outcomes of text mining analyses and the insights they provide. For example, a text mining analysis might rely on incomplete or biased data, leading to inaccurate or misleading results. To address these challenges, scholars use a range of data collection and analysis techniques, including digitization, transcription, and annotation, to ensure the accuracy and reliability of the data used in text mining analyses.

Another challenge in text mining is the complexity of literary texts and the difficulty of modeling them accurately. Literary texts are often rich in metaphor, symbolism, and other forms of figurative language, which can be challenging to analyze and interpret using computational methods. Additionally, literary texts can be subject to multiple interpretations, which can affect the outcomes of text mining analyses and the insights they provide.

To address these challenges, scholars use a range of modeling techniques, including natural language processing, machine learning, and statistical analysis, to create detailed and accurate representations of literary texts.

Text mining also faces ethical and methodological challenges, particularly in relation to the interpretation and representation of literary texts. Text mining analyses can be subject to bias and interpretation, which can affect the outcomes of the analysis and the insights they provide. For example, a text mining analysis might be influenced by the scholar's own biases and interpretations, leading to a skewed or incomplete representation of the literary text. To address these challenges, scholars use a range of ethical and methodological guidelines, including transparency, peer review, and interdisciplinary collaboration, to ensure the accuracy and reliability of text mining analyses.

Ethical Considerations

Ethical considerations are crucial in the development and use of text mining in literature, as they involve the interpretation and representation of literary texts. One of the primary ethical considerations is the potential for bias and misrepresentation in text mining analyses. Text mining analyses can be influenced by the scholar's own biases and interpretations, leading to a skewed or incomplete representation of the literary text. To address this challenge, scholars use a range of ethical guidelines, including transparency, peer review, and interdisciplinary collaboration, to ensure the accuracy and reliability of text mining analyses. For example, scholars might use peer review to evaluate the assumptions and methods used in a text mining analysis, ensuring that the results are based on sound literary evidence and rigorous analysis.

Another ethical consideration in text mining is the potential for misuse or misinterpretation of the results. Text mining analyses can be used to support a wide range of interpretations and narratives, some of which may be inaccurate or misleading. To address this challenge, scholars use a range of ethical guidelines, including transparency, accountability, and public engagement, to ensure that the results of text mining analyses are interpreted and used responsibly. For example, scholars might use public engagement to share the results of a text mining analysis with a wider audience, providing context and interpretation to ensure that the results are understood and used appropriately.

Text mining also raises ethical considerations related to the representation of marginalized or vulnerable groups. Text mining analyses can inadvertently perpetuate stereotypes or misrepresent the experiences of marginalized groups, leading to harm or injustice. To address this challenge, scholars use a range of ethical guidelines, including inclusivity, representation, and cultural sensitivity, to ensure that text mining analyses are respectful and accurate in their representation of diverse groups. For example, scholars might use inclusive data collection and analysis techniques to ensure that the voices and experiences of marginalized groups are represented in the analysis.

4.2.2 Distant Reading

In the rapidly evolving field of digital humanities, distant reading has emerged as a transformative method for analyzing literature. Coined by literary scholar Franco Moretti, the term "distant reading" challenges the traditional practice of close reading by proposing a large-scale, computational approach to studying texts. Rather than examining a single work in depth, distant reading analyzes vast corpora of texts to identify patterns, trends, and structures that would be difficult or impossible to perceive through manual reading alone. Distant reading has reshaped the landscape of literary studies by offering a powerful set of tools and perspectives for engaging with literature at scale. It challenges traditional notions of literary value, expands the boundaries of research, and enables a more inclusive, data-driven approach to cultural analysis. While it faces important criticisms and limitations, its integration with traditional methods promises a more comprehensive and interdisciplinary future for the humanities.

As digital technologies continue to evolve, distant reading will likely become increasingly sophisticated, incorporating advances in machine learning, artificial intelligence, and digital archiving. Yet its ultimate success will depend not only on technical innovation but on its ability to foster critical thinking, cultural awareness, and interpretive depth. In this way, distant reading stands as a testament to the enduring relevance of the humanities in the digital age—bridging the analytical power of computation with the humanistic pursuit of meaning.

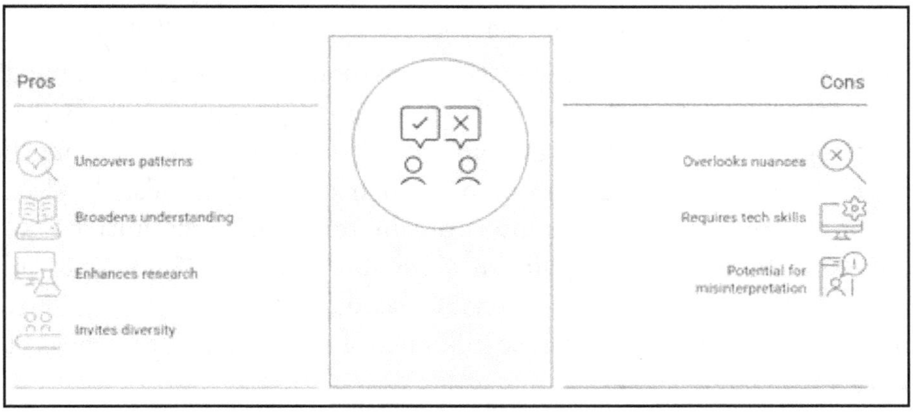

Fig: Distant Reading

Origins and Theoretical Foundations

The concept of distant reading emerged as a critique of the limitations of close reading and canon-focused literary analysis. Franco Moretti, in his influential works, argued that by focusing only on a handful of canonical texts, traditional literary studies overlooked the vast majority of published literature. The literary field, he claimed, had developed a distorted understanding of literary history based on an unrepresentative sample. Distant reading, therefore, was conceived as a way to "read" more by reading less in the traditional sense. Using computational tools to quantify and visualize large datasets, scholars could detect structural shifts, genre evolution, thematic recurrences, and sociolinguistic trends that span across hundreds or thousands of works.

The theoretical foundation of distant reading is built upon the premise that literature, like any cultural artifact, contains measurable patterns. These patterns can be studied through statistical analysis, topic modeling, and other computational methods that extract data from textual corpora. Distant reading is not merely a technical innovation but a conceptual shift in how scholars think about evidence, interpretation, and literary value. It opens the door to a more empirical and inclusive form of literary history, one that includes forgotten or marginalized texts alongside canonical works.

Digital Tools and Methodologies

Distant reading relies on a variety of digital tools and methodologies to process and analyze literary texts. One of the most common approaches is corpus linguistics, which involves the statistical analysis of word frequencies, collocations, and lexical patterns across large collections of texts. This method can reveal stylistic and thematic features characteristic of particular authors, genres, or historical periods. Natural language processing techniques such as named entity recognition, sentiment analysis, and part-of-speech tagging are frequently employed to annotate and categorize text data, enabling more granular analysis.

Topic modeling, a popular machine learning method, is also widely used in distant reading. It identifies latent themes within a corpus by grouping words that tend to appear together, thereby uncovering semantic structures that may not be immediately apparent. Visualization tools such as word clouds, dendrograms, and network graphs help scholars interpret the results of computational analysis and communicate their findings in an accessible manner. Time-series analysis and metadata enrichment further enable scholars to examine the historical development of literary trends and the influence of external factors such as politics, economics, or social movements.

These tools allow researchers to answer new kinds of questions. For example, what themes were most prevalent in novels published during a specific decade? How did the language of emotional expression change over the centuries? Which marginalized authors shared stylistic features with mainstream writers of their time? Distant reading opens the possibility of asking large-scale questions that span literary history in a way that was previously unimaginable.

Reconfiguring Literary Canons and Histories

One of the most significant contributions of distant reading is its potential to reconfigure literary canons and rewrite literary histories. Traditional literary scholarship has often been constrained by the canon—a selection of texts deemed worthy of study based on aesthetic, cultural, or academic value. This canon has historically excluded texts written by women, minorities, and authors from non-Western cultures. By analyzing entire corpora of texts, including those that have been neglected or forgotten, distant reading brings to light the diversity and complexity of literary production.

For instance, distant reading projects have uncovered the sheer volume of popular literature, such as dime novels, romance serials, and colonial adventure stories, that shaped public tastes and cultural values in ways that canonical literature did not. This challenges the traditional narrative that literary value is synonymous with artistic merit or elite approval. It allows scholars to reconsider what constitutes literary significance and how cultural power structures have influenced the preservation and study of texts.

Moreover, distant reading can reveal the contours of literary evolution across time, offering a more comprehensive understanding of how genres emerge, decline, and transform. By analyzing textual features across centuries, scholars can detect patterns that suggest how literary forms respond to broader societal changes. This macro-historical approach enhances our understanding of literature as a dynamic, evolving medium shaped by cultural, technological, and ideological forces.

Challenges and Criticisms

Despite its innovative potential, distant reading has not been without its critics. Some scholars argue that the method's reliance on quantification and abstraction sacrifices the depth, nuance, and contextual sensitivity of traditional literary analysis. By reducing texts to data points, distant reading may overlook the richness of metaphor, irony, ambiguity, and intertextuality that are central to literary meaning. There is also concern about the decontextualization of texts—removing them from their historical, cultural, and authorial frameworks in pursuit of generalizable patterns.

Another significant challenge is the problem of data selection and representation. The quality and scope of a corpus can significantly influence the results of distant reading. If a digital corpus is skewed toward certain genres, periods, or languages, the analysis may inadvertently reproduce existing biases. Additionally, digitization itself is a selective process, often driven by availability, funding, and institutional priorities. These issues underscore the importance of critical engagement with the sources, tools, and assumptions underlying distant reading projects.

The complexity of literary language also presents technical limitations. Algorithms may struggle with figurative language, dialects, or multilingual texts. Furthermore, computational methods require a level of technical expertise that may be inaccessible to many literary scholars. As such, distant reading is most effective when used in collaboration between literary scholars and data scientists, combining domain knowledge with technical skill.

Integration of Distant and Close Reading

Rather than being seen as opposing approaches, distant and close reading can be productively integrated. Distant reading can guide scholars toward specific texts, passages, or patterns that merit deeper investigation through close reading. Conversely, insights from close reading can inform the design of distant reading models, ensuring that computational analysis is grounded in interpretive awareness. This complementary relationship enhances the rigor and depth of literary scholarship. Some of the most innovative digital humanities projects demonstrate the synergy between these methods. For example, a scholar might use distant reading to identify a trend in the depiction of nature in nineteenth-century novels and then apply close reading to explore how individual authors construct ecological imagery. Such an approach combines the breadth of distant reading with the depth of close interpretation, allowing for more robust and multidimensional scholarship.

Applications beyond Academia

Distant reading is not limited to academic research; it has practical applications in education, publishing, and cultural preservation. In classrooms, distant reading tools can help students engage with literature in interactive and exploratory ways. Teachers can use visualizations and text analysis to introduce students to literary trends, genre conventions, or thematic patterns. In the publishing industry, distant reading can support market research, genre classification, and trend prediction by analyzing large datasets of reader preferences and literary content.

Cultural institutions and libraries also benefit from distant reading techniques in their efforts to digitize, catalog, and analyze their collections. By extracting metadata, thematic content, and stylistic features from texts, institutions can create richer digital archives and enhance user access to literary materials. Distant reading, therefore, plays a key role in the broader ecosystem of cultural heritage and knowledge dissemination.

4.3 DIGITAL PHILOSOPHY AND ETHICS

4.3.1 Encoding Logic

The project of encoding logic in digital systems ultimately raises deeper questions about what aspects of human thought and morality can and should be translated into computational forms. While digital technologies offer powerful tools for extending human cognition and improving decision-making, they also risk oversimplifying the complexity of moral reasoning and lived experience. A balanced digital philosophy must acknowledge both the potentials and limitations of formal systems, recognizing that some aspects of wisdom may resist complete encoding.

As we delegate increasingly significant decisions to algorithms, we must ensure that our digital systems reflect not just logical rigor but also ethical depth and philosophical sophistication. The challenge for the coming decades will be to develop digital infrastructures that enhance rather than diminish human flourishing, creating technologies that are not only smart but also wise—a task that will require the combined insights of philosophers, technologists, and society at large.

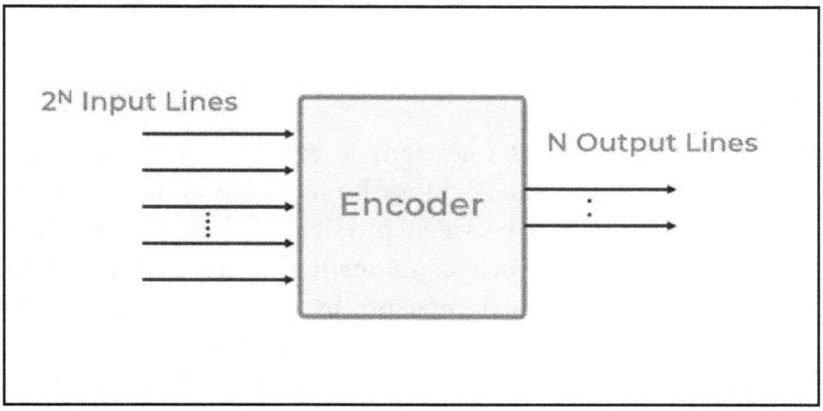

Fig: Encoder in Digital Logic

Nature

At the core of digital philosophy lies the study of computational logic—the formal systems that enable machines to process information, draw inferences, and execute commands. Unlike classical Aristotelian logic, which operates on binary true/false distinctions, computational logic often incorporates probabilistic reasoning, fuzzy logic, and machine learning algorithms that deal with uncertainty and approximation. This shift challenges traditional philosophical notions of determinism and causality, as digital systems increasingly rely on statistical correlations rather than deductive certainty. The question of whether machines can truly "understand" logic in the way humans do remains a subject of debate, with some arguing that computation merely simulates reasoning while others suggest that sufficiently complex algorithms may develop a form of synthetic cognition. These discussions have profound implications for fields such as artificial intelligence, where the line between programmed responses and genuine understanding continues to blur.

Ethical Dimensions of Algorithmic Decision-Making

As digital systems take on greater roles in governance, healthcare, and social interaction, the ethical implications of encoded logic become increasingly urgent. Algorithms designed to optimize efficiency often inadvertently encode biases present in their training data, perpetuating discrimination in areas like criminal sentencing, loan approvals, and hiring practices. The opacity of many machine learning models—commonly referred to as the "black box" problem—further complicates accountability, making it difficult to determine how or why a system arrived at a particular decision. Digital ethics must address these challenges by developing frameworks for transparent, auditable, and fair algorithmic design. Philosophers and computer scientists are collaborating to establish principles such as explainable AI (XAI), which seeks to make machine decision-making processes interpretable to human users, ensuring that automated systems remain accountable to ethical standards.

Ontology of Digital Existence

Digital philosophy also explores questions about the nature of existence and identity in virtual environments. As more human interactions and experiences migrate online, the distinction between physical and digital realities becomes increasingly porous. Virtual worlds, augmented reality, and digital avatars challenge traditional metaphysical concepts by creating spaces where identity can be fluid, multiple, and deliberately constructed. This raises ethical questions about authenticity, consent, and agency in digital interactions. For instance, if an AI system generates a convincing simulation of a deceased individual, does that simulation have any moral status? Similarly, the rise of deepfake technology forces us to reconsider the nature of truth and representation in an era where digital content can be easily manipulated. These issues demand a reevaluation of classical philosophical categories in light of new technological capabilities.

Information Ethics and Digital Rights

The encoding of information in digital systems has given birth to a new branch of ethics concerned with the moral dimensions of data creation, storage, and dissemination. Information ethics addresses questions about privacy, intellectual property, and the right to be forgotten in an age of pervasive digital recording. The European Union's General Data Protection Regulation (GDPR) represents one attempt to codify these ethical concerns into law, establishing principles such as data minimization and purpose limitation. However, philosophical debates continue about the nature of digital property—whether data should be considered a form of personal expression, a commodity, or a public good. The increasing concentration of data in the hands of a few technology corporations has led some philosophers to argue for reconceptualizing data rights as fundamental human rights, necessary for preserving autonomy and democracy in the digital age.

Epistemology of Digital Knowledge

Digital technologies have transformed how knowledge is produced, validated, and disseminated, creating new epistemological challenges. Traditional criteria for assessing truth and reliability—such as peer review in academia or editorial oversight in journalism—compete with algorithmic content curation and crowdsourced knowledge bases like Wikipedia. The speed at which information spreads through digital networks often outpaces verification processes, leading to phenomena like misinformation epidemics and "fake news." Philosophers are examining how digital environments reshape our understanding of justification and belief, particularly when social media algorithms prioritize engagement over accuracy. Some propose developing new digital literacy skills to navigate this landscape, while others suggest redesigning information architectures to better support epistemic virtues like intellectual humility and source criticism. These discussions are crucial for maintaining the integrity of public discourse in increasingly digitized societies.

Artificial Consciousness and Moral Patienthood

One of the most profound questions in digital philosophy concerns the possibility of artificial consciousness and its ethical implications. If a machine were to achieve genuine awareness—as opposed to merely simulating intelligent behavior—would it deserve moral consideration? This debate draws from centuries of philosophical discourse about the nature of consciousness while introducing new dimensions specific to digital systems. Some theorists argue that certain properties of information processing, such as integrated information or self-modeling capabilities, might constitute sufficient conditions for consciousness in machines. Others maintain that biological substrates are essential for true experience. These discussions have practical consequences for how we design and treat advanced AI systems, particularly as they become more sophisticated in their interactions. Establishing criteria for artificial moral patienthood—the status of being worthy of ethical consideration—remains an urgent challenge as technology progresses toward potentially sentient machines.

Digital Virtue Ethics in Algorithm Design

Recent philosophical work has applied virtue ethics—the moral framework emphasizing character and flourishing—to the design of digital systems. Rather than focusing solely on rule-based approaches to AI ethics, some theorists propose cultivating "digital virtues" in both human users and artificial agents. This might involve programming systems to demonstrate patience in interactions, humility in uncertainty, or creativity in problem-solving. The concept raises intriguing questions about whether virtues can be formally encoded and how they might manifest differently in artificial versus human cognition. Digital virtue ethics also examines how technology design can support or undermine human virtues, considering how social media platforms might encourage either narcissism or empathy depending on their architecture. This approach offers a more holistic vision for ethical technology that goes beyond compliance with rules to foster positive moral ecosystems in digital spaces.

4.3.2 Analyzing Discourse

The analysis of digital discourse offers a powerful lens through which to explore the philosophical and ethical dimensions of contemporary life. As technology continues to reshape how we speak, think, and relate to one another, the need for rigorous, reflective, and interdisciplinary approaches to digital ethics becomes ever more urgent. Digital philosophy challenges us to rethink foundational concepts such as truth, identity, and responsibility, while discourse analysis provides the tools to examine how these concepts are enacted in practice. Together, they form a dynamic field that bridges the abstract and the empirical, the normative and the descriptive. By analyzing digital discourse, scholars can better understand the moral contours of the digital age and contribute to the creation of a more thoughtful, equitable, and ethically grounded digital future.

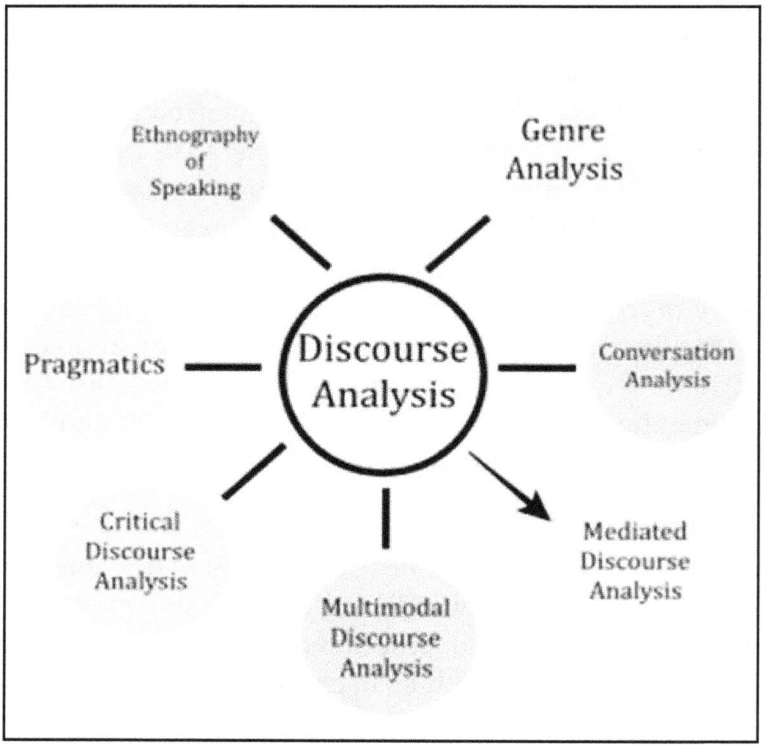

Fig: Analyzing Discourse

Foundations of Digital Philosophy and the Role of Discourse

Digital philosophy is an emerging discipline that interrogates the ontological and epistemological assumptions of the digital age. It draws upon classical philosophical traditions while responding to new questions posed by the proliferation of digital tools and environments. One of the foundational concerns of digital philosophy is the nature of being in a technologically saturated world. What does it mean to exist when our identities are increasingly mediated by digital profiles, data streams, and virtual representations? How do we understand knowledge when vast quantities of information are algorithmically curated, personalized, and often distorted? These questions are deeply entwined with the discourses that unfold across digital platforms, as language becomes both a vehicle and a battleground for shaping reality. Discourse, in this philosophical framework, is not neutral. It constructs and reflects power dynamics, ideologies, and social hierarchies. The digital realm amplifies this effect, as algorithms and platform policies often determine whose voices are heard, whose narratives are elevated, and which ethical norms are reinforced or challenged. Therefore, analyzing discourse becomes a means of uncovering the underlying philosophical currents that shape digital life. By examining the way people speak, write, and interact online, scholars can trace how values such as truth, justice, autonomy, and dignity are negotiated, contested, or undermined in the digital sphere.

Ethical Challenges in the Age of Digital Discourse

The rise of digital discourse has brought with it numerous ethical challenges that require careful analysis and philosophical reflection. One of the most pressing issues is the erosion of truth in an era of misinformation, disinformation, and algorithmic amplification. Social media platforms, in their pursuit of engagement and profit, often prioritize sensational or emotionally charged content, which can distort public discourse and create echo chambers. The philosophical concept of truth, long debated by thinkers from Plato to Foucault, is now reconfigured within digital contexts where credibility is measured by likes, shares, and visibility rather than evidence or logical coherence.

Another ethical concern is the loss of privacy and the commodification of personal data. Digital discourse often unfolds in spaces where users are both speakers and subjects of surveillance. Every post, comment, or search contributes to a data profile that is analyzed, monetized, and potentially exploited. Philosophers question the implications of this for individual autonomy and informed consent. Is it ethical to use personal data for targeted advertising or political manipulation without explicit knowledge or permission? How do digital discourses about privacy shape public attitudes and legislative responses to surveillance capitalism?

Moreover, digital discourse raises questions about responsibility and accountability. The anonymity or pseudonymity of online platforms can embolden users to engage in harmful behaviors, such as hate speech, harassment, or cyberbullying. At the same time, the decentralized and global nature of the internet complicates efforts to enforce ethical norms or legal consequences. Philosophers and ethicists must grapple with the tension between freedom of expression and the need to protect individuals and communities from harm. Analyzing the ways in which these debates are framed and contested within digital discourse helps reveal the shifting boundaries of moral responsibility in networked societies.

Power, Language, and the Politics of Digital Expression

Digital discourse is inherently political, as it shapes and is shaped by relations of power. Language on digital platforms does not merely reflect reality; it constitutes it by framing issues, defining identities, and legitimating certain worldviews. The way discourse is structured—what is said, what is omitted, and how it is received—plays a critical role in shaping public consciousness and social action. This dynamic can be seen in the rise of social movements that rely heavily on digital platforms to mobilize, communicate, and challenge dominant narratives. From #MeToo to Black Lives Matter, digital discourse has become a powerful tool for articulating resistance and demanding justice.

Yet, these same platforms are often governed by opaque algorithms and corporate interests that can suppress dissenting voices or promote harmful content. The politics of visibility—who gets to speak, who is heard, and who is silenced—are central to the ethical analysis of digital discourse. Philosophers must ask: how do technological infrastructures influence whose discourse is amplified? What ethical responsibilities do tech companies have in moderating content or designing algorithms that shape public debate? Analyzing these questions through the lens of discourse allows scholars to uncover the mechanisms by which language becomes a site of power struggle in the digital age.

Digital Discourse and the Construction of Ethical Norms

Ethical norms are not static; they evolve in response to cultural, technological, and historical changes. Digital discourse plays a key role in this process by serving as a space where values are negotiated, reinterpreted, or challenged. Online discussions about issues such as artificial intelligence, climate change, gender identity, and racial justice reveal how digital communities collectively make sense of complex moral questions. These discourses often involve conflicting perspectives, emotional appeals, and contested definitions, making them fertile ground for ethical inquiry.

For example, debates about AI ethics frequently revolve around concepts like fairness, transparency, and human-centered design. Analyzing the language used in these debates—how terms are defined, what assumptions are made, and whose interests are prioritized—can illuminate the ethical frameworks that underpin technological development. Similarly, digital discourse about online harassment or cancel culture can reveal tensions between competing values such as accountability and forgiveness, freedom and safety, or justice and retribution. By studying how these conversations unfold, philosophers can gain insight into the ethical landscape of the digital age and contribute to the development of more just and inclusive norms.

Role of Artificial Intelligence in Shaping Discourse

Artificial intelligence, particularly in the form of language models, recommendation systems, and content moderation tools, increasingly plays a role in shaping digital discourse. AI systems determine what content users see, how conversations are structured, and even how language is interpreted or flagged for potential violations. This raises profound philosophical questions about agency, authorship, and bias. When an algorithm curates a user's news feed or suggests search results, it is participating in the construction of meaning and influencing the flow of information.

Analyzing discourse in this context requires an understanding of how AI technologies mediate communication and embed certain values or assumptions. For instance, if an AI moderation tool disproportionately flags content from marginalized communities as offensive, it reflects and perpetuates existing biases in language recognition. Philosophers must ask whether machines can truly understand discourse in its full social and ethical complexity, or whether human oversight is essential to ensure fairness and contextual sensitivity. Ethical frameworks must also account for the unintended consequences of automated systems and the responsibilities of those who design and deploy them.

Towards a Digital Ethics of Discourse

In light of these challenges and transformations, there is a growing need for a coherent digital ethics of discourse. Such an ethics would provide guiding principles for individuals, communities, platforms, and policymakers to navigate the complexities of digital communication. It would affirm the importance of truthfulness, respect, inclusivity, and accountability in online interactions while acknowledging the unique affordances and constraints of digital environments.

Philosophers and ethicists must work in dialogue with technologists, sociologists, legal scholars, and users themselves to develop ethical norms that are both principled and practical. This involves not only analyzing discourse but also participating in it—contributing to public debates, crafting ethical guidelines, and fostering cultures of critical reflection and digital literacy. The goal is not to impose a single moral code but to cultivate a shared commitment to ethical communication and mutual understanding in a diverse and interconnected world.

4.4 DIGITAL ART HISTORY

4.4.1 Image Recognition

Image recognition is a technology that employs artificial intelligence and machine learning algorithms to recognize and categorize objects, individuals, or other visual components in digital images or videos (places, actions, animals, or text from images or videos). The process involves examining and interpreting various visual characteristics of the image or video, including its color, texture, shape, and context, in order to determine its contents.

Fig: Image Recognition - Techniques

Image recognition includes classification, labeling, segmentation, and object detection.

- **Classification:** The goal is to select images and identify the category they fit.
- **Labeling (or Tagging):** Several objects can be labeled within one image. Labeling is a type of classification with a higher level of precision.
- **Segmentation:** We can identify the elements of an image to the nearest pixel using segmentation as a classification technique.
- **Object Detection:** Detection is used for locating a specific object within images. Once the objects are detected, a box appears around them.

Compared to manual image inspection, image recognition speeds up tasks and processes images more precisely. In many applications, image recognition is a vital technique and is the primary driver in deep learning image apps, as follows:

- **Image Classification:** Based on the image content, images are categorized using this technique. Image classification is helpful in e-commerce applications, like recommender systems and image retrieval.
- **Automated Driving:** Automated driving is vital to autonomous driving applications and can recognize pedestrians and road or traffic signs in images.
- **Visual Inspection:** Visual inspection quickly identifies parts as non-defective and defective. For this reason, thousands of pieces of assembly lines can be inspected quickly.
- **Robotics:** Image recognition is used in robotics to detect objects and enhance autonomous navigation by identifying objects on their path or locations.

By identifying scenes or objects in images, image recognition is the core technology at the base of the following deep-learning image applications. After identifying objects and scenes, all this information can be used to make decisions as part of a larger system. In other words, it enables better decisions by offering insight into the system.

Benefits

Image recognition technology significantly benefits various industries, such as improved accuracy, efficiency, and security. Companies can streamline their operations and provide their clients with better services and products using advanced AI models, recognition software, and neural network architectures. Here are some of the image recognition benefits:

- **Efficiency and Automation:** Image annotation techniques are used to identify and label data, improving efficiency simultaneously. Recognition software automates the process of analyzing large amounts of data by processing images efficiently and quickly.
- **Improved Accuracy:** Image recognition uses advanced AI models and neural network architecture to classify and label images. This process includes pattern recognition, feature extraction, and activation functions, offering accuracy and high precision.
- **Enhances Security:** This technology is used in surveillance and security system: By using recognition models to track and detect vehicles or persons To identify potential threats.
- **Personalization:** Image recognition software can also be used to personalize users' experiences in social media, advertising, and e-commerce. This is possible by analyzing user-generated labels and images - the software offer relevant content and product recommendations.

- **Medical Domain:** Image recognition is used in medical diagnosis - medical image analysis. This software can identify and diagnose with high accuracy medical conditions. In addition, AI models can be trained to recognize specific patterns in medical images, helping doctors offer more accurate diagnoses and better care and treatments for their patients.

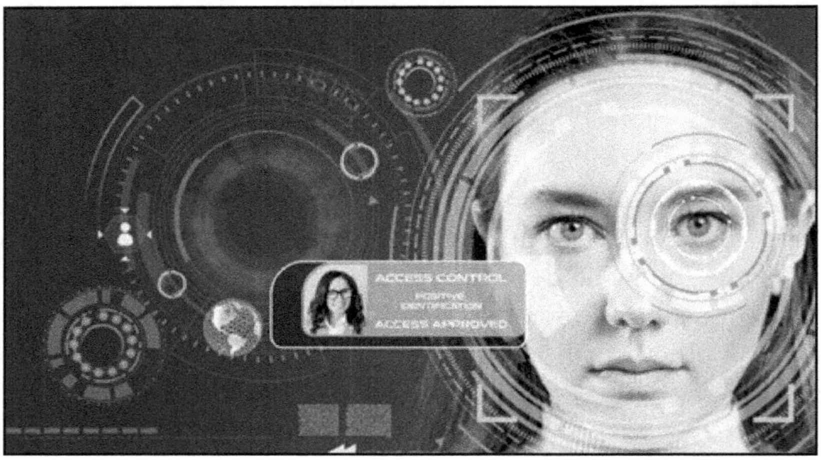

4.4.2 Art Digitization

Art digitization represents a powerful and innovative approach to preserving, disseminating, and analyzing artworks. By leveraging the power of digital technologies, scholars and conservators can create detailed and accurate digital representations of artworks, enabling new forms of scholarly and public engagement. Art digitization has a wide range of applications, from academic research to public education and cultural heritage preservation. The techniques and technologies used in art digitization, including high-resolution photography, 3D scanning, and digital restoration, have evolved significantly over the past few decades, driven by advancements in digital imaging, data storage, and computational power.

Despite its potential, art digitization faces several challenges, including the availability and quality of art digitization data, the complexity of artworks, and ethical and methodological considerations. To address these challenges, scholars and conservators use a range of data collection and analysis techniques, modeling techniques, and ethical guidelines to ensure the accuracy, reliability, and ethical integrity of digital representations.

The future of art digitization lies in the integration of AI and ML, the development of immersive and interactive digital representations, and the creation of collaborative and participatory digital representations that engage a wider range of stakeholders in the preservation, dissemination, and analysis of artworks. As digital technologies continue to evolve, art digitization will play an increasingly important role in the preservation, dissemination, and analysis of artworks. By addressing the challenges and exploring new directions, scholars and conservators can ensure that art digitization is accurate, reliable, and ethically sound, providing new insights and perspectives on artworks. The principles of art digitization, with their dynamic and interactive representations of artworks, will continue to influence the development of digital art and cultural heritage studies, ensuring that the study of art is engaging, inclusive, and relevant to a wider audience. Through the use of art digitization, scholars and conservators can create a more comprehensive and nuanced understanding of artworks, providing new insights and perspectives on the themes, motifs, and stylistic features that shape our artistic heritage.

Fig: Art Digitization

Techniques and Technologies

The techniques and technologies used in art digitization have evolved significantly over the past few decades, driven by advancements in digital imaging, 3D scanning, and data storage. One of the most common techniques for digitizing two-dimensional artworks is high-resolution photography. This involves using specialized cameras and lighting equipment to capture detailed images of the artwork. The images are then processed using software to enhance their quality and accuracy, ensuring that the digital representation is as faithful as possible to the original artwork. High-resolution photography is particularly useful for capturing the fine details and textures of paintings, drawings, and prints, making it an essential tool for art digitization.

For three-dimensional artworks, 3D scanning technologies are employed to create accurate digital replicas. 3D scanning involves using laser or structured light to capture the surface geometry of an object, generating a point cloud of data that can be used to create a 3D model. This process can be used to digitize a wide range of artworks, from sculptures and architectural structures to archaeological artifacts and cultural heritage sites. 3D scanning technologies have revolutionized the way three-dimensional artworks are documented and preserved, enabling scholars and conservators to study and analyze them in new and innovative ways. For example, 3D scanning can be used to create virtual reconstructions of damaged or incomplete artworks, providing insights into their original appearance and function.

Another important technology in art digitization is digital restoration, which involves using software to restore and enhance digital images of artworks. Digital restoration techniques can be used to remove stains, cracks, and other imperfections from digital images, restoring them to their original condition. This process can be particularly useful for preserving and studying damaged or deteriorating artworks, as it allows scholars and conservators to analyze and interpret them without causing further damage. Digital restoration can also be used to enhance the visual quality of digital images, making them more suitable for display and dissemination. For example, digital restoration can be used to improve the contrast, brightness, and color balance of digital images, making them more visually appealing and accessible to a wider audience.

Applications

Art digitization has a wide range of applications, from academic research to public education and cultural heritage preservation. In academic research, art digitization is used to facilitate the study and analysis of artworks, providing scholars with access to high-quality digital images and 3D models. These digital resources can be used to conduct detailed visual analyses, compare and contrast different artworks, and explore the cultural and historical contexts that shaped them. For example, a scholar might use digital images of a painting to analyze its composition, style, and iconography, providing new insights into the artist's techniques and intentions. Similarly, a scholar might use 3D models of a sculpture to study its form, structure, and function, providing a more comprehensive understanding of its cultural and historical significance.

In public education, art digitization is used to create interactive and immersive learning experiences that engage students and the public in the study of art and cultural heritage. For example, a digital exhibition might allow visitors to explore a virtual gallery, interacting with digital images and 3D models of artworks. This hands-on approach to learning can help students to understand the complexities of art and the factors that shaped its development. Similarly, a digital restoration project might allow students to participate in the restoration of a digital image, providing a more engaging and interactive learning experience. Art digitization can also be used to create virtual tours of museums and cultural heritage sites, allowing visitors to explore and interact with artworks in a more immersive and engaging way.

Art digitization is also used in cultural heritage preservation, where it is used to document, preserve, and restore artworks and cultural heritage sites. For example, a digital archive might be created to preserve and document a collection of historical photographs, providing a record of the past that can be accessed and studied by future generations. Similarly, a digital restoration project might be used to restore and preserve a damaged or deteriorating artwork, ensuring its long-term preservation and accessibility. Art digitization can also be used to create virtual reconstructions of cultural heritage sites, providing a record of their original appearance and function. This process can be particularly useful for preserving and studying sites that have been damaged or destroyed, as it allows scholars and conservators to analyze and interpret them without causing further damage.

Role of Data

Data plays a crucial role in art digitization, providing the foundation for digital representations and enabling scholars and conservators to analyze and interpret artworks in new and innovative ways. The data used in art digitization can include a wide range of information, from high-resolution images and 3D models to metadata and contextual data.

This data is used to create detailed and accurate digital representations of artworks, allowing scholars and conservators to study and analyze them in ways that were previously impossible. For example, a digital image of a painting might include metadata on its provenance, condition, and conservation history, providing a more comprehensive understanding of its cultural and historical significance.

The quality and accuracy of art digitization depend on the quality and accuracy of the data used. Art digitization data can be incomplete, biased, or subject to interpretation, which can affect the outcomes of digital representations and the insights they provide. To address these challenges, scholars and conservators use a range of data collection and analysis techniques, including high-resolution photography, 3D scanning, and digital restoration. Additionally, scholars and conservators use data visualization tools to explore and interpret art digitization data, providing new insights and perspectives on artworks. For example, a data visualization might use 3D models to explore the form and structure of a sculpture, providing a more comprehensive understanding of its cultural and historical significance.

Challenges

Despite its potential, art digitization faces several challenges that can limit its effectiveness and accuracy. One of the primary challenges is the availability and quality of art digitization data. Art digitization data can be incomplete, biased, or subject to interpretation, which can affect the outcomes of digital representations and the insights they provide. For example, a digital image of a painting might be incomplete or biased, leading to inaccurate or misleading results. To address these challenges, scholars and conservators use a range of data collection and analysis techniques, including high-resolution photography, 3D scanning, and digital restoration, to ensure the accuracy and reliability of the data used in art digitization.

Another challenge in art digitization is the complexity of artworks and the difficulty of modeling them accurately. Artworks are often rich in detail, texture, and color, which can be challenging to capture and represent digitally. Additionally, artworks can be subject to multiple interpretations, which can affect the outcomes of digital representations and the insights they provide. To address these challenges, scholars and conservators use a range of modeling techniques, including high-resolution photography, 3D scanning, and digital restoration, to create detailed and accurate digital representations of artworks. For example, a 3D model of a sculpture might be used to explore its form and structure, providing a more comprehensive understanding of its cultural and historical significance.

Art digitization also faces ethical and methodological challenges, particularly in relation to the interpretation and representation of artworks. Digital representations can be subject to bias and interpretation, which can affect the outcomes of the representation and the insights they provide. For example, a digital image of a painting might be influenced by the scholar's own biases and interpretations, leading to a skewed or incomplete representation of the artwork. To address these challenges, scholars and conservators use a range of ethical and methodological guidelines, including transparency, peer review, and interdisciplinary collaboration, to ensure the accuracy and reliability of digital representations.

Ethical Considerations

Ethical considerations are crucial in the development and use of art digitization, as they involve the interpretation and representation of artworks. One of the primary ethical considerations is the potential for bias and misrepresentation in digital representations. Digital representations can be influenced by the scholar's own biases and interpretations, leading to a skewed or incomplete representation of the artwork. To address this challenge, scholars and conservators use a range of ethical guidelines, including transparency, peer review, and interdisciplinary collaboration, to ensure the accuracy and reliability of digital representations. For example, scholars and conservators might use peer review to evaluate the assumptions and methods used in a digital representation, ensuring that the results are based on sound artistic evidence and rigorous analysis.

Another ethical consideration in art digitization is the potential for misuse or misinterpretation of the results. Digital representations can be used to support a wide range of interpretations and narratives, some of which may be inaccurate or misleading. To address this challenge, scholars and conservators use a range of ethical guidelines, including transparency, accountability, and public engagement, to ensure that the results of digital representations are interpreted and used responsibly. For example, scholars and conservators might use public engagement to share the results of a digital representation with a wider audience, providing context and interpretation to ensure that the results are understood and used appropriately.

Art digitization also raises ethical considerations related to the representation of marginalized or vulnerable groups. Digital representations can inadvertently perpetuate stereotypes or misrepresent the experiences of marginalized groups, leading to harm or injustice. To address this challenge, scholars and conservators use a range of ethical guidelines, including inclusivity, representation, and cultural sensitivity, to ensure that digital representations are respectful and accurate in their representation of diverse groups. For example, scholars and conservators might use inclusive data collection and analysis techniques to ensure that the voices and experiences of marginalized groups are represented in the digital representation.

4.4.3 Provenance Tracking

Provenance is the chronology of the ownership, custody or location of a historical object. The term was originally mostly used in relation to works of art, but is now used in similar senses in a wide range of fields, including archaeology, paleontology, archival science, economy, computing, and scientific inquiry in general.

The primary purpose of tracing the provenance of an object or entity is normally to provide contextual and circumstantial evidence for its original production or discovery, by establishing, as far as practicable, its later history, especially the sequences of its formal ownership, custody and places of storage.

The practice has a particular value in helping authenticate objects. Comparative techniques, expert opinions and the results of scientific tests may also be used to these ends, but establishing provenance is essentially a matter of documentation. The term dates to the 1780s in English. Provenance is conceptually comparable to the legal term chain of custody. For museums and the art trade, in addition to helping establish the authorship and authenticity of an object, provenance has become increasingly important in helping establish the moral and legal validity of a chain of custody, given the increasing amount of looted art. These issues first became a major concern regarding works that had changed hands in Nazi-controlled areas in Europe before and during World War II. Many museums began compiling pro-active registers of such works and their history. Recently the same concerns have come to prominence for works of African art, often exported illegally, and antiquities from many parts of the world, but currently especially in Iraq, and then Syria.

In archaeology and paleontology, the derived term provenience is used with a related but very particular meaning, to refer to the location (in modern research, recorded precisely in three dimensions) where an artifact or other ancient item was found. Provenance covers an object's complete documented history. An artifact may thus have both a provenience and a provenance.

Works of Art and Antiques

The provenance of works of fine art, antiques and antiquities is of great importance, especially to their owner. There are a number of reasons why painting provenance is important, which mostly also apply to other types of fine art. A good provenance increases the value of a painting, and establishing provenance may help confirm the date, artist and, especially for portraits, the subject of a painting. It may confirm whether a painting is genuinely of the period it seems to date from. The provenance of paintings can help resolve ownership disputes. For example, provenance between 1933 and 1945 can determine whether a painting was looted by the Nazis.

Many galleries are putting a great deal of effort into researching the provenance of paintings in their collections for which there is no firm provenance during that period. Documented evidence of provenance for an object can help to establish that it has not been altered and is not a forgery, a reproduction, stolen or looted art. Provenance helps assign the work to a known artist, and a documented history can be of use in helping to prove ownership. An example of a detailed provenance is given in the Arnolfini portrait.

The quality of provenance of an important work of art can make a considerable difference to its selling price in the market. This is affected by the degree of certainty of the provenance, the status of past owners as collectors, and in many cases by the strength of evidence that an object has not been illegally excavated or exported from another country. The provenance of a work of art may vary greatly in length, depending on context or the amount that is known, from a single name to an entry in a scholarly catalogue some thousands of words long.

An expert certification can mean the difference between an object having no value and being worth a fortune. Certifications themselves may be open to question. Jacques van Meegeren forged the work of his father Han van Meegeren, who had forged the work of Vermeer. Jacques sometimes produced a certificate with his forgeries, stating that a work was created by his father.

John Drewe was able to pass off as genuine paintings, a large number of forgeries that would have easily been recognised as such by scientific examination. He established an impressive, but false provenance. Because of this, galleries and dealers accepted the paintings as genuine. He created this false provenance by forging letters and other documents, including false entries in earlier exhibition catalogues.

Sometimes provenance can be as simple as a photograph of the item with its original owner. Simple yet definitive documentation such as that can increase its value by an order of magnitude, but only if the owner was of high renown. Many items that were sold at auction have gone far past their estimates because of a photograph showing that item with a famous person. Some examples include antiques owned by politicians, musicians, artists, actors, etc.

Researching the Provenance of Paintings

The objective of provenance research is to produce a complete list of owners (together, where possible, with the supporting documentary proof) from when the painting was commissioned or in the artist's studio through to the present time. In practice, there are likely to be gaps in the list and documents that are missing or lost. The documented provenance should also list when the painting has been part of an exhibition and a bibliography of when it has been discussed, or illustrated in print.

Where the research is proceeding backwards, to discover the previous provenance of a painting whose current ownership and location are known, it is important to record the physical details of the painting – style, subject, signature, materials, dimensions, frame, etc. The titles of paintings and the attribution to a particular artist may change over time. The size of the work and its description can be used to identify earlier references to the painting. The back of a painting can contain significant provenance information.

There may be exhibition marks, dealer stamps, gallery labels and other indications of previous ownership. There may be shipping labels. In the BBC TV programme Fake or Fortune? the provenance of the painting Bords de la Seine à Argenteuil was investigated using a gallery sticker and shipping label on the back. Early provenance can sometimes be indicated by a cartellino, a trompe-l'œil representation of an inscribed label, added to the front of a painting. However, these can be forged, or can fade or be painted over.

Auction records are an important resource to assist in researching the provenance of paintings.

- The Witt Library houses a collection of cuttings from auction catalogs which enables the researcher to identify occasions when a picture has been sold.
- The Heinz Library at the National Portrait Gallery, London maintains a similar collection, but restricted to portraits.
- The National Art Library at the Victoria and Albert Museum has a collection of UK sales catalogues.
- The University of York is establishing a web site with on-line resources for investigating art history in the period 1660–1735. This includes diaries, sales catalogues, bills, correspondence and inventories.
- The Getty Research Institute in Los Angeles has a Project for the Study of Collecting and Provenance (PSCP) which includes an on-line database, still being compiled, of auction and other records relating to painting provenance.
- The Frick Art Reference Library in New York has an extensive collection of auction and exhibition catalogues.
- The Netherlands Institute for Art History (RKD) has a number of databases related to artists from the Netherlands.

If a painting has been in private hands for an extended period and on display in a stately home, it may be recorded in an inventory – for example, the Lumley inventory. The painting may also have been noticed by a visitor who subsequently wrote about it. It may have been mentioned in a will or a diary. Where the painting has been bought from a dealer, or changed hands in a private transaction, there may be a bill of sale or sales receipt that provides evidence of provenance. Where the artist is known, there may be a catalogue raisonne listing all the artist's known works and their location at the time of writing. A database of catalogues raisonne is available at the International Foundation for Art Research.

Historic photos of the painting may be discussed and illustrated in a more general work on the artist, period or genre. Similarly, a photograph of a painting may show inscriptions (or a signature) that subsequently became lost as a result of overzealous restoration. Conversely, a photograph may show that an inscription was not visible at an earlier date. One of the disputed aspects of the "Rice" portrait of Jane Austen concerns apparent inscriptions identifying artist and sitter.

Archives

Provenance – also known as custodial history – is a core concept within archival science and archival processing. The term refers to the individuals, groups, or organizations that originally created or received the items in an accumulation of records, and to the items' subsequent chain of custody. The principle of provenance, also termed the principle of "archival integrity", and a major strand in the broader principle of respect des fonds, stipulates that records originating from a common source, or fonds, should be kept together – where practicable, physically, but in all cases intellectually, in the way in which they are catalogued and arranged in finding aids.

Conversely, records of different provenance should be preserved and documented separately. In archival practice, proof of provenance is provided by the operation of control systems that document the history of records kept in archives, including details of amendments made to them. The authority of an archival document or set of documents of which the provenance is uncertain, because of gaps in the recorded chain of custody, will be considered to be severely compromised.

The principles of archival provenance were developed in the 19th century by both French and Prussian archivists, and gained widespread acceptance on the basis of their formulation in the Manual for the Arrangement and Description of Archives by Dutch state archivists Samuel Muller, J. A. Feith, and R. Fruin, published in the Netherlands in 1898, often referred to as the "Dutch Manual". Seamus Ross has argued a case for adapting established principles and theories of archival provenance to the field of modern digital preservation and curation. Provenance is also the title of the journal published by the Society of Georgia Archivists.

Science

Archaeology, Anthropology, and Paleontology

Archaeology and anthropology researchers use provenience to refer to the exact location (or find-spot) of an artifact, a bone or other remains, a soil sample, or a feature within an ancient site, whereas provenance covers an object's complete documented history. Ideally, in modern excavations, the provenience is recorded in three dimensions on a site grid with great precision, and may also be recorded on video to provide additional proof and context.

In older work, often undertaken by amateurs, only the general site or approximate area may be known, especially when an artifact was found outside a professional excavation and its specific position not recorded. The term provenience appeared in the 1880s, about a century after provenance. Outside of academic contexts, it has been used as a synonymous variant spelling of provenance, especially in American English.

Any given antiquity may have both a provenience, where it was found, and a provenance, where it has been since it was found. A summary of the distinction is that "provenience is a fixed point, while provenance can be considered an itinerary that an object follows as it moves from hand to hand." Another metaphor is that provenience is an artifact's "birthplace", while provenance is its "resume". This can be imprecise. Many artifacts originated as trade goods created in one region, but were used and finally deposited in another. Aside from scientific precision, a need for the distinction in these fields has been described thus:

- Archaeologists ... don't care who owned an object—they are more interested in the context of an object within the community of its (mostly original) users. ... [W]e are interested in why a Roman coin turned up in a shipwreck 400 years after it was made; while art historians don't really care, since they can generally figure out what mint a coin came from by the information stamped on its surface. "It's a Roman coin, what else do we need to know?" says an art historian; "The shipping trade in the Mediterranean region during late Roman times" says an archaeologist. ... [P]rovenance for an art historian is important to establish ownership, but provenience is interesting to an archaeologist to establish meaning.

In this context, the provenance can occasionally be the detailed history of where an object has been since its creation, as in art history contexts - not just since its modern finding. In some cases, such as where there is an inscription on the object, or an account of it in written materials from the same era, an object of study in archaeology or cultural anthropology may have an early provenance - a known history that predates modern research - then a provenience from its modern finding, and finally a continued provenance relating to its handling and storage or display after the modern acquisition.

Evidence of provenance in the more general sense can be of importance in archaeology. Fakes are not unknown, and finds are sometimes removed from the context in which they were found without documentation, reducing their value to science. Even when apparently discovered in situ, archaeological finds are treated with caution. The provenience of a find may not be properly represented by the context in which it was found, e.g. due to stratigraphic layers being disturbed by erosion, earthquakes, or ancient reconstruction or other disturbance at a site.

Artifacts can be moved through looting as well as trade, far from their place of origin and long before modern rediscovery. Many source nations have passed legislation forbidding the domestic trade in cultural heritage. Further research is often required to establish the true provenance and legal status of a find, and what the relationship is between the exact provenience and the overall provenance.

In paleontology and paleoanthropology, it is recognized that fossils can also move from their primary context and are sometimes found, apparently in-situ, in deposits to which they do not belong because they have been moved, for example, by the erosion of nearby but different outcrops. It is unclear how strictly paleontology maintains the provenience and provenance distinction. For example, a short glossary at a website, primarily aimed at young students, of the American Museum of Natural History treats the terms as synonymous, while scholarly paleontology works make frequent use of provenience in the same precise sense as used in archaeology and paleoanthropology.

While exacting details of a find's provenience are primarily of use to scientific researchers, most natural history and archaeology museums also make strenuous efforts to record how the items in their collections were acquired. These records are often of use in helping to establish a chain of provenance.

Data Provenance

Scientific research is generally held to be of good provenance when it is documented in detail sufficient to allow reproducibility. Scientific workflow systems assist scientists and programmers with tracking their data through all transformations, analyses, and interpretations. Data sets are reliable when the processes used to create them are reproducible and analyzable for defects. Security researchers are interested in data provenance because it can analyze suspicious data and make large opaque systems transparent.

Current initiatives to effectively manage, share, and reuse ecological data are indicative of the increasing importance of data provenance. Examples of these initiatives are National Science Foundation Datanet projects, DataONE and Data Conservancy, as well as the U.S. Global Change Research Program. Some international academic consortia, such as the Research Data Alliance, have specific groups to tackle issues of provenance. In that case it is the Research Data Provenance Interest Group.

Computer Science

Within computer science, informatics uses the term "provenance" to mean the lineage of data, as per data provenance, with research in the last decade extending the conceptual model of causality and relation to include processes that act on data and agents that are responsible for those processes. Semantic web standards bodies, including the World Wide Web Consortium in 2014, have ratified a standard data model for provenance representation known as PROV which draws from many of the better-known provenance representation systems that preceded it, such as the Proof Markup Language and the Open Provenance Model.

Interoperability is a design goal of most recent computer science provenance theories and models, for example the Open Provenance Model (OPM) 2008 generation workshop aimed at "establishing inter-operability of systems" through information exchange agreements. Data models and serialisation formats for delivering provenance information typically reuse existing metadata models where possible to enable this. Both the OPM Vocabulary and the PROV Ontology make extensive use of metadata models such as Dublin Core and Semantic Web technologies such as the Web Ontology Language (OWL). Current practice is to rely on the W3C PROV data model, OPM's successor.

There are several maintained and open-source provenance capture implementation at the operating system level such as CamFlow, Progger for Linux and MS Windows, and SPADE for Linux, MS Windows, and MacOS. Operating system level provenance have gained interest in the security community notably to develop novel intrusion detection techniques. Other implementations exist for specific programming and scripting languages, such as RDataTracker for R, and NoWorkflow for Python. Whole-system provenance implementation for Linux:

- PASS – closed source – not maintained – kernel v2.6.X
- Hi-Fi – open source – not maintained – kernel v3.2.x
- Flogger – closed source – not maintained – kernel v2.6.x
- S2Logger – closed source – not maintained – kernel v2.6.x
- LPM – open source – not maintained – kernel v2.6.x
- Progger – open source – not maintained – kernel v2.6.x and kernel v.4.14.x
- CamFlow – open source – maintained – kernel v6.0.X

Computers and Law

The term provenance is used when ascertaining the source of goods such as computer hardware to assess if they are genuine or counterfeit. Chain of custody is an equivalent term used in law, especially for evidence in criminal or commercial cases. Software provenance encompasses the origin of software and its licensing terms. For example, when incorporating a free, open source or proprietary software component in an application, one may wish to understand its provenance to ensure that licensing requirements are fulfilled and that other software characteristics can be understood.

Data provenance covers the provenance of computerized data. There are two main aspects of data provenance: ownership of the data and data usage. Ownership will tell the user who is responsible for the source of the data, ideally including information on the originator of the data. Data usage gives details regarding how the data has been used and modified and often includes information on how to cite the data source or sources. Data provenance is of particular concern with electronic data, as data sets are often modified and copied without proper citation or acknowledgement of the originating data set. Databases make it easy to select specific information from data sets and merge this data with other data sources without any documentation of how the data was obtained or how it was modified from the original data set or sets. The automated analysis of data provenance graphs has been described as a mean to verify compliance with regulations regarding data usage such as introduced by the EU GDPR.

Secure Provenance refers to providing integrity and confidentiality guarantees to provenance information. In other words, secure provenance means to ensure that history cannot be rewritten, and users can specify who else can look into their actions on the object. A simple method of ensuring data provenance in computing is to mark a file as read only. This allows the user to view the contents of the file, but not edit or otherwise modify it. Read only can also in some cases prevent the user from accidentally or intentionally deleting the file.

4.5 DIGITAL LINGUISTICS AND CORPUS ANALYSIS

Digital linguistics and corpus analysis represent a paradigm shift in how language is studied, understood, and applied. They offer unparalleled access to real-world language data, empower researchers to identify patterns at scale, and open up new avenues for linguistic discovery across time, space, and social context. At the same time, they challenge traditional assumptions and call for new ethical frameworks and interdisciplinary collaboration. As language continues to evolve in digital spaces, the tools and insights provided by digital linguistics will be essential not only for academic research but also for navigating communication in the digital age. Embracing this digital turn enables a more nuanced, inclusive, and dynamic understanding of human language in all its diversity.

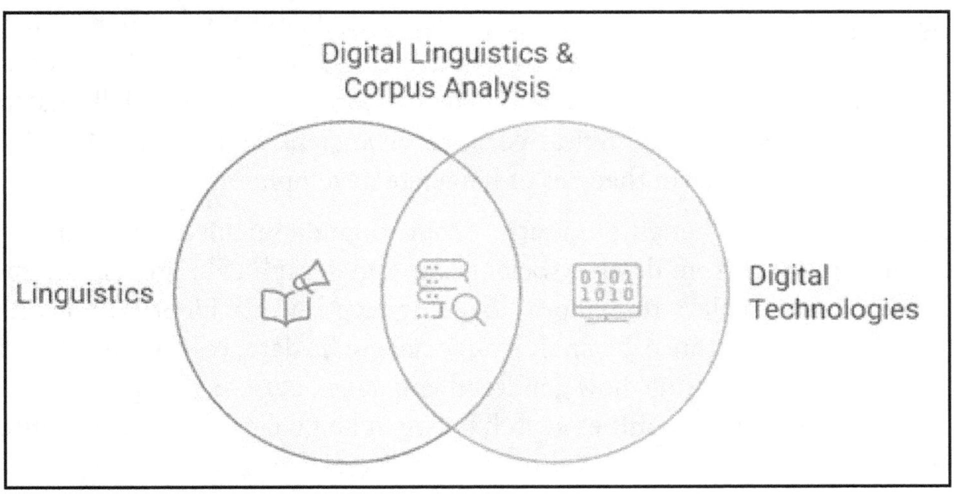

Fig: Unlocking Language Insights through Digital Methods

4.5.1 Evolution of Corpus Linguistics into the Digital Realm

Corpus linguistics has its roots in the manual collection and study of texts to investigate language features such as syntax, semantics, and phonology. Traditional corpora were often compiled by hand, limited in size, and constrained by the availability of printed materials. With the development of computing technologies, however, corpus linguistics has evolved into a dynamic and expansive digital discipline. The digital transformation has enabled the creation of massive corpora, including billions of words, drawn from a wide array of genres, regions, and time periods. These digital corpora can be searched, annotated, and analyzed with computational precision, allowing linguists to examine language use on a scale previously unimaginable.

Digital corpora differ from their traditional counterparts not only in size but also in their interactivity and accessibility. Today, researchers can instantly search for linguistic patterns, generate frequency lists, visualize collocations, and examine discourse structures using sophisticated software. This technological advancement has broadened the scope of linguistic inquiry, making it possible to conduct comparative studies across languages, trace historical language changes, and analyze language in real-time social contexts such as social media, news outlets, and blogs. Digital corpus analysis, therefore, not only accelerates the research process but also deepens the insights that can be gained from textual data.

4.5.2 Applications of Digital Linguistics in Language Research

Digital linguistics has found diverse applications across multiple branches of linguistics, including syntax, semantics, phonetics, sociolinguistics, and discourse analysis. One significant area is the study of language variation and change. By examining large digital corpora, researchers can identify how particular words, phrases, or grammatical structures evolve over time. For example, changes in verb conjugations, shifts in word meanings, and the rise or fall of certain idiomatic expressions can all be tracked through corpus data. This is especially useful in historical linguistics, where digital corpora of ancient and medieval texts can reveal patterns that inform theories of language development.

Sociolinguistics also benefits greatly from digital linguistic methods. The accessibility of texts from diverse social groups, geographical regions, and media platforms allows scholars to explore how language reflects identity, power, and cultural norms. For instance, by analyzing social media data, researchers can study how dialects are used online, how gendered language operates in digital discourse, or how multilingual communities switch between languages in different contexts. These findings offer valuable insights into the social dimensions of language and the dynamics of linguistic diversity in the digital age. Another key application is in lexicography and dictionary-making. Digital corpora enable lexicographers to identify neologisms, slang, and evolving meanings with much greater accuracy. Real-world usage data helps in defining words not just according to traditional rules but based on how they are actually employed by speakers and writers. This leads to the development of more comprehensive and user-relevant dictionaries, such as those regularly updated by major publishers using corpus-based evidence.

4.5.3 Corpus Analysis Tools and Methodologies

Digital corpus analysis relies on a range of tools and techniques that support both qualitative and quantitative research. Corpus management software such as AntConc, Sketch Engine, and WordSmith Tools allows researchers to perform key linguistic tasks, including concordance generation, collocation analysis, keyword extraction, and part-of-speech tagging. These tools can identify not only what words appear in a corpus, but how they function in context, how often they co-occur with other words, and what roles they play in syntactic structures.

One important methodology is frequency analysis, which identifies the most commonly used words and phrases in a given corpus. This can reveal the core vocabulary of a language or register, highlight stylistic features of a particular author or genre, or show how frequently certain grammatical constructions occur. Collocation analysis, on the other hand, focuses on word associations and helps in uncovering patterns of meaning and usage. For example, by analyzing the collocates of the word "climate," researchers can study the discourse surrounding environmental issues and how they have shifted over time.

Concordancing is another powerful technique, where every instance of a word or phrase is presented within its textual context. This allows researchers to observe how a word is used in different grammatical or semantic environments, aiding in the construction of accurate definitions or the analysis of stylistic trends. More advanced computational techniques, such as topic modeling, sentiment analysis, and machine learning classification, are also increasingly applied to large-scale corpus data to reveal deeper patterns and thematic structures.

4.5.4 Ethical Considerations and Challenges in Digital Linguistics

While digital linguistics and corpus analysis offer many opportunities, they also raise important ethical and methodological questions. One key issue concerns data privacy and consent. Many modern corpora include texts from the internet, such as social media posts, blogs, and forums. Even when such data is publicly available, researchers must consider the ethical implications of using personal communications for analysis. Anonymization, informed consent, and sensitivity to cultural and contextual factors are crucial to ensure responsible research practices.

Another challenge is representativeness. Not all languages, dialects, or social groups are equally represented in digital corpora. Dominant languages like English often have extensive corpora, while minority or endangered languages may be underrepresented or absent. This can skew linguistic analysis and perpetuate biases in language research. Efforts must be made to develop more inclusive and diverse corpora, as well as to support digital documentation of lesser-known languages to preserve linguistic heritage. Technical challenges also exist, such as the need for high-quality annotation, reliable metadata, and standardized formats. Errors in tagging or transcription can affect the validity of corpus-based findings. Moreover, the sheer volume of data can sometimes obscure subtle linguistic phenomena, necessitating a balance between large-scale quantitative analysis and close qualitative examination. Researchers must be trained not only in linguistic theory but also in computational methods to effectively navigate the complexities of digital data.

4.5.5 Interdisciplinary Impact and Future Directions

Digital linguistics is inherently interdisciplinary, drawing on insights from computer science, data analytics, cognitive science, and the humanities. Its applications extend beyond academia into fields such as education, forensic linguistics, language technology, and artificial intelligence. In education, corpus-based approaches are used to develop teaching materials that reflect authentic language use. In forensic linguistics, digital analysis helps in authorship attribution and the interpretation of legal texts. Language technology applications include speech recognition, machine translation, and natural language processing systems that rely heavily on corpus data to improve accuracy and performance.

The future of digital linguistics promises even more integration with artificial intelligence and machine learning. As language models become more sophisticated, they can both analyze and generate human-like language, raising new questions about the nature of meaning, creativity, and linguistic competence. Corpus analysis will continue to play a central role in training, evaluating, and refining these models. Additionally, emerging fields like computational sociolinguistics and linguistic data science will further enrich the study of language in digital environments.

4.6 DIGITAL RELIGIOUS STUDIES AND THEOLOGY

4.6.1 Sacred Text Analysis

Sacred text analysis represents a powerful and innovative approach to understanding and interpreting sacred texts. By leveraging the power of computational models, data analysis, and visualization tools, scholars can uncover patterns, themes, and insights that might not be immediately apparent through traditional close reading. Sacred text analysis enables researchers to explore vast corpora of sacred texts efficiently, identifying key themes, motifs, and stylistic features. This method can also help in comparing and contrasting different works, authors, or genres, providing a more comprehensive view of sacred texts and their significance. The evolution of sacred text analysis has been driven by advancements in computational power, data availability, and digital technologies. From traditional exegetical methods to sophisticated machine learning and AI-driven models, sacred text analysis has become more nuanced and context-aware, allowing scholars to delve deeper into the complexities of sacred texts. The integration of digital corpora and repositories has made it possible for scholars to conduct large-scale sacred text analyses, exploring patterns and trends across entire religious traditions or genres.

Despite its potential, sacred text analysis faces several challenges, including the availability and quality of sacred text data, the complexity of sacred texts, and ethical and methodological considerations. To address these challenges, scholars use a range of data collection and analysis techniques, modeling techniques, and ethical guidelines to ensure the accuracy, reliability, and ethical integrity of sacred text analyses. The future of sacred text analysis lies in the integration of AI and ML, the development of immersive and interactive sacred text analyses, and the creation of collaborative and participatory sacred text analyses that engage a wider range of stakeholders in the study and interpretation of sacred texts.

As digital technologies continue to evolve, sacred text analysis will play an increasingly important role in the study and interpretation of sacred texts. By addressing the challenges and exploring new directions, scholars can ensure that sacred text analyses are accurate, reliable, and ethically sound, providing new insights and perspectives on sacred texts. The principles of sacred text analysis, with their dynamic and interactive representations of sacred texts, will continue to influence the development of digital religious studies, ensuring that the study of sacred texts is engaging, inclusive, and relevant to a wider audience. Through the use of sacred text analysis, scholars can create a more comprehensive and nuanced understanding of sacred texts, providing new insights and perspectives on the themes, motifs, and stylistic features that shape our religious heritage.

Traditional Methods

Traditional methods of sacred text analysis have been developed and refined over centuries, drawing on a variety of scholarly disciplines, including theology, linguistics, history, and literary criticism. One of the most common traditional methods is exegetical analysis, which involves a close reading and interpretation of the text. Exegetical analysis seeks to understand the original meaning and context of the text, often by examining the historical, cultural, and linguistic background of the author and the audience. This method requires a deep knowledge of the language, literary conventions, and theological frameworks of the time, as well as an understanding of the broader cultural and historical context. Another traditional method of sacred text analysis is textual criticism, which focuses on the study of the manuscript traditions and textual variants of sacred texts. Textual criticism aims to reconstruct the original text by comparing different manuscript versions and identifying discrepancies and errors. This method is particularly important for texts that have been transmitted over long periods and through multiple copies, as it helps to ensure the accuracy and authenticity of the text. Textual criticism involves a detailed examination of the manuscript evidence, including the dating, provenance, and textual features of the manuscripts.

Literary criticism is another traditional method of sacred text analysis, which examines the literary features and structures of sacred texts. Literary criticism seeks to understand the aesthetic, rhetorical, and narrative techniques used in the text, as well as their theological and cultural significance. This method involves a close reading of the text, paying attention to its style, genre, and literary devices, such as metaphor, symbolism, and allegory. Literary criticism can provide insights into the artistic and literary achievements of sacred texts, as well as their theological and cultural meanings.

Digital Methods

The advent of digital technologies has opened up new possibilities for sacred text analysis, enabling scholars to apply computational and data-driven approaches to the study of sacred texts. One of the most powerful digital methods is text mining, which involves the use of algorithms and statistical techniques to analyze large corpora of textual data. Text mining can identify recurring motifs, track the evolution of theological concepts, and reveal hidden patterns and structures within the texts. For example, a text mining analysis of the Quran might uncover the frequency and distribution of certain keywords, providing insights into the theological emphases of different surahs or chapters.

Natural language processing (NLP) is another digital method that has revolutionized sacred text analysis. NLP involves the use of computational techniques to analyze and interpret human language, enabling scholars to study the linguistic features and structures of sacred texts. NLP can be used to identify and classify different linguistic phenomena, such as grammatical structures, semantic relationships, and stylistic features. For example, an NLP analysis of the New Testament might reveal the distinctive linguistic features of different authors, providing insights into their theological and literary styles.

Data visualization is a digital method that has become increasingly important in sacred text analysis. Data visualization involves the use of graphical and visual techniques to represent and explore complex data sets, enabling scholars to identify patterns, trends, and relationships within the texts. For example, a data visualization of the Old Testament might use network graphs to represent the relationships between different characters, events, and themes, providing a visual overview of the text's narrative structure. Data visualization can also be used to explore the geographical, historical, and cultural contexts of sacred texts, providing new insights into their significance and relevance.

Applications

Sacred text analysis has a wide range of applications, from academic research to public education and religious practice. In academic research, sacred text analysis is used to explore and interpret the meanings, themes, and structures within sacred texts, providing new insights into their historical, cultural, and theological significance. For example, a scholar might use text mining to analyze the frequency and distribution of certain keywords in the Bhagavad Gita, providing insights into the text's philosophical and theological emphases. Similarly, a scholar might use NLP to study the linguistic features of the Torah, revealing the distinctive literary and rhetorical techniques used in the text.

In public education, sacred text analysis is used to create interactive and immersive learning experiences that engage students and the public in the study of sacred texts. For example, a digital exhibition might allow visitors to explore a virtual library of sacred texts, interacting with digital images and annotations. This hands-on approach to learning can help students to understand the complexities of sacred texts and the factors that shaped their development. Similarly, a digital course might use data visualization to explore the geographical, historical, and cultural contexts of sacred texts, providing a more comprehensive and engaging learning experience.

Sacred text analysis is also used in religious practice, where it is used to deepen understanding and devotion to sacred texts. For example, a religious community might use text mining to analyze the frequency and distribution of certain keywords in their sacred texts, providing insights into their theological and spiritual significance. Similarly, a religious leader might use NLP to study the linguistic features of their sacred texts, revealing the distinctive literary and rhetorical techniques used in the text. This approach can help to enhance the spiritual and devotional practices of the community, providing a deeper understanding and appreciation of their sacred texts.

Role of Data

Data plays a crucial role in sacred text analysis, providing the foundation for computational models and enabling scholars to test hypotheses and explore "what-if" scenarios. Sacred text analysis relies on a wide range of data sources, including digitized manuscripts, translations, and commentaries. This data is used to create detailed and accurate representations of sacred texts, allowing scholars to analyze and interpret them in new and innovative ways. For example, a data set of digitized manuscripts might be used to study the textual variants and manuscript traditions of a sacred text, providing insights into its historical and cultural contexts. The quality and accuracy of sacred text analysis depend on the quality and accuracy of the data used. Sacred text data can be incomplete, biased, or subject to interpretation, which can affect the outcomes of the analysis and the insights they provide. To address these challenges, scholars use a range of data collection and analysis techniques, including digitization, transcription, and annotation. Additionally, scholars use data visualization tools to explore and interpret sacred text data, providing new insights and perspectives on the texts. For example, a data visualization might use network graphs to represent the relationships between different characters, events, and themes in a sacred text, providing a visual overview of the text's narrative structure.

Challenges

Despite its potential, sacred text analysis faces several challenges that can limit its effectiveness and accuracy. One of the primary challenges is the availability and quality of sacred text data. Sacred text data can be incomplete, biased, or subject to interpretation, which can affect the outcomes of the analysis and the insights they provide. For example, a data set of digitized manuscripts might be incomplete or biased, leading to inaccurate or misleading results. To address these challenges, scholars use a range of data collection and analysis techniques, including digitization, transcription, and annotation, to ensure the accuracy and reliability of the data used in sacred text analysis.

Another challenge in sacred text analysis is the complexity of sacred texts and the difficulty of modeling them accurately. Sacred texts are often rich in metaphor, symbolism, and other forms of figurative language, which can be challenging to analyze and interpret using computational methods. Additionally, sacred texts can be subject to multiple interpretations, which can affect the outcomes of the analysis and the insights they provide. To address these challenges, scholars use a range of modeling techniques, including natural language processing, machine learning, and statistical analysis, to create detailed and accurate representations of sacred texts.

Sacred text analysis also faces ethical and methodological challenges, particularly in relation to the interpretation and representation of sacred texts. Sacred text analyses can be subject to bias and interpretation, which can affect the outcomes of the analysis and the insights they provide. For example, a sacred text analysis might be influenced by the scholar's own biases and interpretations, leading to a skewed or incomplete representation of the text. To address these challenges, scholars use a range of ethical and methodological guidelines, including transparency, peer review, and interdisciplinary collaboration, to ensure the accuracy and reliability of sacred text analyses.

Ethical Considerations

Ethical considerations are crucial in the development and use of sacred text analysis, as they involve the interpretation and representation of sacred texts. One of the primary ethical considerations is the potential for bias and misrepresentation in sacred text analyses. Sacred text analyses can be influenced by the scholar's own biases and interpretations, leading to a skewed or incomplete representation of the text. To address this challenge, scholars use a range of ethical guidelines, including transparency, peer review, and interdisciplinary collaboration, to ensure the accuracy and reliability of sacred text analyses. For example, scholars might use peer review to evaluate the assumptions and methods used in a sacred text analysis, ensuring that the results are based on sound textual evidence and rigorous analysis.

Another ethical consideration in sacred text analysis is the potential for misuse or misinterpretation of the results. Sacred text analyses can be used to support a wide range of interpretations and narratives, some of which may be inaccurate or misleading. To address this challenge, scholars use a range of ethical guidelines, including transparency, accountability, and public engagement, to ensure that the results of sacred text analyses are interpreted and used responsibly. For example, scholars might use public engagement to share the results of a sacred text analysis with a wider audience, providing context and interpretation to ensure that the results are understood and used appropriately.

Sacred text analysis also raises ethical considerations related to the representation of marginalized or vulnerable groups. Sacred text analyses can inadvertently perpetuate stereotypes or misrepresent the experiences of marginalized groups, leading to harm or injustice. To address this challenge, scholars use a range of ethical guidelines, including inclusivity, representation, and cultural sensitivity, to ensure that sacred text analyses are respectful and accurate in their representation of diverse groups. For example, scholars might use inclusive data collection and analysis techniques to ensure that the voices and experiences of marginalized groups are represented in the analysis.

4.6.2 Ritual Mapping

Rituals are structured, symbolic actions performed in religious, cultural, political, or social contexts. They range from daily devotional practices to large-scale public festivals, rites of passage, pilgrimages, and ceremonial processions. Rituals often occur in designated sacred spaces such as temples, altars, shrines, or public squares, and are imbued with layers of meaning that connect participants to their communities, ancestors, deities, or spiritual beliefs. To understand the full impact of ritual, one must analyze not only the symbolic elements and the social roles involved but also the spatial settings in which these actions unfold.

Space in ritual is never neutral. It is curated, imagined, and experienced in specific ways that reflect cultural values and cosmologies. For example, the axis mundi in many traditions marks the center of the world and serves as the focal point for rituals that connect heaven and earth. Similarly, thresholds, borders, and liminal spaces often become sites of transformation during rites of passage. Ritual mapping seeks to uncover how space is constructed and consecrated through repeated ritual actions, and how movement through space reflects the internal logic and significance of the ritual itself.

Historical and Ethnographic Dimensions

Traditionally, scholars studied rituals through textual analysis, oral histories, and ethnographic observation. While these methods provided valuable insights, they often lacked the capacity to capture spatial relationships and patterns across time. Ritual mapping supplements these approaches by visually representing how rituals relate to geography, architecture, and movement. In historical studies, this could involve reconstructing the spatial layout of ancient temples and their surrounding areas to better understand the positioning and flow of ritual processions. In ethnographic contexts, mapping contemporary festivals and pilgrimages reveals how communities mobilize space, claim identity, and engage with tradition.

One important application of ritual mapping is the study of pilgrimage routes. Mapping the paths taken by pilgrims—such as the Camino de Santiago in Spain or the Char Dham Yatra in India—sheds light on the spiritual geographies constructed through movement and devotion. These routes are not just paths to a destination but become sacred landscapes imbued with stories, memories, and rituals performed along the way. Mapping these experiences allows scholars to see how meaning is distributed across space and how sacred topographies are sustained over time.

Another historical example is the mapping of religious festivals in medieval Europe or processions in Renaissance Italy. These events often followed fixed routes through cities, moving from one church or shrine to another, while involving various ritual acts at different stations. By reconstructing these routes and their timings, scholars can analyze the interplay between ritual, civic life, and power structures. In doing so, ritual mapping contributes to our understanding of how rituals helped shape urban identities and spatial hierarchies.

Digital Tools and Technologies

With the rise of digital humanities, new tools and technologies have significantly expanded the potential of ritual mapping. Geographic Information Systems (GIS), 3D modeling, augmented reality, and virtual reconstructions are now employed to create interactive maps and simulations of ritual events. These tools not only allow for the visualization of ritual space but also enable the layering of temporal, symbolic, and social data onto geographical representations. GIS, for example, allows scholars to plot ritual locations on digital maps and analyze spatial patterns, proximities, and connections. This can help uncover the logic behind site selection, routes of movement, and spatial symbolism. For instance, in mapping rituals of the ancient Maya civilization, GIS has been used to analyze the alignment of temples and plazas with celestial events, showing how ritual architecture mirrored cosmological beliefs.

3D modeling and digital reconstructions, on the other hand, allow for immersive exploration of ritual spaces that no longer exist or are difficult to access. Through virtual environments, researchers and the public can witness how rituals might have unfolded in reconstructed temples, mosques, or sacred groves. This form of spatial storytelling brings rituals to life and offers a multisensory understanding of the cultural and emotional experiences embedded in them.

Augmented reality also presents opportunities for participatory ritual mapping. Mobile applications can guide users through contemporary or reconstructed ritual routes, providing contextual information, historical images, and audio narratives. This interactive mode of engagement bridges academic research and public heritage, making rituals accessible to broader audiences and preserving intangible cultural heritage in digital formats.

Symbolic and Social Dimensions

Ritual mapping does more than chart physical locations; it seeks to understand how space is imbued with symbolic meaning and how social relations are constructed through ritual acts. Every ritual space is a product of cultural imagination. The position of altars, the direction of movement, the placement of ritual participants—all carry symbolic weight. Mapping these elements reveals how cosmological principles, theological doctrines, and social hierarchies are encoded into spatial arrangements.

In many cultures, the orientation of ritual structures reflects cosmic beliefs. Hindu temples, for example, are typically aligned along cardinal directions to correspond with cosmic order, while Catholic cathedrals often face east toward the rising sun, symbolizing resurrection and hope. Ritual mapping helps visualize these orientations and their intended meanings, showing how ritual space acts as a microcosm of the universe. Social stratification is another aspect often revealed through ritual mapping. In many traditional societies, access to certain ritual spaces is determined by gender, caste, class, or religious status. By mapping who can go where during rituals, scholars gain insight into the social logic of inclusion and exclusion. This spatial segmentation reflects and reinforces social hierarchies, while also offering sites of resistance or negotiation, especially in changing political or cultural contexts.

Ritual Mapping and the Politics of Memory and Identity

Rituals are powerful vehicles for constructing collective memory and identity. By mapping where rituals occur and how they evolve, researchers can trace the ways communities remember their past and assert their cultural presence. Ritual spaces often become sites of contested memory, especially in regions marked by colonization, displacement, or religious conflict. Mapping these spaces reveals the layers of history embedded in them and the tensions surrounding their meanings.

For indigenous communities, ritual mapping can serve as a form of cultural reclamation. By digitally mapping sacred landscapes and traditional ritual routes, communities can preserve ancestral knowledge and assert sovereignty over cultural heritage. This process is not only academic but deeply political, as it involves reclaiming space from erasure, development, or misappropriation.

Ritual mapping can also play a role in reconciliation and heritage preservation. In post-conflict societies, mapping shared ritual practices and sacred sites can highlight intercommunal connections and foster dialogue. In urban contexts, mapping forgotten or hidden ritual histories can revive local traditions and support cultural tourism or community development. Thus, ritual mapping contributes to both scholarly knowledge and social healing.

4.7 CLASSICS AND ARCHAEOLOGY IN THE DIGITAL AGE

The digital age has brought about a profound transformation in the fields of Classics and Archaeology, leveraging advanced technologies to enhance research, preservation, and public engagement. Digital tools and methodologies, such as 3D scanning, virtual reality, augmented reality, and data visualization, have revolutionized the way scholars study and interpret ancient texts, artifacts, and sites. These technologies enable the creation of detailed and accurate digital representations, providing new insights and opportunities for exploration. The applications of digital Classics and Archaeology are vast and varied, ranging from academic research to public education and cultural heritage preservation.

Despite its potential, digital Classics and Archaeology face several challenges, including the availability and quality of digital data, the complexity of ancient texts, artifacts, and sites, and ethical and methodological considerations. To address these challenges, scholars and conservators use a range of data collection and analysis techniques, modeling techniques, and ethical guidelines to ensure the accuracy, reliability, and ethical integrity of digital representations. The future of digital Classics and Archaeology lies in the integration of AI and ML, the development of immersive and interactive digital representations, and the creation of collaborative and participatory digital representations that engage a wider range of stakeholders in the study and interpretation of ancient texts, artifacts, and sites.

As digital technologies continue to evolve, digital Classics and Archaeology will play an increasingly important role in the study and interpretation of ancient cultures. By addressing the challenges and exploring new directions, scholars and conservators can ensure that digital representations are accurate, reliable, and ethically sound, providing new insights and perspectives on ancient texts, artifacts, and sites. The principles of digital Classics and Archaeology, with their dynamic and interactive representations of ancient cultures, will continue to influence the development of digital humanities, ensuring that the study of ancient cultures is engaging, inclusive, and relevant to a wider audience. Through the use of digital tools and methodologies, scholars and conservators can create a more comprehensive and nuanced understanding of ancient cultures, providing new insights and perspectives on the themes, motifs, and stylistic features that shape our cultural heritage.

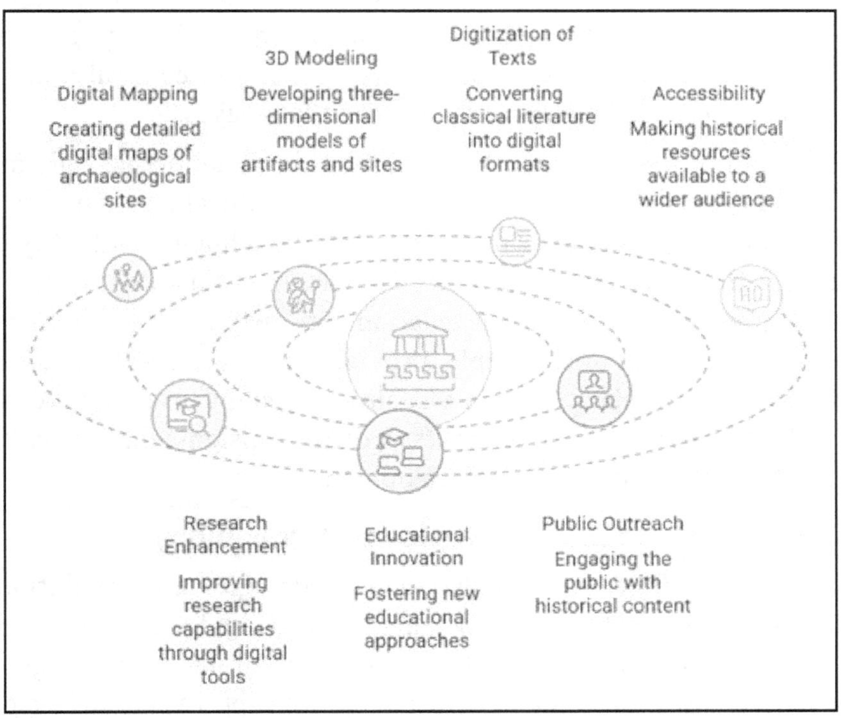

Fig: Transforming Classics and Archaeology with Digital Tools

4.7.1 Digital Tools and Methodologies in Classics

In the field of Classics, digital tools and methodologies have revolutionized the study of ancient texts and languages. One of the most significant developments is the creation of digital corpora, which are comprehensive collections of ancient texts that can be searched, analyzed, and annotated using digital tools. These corpora provide scholars with access to a vast amount of textual data, enabling them to conduct large-scale analyses and identify patterns and trends that might not be immediately apparent through traditional close reading. For example, the Perseus Digital Library is a digital corpus that contains a wide range of ancient Greek and Latin texts, along with translations, commentaries, and other scholarly resources. This digital library allows scholars to search for specific words, phrases, or themes across multiple texts, providing new insights into the literary and cultural contexts of ancient Greece and Rome.

Another important digital tool in Classics is natural language processing (NLP), which involves the use of computational techniques to analyze and interpret human language. NLP can be used to study the linguistic features and structures of ancient languages, providing insights into their grammar, syntax, and semantics.

For example, NLP can be used to analyze the frequency and distribution of certain words or phrases in a corpus of ancient texts, revealing the stylistic and thematic preferences of different authors. Similarly, NLP can be used to study the evolution of ancient languages over time, tracking changes in vocabulary, grammar, and usage. This approach can provide new insights into the cultural and historical contexts that shaped the development of ancient languages.

Data visualization is another digital tool that has become increasingly important in Classics. Data visualization involves the use of graphical and visual techniques to represent and explore complex data sets, enabling scholars to identify patterns, trends, and relationships within the texts. For example, a data visualization might use network graphs to represent the relationships between different characters, events, and themes in an ancient epic, providing a visual overview of the text's narrative structure. Similarly, a data visualization might use maps to represent the geographical contexts of ancient texts, providing insights into the cultural and historical settings that shaped their development.

4.7.2 Digital Tools and Methodologies in Archaeology

In the field of Archaeology, digital tools and methodologies have revolutionized the way ancient sites and artifacts are documented, analyzed, and preserved. One of the most significant developments is the use of 3D scanning and photogrammetry, which involve the use of laser or structured light to capture the surface geometry of an object, generating a point cloud of data that can be used to create a 3D model.

This process can be used to digitize a wide range of artifacts, from sculptures and architectural structures to archaeological sites and cultural heritage sites. 3D scanning and photogrammetry have enabled archaeologists to create detailed and accurate digital replicas of ancient artifacts, allowing them to study and analyze them in new and innovative ways. For example, a 3D model of an ancient sculpture might be used to study its form, structure, and craftsmanship, providing a more comprehensive understanding of its cultural and historical significance. Another important digital tool in Archaeology is Geographic Information Systems (GIS), which involves the use of spatial data to map and analyze archaeological sites and landscapes. GIS allows archaeologists to create detailed and accurate maps of ancient sites, providing insights into their layout, structure, and function. For example, a GIS map of an ancient city might reveal the distribution of buildings, roads, and public spaces, providing a more comprehensive understanding of the city's urban planning and social organization. Similarly, a GIS map of an ancient landscape might reveal the distribution of archaeological sites, natural features, and cultural resources, providing insights into the environmental and cultural contexts that shaped their development.

Virtual reality (VR) and augmented reality (AR) technologies have also become increasingly important in Archaeology, enabling the creation of immersive and interactive experiences that allow users to explore ancient sites and artifacts in a more engaging and experiential way. For example, a VR-based archaeological project might allow users to walk through a reconstructed ancient city, interacting with virtual buildings, artifacts, and residents. Similarly, an AR-based archaeological project might overlay digital images and visualizations onto the real world, allowing users to explore and interact with ancient sites and artifacts in their immediate environment. This approach can help to preserve and protect ancient sites and artifacts, as it allows users to experience them without causing physical damage or disturbance.

4.7.3 Applications of Digital Classics and Archaeology

The applications of digital Classics and Archaeology are vast and varied, ranging from academic research to public education and cultural heritage preservation. In academic research, digital tools and methodologies are used to explore and analyze ancient texts, artifacts, and sites, providing new insights into their historical, cultural, and linguistic contexts. For example, a digital analysis of an ancient text might reveal the frequency and distribution of certain words or phrases, providing insights into the author's stylistic and thematic preferences. Similarly, a digital analysis of an ancient artifact might reveal its form, structure, and craftsmanship, providing a more comprehensive understanding of its cultural and historical significance.

In public education, digital tools and methodologies are used to create interactive and immersive learning experiences that engage students and the public in the study of ancient cultures. For example, a digital exhibition might allow visitors to explore a virtual museum, interacting with digital images and 3D models of ancient artifacts. This hands-on approach to learning can help students to understand the complexities of ancient cultures and the factors that shaped their development. Similarly, a digital course might use data visualization to explore the geographical, historical, and cultural contexts of ancient sites, providing a more comprehensive and engaging learning experience. Digital tools and methodologies are also used in cultural heritage preservation, where they are used to document, preserve, and restore ancient sites and artifacts. For example, a digital archive might be created to preserve and document a collection of ancient manuscripts, providing a record of the past that can be accessed and studied by future generations.

Similarly, a digital restoration project might be used to restore and preserve a damaged or deteriorating ancient artifact, ensuring its long-term preservation and accessibility. Digital tools and methodologies can also be used to create virtual reconstructions of ancient sites, providing a record of their original appearance and function. This process can be particularly useful for preserving and studying sites that have been damaged or destroyed, as it allows scholars and conservators to analyze and interpret them without causing further damage.

4.7.4 Role of Data in Digital Classics and Archaeology

Data plays a crucial role in digital Classics and Archaeology, providing the foundation for digital representations and enabling scholars to analyze and interpret ancient texts, artifacts, and sites in new and innovative ways. The data used in digital Classics and Archaeology can include a wide range of information, from high-resolution images and 3D models to metadata and contextual data. This data is used to create detailed and accurate digital representations of ancient texts, artifacts, and sites, allowing scholars to study and analyze them in ways that were previously impossible. For example, a digital image of an ancient manuscript might include metadata on its provenance, condition, and conservation history, providing a more comprehensive understanding of its cultural and historical significance.

The quality and accuracy of digital Classics and Archaeology depend on the quality and accuracy of the data used. Digital data can be incomplete, biased, or subject to interpretation, which can affect the outcomes of digital representations and the insights they provide. To address these challenges, scholars and conservators use a range of data collection and analysis techniques, including digitization, transcription, and annotation. Additionally, scholars and conservators use data visualization tools to explore and interpret digital data, providing new insights and perspectives on ancient texts, artifacts, and sites. For example, a data visualization might use 3D models to explore the form and structure of an ancient artifact, providing a more comprehensive understanding of its cultural and historical significance.

4.7.5 Challenges in Digital Classics and Archaeology

Despite its potential, digital Classics and Archaeology face several challenges that can limit their effectiveness and accuracy. One of the primary challenges is the availability and quality of digital data. Digital data can be incomplete, biased, or subject to interpretation, which can affect the outcomes of digital representations and the insights they provide. For example, a digital image of an ancient artifact might be incomplete or biased, leading to inaccurate or misleading results. To address these challenges, scholars and conservators use a range of data collection and analysis techniques, including digitization, transcription, and annotation, to ensure the accuracy and reliability of the data used in digital Classics and Archaeology.

Another challenge in digital Classics and Archaeology is the complexity of ancient texts, artifacts, and sites, and the difficulty of modeling them accurately. Ancient texts, artifacts, and sites are often rich in detail, texture, and context, which can be challenging to capture and represent digitally. Additionally, ancient texts, artifacts, and sites can be subject to multiple interpretations, which can affect the outcomes of digital representations and the insights they provide. To address these challenges, scholars and conservators use a range of modeling techniques, including 3D scanning, photogrammetry, and data visualization, to create detailed and accurate digital representations of ancient texts, artifacts, and sites. For example, a 3D model of an ancient site might be used to explore its layout, structure, and function, providing a more comprehensive understanding of its cultural and historical significance.

Digital Classics and Archaeology also face ethical and methodological challenges, particularly in relation to the interpretation and representation of ancient texts, artifacts, and sites. Digital representations can be subject to bias and interpretation, which can affect the outcomes of the representation and the insights they provide. For example, a digital image of an ancient artifact might be influenced by the scholar's own biases and interpretations, leading to a skewed or incomplete representation of the artifact. To address these challenges, scholars and conservators use a range of ethical and methodological guidelines, including transparency, peer review, and interdisciplinary collaboration, to ensure the accuracy and reliability of digital representations.

4.7.6 Ethical Considerations in Digital Classics and Archaeology

Ethical considerations are crucial in the development and use of digital Classics and Archaeology, as they involve the interpretation and representation of ancient texts, artifacts, and sites. One of the primary ethical considerations is the potential for bias and misrepresentation in digital representations. Digital representations can be influenced by the scholar's own biases and interpretations, leading to a skewed or incomplete representation of the ancient text, artifact, or site. To address this challenge, scholars and conservators use a range of ethical guidelines, including transparency, peer review, and interdisciplinary collaboration, to ensure the accuracy and reliability of digital representations. For example, scholars and conservators might use peer review to evaluate the assumptions and methods used in a digital representation, ensuring that the results are based on sound historical and archaeological evidence and rigorous analysis.

Another ethical consideration in digital Classics and Archaeology is the potential for misuse or misinterpretation of the results. Digital representations can be used to support a wide range of interpretations and narratives, some of which may be inaccurate or misleading. To address this challenge, scholars and conservators use a range of ethical guidelines, including transparency, accountability, and public engagement, to ensure that the results of digital representations are interpreted and used responsibly. For example, scholars and conservators might use public engagement to share the results of a digital representation with a wider audience, providing context and interpretation to ensure that the results are understood and used appropriately.

Digital Classics and Archaeology also raise ethical considerations related to the representation of marginalized or vulnerable groups. Digital representations can inadvertently perpetuate stereotypes or misrepresent the experiences of marginalized groups, leading to harm or injustice. To address this challenge, scholars and conservators use a range of ethical guidelines, including inclusivity, representation, and cultural sensitivity, to ensure that digital representations are respectful and accurate in their representation of diverse groups. For example, scholars and conservators might use inclusive data collection and analysis techniques to ensure that the voices and experiences of marginalized groups are represented in the digital representation.

4.7.7 Future Directions in Digital Classics and Archaeology

As digital technologies continue to evolve, digital Classics and Archaeology are poised to play an increasingly important role in the study and interpretation of ancient texts, artifacts, and sites. One of the key future directions in digital Classics and Archaeology is the integration of artificial intelligence (AI) and machine learning (ML) to enhance the accuracy and sophistication of digital representations. AI and ML can be used to analyze large and complex datasets, identify patterns and anomalies, and generate insights that would be difficult or impossible to achieve through traditional methods. For example, an AI-driven digital Classics project might use machine learning algorithms to model the evolution of an ancient language, providing new insights into the factors that contributed to its development and influence. Another future direction in digital Classics and Archaeology is the development of immersive and interactive digital representations that engage users in new and innovative ways. Virtual reality (VR) and augmented reality (AR) technologies can be used to create immersive and interactive digital experiences that allow users to explore ancient texts, artifacts, and sites in a more engaging and experiential way. For example, a VR-based digital Classics project might allow users to walk through a reconstructed ancient library, interacting with virtual manuscripts and scholars. Similarly, an AR-based digital Archaeology project might overlay digital images and visualizations onto the real world, allowing users to explore and interact with ancient sites and artifacts in their immediate environment.

The future of digital Classics and Archaeology also lies in the development of collaborative and participatory digital representations that engage a wider range of stakeholders in the study and interpretation of ancient texts, artifacts, and sites. Collaborative digital representations can bring together scholars, conservators, and the public to co-create and co-interpret digital representations, providing a more inclusive and democratic approach to the study of ancient cultures. For example, a collaborative digital Classics project might involve scholars, conservators, and community members working together to digitize and preserve a collection of ancient manuscripts, providing new insights and perspectives on the past. Participatory digital representations can also be used to engage the public in the study of ancient cultures, providing opportunities for learning, reflection, and action.

CHAPTER 5

Pedagogy and Education in Digital Humanities

5.1 TEACHING WITH DIGITAL TOOLS

Teaching with digital tools has revolutionized the way education is conducted, providing educators with new methods to enhance the delivery of content, engage students, and support personalized learning. Digital tools, ranging from multimedia presentations to virtual reality simulations, have transformed traditional classrooms into dynamic and interactive learning environments. The evolution of teaching with digital tools has been driven by advancements in technology, changes in educational philosophies, and the need to adapt to the digital age. Despite their potential, teaching with digital tools faces several challenges, including the digital divide, the need for digital literacy, and ethical and methodological considerations.

To address these challenges, educators must ensure equitable access to digital tools and resources, provide ongoing training and support in digital literacy, and adhere to ethical guidelines and best practices. The future of teaching with digital tools lies in the integration of AI and ML, the development of immersive and interactive educational experiences, and the creation of collaborative and participatory educational experiences that engage a wider range of stakeholders in the learning process. By addressing the challenges and exploring new directions, educators can ensure that teaching with digital tools is effective, inclusive, and ethically sound, providing new opportunities for learning, growth, and success. The principles of teaching with digital tools, with their dynamic and interactive learning experiences, will continue to influence the development of education, ensuring that the learning process is engaging, inclusive, and relevant to a wider audience. Through the use of digital tools, educators can create a more comprehensive and nuanced understanding of educational content, providing new insights and perspectives on the themes, motifs, and stylistic features that shape our educational heritage.

5.1.1 Types of Digital Tools in Education

Digital tools in education encompass a wide range of technologies and applications, each serving different purposes and addressing various educational needs. One of the most common types of digital tools is multimedia, which includes the use of images, audio, video, and animations to enhance the delivery of content. Multimedia tools can make learning more engaging and interactive, catering to different learning styles and preferences. For example, a multimedia presentation on the solar system might include images of planets, videos of space missions, and animations of planetary movements, providing a comprehensive and visually appealing learning experience.

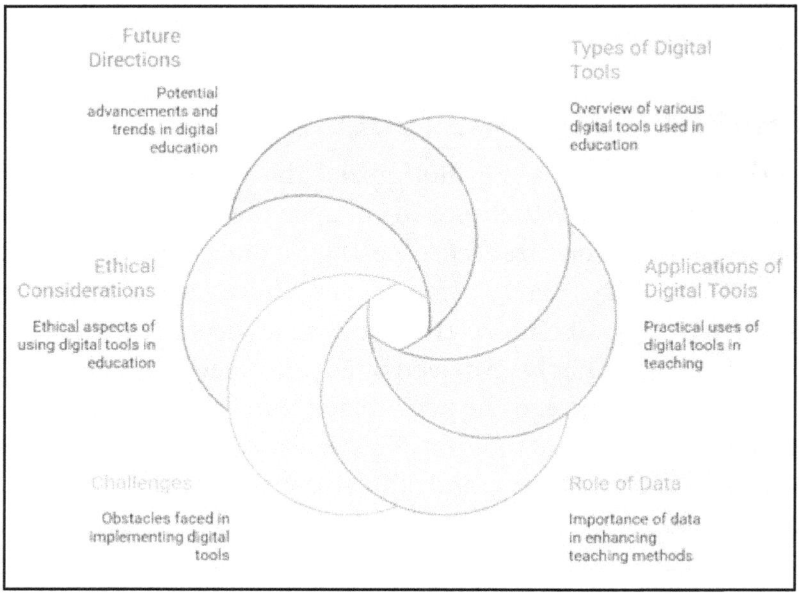

Fig: Exploring Digital Tools in Education

Another important type of digital tool is learning management systems (LMS), which are software platforms designed to manage and deliver educational content. LMS platforms provide a centralized hub for course materials, assessments, and communication, enabling educators to organize and deliver content more effectively. LMS platforms also facilitate collaboration and interaction, allowing students to engage with each other and with their instructors through discussion forums, group projects, and online assessments. Examples of popular LMS platforms include Moodle, Blackboard, and Canvas, which are used by educational institutions worldwide to support online and blended learning.

Virtual reality (VR) and augmented reality (AR) are emerging digital tools that are transforming the way students learn and interact with educational content. VR tools create immersive virtual environments, allowing students to experience and explore concepts in a three-dimensional space. For example, a VR simulation of a historical event might allow students to virtually visit a historical site, interact with virtual characters, and observe the dynamics of the event. AR tools, on the other hand, overlay digital information onto the real world, providing students with interactive and context-rich learning experiences. For example, an AR application might allow students to scan a historical artifact and view additional information, such as its history, significance, and cultural context.

5.1.2 Applications of Digital Tools in Education

Digital tools have a wide range of applications in education, from K-12 classrooms to higher education and professional development. In K-12 education, digital tools are used to enhance the delivery of content, engage students, and support personalized learning. For example, interactive whiteboards and educational software can make learning more interactive and engaging, catering to different learning styles and preferences. Digital tools can also support the development of 21st-century skills, such as digital literacy, critical thinking, and collaboration, preparing students for the challenges of the digital age.

In higher education, digital tools are used to support online and blended learning, providing students with flexible and accessible learning opportunities. For example, online learning platforms and virtual classrooms enable students to access educational content and interact with their instructors and peers from anywhere at any time. Digital tools can also support research and collaboration, enabling students and faculty to work together on projects, share resources, and engage in scholarly discussions. For example, digital repositories and collaboration tools can facilitate the sharing of research data, publications, and other academic resources, enhancing the quality and impact of scholarly work.

In professional development, digital tools are used to provide educators with ongoing training and support, enabling them to stay up-to-date with the latest educational practices and technologies. For example, online courses and webinars can provide educators with access to expert-led training and professional development opportunities, allowing them to enhance their skills and knowledge. Digital tools can also support the development of professional learning communities, enabling educators to collaborate, share best practices, and engage in continuous learning and improvement. For example, online forums and social media groups can facilitate the sharing of ideas, resources, and experiences, fostering a culture of collaboration and innovation in education.

5.1.3 Role of Data in Teaching with Digital Tools

Data plays a crucial role in teaching with digital tools, providing educators with valuable insights into student learning and performance. Digital tools generate a wealth of data, including student interactions, assessments, and feedback, which can be analyzed to inform instructional practices and improve learning outcomes. For example, learning analytics can be used to track student progress, identify learning gaps, and provide personalized recommendations for improvement. This data-driven approach to education enables educators to make informed decisions, tailor instruction to meet individual needs, and enhance the overall quality of education. The quality and accuracy of data in teaching with digital tools depend on the quality and accuracy of the data collection and analysis processes. Educational data can be incomplete, biased, or subject to interpretation, which can affect the outcomes of data analysis and the insights they provide.

To address these challenges, educators use a range of data collection and analysis techniques, including surveys, assessments, and learning analytics, to ensure the accuracy and reliability of the data used in teaching with digital tools. Additionally, educators use data visualization tools to explore and interpret educational data, providing new insights and perspectives on student learning and performance.

5.1.4 Challenges in Teaching with Digital Tools

Despite their potential, teaching with digital tools faces several challenges that can limit their effectiveness and impact. One of the primary challenges is the digital divide, which refers to the gap between those who have access to digital tools and those who do not. The digital divide can limit the benefits of digital tools in education, as students and educators without access to digital tools may be at a disadvantage. To address this challenge, educational institutions and policymakers must ensure equitable access to digital tools and resources, providing all students and educators with the opportunity to benefit from digital learning.

Another challenge in teaching with digital tools is the need for digital literacy, which refers to the ability to use digital tools and technologies effectively and responsibly. Digital literacy is essential for both students and educators, as it enables them to navigate the digital landscape, evaluate information, and communicate effectively. To address this challenge, educational institutions must provide ongoing training and support in digital literacy, ensuring that all students and educators have the skills and knowledge needed to succeed in the digital age. Additionally, educators must integrate digital literacy into the curriculum, providing students with opportunities to develop and apply digital skills in meaningful and relevant contexts.

Teaching with digital tools also faces ethical and methodological challenges, particularly in relation to the use of data and the protection of privacy. Digital tools generate a wealth of data, including student interactions, assessments, and feedback, which can be used to inform instructional practices and improve learning outcomes.

However, the use of this data raises important ethical considerations, including the protection of student privacy and the responsible use of data. To address these challenges, educators must adhere to ethical guidelines and best practices, ensuring the responsible and ethical use of data in teaching with digital tools.

Additionally, educators must be transparent and accountable in their use of data, providing students and parents with clear and accurate information about data collection, use, and protection.

5.1.5 Ethical Considerations in Teaching with Digital Tools

Ethical considerations are crucial in the development and use of digital tools in education, as they involve the collection, use, and protection of student data. One of the primary ethical considerations is the protection of student privacy, which refers to the right of students to control the collection, use, and disclosure of their personal information. Digital tools generate a wealth of data, including student interactions, assessments, and feedback, which can be used to inform instructional practices and improve learning outcomes. However, the use of this data raises important ethical considerations, including the protection of student privacy and the responsible use of data. To address this challenge, educators must adhere to ethical guidelines and best practices, ensuring the responsible and ethical use of data in teaching with digital tools.

Another ethical consideration in teaching with digital tools is the potential for bias and discrimination, which can occur when digital tools are used to make decisions about student learning and performance. For example, algorithms and artificial intelligence (AI) can be used to analyze student data and provide personalized recommendations for improvement. However, these tools can be subject to bias and discrimination, as they may rely on incomplete or inaccurate data, or may be designed with inherent biases. To address this challenge, educators must be aware of the potential for bias and discrimination in digital tools, and must take steps to mitigate these risks. For example, educators can use diverse and representative data sets, and can design algorithms and AI tools with fairness and equity in mind.

Teaching with digital tools also raises ethical considerations related to the representation of marginalized or vulnerable groups. Digital tools can inadvertently perpetuate stereotypes or misrepresent the experiences of marginalized groups, leading to harm or injustice. To address this challenge, educators must use a range of ethical guidelines, including inclusivity, representation, and cultural sensitivity, to ensure that digital tools are respectful and accurate in their representation of diverse groups. For example, educators can use inclusive data collection and analysis techniques to ensure that the voices and experiences of marginalized groups are represented in digital tools. Additionally, educators can design digital tools with cultural sensitivity in mind, ensuring that they are appropriate and relevant for diverse student populations.

5.1.6 Future Directions in Teaching with Digital Tools

As digital technologies continue to evolve, teaching with digital tools is poised to play an increasingly important role in education. One of the key future directions in teaching with digital tools is the integration of artificial intelligence (AI) and machine learning (ML) to enhance the accuracy and sophistication of educational practices. AI and ML can be used to analyze large and complex datasets, identify patterns and anomalies, and generate insights that would be difficult or impossible to achieve through traditional methods. For example, an AI-driven educational tool might use machine learning algorithms to model student learning and provide personalized recommendations for improvement. Additionally, AI and ML can be used to enhance the delivery of content, providing students with adaptive and personalized learning experiences.

Another future direction in teaching with digital tools is the development of immersive and interactive educational experiences that engage students in new and innovative ways. Virtual reality (VR) and augmented reality (AR) technologies can be used to create immersive and interactive learning experiences that allow students to explore educational content in a more engaging and experiential way. For example, a VR-based educational tool might allow students to walk through a virtual historical site, interacting with virtual artifacts and characters. Similarly, an AR-based educational tool might overlay digital information onto the real world, allowing students to explore and interact with educational content in their immediate environment. This approach can help to enhance student engagement, motivation, and learning outcomes.

The future of teaching with digital tools also lies in the development of collaborative and participatory educational experiences that engage a wider range of stakeholders in the learning process. Collaborative educational tools can bring together students, educators, and the community to co-create and co-interpret educational content, providing a more inclusive and democratic approach to education. For example, a collaborative educational tool might involve students, educators, and community members working together to create a digital story or multimedia presentation. Participatory educational tools can also be used to engage students in the learning process, providing opportunities for collaboration, creativity, and critical thinking. For example, participatory educational tools can be used to facilitate group projects, peer-to-peer learning, and community-based learning, fostering a culture of collaboration and innovation in education.

5.2 DIGITAL LITERACY IN THE HUMANITIES CURRICULUM

Digital literacy is not a threat to the humanities; it is a powerful extension of its mission. By embracing digital tools and methods, humanities educators can engage students in new ways, expand the boundaries of scholarly inquiry, and equip future generations with the skills and insights needed to understand and shape a complex digital world. As technology continues to influence every aspect of human life, the humanities have a vital role to play in ensuring that digital culture is thoughtful, inclusive, and ethically grounded. Integrating digital literacy into the humanities curriculum is not only a response to current trends but a visionary step toward a more engaged, critical, and creative future for the humanities.

Digital literacy in the context of the humanities refers to the ability to effectively use digital tools and platforms to research, analyze, produce, and communicate knowledge. It includes the competence to locate and evaluate digital sources, understand the ethical implications of digital communication, and employ digital media to interpret and present humanistic content. Unlike general computer literacy, which focuses on basic operational skills, digital literacy in the humanities emphasizes the critical use of digital technologies in the context of cultural, historical, and philosophical inquiry. It is about knowing how to use technology not only functionally but thoughtfully, in ways that enhance rather than dilute humanistic understanding.

In the humanities, digital literacy allows students to explore new forms of representation and meaning-making. For example, it enables the analysis of vast textual corpora using digital tools, the creation of digital archives for historical materials, and the visualization of philosophical ideas through interactive media. It also involves familiarity with online scholarly communication, from academic blogging to open-access publishing. In short, digital literacy reshapes the boundaries of the humanities by opening up new avenues for interpretation, collaboration, and dissemination of knowledge.

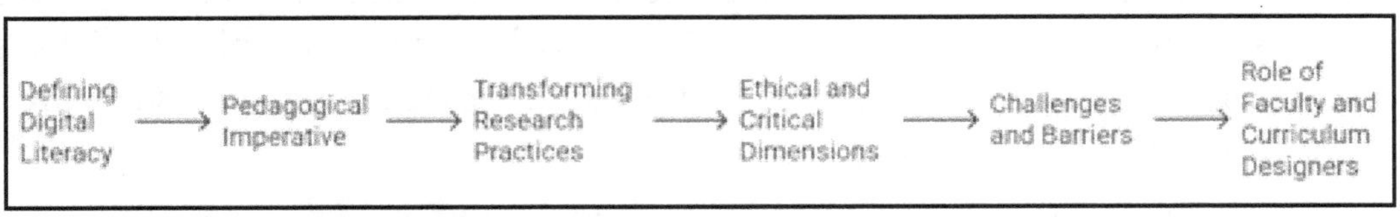

Fig: Digital Literacy in Humanities Curriculum

5.2.1 Pedagogical Imperative for Digital Integration

The inclusion of digital literacy in the humanities curriculum is not just a response to technological change but a proactive educational strategy. As students increasingly interact with information through digital platforms, educators must adapt their teaching methods to ensure that critical thinking extends into the digital realm.

Humanities education has always been about understanding human culture, thought, and expression; in the digital age, this includes understanding how these are mediated by technology. A curriculum that incorporates digital literacy empowers students to engage with contemporary forms of communication while remaining anchored in the core values of the humanities: empathy, ethics, interpretation, and critical inquiry. By integrating digital tools into assignments and classroom activities, instructors can foster a more dynamic and participatory learning environment. Students might analyze social media narratives in literature courses, map historical events using GIS software, or curate virtual museum exhibits as part of art history projects. These practices not only develop digital skills but also deepen disciplinary understanding by applying theoretical knowledge in innovative and practical ways. The result is a more engaged form of learning that connects traditional humanities scholarship with real-world contexts and challenges.

5.2.2 Transforming Research Practices through Digital Literacy

Digital literacy is reshaping how humanities research is conducted. Students and scholars now have access to a wealth of digital archives, databases, and scholarly networks that expand the scope of research far beyond the physical library. With the use of digital tools, researchers can analyze massive datasets, trace intertextual relationships, and visualize complex historical phenomena. For example, text mining allows the analysis of patterns across thousands of documents, while digital mapping techniques reveal spatial dimensions of historical or cultural narratives.

Digital literacy also encourages interdisciplinary collaboration. Projects in the digital humanities often involve teams composed of historians, computer scientists, designers, and librarians. Students trained in both humanistic thinking and digital skills are better prepared to participate in such collaborations and to contribute meaningfully to multi-faceted research initiatives. Furthermore, digital literacy enhances students' ability to communicate their research findings through diverse formats, including websites, podcasts, digital exhibits, and interactive timelines. These new modes of expression align with the ways in which audiences increasingly consume and engage with information, making humanities research more accessible and impactful.

5.2.3 Ethical and Critical Dimensions of Digital Literacy

One of the essential components of digital literacy in the humanities is the capacity to think critically about the digital world itself. This includes an understanding of the ethical, political, and cultural implications of digital technologies. Students must be equipped to ask important questions about data privacy, algorithmic bias, digital surveillance, and the digital divide.

They must learn to evaluate the credibility of online sources, recognize the influence of platform design on user behavior, and reflect on how digital media shapes public discourse and cultural memory. Incorporating these critical dimensions into the curriculum ensures that digital literacy is not reduced to technical proficiency. Instead, it becomes a means of fostering digital citizenship—responsible and reflective participation in digital culture. Humanities students are uniquely positioned to lead such discussions because their training emphasizes the analysis of meaning, power, and representation. A digitally literate humanities curriculum should therefore include discussions on digital ethics, intellectual property, and the social impact of technology, preparing students to navigate and shape the digital world with integrity and insight.

5.2.4 Challenges and Barriers to Implementation

Despite its importance, integrating digital literacy into the humanities curriculum poses several challenges. Many institutions lack the resources, infrastructure, or faculty expertise needed to implement digital humanities courses and projects. There may be resistance from departments that view digital tools as incompatible with traditional scholarship or fear that technological skills will overshadow critical thinking. In addition, students may enter university with highly uneven levels of digital preparedness, requiring differentiated instruction and support. Addressing these challenges requires institutional commitment and strategic investment. Universities must provide training opportunities for faculty, create interdisciplinary digital humanities centers, and ensure access to the necessary software and equipment. Curricular reform should be inclusive and collaborative, involving stakeholders from across departments and disciplines. Furthermore, digital literacy should not be confined to specialized electives but embedded throughout the humanities curriculum—from introductory courses to advanced seminars—so that it becomes a foundational component of humanities education rather than an optional add-on.

5.2.5 The Role of Faculty and Curriculum Designers

Faculty members play a central role in fostering digital literacy in the humanities. As educators, they must model the integration of digital tools into research and pedagogy, guiding students through the complexities of digital scholarship. Curriculum designers must work with faculty to develop modules, assignments, and learning outcomes that incorporate digital literacy in meaningful ways. This may involve redesigning traditional assignments to include digital components, such as multimedia presentations or collaborative online projects. Professional development is crucial in this process. Workshops, seminars, and collaborative teaching initiatives can help faculty gain confidence in using digital tools and understanding their pedagogical potential. Peer support and interdisciplinary collaboration can also encourage experimentation and innovation in teaching practices. Ultimately, building a culture of digital literacy in the humanities requires collective effort, institutional support, and a shared vision of what humanistic education can and should be in the digital era.

5.3 ONLINE AND HYBRID HUMANITIES COURSES

The expansion of online and hybrid humanities courses represents not a diminishment of the discipline's value but rather its evolution and democratization. While digital formats require adjustments to traditional teaching methods, they also create opportunities to make humanistic ways of thinking accessible to broader populations and applicable to contemporary digital culture.

The most successful digital humanities courses don't merely transmit information about culture, history, and ideas—they create spaces where students develop the habits of mind that define humanistic inquiry: careful attention to language and form, sensitivity to historical context, awareness of multiple perspectives, and comfort with ambiguity. As educational institutions continue to refine their online and hybrid offerings, the measure of success should be whether these digital learning environments foster the same depth of engagement, intellectual community, and transformative encounters with ideas that have always been the hallmark of excellent humanities education. In this way, digital humanities education can fulfill its promise of expanding access while maintaining the discipline's essential role in cultivating thoughtful, ethically engaged citizens for the digital age.

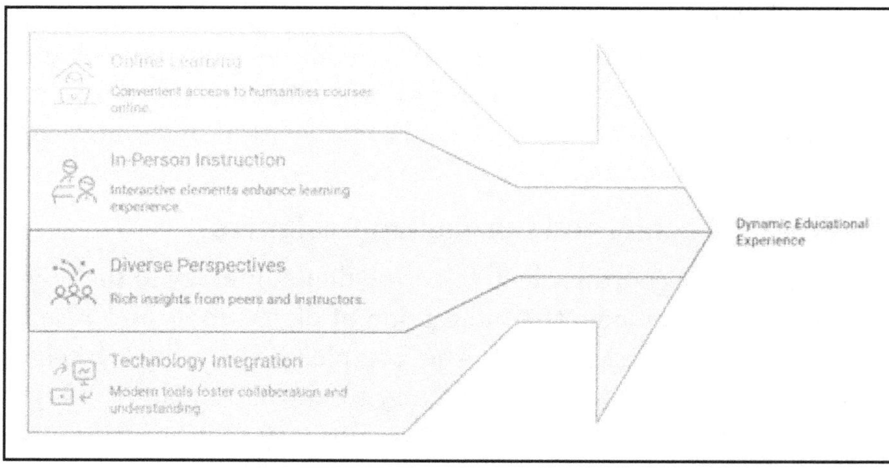

Fig: Pathways to Humanities Engagement

5.3.1 Pedagogical Approaches in Virtual Humanities Classrooms

Teaching humanities in online environments requires fundamentally rethinking instructional methodologies that were developed for physical classrooms. Successful virtual humanities courses employ multimodal strategies that compensate for the absence of shared physical space while leveraging unique affordances of digital tools. Asynchronous discussion forums have become central to replicating the seminar-style dialogue characteristic of humanities education, allowing students time for reflective responses that often demonstrate greater depth than spontaneous classroom comments. Synchronous video sessions using platforms like Zoom enable real-time textual analysis and debate, with breakout rooms facilitating small-group close reading exercises. Innovative instructors incorporate collaborative annotation tools such as Hypothesis to create layered conversations directly on digital texts, while virtual whiteboards allow for visual mapping of complex philosophical arguments or historical timelines. These adapted methodologies demonstrate that the core activities of humanities education—careful reading, contextual analysis, and interpretive debate—can be effectively translated into digital formats with thoughtful pedagogical design.

5.3.2 Hybrid Models and Their Impact on Learning Outcomes

Hybrid humanities courses, which blend in-person and online components, have emerged as particularly effective models for maintaining the strengths of traditional instruction while incorporating digital enhancements. In these configurations, classroom time focuses on activities that benefit most from physical co-presence—such as performance-based learning in theater studies or object-based learning in material culture courses—while online modules handle content delivery and preliminary analysis.

Research indicates that well-designed hybrid humanities courses achieve comparable or superior learning outcomes to fully in-person equivalents, particularly in developing writing and research skills. The online components allow students to engage with primary sources and secondary literature at their own pace, while face-to-face sessions deepen understanding through embodied interaction. This model has proven especially valuable for teaching archival research methods, where students can digitally access rare materials before working with physical collections, maximizing the productivity of limited time in special collections libraries.

5.3.3 Digital Tools Enhancing Humanities Pedagogy

The proliferation of specialized digital tools has created unprecedented opportunities for enriching online humanities instruction. Virtual reality reconstructions of historical sites enable immersive study of architectural history, allowing students to explore ancient Roman forums or medieval cathedrals with scholarly annotations. Text analysis platforms like Voyant Tools facilitate distant reading exercises across large corpora of literature, helping students identify patterns and themes that might escape traditional close reading.

Digital storytelling applications empower students to create multimedia interpretations of philosophical concepts or historical events, developing both technical and interpretive skills simultaneously. Perhaps most significantly, collaborative platforms such as Omeka and Scalar have transformed how students engage with primary source materials, enabling the creation of digital exhibitions and scholarly editions that would be impossible in analog formats. These tools don't merely replicate traditional humanities methods digitally—they expand the very possibilities of humanistic inquiry and expression.

5.3.4 Addressing Equity and Access through Online Humanities

The expansion of online humanities education has brought both promises and challenges regarding educational equity. On one hand, digital delivery eliminates geographical barriers, enabling students from rural areas, working professionals, and those with caregiving responsibilities to access high-quality humanities instruction that was previously restricted to residential programs. Many institutions have reported increased enrollment from historically underserved populations in their online humanities offerings.

However, the digital divide persists as a significant obstacle, with students from low-income backgrounds often lacking reliable internet access or adequate devices for participating fully in digital learning. Innovative solutions such as low-bandwidth course designs, offline-accessible materials, and institutional device loan programs have helped mitigate these disparities. Additionally, the asynchronous nature of many online humanities courses can accommodate neurodiverse learners and non-traditional students who benefit from flexible pacing, though it requires careful instructional design to maintain academic rigor and community building in self-paced environments.

5.3.5 Building Intellectual Community in Digital Spaces

One of the most persistent critiques of online humanities education concerns its potential to isolate learners and diminish the communal aspects of humanistic study. Traditional humanities pedagogy emphasizes the social construction of knowledge through lively debate and shared intellectual discovery—qualities that many fear get lost in virtual formats. However, forward-thinking programs have developed effective strategies for cultivating robust intellectual communities online.

Semester-long collaborative research projects using shared digital workspaces create sustained academic relationships, while virtual reading groups and writing workshops maintain the social dimensions of scholarship. Some institutions have implemented synchronous "digital humanities labs" where students work simultaneously on independent projects while maintaining open video connections for spontaneous consultation. The most successful online humanities programs also create intentional spaces for informal interaction, from discipline-specific discussion channels to virtual coffee hours, recognizing that the serendipitous conversations outside formal class time often spark the most profound intellectual growth.

5.3.6 Assessment and Evaluation in Digital Humanities Courses

The shift to online and hybrid formats has necessitated reimagining how student learning is assessed in humanities disciplines. Traditional evaluation methods like timed in-class essays and oral presentations have given way to innovative digital alternatives that often provide richer demonstrations of student learning. Portfolio-based assessments allow students to compile and reflect on their work across a semester, showcasing the development of their analytical abilities. Digital annotation assignments make visible the close reading process itself, enabling instructors to assess how students engage with texts at the sentence level.

Collaborative digital projects—such as building online exhibitions or contributing to crowd-sourced textual archives—develop both subject mastery and digital literacy skills simultaneously. Many instructors report that online assessment actually provides better documentation of the learning process through automatically time-stamped discussion posts and version-controlled writing projects, offering insights into student thinking that were difficult to capture in traditional classroom settings.

5.3.7 Faculty Development for Digital Humanities Instruction

The successful implementation of online and hybrid humanities courses requires significant investment in faculty development, as the transition demands both technological upskilling and pedagogical retooling. Effective professional development programs move beyond simple platform training to address the philosophical and methodological challenges of translating humanistic teaching practices to digital environments. Many institutions have created humanities-specific teaching centers that pair instructional designers with disciplinary experts to co-develop courses.

Mentorship programs where experienced online humanities instructors guide their colleagues through course design have proven particularly effective. Ongoing communities of practice allow faculty to share successful strategies for facilitating Socratic dialogue via video conference or designing authentic assessments for virtual environments. This support is crucial for helping humanities professors—who often have deep reservations about digital mediation of their disciplines—become confident and innovative online educators while maintaining the intellectual rigor central to their fields.

5.4 STUDENT-CENTERED DH PROJECTS AND LABS

Student-centered DH projects and labs represent a powerful and innovative approach to education, prioritizing the active involvement of students in the research process. By leveraging the power of digital tools and methodologies, student-centered DH projects and labs provide students with the skills, knowledge, and resources needed to engage with digital technologies in meaningful and impactful ways. These initiatives not only enhance the educational outcomes but also contribute to the broader goals of digital humanities, such as democratizing access to knowledge and promoting digital literacy. Student-centered DH projects and labs are characterized by collaboration, hands-on learning, and a focus on student agency, fostering a sense of community and belonging, and developing critical thinking and problem-solving skills.

Despite their potential, student-centered DH projects and labs face several challenges, including the need for digital literacy, the availability and quality of digital tools and resources, and ethical and methodological considerations. To address these challenges, educators must provide ongoing training and support in digital literacy, invest in high-quality digital tools and resources, and adhere to ethical guidelines and best practices. The future of student-centered DH projects and labs lies in the integration of AI and ML, the development of immersive and interactive educational experiences, and the creation of collaborative and participatory educational experiences that engage a wider range of stakeholders in the learning process.

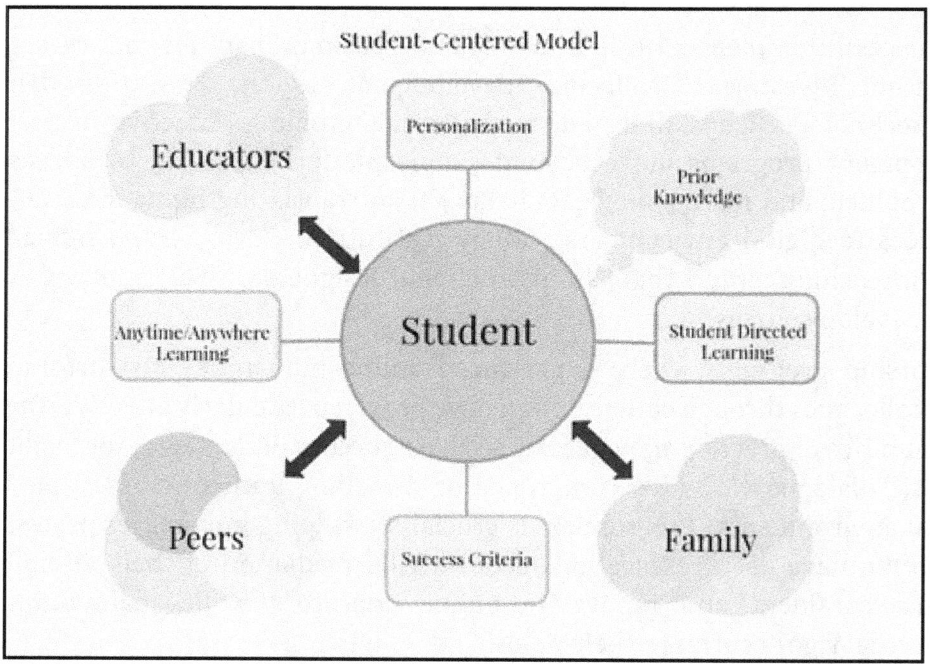

Fig: Student-Centered Design

vBy addressing the challenges and exploring new directions, educators can ensure that student-centered DH projects and labs are effective, inclusive, and ethically sound, providing new opportunities for learning, growth, and success. The principles of student-centered DH projects and labs, with their dynamic and interactive learning experiences, will continue to influence the development of education, ensuring that the learning process is engaging, inclusive, and relevant to a wider audience. Through the use of digital tools and methodologies, educators can create a more comprehensive and nuanced understanding of educational content, providing new insights and perspectives on the themes, motifs, and stylistic features that shape our educational heritage.

5.4.1 Characteristics

Student-centered DH projects and labs are characterized by several key features, including collaboration, hands-on learning, and a focus on student agency. Collaboration is a fundamental aspect of student-centered DH projects and labs, as they often involve teamwork and the sharing of ideas, resources, and expertise. This collaborative approach not only enhances the learning experience but also fosters a sense of community and belonging, as students work together towards a common goal.

Hands-on learning is another key feature of student-centered DH projects and labs, as they prioritize the active involvement of students in the research process. This hands-on approach allows students to apply theoretical knowledge to practical problems, developing the skills and confidence needed to succeed in the digital age. A focus on student agency is also a key characteristic of student-centered DH projects and labs, as they prioritize the voices, experiences, and perspectives of students. This focus on student agency empowers students to take ownership of their learning, making decisions and taking actions that reflect their interests, needs, and goals.

Another important characteristic of student-centered DH projects and labs is the integration of interdisciplinary approaches, which combine methods and perspectives from various fields, such as computer science, history, literature, and art. This interdisciplinary approach allows students to explore complex problems from multiple angles, developing a more comprehensive and nuanced understanding of the subject matter.

For example, a student-centered DH project might involve the use of text mining to analyze a corpus of historical documents, combining methods from computer science and history to uncover patterns and themes that might not be immediately apparent through traditional methods. Similarly, a student-centered DH lab might involve the use of data visualization to explore the relationships between different characters in a literary work, combining methods from literature and computer science to create a more engaging and interactive learning experience.

5.4.2 Examples

Student-centered DH projects and labs can take many forms, from small-scale classroom activities to large-scale research initiatives. One example of a student-centered DH project is the development of a digital archive, which involves the collection, digitization, and curation of historical or cultural materials. For example, a group of students might work together to create a digital archive of local history, collecting and digitizing photographs, documents, and artifacts from the community. This project not only provides students with the opportunity to engage with digital technologies and methodologies but also contributes to the preservation and dissemination of local history. Similarly, a student-centered DH lab might involve the use of virtual reality to create an immersive learning experience, allowing students to explore a historical site or cultural artifact in a more engaging and interactive way.

Another example of a student-centered DH project is the creation of a digital storytelling project, which involves the use of multimedia tools to tell a story or convey a message. For example, a group of students might work together to create a digital story about a historical event or cultural practice, using images, audio, and video to create a more engaging and interactive learning experience. This project not only provides students with the opportunity to develop digital literacy skills but also fosters creativity, critical thinking, and collaboration.

Similarly, a student-centered DH lab might involve the use of data visualization to explore a complex data set, allowing students to uncover patterns, themes, and insights that might not be immediately apparent through traditional methods. For example, a data visualization project might involve the use of network graphs to explore the relationships between different characters in a literary work, providing a more comprehensive and nuanced understanding of the text.

5.4.3 Role of Technology

Technology plays a crucial role in student-centered DH projects and labs, providing the tools and resources needed to engage with digital methodologies and explore complex data sets. Digital tools and technologies, such as text mining, data visualization, and virtual reality, enable students to analyze and interpret data in new and innovative ways, uncovering patterns, themes, and insights that might not be immediately apparent through traditional methods.

For example, text mining tools can be used to analyze a corpus of historical documents, identifying recurring motifs, tracking the evolution of themes, and revealing hidden patterns and structures within the texts. Similarly, data visualization tools can be used to explore the relationships between different characters, events, and themes in a literary work, providing a visual overview of the text's narrative structure.

Virtual reality (VR) and augmented reality (AR) technologies are also important in student-centered DH projects and labs, as they enable the creation of immersive and interactive learning experiences. VR tools can be used to create virtual environments, allowing students to explore historical sites, cultural artifacts, and scientific phenomena in a more engaging and experiential way. For example, a VR-based DH project might allow students to walk through a reconstructed historical city, interacting with virtual residents and observing the dynamics of urban life. Similarly, an AR-based DH project might overlay digital information onto the real world, allowing students to explore and interact with historical sites and cultural artifacts in their immediate environment. This approach can help to enhance student engagement, motivation, and learning outcomes, as it provides a more immersive and interactive learning experience.

5.4.4 Benefits

Student-centered DH projects and labs offer numerous benefits, both for students and for the broader field of digital humanities. One of the primary benefits is the development of digital literacy skills, which are essential for navigating the digital age. By engaging with digital tools and methodologies, students develop the skills and knowledge needed to analyze and interpret complex data sets, uncovering patterns, themes, and insights that might not be immediately apparent through traditional methods. This digital literacy is not only important for academic success but also for personal and professional development, as it enables students to communicate, collaborate, and create in the digital age.

Another benefit of student-centered DH projects and labs is the enhancement of critical thinking and problem-solving skills. By engaging with complex problems and data sets, students develop the ability to analyze, evaluate, and synthesize information, drawing on multiple perspectives and approaches. This critical thinking and problem-solving is essential for academic success, as it enables students to tackle complex problems and challenges in their studies. Additionally, this skill set is important for personal and professional development, as it enables students to adapt to changing circumstances, make informed decisions, and solve problems in their personal and professional lives.

Student-centered DH projects and labs also foster a sense of community and belonging, as they prioritize the active involvement of students in the research process. This collaborative approach not only enhances the learning experience but also fosters a sense of community and belonging, as students work together towards a common goal. This sense of community and belonging is important for academic success, as it provides students with the support and encouragement needed to succeed in their studies. Additionally, this sense of community and belonging is important for personal and professional development, as it provides students with the networks and connections needed to succeed in their personal and professional lives.

5.4.5 Challenges

Despite their potential, student-centered DH projects and labs face several challenges that can limit their effectiveness and impact. One of the primary challenges is the need for digital literacy, which refers to the ability to use digital tools and technologies effectively and responsibly. Digital literacy is essential for both students and educators, as it enables them to navigate the digital landscape, evaluate information, and communicate effectively. To address this challenge, educational institutions must provide ongoing training and support in digital literacy, ensuring that all students and educators have the skills and knowledge needed to succeed in the digital age. Additionally, educators must integrate digital literacy into the curriculum, providing students with opportunities to develop and apply digital skills in meaningful and relevant contexts.

Another challenge in student-centered DH projects and labs is the availability and quality of digital tools and resources. Digital tools and resources can be expensive, and their quality can vary widely, which can affect the outcomes of student-centered DH projects and labs. To address this challenge, educational institutions must invest in high-quality digital tools and resources, ensuring that students and educators have access to the tools and resources needed to succeed in the digital age. Additionally, educators must be aware of the potential biases and limitations of digital tools and resources, ensuring that they are used in a responsible and ethical manner.

Student-centered DH projects and labs also face ethical and methodological challenges, particularly in relation to the interpretation and representation of data. Digital representations can be subject to bias and interpretation, which can affect the outcomes of the representation and the insights they provide. For example, a digital representation of a historical event might be influenced by the student's own biases and interpretations, leading to a skewed or incomplete representation of the event. To address these challenges, educators must use a range of ethical and methodological guidelines, including transparency, peer review, and interdisciplinary collaboration, to ensure the accuracy and reliability of digital representations.

5.4.6 Ethical Considerations

Ethical considerations are crucial in the development and use of student-centered DH projects and labs, as they involve the interpretation and representation of data. One of the primary ethical considerations is the potential for bias and misrepresentation in digital representations. Digital representations can be influenced by the student's own biases and interpretations, leading to a skewed or incomplete representation of the data. To address this challenge, educators must use a range of ethical guidelines, including transparency, peer review, and interdisciplinary collaboration, to ensure the accuracy and reliability of digital representations. For example, educators might use peer review to evaluate the assumptions and methods used in a digital representation, ensuring that the results are based on sound evidence and rigorous analysis.

Another ethical consideration in student-centered DH projects and labs is the potential for misuse or misinterpretation of the results. Digital representations can be used to support a wide range of interpretations and narratives, some of which may be inaccurate or misleading. To address this challenge, educators must use a range of ethical guidelines, including transparency, accountability, and public engagement, to ensure that the results of digital representations are interpreted and used responsibly. For example, educators might use public engagement to share the results of a digital representation with a wider audience, providing context and interpretation to ensure that the results are understood and used appropriately.

Student-centered DH projects and labs also raise ethical considerations related to the representation of marginalized or vulnerable groups. Digital representations can inadvertently perpetuate stereotypes or misrepresent the experiences of marginalized groups, leading to harm or injustice. To address this challenge, educators must use a range of ethical guidelines, including inclusivity, representation, and cultural sensitivity, to ensure that digital representations are respectful and accurate in their representation of diverse groups. For example, educators might use inclusive data collection and analysis techniques to ensure that the voices and experiences of marginalized groups are represented in the digital representation.

5.4.7 Future Directions

As digital technologies continue to evolve, student-centered DH projects and labs are poised to play an increasingly important role in education. One of the key future directions in student-centered DH projects and labs is the integration of artificial intelligence (AI) and machine learning (ML) to enhance the accuracy and sophistication of educational practices. AI and ML can be used to analyze large and complex datasets, identify patterns and anomalies, and generate insights that would be difficult or impossible to achieve through traditional methods. For example, an AI-driven student-centered DH project might use machine learning algorithms to model student learning and provide personalized recommendations for improvement. Additionally, AI and ML can be used to enhance the delivery of content, providing students with adaptive and personalized learning experiences.

Another future direction in student-centered DH projects and labs is the development of immersive and interactive educational experiences that engage students in new and innovative ways. Virtual reality (VR) and augmented reality (AR) technologies can be used to create immersive and interactive learning experiences that allow students to explore educational content in a more engaging and experiential way. For example, a VR-based student-centered DH project might allow students to walk through a virtual historical site, interacting with virtual artifacts and characters. Similarly, an AR-based student-centered DH project might overlay digital information onto the real world, allowing students to explore and interact with educational content in their immediate environment. This approach can help to enhance student engagement, motivation, and learning outcomes.

The future of student-centered DH projects and labs also lies in the development of collaborative and participatory educational experiences that engage a wider range of stakeholders in the learning process. Collaborative educational tools can bring together students, educators, and the community to co-create and co-interpret educational content, providing a more inclusive and democratic approach to education. For example, a collaborative student-centered DH project might involve students, educators, and community members working together to create a digital story or multimedia presentation. Participatory educational tools can also be used to engage students in the learning process, providing opportunities for collaboration, creativity, and critical thinking. For example, participatory educational tools can be used to facilitate group projects, peer-to-peer learning, and community-based learning, fostering a culture of collaboration and innovation in education.

5.5 GAMIFICATION AND INTERACTIVE LEARNING ENVIRONMENTS

As gamification matures from educational novelty to established practice, the field faces the critical challenge of maintaining equilibrium between engagement and academic rigor. The most effective implementations demonstrate that game elements need not trivialize learning but can instead deepen intellectual engagement when thoughtfully integrated with substantive content. Successful gamified learning environments achieve the delicate balance where students become so absorbed in challenges that they forget they're learning while simultaneously developing robust knowledge and skills.

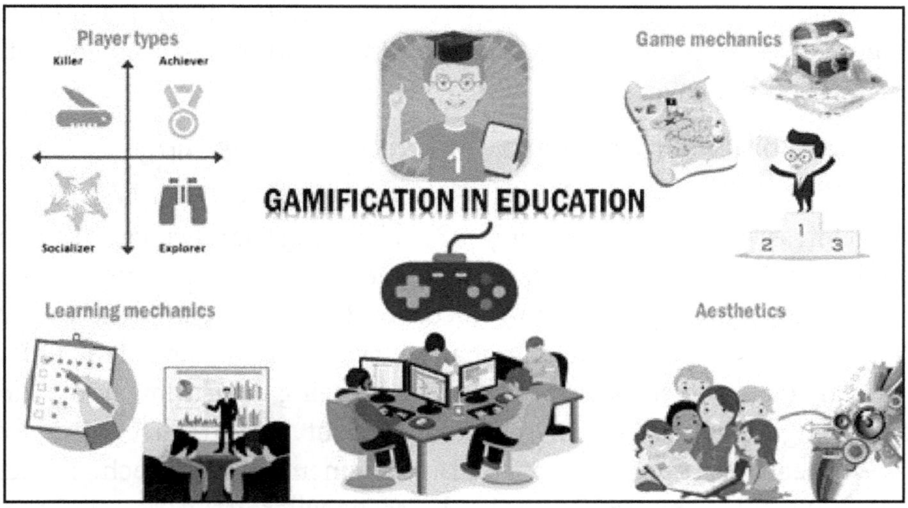

Fig: Gamification in Education

This requires resisting the temptation to prioritize flashy aesthetics over meaningful interaction and ensuring game mechanics align with rather than distract from learning objectives. As digital technologies continue evolving and student expectations shift, gamification will likely become not just an occasional teaching strategy but a fundamental organizing principle for education design. The institutions that thrive in this new landscape will be those that harness the motivational power of games while preserving the depth, nuance, and critical inquiry that define quality education, creating interactive learning environments that are as intellectually substantial as they are engaging.

5.5.1 Core Principles of Effective Learning Gamification

Successful implementation of gamification in education requires more than superficial additions of game-like elements to traditional coursework. The most effective systems build upon established psychological theories of motivation and learning, particularly Self-Determination Theory which emphasizes competence, autonomy, and relatedness as fundamental human needs. Well-designed educational gamification provides learners with clear pathways to demonstrate mastery (competence), meaningful choices in their learning journey (autonomy), and opportunities for collaborative achievement (relatedness).

These systems often incorporate progression mechanics that make skill development visible through leveling systems, narrative structures that contextualize learning within compelling storylines, and reward schedules that balance intrinsic and extrinsic motivation. The most sophisticated implementations create what game designers call "magic circles"—psychological spaces where learners voluntarily accept challenges and find inherent satisfaction in overcoming them. When properly constructed, these gamified environments transform the learning process from obligatory task to engaging experience while maintaining academic integrity and depth of content coverage.

5.5.2 Technological Frameworks for Interactive Learning Environments

The digital infrastructure supporting gamified learning has advanced dramatically, enabling increasingly immersive and responsive educational experiences. Modern learning management systems now incorporate native gamification features including experience point tracking, leaderboards, and achievement unlocking. More specialized platforms leverage adaptive learning algorithms to dynamically adjust challenge levels based on real-time student performance data, creating personalized learning trajectories. Virtual and augmented reality technologies have begun enabling fully immersive gamified lessons where students might explore historical sites in VR or manipulate molecular structures in AR space. Application programming interfaces (APIs) allow integration between learning platforms and game engines, facilitating the development of sophisticated educational games with robust analytics capabilities. These technological advancements support the creation of persistent learning worlds where student progress accumulates across courses and semesters, building comprehensive learner profiles that inform instructional design. The most cutting-edge implementations incorporate elements from massively multiplayer online games, creating educational ecosystems where hundreds of students collaborate and compete in knowledge-building activities.

5.5.3 Cognitive and Behavioral Impacts of Gamified Learning

Research into the effects of gamification on learning processes reveals complex interactions between game mechanics and cognitive development. The immediate feedback loops characteristic of well-designed gamified systems appear to strengthen neural pathways associated with skill acquisition and knowledge retention. The dopamine release triggered by achievement milestones may enhance memory consolidation while simultaneously building positive associations with the learning process.

Behavioral studies demonstrate increased time-on-task for students in gamified environments compared to traditional instructional formats, along with higher rates of voluntary engagement with supplementary materials. The social components of many gamified systems—including team challenges and peer recognition features—appear to foster collaborative learning behaviors and reduce classroom anxiety. Neuroeducational research suggests that the emotional engagement stimulated by game elements may activate broader neural networks during learning tasks, potentially leading to more flexible knowledge application. However, scholars caution against over-reliance on extrinsic reward systems, which may undermine intrinsic motivation if not carefully balanced with meaningful learning experiences and authentic mastery opportunities.

5.5.4 Disciplinary Applications across the Curriculum

The versatility of gamification strategies allows for tailored implementation across virtually all academic disciplines, each requiring distinct adaptations of core game mechanics. In STEM fields, gamification often takes the form of simulation-based challenges where students apply mathematical or scientific principles to solve progressively complex problems, such as managing virtual ecosystems or programming robot swarms.

Language arts curricula increasingly incorporate role-playing game elements where students assume character identities to explore literary texts or accumulate "writing power" through drafting and revision cycles. History education has seen success with alternate reality games that position students as historical agents making period-authentic decisions with consequential outcomes. Even traditionally lecture-based disciplines like philosophy have implemented gamified systems where students earn "wisdom points" for constructing logically valid arguments or identifying fallacies in contemporary media. Professional programs in fields such as medicine and engineering employ serious games that simulate high-stakes scenarios requiring the application of technical knowledge under time pressure. This disciplinary diversity demonstrates gamification's adaptability while highlighting the importance of content-specific design principles that align game mechanics with subject matter learning objectives.

5.5.5 Assessment and Evaluation in Gamified Systems

The integration of gamification necessitates rethinking traditional assessment paradigms to align with interactive learning environments. Rather than relying solely on summative exams, gamified courses often employ continuous assessment through experience point accumulation tied to specific competencies. Digital badges frequently serve as micro-credentials that validate discrete skill acquisitions while providing visible markers of progress.

The rich data generated by gamified platforms enables learning analytics that track not just outcomes but the learning process itself—recording time spent on tasks, patterns of error and correction, and pathways through content. Some systems employ stealth assessment techniques where evaluation occurs seamlessly during gameplay, reducing test anxiety while providing more authentic demonstrations of capability. Narrative-driven assessments position students as protagonists who must apply knowledge to advance a storyline, creating contextualized demonstrations of understanding. These alternative assessment strategies frequently provide more nuanced pictures of student learning than traditional exams while maintaining academic rigor through carefully calibrated challenge levels and mastery thresholds.

5.5.6 Equity and Accessibility Considerations

While gamification offers numerous educational benefits, its implementation raises important questions regarding equity and accessibility that demand careful consideration. The competitive elements present in many gamified systems—such as leaderboards and achievement rankings—may inadvertently disadvantage students with different learning needs or prior knowledge bases.

Cultural variations in attitudes toward competition and public recognition require sensitivity in system design. Technological access disparities create potential barriers for students lacking reliable devices or high-speed internet connections necessary for sophisticated gamified platforms. Students with certain cognitive or sensory processing differences may find some game mechanics overwhelming rather than motivating. Thoughtful implementation strategies include providing multiple pathways to achievement, balancing competitive and collaborative elements, offering offline alternatives for digital components, and building in flexibility for individual pacing. The most inclusive gamified systems incorporate universal design principles from their inception rather than retrofitting accessibility features, ensuring all students can benefit from interactive learning environments regardless of background or ability.

5.5.7 Faculty Development and Institutional Support

Successful institutional adoption of gamification in education requires comprehensive support structures for faculty transitioning to interactive teaching methodologies. Effective professional development programs move beyond technical training to address pedagogical redesign, helping instructors reconceptualize their courses through game design lenses. Many institutions have established faculty learning communities where educators across disciplines collaborate on gamification strategies and share best practices.

Instructional design support proves crucial for balancing entertainment value with academic substance, ensuring game elements enhance rather than distract from learning objectives. Resource allocation must account for the substantial development time required to create quality gamified experiences, with institutional incentives recognizing this labor in promotion and tenure considerations. Some forward-thinking universities have established serious game development studios that partner with faculty to produce high-quality interactive learning modules. These support structures acknowledge that effective gamification represents not merely a technological add-on but a fundamental rethinking of instructional practice requiring sustained institutional commitment.

CHAPTER

Project Design and Management

6

6.1 PLANNING AND DEVELOPING A DH PROJECT

Planning and developing a Digital Humanities (DH) project involves a systematic and collaborative approach to leveraging digital tools and methodologies to explore and interpret humanities data. The process typically involves several key stages, from conceptualization and planning to implementation and evaluation. During the conceptualization stage, researchers identify a research question or problem, define the project's goals, objectives, and scope, and consider the potential impact and relevance of the project.

The next stage involves defining the scope and objectives of the project, specifying the project's boundaries, and identifying the key research questions and hypotheses to be addressed. Identifying and gathering data is a critical aspect of planning and developing a DH project, involving the identification of data sources, methods for collecting and digitizing the data, and ethical and legal considerations.

Selecting and implementing digital tools and methodologies are crucial for the success of a DH project, involving the identification of appropriate tools and techniques, as well as the methods for presenting and disseminating the findings. Ethical considerations are crucial in the planning and development of DH projects, involving the potential for bias and misrepresentation, the potential for misuse or misinterpretation of the results, and the representation of marginalized or vulnerable groups. Collaborative and participatory approaches are essential for the success of DH projects, involving the active engagement of various stakeholders in the research process. Evaluation and dissemination are crucial stages in the planning and development of a DH project, involving the assessment of the project's outcomes and sharing the findings with a wider audience.

As digital technologies continue to evolve, DH projects are poised to play an increasingly important role in the humanities. The future of DH projects lies in the integration of AI and ML, the development of immersive and interactive research experiences, and the creation of collaborative and participatory research experiences that engage a wider range of stakeholders in the research process. By addressing the challenges and exploring new directions, researchers can ensure that DH projects are effective, inclusive, and ethically sound, providing new opportunities for research, learning, and growth. The principles of DH projects, with their dynamic and interactive research experiences, will continue to influence the development of the humanities, ensuring that the research process is engaging, inclusive, and relevant to a wider audience. Through the use of digital tools and methodologies, researchers can create a more comprehensive and nuanced understanding of humanities data, providing new insights and perspectives on the themes, motifs, and stylistic features that shape our cultural heritage.

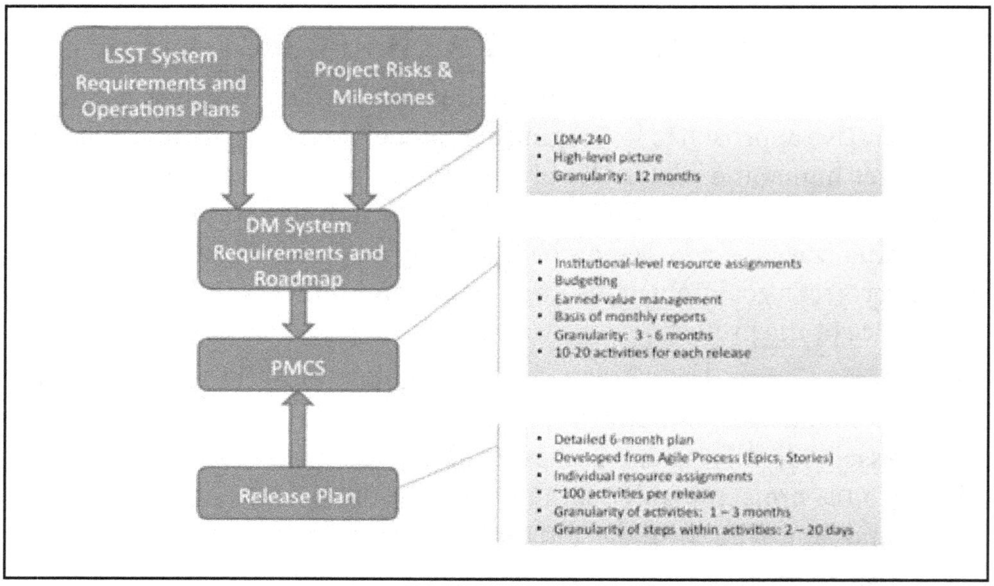

Fig: The Ultimate R&D Plan Timeline: From Idea to Product

As digital technologies continue to evolve, DH projects are poised to play an increasingly important role in the humanities. One of the key future directions in DH projects is the integration of artificial intelligence (AI) and machine learning (ML) to enhance the accuracy and sophistication of research practices.

AI and ML can be used to analyze large and complex datasets, identify patterns and anomalies, and generate insights that would be difficult or impossible to achieve through traditional methods. For example, an AI-driven DH project might use machine learning algorithms to model the evolution of a particular literary style, providing new insights into the factors that contributed to its development and influence. Additionally, AI and ML can be used to enhance the delivery of content, providing researchers with adaptive and personalized research experiences.

Another future direction in DH projects is the development of immersive and interactive research experiences that engage users in new and innovative ways. Virtual reality (VR) and augmented reality (AR) technologies can be used to create immersive and interactive research experiences that allow users to explore humanities data in a more engaging and experiential way. For example, a VR-based DH project might allow users to walk through a reconstructed historical site, interacting with virtual artifacts and characters. Similarly, an AR-based DH project might overlay digital information onto the real world, allowing users to explore and interact with humanities data in their immediate environment. This approach can help to enhance user engagement, motivation, and learning outcomes, as it provides a more immersive and interactive research experience.

The future of DH projects also lies in the development of collaborative and participatory research experiences that engage a wider range of stakeholders in the research process. Collaborative research experiences can bring together scholars, institutions, and communities to co-create and co-interpret research findings, providing a more inclusive and democratic approach to the humanities. For example, a collaborative DH project might involve scholars, institutions, and community members working together to analyze the cultural significance of a historical event, providing new insights and perspectives on the event. Participatory research experiences can also be used to engage the public in the research process, providing opportunities for learning, reflection, and action.

6.1.1 Defining the Scope and Objectives

Once the conceptualization stage is complete, the next step is to define the scope and objectives of the DH project. This involves specifying the project's boundaries, including the time period, geographical area, and types of data to be analyzed. For example, a DH project might focus on a specific historical period, such as the Renaissance, or a particular geographical region, such as Europe. Similarly, the project might involve the analysis of various types of data, including textual documents, images, and artifacts. Defining the scope and objectives is crucial for ensuring that the project is manageable and focused, as well as for identifying the key research questions and hypotheses to be addressed.

During this stage, researchers should also consider the project's objectives, which outline the specific outcomes and deliverables to be achieved. For example, the objectives might include the creation of a digital archive, the development of a data visualization tool, or the publication of a scholarly article. Additionally, researchers should consider the project's timeline, including the key milestones and deadlines, as well as the resources and budget required for its completion. This information is essential for planning and managing the project effectively, ensuring that it is completed on time and within budget.

6.1.2 Identifying and Gathering Data

One of the most critical aspects of planning and developing a DH project is identifying and gathering the data to be analyzed. This stage involves identifying the sources of data, including archives, libraries, and museums, as well as the methods for collecting and digitizing the data. For example, a DH project might involve the digitization of historical documents, the collection of oral histories, or the creation of 3D models of artifacts. During this stage, researchers should also consider the ethical and legal implications of data collection, including issues related to copyright, privacy, and cultural sensitivity. Additionally, researchers should ensure that the data is accurate, complete, and representative, as this is essential for the validity and reliability of the project's findings.

Gathering data for a DH project often involves collaboration with various stakeholders, including scholars, institutions, and communities. For example, researchers might collaborate with archivists to access and digitize historical documents, or with community members to collect oral histories. This collaborative approach not only enhances the quality and relevance of the data but also fosters a sense of ownership and engagement among the stakeholders. Additionally, researchers should consider the long-term preservation and accessibility of the data, ensuring that it is stored and managed in a way that supports future research and use.

6.1.3 Selecting and Implementing Digital Tools and Methodologies

The selection and implementation of digital tools and methodologies are crucial for the success of a DH project. This stage involves identifying the appropriate tools and techniques for analyzing and interpreting the data, as well as the methods for presenting and disseminating the findings. For example, a DH project might involve the use of text mining to analyze a corpus of literary works, or the use of data visualization to explore the relationships between different historical events. During this stage, researchers should also consider the technical requirements and constraints, including the availability of software and hardware, as well as the skills and expertise of the project team.

Implementing digital tools and methodologies in a DH project requires a systematic and iterative approach, involving the development, testing, and refinement of the tools and techniques. For example, researchers might develop a prototype of a data visualization tool, test it with a sample dataset, and refine it based on the feedback and results. This iterative approach ensures that the tools and methodologies are effective, efficient, and user-friendly, as well as for identifying and addressing any technical or methodological challenges. Additionally, researchers should consider the long-term sustainability and scalability of the tools and methodologies, ensuring that they can be adapted and expanded to support future research and use.

6.1.4 Ethical Considerations in DH Projects

Ethical considerations are crucial in the planning and development of DH projects, as they involve the interpretation and representation of humanities data. One of the primary ethical considerations is the potential for bias and misrepresentation in the data and findings. DH projects can be influenced by the researcher's own biases and interpretations, leading to a skewed or incomplete representation of the data. To address this challenge, researchers should use a range of ethical guidelines, including transparency, peer review, and interdisciplinary collaboration, to ensure the accuracy and reliability of the data and findings. For example, researchers might use peer review to evaluate the assumptions and methods used in the project, ensuring that the results are based on sound evidence and rigorous analysis.

Another ethical consideration in DH projects is the potential for misuse or misinterpretation of the results. DH projects can be used to support a wide range of interpretations and narratives, some of which may be inaccurate or misleading. To address this challenge, researchers should use a range of ethical guidelines, including transparency, accountability, and public engagement, to ensure that the results of the project are interpreted and used responsibly. For example, researchers might use public engagement to share the results of the project with a wider audience, providing context and interpretation to ensure that the results are understood and used appropriately.

DH projects also raise ethical considerations related to the representation of marginalized or vulnerable groups. DH projects can inadvertently perpetuate stereotypes or misrepresent the experiences of marginalized groups, leading to harm or injustice. To address this challenge, researchers should use a range of ethical guidelines, including inclusivity, representation, and cultural sensitivity, to ensure that the project is respectful and accurate in its representation of diverse groups. For example, researchers might use inclusive data collection and analysis techniques to ensure that the voices and experiences of marginalized groups are represented in the project.

6.1.5 Collaborative and Participatory Approaches

Collaborative and participatory approaches are essential for the success of DH projects, as they involve the active engagement of various stakeholders in the research process. Collaboration involves working with other scholars, institutions, and communities to share resources, expertise, and knowledge. For example, researchers might collaborate with archivists to access and digitize historical documents, or with community members to collect oral histories. This collaborative approach not only enhances the quality and relevance of the project but also fosters a sense of ownership and engagement among the stakeholders. Additionally, collaboration can provide access to additional resources and expertise, as well as opportunities for networking and professional development. Participatory approaches involve engaging the public and other stakeholders in the research process, providing them with opportunities to contribute to the project's goals, methods, and findings. For example, researchers might involve community members in the collection and analysis of data, or in the development and dissemination of the project's findings. This participatory approach not only enhances the relevance and impact of the project but also fosters a sense of ownership and engagement among the stakeholders. Additionally, participatory approaches can provide new insights and perspectives, as well as opportunities for learning and reflection.

6.1.6 Evaluating and Disseminating the Project

Evaluation and dissemination are crucial stages in the planning and development of a DH project, as they involve assessing the project's outcomes and sharing the findings with a wider audience. Evaluation involves assessing the project's goals, objectives, and deliverables, as well as the methods and tools used to achieve them.

For example, researchers might evaluate the effectiveness of a data visualization tool, the accuracy of the data, or the impact of the project on the stakeholders. This evaluation is essential for identifying the project's strengths and weaknesses, as well as for informing future research and practice. Additionally, evaluation can provide valuable feedback and insights, as well as opportunities for learning and improvement.

Dissemination involves sharing the project's findings with a wider audience, including scholars, students, and the public. Dissemination can take various forms, including publications, presentations, exhibitions, and digital platforms. For example, researchers might publish a scholarly article, present the findings at a conference, or create a digital exhibition. This dissemination is essential for communicating the project's findings and impact, as well as for engaging the public and other stakeholders in the research process. Additionally, dissemination can provide opportunities for collaboration, networking, and professional development.

6.2 DATA CURATION AND MANAGEMENT

In the era of big data, the importance of data curation and management has grown exponentially across academic, scientific, business, and cultural domains. As information becomes a vital resource, how it is collected, organized, preserved, and made accessible plays a crucial role in determining its value and usability.

Data curation and management refer to the processes involved in maintaining and ensuring the quality, integrity, accessibility, and usability of data throughout its lifecycle. These activities are particularly significant in research-intensive environments where data serves as the foundation for analysis, insight, and innovation. With the expansion of digital technologies, managing vast and diverse datasets has become both a challenge and a necessity.

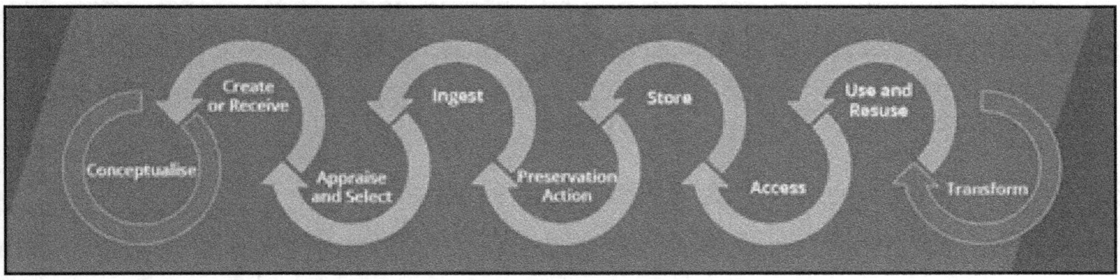

Fig: Data Curation

Data curation and management are no longer peripheral concerns but central pillars of digital knowledge infrastructure. They ensure that data, one of the most valuable assets of our time, remains reliable, accessible, and usable across generations. Whether in the sciences, humanities, or public sector, responsible data practices are essential for knowledge production, collaboration, innovation, and accountability.

By investing in robust curation and management systems, institutions can safeguard their digital heritage and empower their communities to make informed, data-driven decisions. As we move deeper into the digital age, the role of data curators and managers will only become more critical in shaping the landscape of information and knowledge.

Looking ahead, the field of data curation and management is poised to evolve in response to new technological, legal, and societal developments. Advances in artificial intelligence and machine learning may automate parts of the curation process, enabling the handling of even larger and more complex datasets. At the same time, new regulations on data protection, such as the General Data Protection Regulation (GDPR), will continue to shape the legal landscape.

The growth of open science and open data movements is also transforming expectations around data sharing and transparency. In this changing environment, the principles of good data curation—accuracy, accessibility, accountability, and ethics—will remain essential. Future curators will need to be agile, informed, and proactive in responding to emerging challenges while upholding these enduring values.

6.2.1 Scope

Data curation encompasses a broad range of activities aimed at maintaining the long-term value of data. It begins with the creation and initial documentation of data and continues through its processing, organization, preservation, and reuse. It is not merely a technical or logistical process but involves critical decision-making to determine what data to keep, how to structure it, and how to maintain its integrity. Curation also involves metadata creation, standardization, version control, and assigning proper licensing and permissions. These steps ensure that data is not only stored but is also discoverable and understandable to future users. The curated data thus becomes part of an ecosystem where it can be reused and reinterpreted across different contexts and disciplines.

6.2.2 Data Management as a Strategic Framework

While data curation focuses on the handling and enrichment of data, data management encompasses the broader framework in which data is governed. It includes planning for data storage, security, access control, backup procedures, and compliance with legal and ethical standards. Effective data management ensures that data is handled in a way that meets institutional, national, and international policies.

It includes the development of data management plans (DMPs), which are often required by research funding agencies. These plans outline how data will be created, stored, shared, and preserved, providing a strategic roadmap for responsible data stewardship. Good data management practices reduce redundancy, enhance collaboration, and protect sensitive or proprietary information.

6.2.3 Role of Metadata

Metadata, often referred to as "data about data," plays a central role in data curation. It provides context, structure, and meaning to datasets, allowing users to understand, locate, and utilize the data effectively. Metadata can include information about the data's origin, purpose, format, time of creation, and methods of collection.

It also provides insights into the limitations, accuracy, and potential uses of the data. Standardized metadata schemas, such as Dublin Core or METS, help in the interoperability and integration of data across different platforms and systems. Without proper metadata, even well-preserved data can become unintelligible or unusable over time. Thus, metadata creation is not a mere technicality but a critical component of making data accessible and meaningful.

6.2.4 Lifecycle Approach

Data curation and management are most effective when approached as a continuous, lifecycle-oriented process. This approach views data as evolving through various stages, including creation, active use, dissemination, preservation, and long-term archiving. At each stage, different curation and management actions are necessary.

For example, during the data creation stage, researchers must ensure data is well-documented and structured according to best practices. During active use, data must be backed up regularly and stored in secure environments. When data is shared or published, it needs to be accompanied by metadata and clear usage rights. In the preservation phase, strategies must be developed for long-term access, including the use of stable formats and trusted repositories. A lifecycle approach ensures that data remains usable and relevant, not just during a project's duration but for years or decades afterward.

6.2.5 Technological Tools and Platforms

The practice of data curation and management is supported by a wide range of technological tools and platforms. Institutional repositories, cloud storage systems, data catalogs, and digital preservation tools all contribute to the infrastructure needed for managing data effectively. Tools like Dataverse, DSpace, Figshare, and Zenodo allow researchers to deposit, share, and cite datasets, while version control systems like Git help track changes and collaborations. Data management systems also provide automated workflows for ingest, validation, and access control. However, technology alone is not sufficient; human expertise is essential to interpret, refine, and maintain data in context. The best results come from combining automated processes with curatorial judgment and domain-specific knowledge.

6.2.6 Ethical Considerations

The ethical dimensions of data curation and management are increasingly under scrutiny, especially as data becomes more personal, pervasive, and powerful. Issues of privacy, consent, data ownership, and digital rights must be considered carefully. Curators must ensure that data collected from individuals or communities is handled respectfully and transparently. This involves obtaining informed consent, anonymizing personal identifiers, and adhering to ethical standards in data sharing and reuse. Additionally, questions arise about who has access to curated data and whose voices or experiences are represented in the data. Ethical data curation goes beyond technical stewardship and includes a responsibility to consider the societal and cultural implications of data practices. It challenges curators to think about power dynamics, inclusion, and the potential misuse of information.

6.2.7 Interdisciplinary Nature

Data curation and management are inherently interdisciplinary activities, drawing on knowledge from information science, computer science, domain-specific expertise, and archival practice. In academic settings, data curation teams often include librarians, IT specialists, subject-matter experts, and researchers. Each brings a unique perspective that enriches the curation process. For instance, librarians may contribute expertise in metadata and classification, while IT professionals manage storage and security protocols. Researchers provide insights into the context and significance of the data. This collaborative model fosters innovation and ensures that data systems are robust, user-friendly, and aligned with scholarly needs. As research becomes increasingly collaborative and data-driven, the interdisciplinary nature of data curation will continue to grow in importance.

6.2.8 Training and Capacity Building

For data curation and management practices to be sustainable, institutions must invest in training and capacity building. This includes formal education programs in data science, information management, and digital curation, as well as professional development opportunities for faculty, researchers, and staff. Workshops, online courses, and certifications can help individuals acquire the necessary skills to curate and manage data effectively. Developing a culture of data stewardship within organizations also involves raising awareness of best practices, encouraging responsible data behaviors, and recognizing data-related contributions in academic and professional settings. As the demand for skilled data professionals rises, educational institutions must take the lead in preparing the next generation of data curators.

6.3 SUSTAINABILITY AND LONG-TERM PRESERVATION

In an era marked by rapid technological advancement and environmental challenges, the concept of sustainability has become inextricably linked with long-term preservation efforts across multiple domains. The need to maintain access to both digital and physical artifacts for future generations while minimizing ecological impact represents one of the most pressing challenges of our time.

Cultural heritage institutions, data centers, and government agencies worldwide are grappling with how to preserve increasingly complex digital assets alongside traditional physical collections in ways that are both environmentally responsible and technologically feasible. This dual mandate requires rethinking traditional preservation paradigms to account for the energy consumption of digital storage, the material durability of physical artifacts, and the evolving nature of how societies value and access preserved materials.

Sustainable long-term preservation ultimately represents an ethical commitment to intergenerational equity—the principle that future generations deserve access to the same breadth of cultural and scientific heritage available today. This expansive view of preservation integrates environmental responsibility with cultural stewardship, recognizing that preserved materials have little value if the ecosystems supporting human civilization collapse. The field is moving toward holistic models that measure success not just in terms of object survival but in terms of ongoing accessibility, contextual integrity, and ecological impact. As preservation professionals navigate this complex landscape, they increasingly serve as mediators between past and future, between technological possibility and environmental limits, and between specialized expertise and public responsibility. The most sustainable preservation strategies will be those that recognize preservation as a dynamic process rather than a static state—one that must continuously adapt to changing environmental conditions, technological capabilities, and societal needs while remaining true to its fundamental mission of safeguarding our shared inheritance for centuries yet to come.

The most promising developments in sustainable preservation emerge at the intersection of multiple technological frontiers. Artificial intelligence applications are enabling predictive preservation—anticipating degradation patterns and optimizing intervention timing to maximize resource efficiency. Quantum computing may eventually revolutionize digital preservation through theoretically unbreakable encryption and massively parallel processing for format migration tasks.

Advanced materials science is yielding new storage media such as 5D quartz glass that can theoretically preserve data for billions of years with minimal energy input. Perhaps most significantly, the convergence of biological and digital technologies suggests future possibilities like using synthetic DNA for both artifact conservation treatments and ultra-dense, durable data storage. These technological synergies must be guided by preservation ethics to ensure they serve rather than distort cultural memory and knowledge transmission. The sustainable preservation systems of the future will likely combine cutting-edge science with time-tested principles of careful stewardship in hybrid analog-digital configurations that hedge against technological obsolescence.

6.3.1 Digital Preservation in the Age of Exponential Data Growth

The explosive growth of digital information has created unprecedented challenges for long-term preservation strategies. Current estimates suggest the global datasphere will exceed 175 zettabytes by 2025, with much of this information requiring active preservation measures to remain accessible. Unlike physical artifacts that may survive passively for centuries if properly stored, digital objects demand continuous intervention to combat format obsolescence, hardware degradation, and software dependency. Sustainable digital preservation requires multilayered approaches including format migration, emulation strategies, and robust metadata standards that maintain contextual understanding across technological generations. The environmental impact of massive data storage infrastructures adds another dimension to these challenges, with data centers currently consuming approximately 1% of global electricity production. Emerging solutions such as DNA-based data storage and ceramic nanolithography promise dramatically reduced energy requirements and vastly extended lifespan potential, though these technologies remain in developmental stages. The field must balance immediate practical concerns with visionary experimentation to create preservation systems capable of enduring across centuries rather than just decades.

6.3.2 Material Science and the Preservation of Physical Artifacts

While digital preservation dominates contemporary discourse, the conservation of physical artifacts remains equally critical to maintaining humanity's cultural and scientific legacy. Advances in material science are revolutionizing approaches to artifact preservation through nanotechnology-based consolidants for fragile materials, environmentally responsive storage systems, and non-invasive analysis techniques. The development of passive preservation environments that maintain stable temperature and humidity without energy-intensive climate control represents a major sustainability breakthrough. Researchers are exploring biomimetic solutions inspired by natural preservation phenomena—such as the chemical processes that preserve fossils—to develop new treatments for paper, textiles, and organic artifacts. Perhaps most importantly, the field is shifting toward preventive conservation strategies that emphasize proper storage and handling over invasive restoration, reducing both environmental impact and long-term maintenance requirements. These material innovations must be paired with sustainable sourcing practices to ensure preservation methods don't inadvertently contribute to resource depletion or ecological harm through their supply chains.

6.3.3 Policy Frameworks for Sustainable Preservation

Effective long-term preservation requires robust policy frameworks that align institutional practices with sustainability principles at local, national, and international levels. UNESCO's Recommendation on Historic Urban Landscapes exemplifies the growing recognition that preservation must be integrated with sustainable development goals rather than treated as separate concern. Digital preservation faces particular policy challenges regarding intellectual property rights, privacy regulations, and cross-border data flows that can hinder collaborative preservation efforts. Emerging policy models emphasize the concept of "stewardship ecosystems" where multiple stakeholders share responsibility for preservation according to their capacities and interests. Climate change adaptation policies increasingly incorporate cultural heritage protection measures, recognizing that historic sites and collections represent both vulnerable assets and potential resources for sustainable community development. The most forward-thinking policies treat preservation not as a cost center but as an investment in social resilience and sustainable economic development through cultural tourism and educational resources.

6.3.4 Community-Centered Approaches to Preservation

The most sustainable preservation strategies actively engage the communities most connected to and affected by the materials being preserved. Indigenous knowledge systems in particular offer valuable models for intergenerational preservation that integrates cultural practice with environmental stewardship. Community archives and decentralized preservation networks are proving particularly effective for safeguarding intangible heritage and marginalized histories that formal institutions have traditionally neglected. These participatory models often demonstrate greater sustainability than top-down approaches by creating local ownership and aligning preservation with community needs and values.

Digital tools have enabled new forms of community engagement with preservation through crowdsourced transcription projects, collaborative metadata creation, and virtual volunteer programs. However, true sustainability requires moving beyond extractive models of community participation to establish equitable partnerships that share authority and benefits. The growing "citizen archivist" movement demonstrates how public involvement can simultaneously expand preservation capacity and strengthen societal connections to cultural heritage.

6.3.5 Economic Models for Sustainable Stewardship

The financial sustainability of preservation initiatives remains one of the field's most persistent challenges, requiring innovative approaches to funding and valuation. Traditional models relying on government appropriations or philanthropic giving prove increasingly inadequate for maintaining preservation infrastructure amid growing collections and rising costs. Alternative economic strategies include monetizing preservation byproducts like digitization metadata for research applications, developing preservation-as-a-service offerings for private collectors, and creating cultural heritage impact investment funds.

Some institutions are experimenting with blockchain-based models for decentralized funding of preservation projects through micro-patronage and non-fungible tokens (NFTs) representing shares in conservation efforts. The most comprehensive approaches seek to quantify the full economic value of preservation—including its contributions to education, research, community identity, and creative industries—to justify sustained investment. These economic innovations must be carefully balanced against ethical considerations to prevent commercialization from distorting preservation priorities or creating inequitable access to cultural materials.

6.3.6 Climate Change and Preservation Imperatives

The accelerating impacts of climate change have made sustainable preservation not just an ideal but an urgent necessity. Rising sea levels threaten coastal archives and historic sites, while increasing temperature volatility destabilizes preservation environments for both physical and digital collections. Wildfires, floods, and extreme weather events demand new approaches to disaster preparedness that account for climate projections rather than historical patterns. Preservation strategies are adapting through climate-resilient storage facility design, decentralized digital preservation networks that reduce single-point vulnerability, and managed retreat protocols for immovable heritage. Paradoxically, preservation institutions must also address their own contributions to climate change through energy-intensive conservation practices and facility operations. Life cycle assessment methodologies are being applied to preservation activities to identify high-impact areas for emissions reduction while maintaining collection safety. The field is increasingly recognizing that truly sustainable preservation must simultaneously mitigate climate impacts on collections and mitigate preservation's impacts on the climate.

6.3.7 Education and Professional Development for Sustainable Preservation

Building capacity for sustainable preservation requires transformative approaches to professional education and public awareness. Traditional conservation training programs are expanding to incorporate sustainability literacy, materials life cycle analysis, and energy-efficient preservation technologies. Interdisciplinary programs are emerging that bridge preservation science with environmental studies, data science, and sustainable design. Professional certification systems are beginning to incorporate sustainability standards for archival storage, digital preservation, and conservation treatment.

Public education initiatives aim to cultivate broader understanding of preservation as a shared responsibility with environmental dimensions, moving beyond the perception of preservation as an elite or esoteric concern. These educational efforts must address the tension between established preservation orthodoxies and emerging sustainable practices, preparing professionals to navigate ethical dilemmas where perfect preservation may conflict with environmental responsibility. The development of open educational resources in sustainable preservation helps democratize access to this critical knowledge across institutional and national boundaries.

6.4 COLLABORATION AND CROWDSOURCING IN DH

Collaboration and crowdsourcing have become integral components of Digital Humanities, transforming the way research is conducted, data is collected, and knowledge is disseminated. Collaboration in DH involves working with other scholars, institutions, and communities to share resources, expertise, and knowledge. Crowdsourcing, on the other hand, involves engaging the public and other stakeholders in the research process, providing them with opportunities to contribute to the project's goals, methods, and findings. Together, collaboration and crowdsourcing foster a more inclusive, democratic, and participatory approach to the humanities, enhancing the quality and impact of research, as well as the engagement, education, and outreach of the public.

Collaboration and crowdsourcing in DH can take many forms, from interdisciplinary collaboration to institutional and community collaboration, as well as from citizen science to community-based and global crowdsourcing. These approaches offer numerous benefits, including the enhancement of research quality and impact, the enhancement of public engagement, education, and outreach, and the fostering of a sense of community and belonging. However, collaboration and crowdsourcing in DH also face several challenges, including the need for effective communication and coordination, the need for ethical and responsible practices, and technical and methodological challenges.

To address these challenges, researchers should use a range of communication and coordination tools, ethical and responsible practices, and technical and methodological tools, as well as establish clear and transparent protocols for communication, coordination, ethics, and methodology. The future of collaboration and crowdsourcing in DH lies in the integration of AI and ML, the development of immersive and interactive research experiences, and the creation of collaborative and participatory research experiences that engage a wider range of stakeholders in the research process.

By addressing the challenges and exploring new directions, researchers can ensure that collaboration and crowdsourcing in DH are effective, inclusive, and ethically sound, providing new opportunities for research, learning, and growth. The principles of collaboration and crowdsourcing in DH, with their dynamic and interactive research experiences, will continue to influence the development of the humanities, ensuring that the research process is engaging, inclusive, and relevant to a wider audience. Through the use of digital tools and methodologies, researchers can create a more comprehensive and nuanced understanding of humanities data, providing new insights and perspectives on the themes, motifs, and stylistic features that shape our cultural heritage.

As digital technologies continue to evolve, collaboration and crowdsourcing in Digital Humanities are poised to play an increasingly important role in the humanities. One of the key future directions in collaboration and crowdsourcing in DH is the integration of artificial intelligence (AI) and machine learning (ML) to enhance the accuracy and sophistication of research practices. AI and ML can be used to analyze large and complex datasets, identify patterns and anomalies, and generate insights that would be difficult or impossible to achieve through traditional methods. For example, an AI-driven collaborative project might use machine learning algorithms to model the evolution of a particular literary style, providing new insights into the factors that contributed to its development and influence. Additionally, AI and ML can be used to enhance the delivery of content, providing researchers with adaptive and personalized research experiences.

Another future direction in collaboration and crowdsourcing in DH is the development of immersive and interactive research experiences that engage users in new and innovative ways. Virtual reality (VR) and augmented reality (AR) technologies can be used to create immersive and interactive research experiences that allow users to explore humanities data in a more engaging and experiential way.

For example, a VR-based collaborative project might allow users to walk through a reconstructed historical site, interacting with virtual artifacts and characters. Similarly, an AR-based collaborative project might overlay digital information onto the real world, allowing users to explore and interact with humanities data in their immediate environment. This approach can help to enhance user engagement, motivation, and learning outcomes, as it provides a more immersive and interactive research experience.

The future of collaboration and crowdsourcing in DH also lies in the development of collaborative and participatory research experiences that engage a wider range of stakeholders in the research process. Collaborative research experiences can bring together scholars, institutions, and communities to co-create and co-interpret research findings, providing a more inclusive and democratic approach to the humanities. For example, a collaborative project might involve scholars, institutions, and community members working together to analyze the cultural significance of a historical event, providing new insights and perspectives on the event. Participatory research experiences can also be used to engage the public in the research process, providing opportunities for learning, reflection, and action.

6.4.1 Types

Collaboration in Digital Humanities can take many forms, from small-scale partnerships to large-scale, interdisciplinary projects. One of the most common types of collaboration in DH is interdisciplinary collaboration, which involves working with scholars from different disciplines to share resources, expertise, and knowledge. For example, a DH project might involve collaboration between historians, computer scientists, and digital archivists to analyze and interpret a collection of historical documents. This interdisciplinary approach allows scholars to explore complex problems from multiple angles, developing a more comprehensive and nuanced understanding of the subject matter. Additionally, interdisciplinary collaboration can provide access to additional resources and expertise, as well as opportunities for networking and professional development.

Another type of collaboration in DH is institutional collaboration, which involves working with other institutions, such as universities, museums, and libraries, to share resources, expertise, and knowledge. For example, a DH project might involve collaboration between a university and a museum to digitize and analyze a collection of artifacts. This institutional collaboration can provide access to additional resources and expertise, as well as opportunities for networking and professional development. Additionally, institutional collaboration can enhance the visibility and impact of the project, as it involves the participation of multiple institutions and stakeholders. For example, a collaborative project between a university and a museum can provide opportunities for public engagement, education, and outreach, as well as for the preservation and dissemination of cultural heritage.

Community collaboration is another important type of collaboration in DH, which involves working with local communities to share resources, expertise, and knowledge. For example, a DH project might involve collaboration with a local community to collect and analyze oral histories, providing insights into the community's cultural and historical contexts. This community collaboration can provide access to additional resources and expertise, as well as opportunities for networking and professional development. Additionally, community collaboration can enhance the relevance and impact of the project, as it involves the participation of the community and addresses their needs and interests. For example, a collaborative project with a local community can provide opportunities for education, outreach, and empowerment, as well as for the preservation and dissemination of local history and culture.

6.4.2 Types of Crowdsourcing

Crowdsourcing in Digital Humanities can also take many forms, from small-scale, community-based projects to large-scale, global initiatives. One of the most common types of crowdsourcing in DH is citizen science, which involves engaging the public in the collection and analysis of scientific data. For example, a citizen science project might involve the public in the collection of environmental data, such as water quality or air pollution, providing insights into the environmental conditions of a particular region. This citizen science approach can provide access to additional data and expertise, as well as opportunities for public engagement, education, and outreach. Additionally, citizen science can enhance the relevance and impact of the project, as it involves the participation of the public and addresses their needs and interests.

Another type of crowdsourcing in DH is community-based crowdsourcing, which involves engaging local communities in the collection and analysis of data. For example, a community-based crowdsourcing project might involve the collection of oral histories, providing insights into the cultural and historical contexts of a particular community. This community-based approach can provide access to additional data and expertise, as well as opportunities for public engagement, education, and outreach. Additionally, community-based crowdsourcing can enhance the relevance and impact of the project, as it involves the participation of the community and addresses their needs and interests. For example, a community-based crowdsourcing project can provide opportunities for education, outreach, and empowerment, as well as for the preservation and dissemination of local history and culture.

Global crowdsourcing is another important type of crowdsourcing in DH, which involves engaging a global community in the collection and analysis of data. For example, a global crowdsourcing project might involve the transcription of historical documents, providing access to a wide range of historical sources and insights. This global approach can provide access to additional data and expertise, as well as opportunities for public engagement, education, and outreach. Additionally, global crowdsourcing can enhance the relevance and impact of the project, as it involves the participation of a global community and addresses their needs and interests. For example, a global crowdsourcing project can provide opportunities for collaboration, networking, and professional development, as well as for the preservation and dissemination of global history and culture.

6.4.3 Benefits

Collaboration and crowdsourcing in Digital Humanities offer numerous benefits, both for researchers and for the broader field of the humanities. One of the primary benefits is the enhancement of research quality and impact, as collaboration and crowdsourcing provide access to additional resources, expertise, and data. For example, a collaborative project might involve the participation of scholars from different disciplines, providing a more comprehensive and nuanced understanding of the subject matter. Similarly, a crowdsourcing project might involve the participation of the public, providing access to additional data and insights. This enhancement of research quality and impact can lead to more innovative, relevant, and impactful research, as well as to the development of new methods, tools, and approaches.

Another benefit of collaboration and crowdsourcing in DH is the enhancement of public engagement, education, and outreach. Collaboration and crowdsourcing provide opportunities for the public to engage with research, providing them with opportunities to contribute to the project's goals, methods, and findings. For example, a collaborative project might involve the participation of local communities, providing them with opportunities to learn about and contribute to the preservation and dissemination of local history and culture. Similarly, a crowdsourcing project might involve the participation of a global community, providing them with opportunities to learn about and contribute to the preservation and dissemination of global history and culture. This enhancement of public engagement, education, and outreach can lead to a more inclusive, democratic, and participatory approach to the humanities, as well as to the development of new methods, tools, and approaches for public engagement.

Collaboration and crowdsourcing in DH also foster a sense of community and belonging, as they involve the active participation of a diverse range of stakeholders in the research process. This collaborative and participatory approach not only enhances the quality and impact of the research but also fosters a sense of ownership and engagement among the stakeholders. For example, a collaborative project might involve the participation of scholars, institutions, and communities, providing them with opportunities to share resources, expertise, and knowledge. Similarly, a crowdsourcing project might involve the participation of the public, providing them with opportunities to contribute to the project's goals, methods, and findings. This sense of community and belonging is important for the success of the project, as it provides the support and encouragement needed to achieve the project's goals and objectives.

6.4.4 Challenges

Despite their potential, collaboration and crowdsourcing in Digital Humanities face several challenges that can limit their effectiveness and impact. One of the primary challenges is the need for effective communication and coordination, as collaboration and crowdsourcing involve the participation of a diverse range of stakeholders. Effective communication and coordination are essential for ensuring that the project's goals, methods, and findings are shared and understood by all stakeholders, as well as for resolving any conflicts or disagreements that may arise. To address this challenge, researchers should use a range of communication and coordination tools, including email, social media, and project management software, to ensure effective and efficient communication and coordination. Additionally, researchers should establish clear and transparent communication and coordination protocols, ensuring that all stakeholders are informed and involved in the decision-making process.

Another challenge in collaboration and crowdsourcing in DH is the need for ethical and responsible practices, as these approaches involve the participation of a diverse range of stakeholders. Ethical and responsible practices are essential for ensuring that the project's goals, methods, and findings are respectful and accurate in their representation of diverse groups, as well as for protecting the privacy and security of the data and participants. To address this challenge, researchers should use a range of ethical and responsible practices, including informed consent, data protection, and cultural sensitivity, to ensure the ethical and responsible conduct of the project. Additionally, researchers should establish clear and transparent ethical and responsible practices protocols, ensuring that all stakeholders are informed and involved in the decision-making process.

Collaboration and crowdsourcing in DH also face technical and methodological challenges, particularly in relation to the collection, analysis, and interpretation of data. These approaches involve the participation of a diverse range of stakeholders, who may have different levels of expertise, skills, and knowledge. To address this challenge, researchers should use a range of technical and methodological tools, including data collection, analysis, and visualization tools, to ensure the accuracy and reliability of the data and findings. Additionally, researchers should establish clear and transparent technical and methodological protocols, ensuring that all stakeholders are informed and involved in the decision-making process.

6.4.5 Ethical Considerations

Ethical considerations are crucial in the development and use of collaboration and crowdsourcing in Digital Humanities, as they involve the participation of a diverse range of stakeholders. One of the primary ethical considerations is the potential for bias and misrepresentation in the data and findings. Collaboration and crowdsourcing can be influenced by the participants' own biases and interpretations, leading to a skewed or incomplete representation of the data. To address this challenge, researchers should use a range of ethical guidelines, including transparency, peer review, and interdisciplinary collaboration, to ensure the accuracy and reliability of the data and findings. For example, researchers might use peer review to evaluate the assumptions and methods used in the project, ensuring that the results are based on sound evidence and rigorous analysis.

Another ethical consideration in collaboration and crowdsourcing in DH is the potential for misuse or misinterpretation of the results. Collaboration and crowdsourcing can be used to support a wide range of interpretations and narratives, some of which may be inaccurate or misleading. To address this challenge, researchers should use a range of ethical guidelines, including transparency, accountability, and public engagement, to ensure that the results of the project are interpreted and used responsibly. For example, researchers might use public engagement to share the results of the project with a wider audience, providing context and interpretation to ensure that the results are understood and used appropriately. Collaboration and crowdsourcing in DH also raise ethical considerations related to the representation of marginalized or vulnerable groups. Collaboration and crowdsourcing can inadvertently perpetuate stereotypes or misrepresent the experiences of marginalized groups, leading to harm or injustice. To address this challenge, researchers should use a range of ethical guidelines, including inclusivity, representation, and cultural sensitivity, to ensure that the project is respectful and accurate in its representation of diverse groups. For example, researchers might use inclusive data collection and analysis techniques to ensure that the voices and experiences of marginalized groups are represented in the project.

6.5 PROJECT EVALUATION AND IMPACT ASSESSMENT

Project evaluation and impact assessment are crucial components of Digital Humanities projects, ensuring that the research is conducted effectively, efficiently, and ethically. These processes involve systematically assessing the outcomes, impact, and sustainability of DH projects, providing valuable insights into their strengths, weaknesses, and areas for improvement. Project evaluation focuses on assessing the project's goals, objectives, and deliverables, as well as the methods and tools used to achieve them. Impact assessment, on the other hand, focuses on evaluating the broader implications and effects of the project, including its social, cultural, and economic impacts. Together, project evaluation and impact assessment provide a comprehensive understanding of the project's success and its contributions to the field of Digital Humanities.

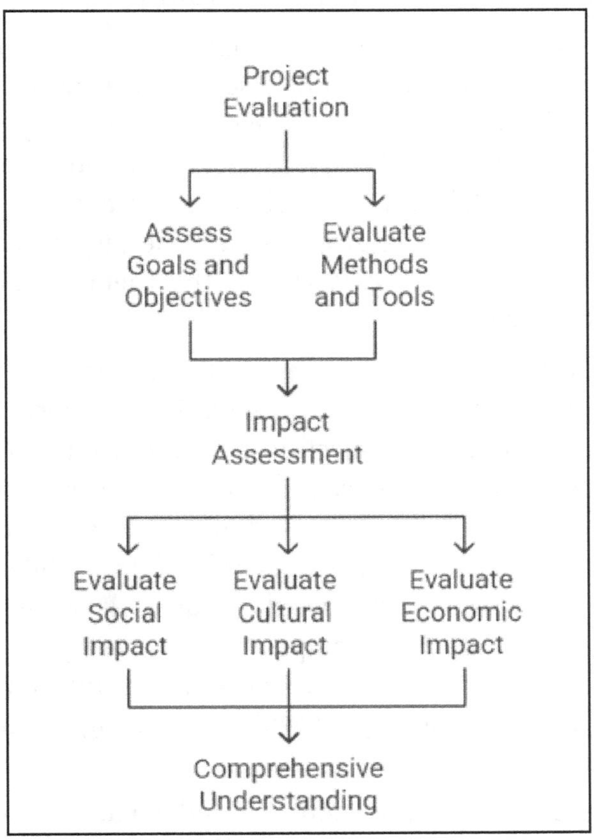

Fig: Project Evaluation and Impact Assessment in Digital Humanities

Project evaluation and impact assessment in DH involve several key components, including the assessment of the project's goals and objectives, methods and tools, and deliverables, as well as the assessment of the project's social, cultural, and economic impacts. These processes employ a range of methods and tools, including qualitative evaluation, quantitative evaluation, and mixed-methods evaluation, to assess the project's outcomes, impact, and sustainability. Ethical considerations are crucial in the development and use of project evaluation and impact assessment in DH, involving the potential for bias and misrepresentation, the potential for misuse or misinterpretation of the results, and the representation of marginalized or vulnerable groups.

The future of project evaluation and impact assessment in DH lies in the integration of AI and ML, the development of immersive and interactive evaluation and assessment experiences, and the creation of collaborative and participatory evaluation and assessment experiences that engage a wider range of stakeholders in the evaluation and assessment process. By addressing the challenges and exploring new directions, researchers can ensure that project evaluation and impact assessment in DH are effective, inclusive, and ethically sound, providing new opportunities for research, learning, and growth.

The principles of project evaluation and impact assessment in DH, with their dynamic and interactive evaluation and assessment experiences, will continue to influence the development of the humanities, ensuring that the research process is engaging, inclusive, and relevant to a wider audience. Through the use of digital tools and methodologies, researchers can create a more comprehensive and nuanced understanding of the project's outcomes, impact, and sustainability, providing new insights and perspectives on the themes, motifs, and stylistic features that shape our cultural heritage.

As digital technologies continue to evolve, project evaluation and impact assessment in Digital Humanities are poised to play an increasingly important role in the field. One of the key future directions in project evaluation and impact assessment in DH is the integration of artificial intelligence (AI) and machine learning (ML) to enhance the accuracy and sophistication of the evaluation and assessment processes. AI and ML can be used to analyze large and complex datasets, identify patterns and anomalies, and generate insights that would be difficult or impossible to achieve through traditional methods. For example, an AI-driven project evaluation and impact assessment might use machine learning algorithms to model the project's outcomes, impact, and sustainability, providing new insights into the factors that contributed to its success or failure.

Another future direction in project evaluation and impact assessment in DH is the development of immersive and interactive evaluation and assessment experiences that engage users in new and innovative ways. Virtual reality (VR) and augmented reality (AR) technologies can be used to create immersive and interactive evaluation and assessment experiences that allow users to explore the project's outcomes, impact, and sustainability in a more engaging and experiential way. For example, a VR-based project evaluation and impact assessment might allow users to walk through a virtual representation of the project, interacting with virtual artifacts and characters. Similarly, an AR-based project evaluation and impact assessment might overlay digital information onto the real world, allowing users to explore and interact with the project's outcomes, impact, and sustainability in their immediate environment. This approach can help to enhance user engagement, motivation, and learning outcomes, as it provides a more immersive and interactive evaluation and assessment experience.

The future of project evaluation and impact assessment in DH also lies in the development of collaborative and participatory evaluation and assessment experiences that engage a wider range of stakeholders in the evaluation and assessment process. Collaborative evaluation and assessment experiences can bring together scholars, institutions, and communities to co-create and co-interpret the project's outcomes, impact, and sustainability, providing a more inclusive and democratic approach to the evaluation and assessment process. For example, a collaborative project evaluation and impact assessment might involve scholars, institutions, and community members working together to analyze the project's outcomes, impact, and sustainability, providing new insights and perspectives on the project. Participatory evaluation and assessment experiences can also be used to engage the public in the evaluation and assessment process, providing opportunities for learning, reflection, and action.

6.5.1 Key Components of Project Evaluation in Digital Humanities

Project evaluation in Digital Humanities involves several key components, each focusing on different aspects of the project. One of the primary components is the assessment of the project's goals and objectives, which involves evaluating the clarity, relevance, and feasibility of the project's aims. This assessment ensures that the project's goals and objectives are well-defined, achievable, and aligned with the project's overall mission and vision. For example, a DH project might aim to digitize and analyze a collection of historical documents, providing new insights into the cultural and historical contexts that shaped their development. The assessment of the project's goals and objectives would involve evaluating the clarity, relevance, and feasibility of this aim, ensuring that it is well-defined, achievable, and aligned with the project's overall mission and vision.

Another key component of project evaluation in DH is the assessment of the project's methods and tools, which involves evaluating the effectiveness, efficiency, and appropriateness of the methods and tools used to achieve the project's goals and objectives. This assessment ensures that the project's methods and tools are well-designed, feasible, and aligned with the project's goals and objectives. For example, a DH project might use text mining to analyze a corpus of literary works, identifying recurring motifs, tracking the evolution of themes, and revealing hidden patterns and structures within the texts. The assessment of the project's methods and tools would involve evaluating the effectiveness, efficiency, and appropriateness of this method, ensuring that it is well-designed, feasible, and aligned with the project's goals and objectives.

The assessment of the project's deliverables is also a crucial component of project evaluation in DH, which involves evaluating the quality, relevance, and impact of the project's outcomes and outputs. This assessment ensures that the project's deliverables are well-designed, feasible, and aligned with the project's goals and objectives. For example, a DH project might produce a digital archive, a data visualization tool, or a scholarly publication. The assessment of the project's deliverables would involve evaluating the quality, relevance, and impact of these outcomes and outputs, ensuring that they are well-designed, feasible, and aligned with the project's goals and objectives.

6.5.2 Key Components of Impact Assessment in Digital Humanities

Impact assessment in Digital Humanities involves several key components, each focusing on different aspects of the project's broader implications and effects. One of the primary components is the assessment of the project's social impact, which involves evaluating the project's effects on society, including its contributions to social justice, equity, and inclusion. This assessment ensures that the project's social impact is positive, sustainable, and aligned with the project's goals and objectives. For example, a DH project might aim to preserve and disseminate the cultural heritage of a marginalized community, providing new insights into their history, culture, and identity. The assessment of the project's social impact would involve evaluating the project's contributions to social justice, equity, and inclusion, ensuring that they are positive, sustainable, and aligned with the project's goals and objectives.

Another key component of impact assessment in DH is the assessment of the project's cultural impact, which involves evaluating the project's effects on culture, including its contributions to cultural preservation, dissemination, and innovation. This assessment ensures that the project's cultural impact is positive, sustainable, and aligned with the project's goals and objectives. For example, a DH project might aim to digitize and analyze a collection of artifacts, providing new insights into their cultural significance and historical contexts. The assessment of the project's cultural impact would involve evaluating the project's contributions to cultural preservation, dissemination, and innovation, ensuring that they are positive, sustainable, and aligned with the project's goals and objectives. The assessment of the project's economic impact is also a crucial component of impact assessment in DH, which involves evaluating the project's effects on the economy, including its contributions to economic development, innovation, and sustainability. This assessment ensures that the project's economic impact is positive, sustainable, and aligned with the project's goals and objectives. For example, a DH project might aim to develop a new digital tool or technology, providing new opportunities for economic development, innovation, and sustainability. The assessment of the project's economic impact would involve evaluating the project's contributions to economic development, innovation, and sustainability, ensuring that they are positive, sustainable, and aligned with the project's goals and objectives.

6.5.3 Methods and Tools for Project Evaluation and Impact Assessment

Project evaluation and impact assessment in Digital Humanities employ a range of methods and tools to assess the outcomes, impact, and sustainability of DH projects. One of the most common methods is qualitative evaluation, which involves the use of qualitative data, such as interviews, focus groups, and case studies, to assess the project's outcomes and impact. Qualitative evaluation provides in-depth, context-rich insights into the project's strengths, weaknesses, and areas for improvement, as well as into the perspectives and experiences of the project's stakeholders. For example, a qualitative evaluation of a DH project might involve conducting interviews with the project's participants, stakeholders, and beneficiaries, providing insights into their experiences, perspectives, and recommendations for improvement.

Quantitative evaluation is another important method for project evaluation and impact assessment in DH, which involves the use of quantitative data, such as surveys, statistical analysis, and performance metrics, to assess the project's outcomes and impact. Quantitative evaluation provides objective, measurable insights into the project's strengths, weaknesses, and areas for improvement, as well as into the project's effectiveness, efficiency, and sustainability. For example, a quantitative evaluation of a DH project might involve conducting a survey of the project's participants, stakeholders, and beneficiaries, providing insights into their satisfaction, engagement, and outcomes.

Mixed-methods evaluation is also a valuable approach for project evaluation and impact assessment in DH, which involves the use of both qualitative and quantitative data to assess the project's outcomes and impact. Mixed-methods evaluation provides a comprehensive, nuanced, and context-rich understanding of the project's strengths, weaknesses, and areas for improvement, as well as into the project's effectiveness, efficiency, and sustainability. For example, a mixed-methods evaluation of a DH project might involve conducting both qualitative and quantitative assessments, providing insights into the project's outcomes, impact, and sustainability from multiple perspectives and angles.

6.5.4 Ethical Considerations in Project Evaluation and Impact Assessment

Ethical considerations are crucial in the development and use of project evaluation and impact assessment in Digital Humanities, as they involve the assessment of the project's outcomes, impact, and sustainability. One of the primary ethical considerations is the potential for bias and misrepresentation in the evaluation and assessment processes. Project evaluation and impact assessment can be influenced by the evaluator's own biases and interpretations, leading to a skewed or incomplete representation of the project's outcomes, impact, and sustainability. To address this challenge, evaluators should use a range of ethical guidelines, including transparency, peer review, and interdisciplinary collaboration, to ensure the accuracy and reliability of the evaluation and assessment processes. For example, evaluators might use peer review to evaluate the assumptions and methods used in the evaluation and assessment, ensuring that the results are based on sound evidence and rigorous analysis.

Another ethical consideration in project evaluation and impact assessment in DH is the potential for misuse or misinterpretation of the results. Project evaluation and impact assessment can be used to support a wide range of interpretations and narratives, some of which may be inaccurate or misleading. To address this challenge, evaluators should use a range of ethical guidelines, including transparency, accountability, and public engagement, to ensure that the results of the evaluation and assessment are interpreted and used responsibly. For example, evaluators might use public engagement to share the results of the evaluation and assessment with a wider audience, providing context and interpretation to ensure that the results are understood and used appropriately.

Project evaluation and impact assessment in DH also raise ethical considerations related to the representation of marginalized or vulnerable groups. Project evaluation and impact assessment can inadvertently perpetuate stereotypes or misrepresent the experiences of marginalized groups, leading to harm or injustice. To address this challenge, evaluators should use a range of ethical guidelines, including inclusivity, representation, and cultural sensitivity, to ensure that the evaluation and assessment are respectful and accurate in their representation of diverse groups. For example, evaluators might use inclusive data collection and analysis techniques to ensure that the voices and experiences of marginalized groups are represented in the evaluation and assessment.

6.6 FUNDING AND GRANT WRITING FOR DH INITIATIVES

Funding and grant writing are central to the growth and sustainability of Digital Humanities initiatives. While the process can be complex and competitive, it also offers significant opportunities for innovation, collaboration, and scholarly impact. By understanding the funding landscape, planning strategically, crafting compelling narratives, and aligning with funders' priorities, DH scholars can greatly increase their chances of securing support. Ultimately, successful grant writing in the DH context is not just about securing resources but about articulating a vision that bridges the digital and the humanistic, opening new pathways for knowledge and engagement in the 21st century.

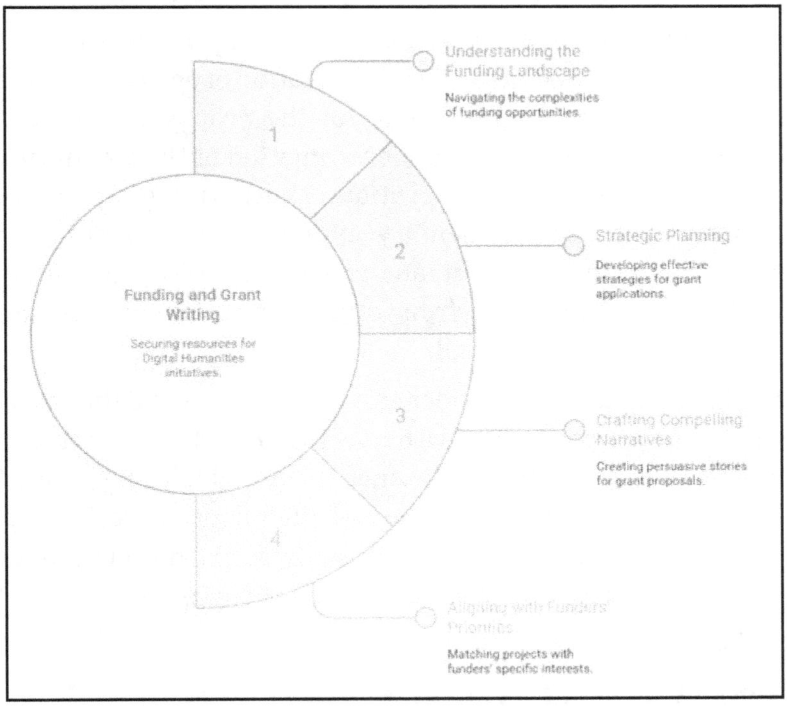

Fig: Unveiling the Dimensions of DH Funding

6.6.1 Funding Landscape for DH

Funding for Digital Humanities comes from a diverse array of sources, including governmental agencies, private foundations, international bodies, educational institutions, and even corporate sponsors. In countries like the United States, the National Endowment for the Humanities (NEH) offers numerous grants specifically tailored to support DH research and infrastructure. Similarly, the European Commission, through its Horizon Europe framework and earlier through Horizon 2020, has been a significant funder of DH projects across Europe. In addition to these large institutional funders, various universities also support DH initiatives through internal research grants and collaborative funding opportunities. Many academic libraries, cultural heritage institutions, and museums also allocate resources for digital preservation and digital storytelling, which are closely linked to DH.

Despite the increasing number of opportunities, obtaining funding for DH projects remains highly competitive. This is due in part to the interdisciplinary nature of DH, which often does not align neatly with traditional funding categories. As a result, DH grant seekers must be particularly strategic in articulating the relevance, innovation, and impact of their proposals. A nuanced understanding of the priorities and expectations of different funding bodies is therefore essential in crafting successful applications.

6.6.2 Importance of Strategic Planning in Grant Writing

Effective grant writing for DH initiatives begins long before the actual writing process. It involves careful planning, clear articulation of objectives, and a thorough understanding of the scope and feasibility of the proposed project. A common pitfall in DH grant applications is the underestimation of the technical and human resources required for successful execution. Thus, strategic planning includes assembling a team with complementary expertise in humanities scholarship, digital technology, data management, and project administration. It also involves identifying potential collaborators from other institutions or disciplines whose inclusion can strengthen the proposal.

The planning phase should also consider sustainability beyond the life of the grant. Funders are increasingly concerned with how DH projects will continue to benefit the academic community and the public once the initial funding period has ended. Applicants must therefore address issues of digital preservation, open access, community engagement, and knowledge dissemination in their proposals. These considerations demonstrate a long-term vision that aligns with the strategic goals of many funding agencies.

6.6.3 Crafting a Compelling Narrative

At the heart of successful grant writing lies the ability to tell a compelling story. A DH proposal must present a clear and engaging narrative that outlines the problem being addressed, the proposed solution, the methodologies to be employed, and the expected outcomes. This narrative must be rooted in rigorous scholarship but also accessible to reviewers who may not be specialists in DH. Clarity, coherence, and conciseness are critical in this regard. The proposal should begin with a strong opening statement that captures the essence of the project and its significance in advancing knowledge, fostering innovation, or addressing a societal need.

A successful narrative also conveys passion and commitment. Funders are more likely to support projects that are not only intellectually sound but also driven by a genuine desire to make a difference. The narrative should therefore reflect the applicant's enthusiasm for the project and their confidence in its feasibility and potential impact. It should also include a detailed timeline, with milestones and deliverables that indicate thoughtful planning and project management skills.

6.6.4 Demonstrating Innovation and Relevance

Digital Humanities projects are often funded on the basis of their innovation. This could mean the development of new digital tools, the application of existing technologies in novel ways, or the exploration of previously unexamined research questions through computational methods. In grant writing, it is essential to emphasize what makes the proposed project innovative. This includes explaining how it builds on or departs from existing work in the field, how it addresses gaps in current research, and how it contributes to the broader landscape of digital scholarship. Equally important is demonstrating the relevance of the project to contemporary academic or societal challenges. Funders want to invest in initiatives that have the potential to generate new knowledge, influence public discourse, or support education and community engagement. Therefore, the proposal should make explicit connections between the project's goals and broader intellectual, cultural, or social issues. This could include themes such as digital equity, cultural preservation, interdisciplinary collaboration, or public access to knowledge.

6.6.5 Budgeting and Justification

A well-prepared budget is a crucial component of any DH grant application. It should be realistic, transparent, and aligned with the project's objectives and timeline. Applicants must account for all anticipated expenses, including personnel costs, software and hardware, travel, dissemination activities, and contingency provisions. Each budget item should be accompanied by a justification that explains its necessity and relevance to the project's success. In many DH projects, a significant portion of the budget goes toward staffing, including hiring research assistants, software developers, or digital archivists. Justifying these costs involves explaining the specific roles and responsibilities of each team member and how their expertise will contribute to achieving the project's outcomes. In addition, proposals should anticipate costs related to data storage, website maintenance, and long-term preservation, which are often overlooked but essential for project sustainability.

6.6.6 Evaluation and Impact Assessment

Grant applications increasingly require applicants to outline how the success of their projects will be evaluated. For DH initiatives, this involves both qualitative and quantitative measures. Evaluation metrics might include the number of digital assets created, user engagement statistics, scholarly publications, citations, or the uptake of tools or platforms developed through the project. In addition, applicants should propose mechanisms for gathering feedback from users, collaborators, or community stakeholders. Articulating the broader impact of the project is another key requirement. Funders want to know how the project will benefit the academic community, contribute to public understanding, or support digital innovation in the humanities. This requires a thoughtful reflection on who the intended audiences are, how the project will reach them, and what kind of long-term legacy it will leave. Strategies might include creating open-access resources, hosting workshops or conferences, partnering with educational institutions, or contributing to policy discussions related to digital culture.

6.6.7 Common Pitfalls and Best Practices

While many DH scholars are excellent researchers, they may not have extensive experience in grant writing. This lack of experience can result in several common pitfalls, such as vague objectives, poor budgeting, insufficient justification of methods, or failure to demonstrate relevance. To avoid these issues, it is advisable to seek mentorship from experienced grant writers, attend grant writing workshops, or consult with research support offices at universities.

Best practices in DH grant writing include tailoring each application to the specific requirements of the funder, following the guidelines meticulously, and submitting drafts for peer review before final submission. Clear writing, consistent formatting, and attention to detail all contribute to the professionalism of the application. Moreover, establishing a track record of smaller, successful projects can build credibility and lay the foundation for larger, more ambitious funding proposals in the future.

CHAPTER 7

Publishing and Dissemination in DH

7.1 DIGITAL EDITIONS AND SCHOLARLY PUBLISHING

Digital editions and scholarly publishing in Digital Humanities have revolutionized the way academic research is conducted, disseminated, and preserved. These initiatives leverage digital tools and technologies to create interactive, multimedia-rich editions of historical and literary texts, providing new insights and perspectives on cultural heritage. Digital editions and scholarly publishing in DH are characterized by interactivity, multimedia richness, and scholarly annotation, fostering a more engaging, inclusive, and democratic approach to the humanities. Digital editions can take many forms, from digital facsimiles to critical and multimedia editions, each offering unique benefits and opportunities for exploration and engagement.

Technology plays a crucial role in digital editions and scholarly publishing in DH, providing the tools and resources needed to create, disseminate, and preserve scholarly works. Digital tools and technologies, such as text mining, data visualization, and virtual reality, enable scholars to analyze and interpret complex data sets, uncovering patterns, themes, and insights that might not be immediately apparent through traditional methods. Digital editions and scholarly publishing in DH offer numerous benefits, including the enhancement of accessibility and usability, the enhancement of scholarly communication and collaboration, and the fostering of a sense of community and belonging.

Despite their potential, digital editions and scholarly publishing in DH face several challenges, including the need for digital literacy, the availability and quality of digital tools and resources, and ethical and methodological challenges. To address these challenges, scholars must provide ongoing training and support in digital literacy, invest in high-quality digital tools and resources, and adhere to ethical guidelines and best practices.

The future of digital editions and scholarly publishing in DH lies in the integration of AI and ML, the development of immersive and interactive scholarly experiences, and the creation of collaborative and participatory scholarly experiences that engage a wider range of stakeholders in the creation and dissemination of scholarly works. By addressing the challenges and exploring new directions, scholars can ensure that digital editions and scholarly publishing in DH are effective, inclusive, and ethically sound, providing new opportunities for research, learning, and growth.

The principles of digital editions and scholarly publishing in DH, with their dynamic and interactive scholarly experiences, will continue to influence the development of the humanities, ensuring that the research process is engaging, inclusive, and relevant to a wider audience. Through the use of digital tools and methodologies, scholars can create a more comprehensive and nuanced understanding of scholarly works, providing new insights and perspectives on the themes, motifs, and stylistic features that shape our cultural heritage.

As digital technologies continue to evolve, digital editions and scholarly publishing in Digital Humanities are poised to play an increasingly important role in the field. One of the key future directions in digital editions and scholarly publishing in DH is the integration of artificial intelligence (AI) and machine learning (ML) to enhance the accuracy and sophistication of scholarly works. AI and ML can be used to analyze large and complex datasets, identify patterns and anomalies, and generate insights that would be difficult or impossible to achieve through traditional methods. For example, an AI-driven digital edition might use machine learning algorithms to model the evolution of a particular literary style, providing new insights into the factors that contributed to its development and influence. Additionally, AI and ML can be used to enhance the delivery of content, providing users with adaptive and personalized learning experiences.

Another future direction in digital editions and scholarly publishing in DH is the development of immersive and interactive scholarly experiences that engage users in new and innovative ways. Virtual reality (VR) and augmented reality (AR) technologies can be used to create immersive and interactive scholarly experiences that allow users to explore scholarly works in a more engaging and experiential way. For example, a VR-based digital edition might allow users to walk through a virtual representation of a historical site, interacting with virtual artifacts and characters. Similarly, an AR-based digital edition might overlay digital information onto the real world, allowing users to explore and interact with scholarly works in their immediate environment. This approach can help to enhance user engagement, motivation, and learning outcomes, as it provides a more immersive and interactive scholarly experience.

The future of digital editions and scholarly publishing in DH also lies in the development of collaborative and participatory scholarly experiences that engage a wider range of stakeholders in the creation and dissemination of scholarly works. Collaborative scholarly experiences can bring together scholars, institutions, and communities to co-create and co-interpret scholarly works, providing a more inclusive and democratic approach to the humanities. For example, a collaborative digital edition might involve scholars, institutions, and community members working together to analyze the cultural significance of a historical event, providing new insights and perspectives on the event. Participatory scholarly experiences can also be used to engage the public in the creation and dissemination of scholarly works, providing opportunities for learning, reflection, and action.

7.1.1 Characteristics of Digital Editions in Digital Humanities

Digital editions in Digital Humanities are characterized by several key features, including interactivity, multimedia richness, and scholarly annotation. Interactivity is a fundamental aspect of digital editions, as they often include interactive elements, such as hyperlinks, searchable databases, and multimedia content, which allow users to explore and engage with the scholarly work in a more dynamic and immersive way.

For example, a digital edition of a historical text might include interactive maps, timelines, and images, providing users with a more comprehensive and engaging learning experience. Multimedia richness is another key feature of digital editions, as they often incorporate a variety of media, including images, audio, video, and animations, to enhance the delivery of content and cater to different learning styles and preferences. For example, a digital edition of a literary work might include images of the original manuscript, audio recordings of the text, and animations of the narrative structure, providing a more immersive and engaging learning experience.

Scholarly annotation is also a crucial feature of digital editions, as they often include detailed and context-rich annotations, which provide users with additional information, insights, and interpretations of the scholarly work. For example, a digital edition of a historical document might include annotations that provide context, analysis, and interpretation of the text, helping users to understand the historical, cultural, and linguistic contexts that shaped its development. Additionally, digital editions often include collaborative and participatory features, which allow users to contribute to the annotation and interpretation of the scholarly work, fostering a more inclusive and democratic approach to the humanities. For example, a digital edition of a literary work might include a collaborative annotation tool, which allows users to add their own annotations, comments, and interpretations, providing a more engaging and interactive learning experience.

7.1.2 Types of Digital Editions in Digital Humanities

Digital editions in Digital Humanities can take many forms, from simple digital facsimiles to complex, multimedia-rich editions. One of the most common types of digital editions is the digital facsimile, which involves the digitization and reproduction of an original text or artifact. Digital facsimiles provide users with a high-quality, accurate, and accessible reproduction of the original work, allowing them to explore and engage with the text or artifact in a more convenient and accessible way. For example, a digital facsimile of a historical manuscript might include high-resolution images of the original text, providing users with a detailed and accurate reproduction of the manuscript. Digital facsimiles are particularly useful for preserving and disseminating fragile or rare texts and artifacts, as they provide a non-invasive and accessible way to explore and engage with the original work.

Another type of digital edition is the critical edition, which involves the creation of a scholarly edition of a text, including detailed annotations, commentary, and analysis. Critical editions provide users with a comprehensive and context-rich understanding of the text, helping them to explore and interpret the text in a more informed and nuanced way. For example, a critical edition of a literary work might include detailed annotations, commentary, and analysis, providing users with insights into the text's literary, cultural, and historical contexts. Critical editions are particularly useful for scholars and students, as they provide a rich and detailed resource for research, teaching, and learning. Additionally, critical editions often include collaborative and participatory features, which allow users to contribute to the annotation and interpretation of the text, fostering a more inclusive and democratic approach to the humanities.

A third type of digital edition is the multimedia edition, which involves the incorporation of a variety of media, including images, audio, video, and animations, to enhance the delivery of content and cater to different learning styles and preferences. Multimedia editions provide users with a more immersive and engaging learning experience, as they incorporate a variety of media to enhance the delivery of content and cater to different learning styles and preferences. For example, a multimedia edition of a historical event might include images, audio recordings, and animations, providing users with a more comprehensive and engaging learning experience. Multimedia editions are particularly useful for public education and outreach, as they provide a more engaging and accessible way to explore and engage with scholarly works.

7.1.3 Role of Technology in Digital Editions and Scholarly Publishing

Technology plays a crucial role in digital editions and scholarly publishing in Digital Humanities, providing the tools and resources needed to create, disseminate, and preserve scholarly works. Digital tools and technologies, such as text mining, data visualization, and virtual reality, enable scholars to analyze and interpret complex data sets, uncovering patterns, themes, and insights that might not be immediately apparent through traditional methods. For example, text mining tools can be used to analyze a corpus of historical documents, identifying recurring motifs, tracking the evolution of themes, and revealing hidden patterns and structures within the texts. Similarly, data visualization tools can be used to explore the relationships between different characters, events, and themes in a literary work, providing a visual overview of the text's narrative structure.

Virtual reality (VR) and augmented reality (AR) technologies are also important in digital editions and scholarly publishing, as they enable the creation of immersive and interactive learning experiences. VR tools can be used to create virtual environments, allowing users to explore historical sites, cultural artifacts, and scientific phenomena in a more engaging and experiential way. For example, a VR-based digital edition might allow users to walk through a reconstructed historical city, interacting with virtual residents and observing the dynamics of urban life. Similarly, an AR-based digital edition might overlay digital information onto the real world, allowing users to explore and interact with historical sites and cultural artifacts in their immediate environment. This approach can help to enhance user engagement, motivation, and learning outcomes, as it provides a more immersive and interactive learning experience.

7.1.4 Benefits of Digital Editions and Scholarly Publishing in Digital Humanities

Digital editions and scholarly publishing in Digital Humanities offer numerous benefits, both for scholars and for the broader field of the humanities. One of the primary benefits is the enhancement of accessibility and usability, as digital editions and scholarly publications provide users with a more convenient, accessible, and engaging way to explore and engage with scholarly works. For example, a digital edition of a historical text might include interactive maps, timelines, and images, providing users with a more comprehensive and engaging learning experience. Similarly, a digital scholarly publication might include multimedia content, such as images, audio, and video, providing users with a more immersive and engaging learning experience. This enhancement of accessibility and usability can lead to a more inclusive and democratic approach to the humanities, as it provides users with a more convenient, accessible, and engaging way to explore and engage with scholarly works.

Another benefit of digital editions and scholarly publishing in DH is the enhancement of scholarly communication and collaboration, as digital tools and technologies enable scholars to share, collaborate, and engage with each other in new and innovative ways. For example, a digital scholarly publication might include interactive and collaborative features, such as discussion forums, comment sections, and annotation tools, providing scholars with a more engaging and interactive way to share, collaborate, and engage with each other. Similarly, a digital edition might include collaborative and participatory features, which allow users to contribute to the annotation and interpretation of the scholarly work, fostering a more inclusive and democratic approach to the humanities. This enhancement of scholarly communication and collaboration can lead to more innovative, relevant, and impactful research, as well as to the development of new methods, tools, and approaches.

Digital editions and scholarly publishing in DH also foster a sense of community and belonging, as they provide users with a more engaging, interactive, and collaborative way to explore and engage with scholarly works. This collaborative and participatory approach not only enhances the learning experience but also fosters a sense of community and belonging, as users work together towards a common goal. For example, a digital edition might include a collaborative annotation tool, which allows users to add their own annotations, comments, and interpretations, providing a more engaging and interactive learning experience. Similarly, a digital scholarly publication might include a discussion forum, which allows users to share, collaborate, and engage with each other, providing a more engaging and interactive learning experience. This sense of community and belonging is important for the success of the project, as it provides users with the support and encouragement needed to achieve the project's goals and objectives.

7.1.5 Challenges in Digital Editions and Scholarly Publishing

Despite their potential, digital editions and scholarly publishing in Digital Humanities face several challenges that can limit their effectiveness and impact. One of the primary challenges is the need for digital literacy, which refers to the ability to use digital tools and technologies effectively and responsibly. Digital literacy is essential for both scholars and users, as it enables them to navigate the digital landscape, evaluate information, and communicate effectively. To address this challenge, educational institutions must provide ongoing training and support in digital literacy, ensuring that all scholars and users have the skills and knowledge needed to succeed in the digital age. Additionally, scholars must integrate digital literacy into the curriculum, providing users with opportunities to develop and apply digital skills in meaningful and relevant contexts.

Another challenge in digital editions and scholarly publishing in DH is the availability and quality of digital tools and resources. Digital tools and resources can be expensive, and their quality can vary widely, which can affect the outcomes of digital editions and scholarly publications. To address this challenge, educational institutions must invest in high-quality digital tools and resources, ensuring that scholars and users have access to the tools and resources needed to succeed in the digital age. Additionally, scholars must be aware of the potential biases and limitations of digital tools and resources, ensuring that they are used in a responsible and ethical manner. Digital editions and scholarly publishing in DH also face ethical and methodological challenges, particularly in relation to the interpretation and representation of scholarly works. Digital representations can be subject to bias and interpretation, which can affect the outcomes of the representation and the insights they provide. For example, a digital representation of a historical event might be influenced by the scholar's own biases and interpretations, leading to a skewed or incomplete representation of the event. To address these challenges, scholars must use a range of ethical and methodological guidelines, including transparency, peer review, and interdisciplinary collaboration, to ensure the accuracy and reliability of digital representations.

7.1.6 Ethical Considerations in Digital Editions and Scholarly Publishing

Ethical considerations are crucial in the development and use of digital editions and scholarly publishing in Digital Humanities, as they involve the interpretation and representation of scholarly works. One of the primary ethical considerations is the potential for bias and misrepresentation in digital representations. Digital representations can be influenced by the scholar's own biases and interpretations, leading to a skewed or incomplete representation of the scholarly work. To address this challenge, scholars must use a range of ethical guidelines, including transparency, peer review, and interdisciplinary collaboration, to ensure the accuracy and reliability of digital representations. For example, scholars might use peer review to evaluate the assumptions and methods used in a digital representation, ensuring that the results are based on sound evidence and rigorous analysis.

Another ethical consideration in digital editions and scholarly publishing in DH is the potential for misuse or misinterpretation of the results. Digital representations can be used to support a wide range of interpretations and narratives, some of which may be inaccurate or misleading. To address this challenge, scholars must use a range of ethical guidelines, including transparency, accountability, and public engagement, to ensure that the results of digital representations are interpreted and used responsibly. For example, scholars might use public engagement to share the results of a digital representation with a wider audience, providing context and interpretation to ensure that the results are understood and used appropriately.

Digital editions and scholarly publishing in DH also raise ethical considerations related to the representation of marginalized or vulnerable groups. Digital representations can inadvertently perpetuate stereotypes or misrepresent the experiences of marginalized groups, leading to harm or injustice. To address this challenge, scholars must use a range of ethical guidelines, including inclusivity, representation, and cultural sensitivity, to ensure that digital representations are respectful and accurate in their representation of diverse groups. For example, scholars might use inclusive data collection and analysis techniques to ensure that the voices and experiences of marginalized groups are represented in the digital representation.

7.2 OPEN ACCESS AND LICENSING

Open Access and licensing represent a significant shift in the way knowledge is created, shared, and used. By removing barriers to access, OA enhances the visibility, reach, and impact of research while promoting a more equitable and inclusive scholarly ecosystem. Licensing mechanisms, particularly those provided by Creative Commons, empower authors to share their work freely and responsibly. However, realizing the full potential of Open Access requires sustained support from institutions, funders, and policymakers, as well as a commitment to education, advocacy, and innovation. As the world becomes increasingly interconnected, the principles of Open Access will continue to shape the future of knowledge and ensure that it remains a public good accessible to all.

The future of Open Access lies in creating inclusive, sustainable, and ethical publishing systems that serve the interests of the global research community. This involves rethinking traditional metrics of scholarly impact, promoting open peer review, and supporting community-led publishing initiatives. The integration of Open Access with other open science practices, such as open data, open educational resources, and open-source software, holds great promise for transforming research and education. As artificial intelligence and digital tools evolve, the reuse and analysis of open content will become even more critical, making licensing choices all the more important.

Efforts to promote equitable OA must also address language barriers, cultural diversity, and regional disparities. This includes supporting multilingual publishing, recognizing diverse forms of scholarship, and investing in local publishing infrastructure. Collaborative global efforts, such as the UNESCO Recommendation on Open Science, provide a framework for advancing OA principles and practices worldwide.

7.2.1 Philosophy

The core philosophy of Open Access lies in the democratization of knowledge. Traditional academic publishing limits access to journal articles and research outputs through high subscription fees, which many institutions, particularly in the Global South, cannot afford. This model perpetuates inequalities in access to knowledge and slows down the pace of scientific advancement and scholarly discourse. Open Access counters this model by enabling free and unrestricted online access to research findings. It operates on the principle that knowledge generated through research should not be locked behind paywalls, especially when that research has been publicly funded. The underlying belief is that the free dissemination of scholarly information accelerates discovery, encourages innovation, and fosters collaboration across borders and disciplines.

7.2.2 Models

Open Access publishing is not monolithic; it comprises various models, each with its own characteristics and implications. The most commonly recognized model is the Gold Open Access, where articles are published in OA journals and made freely available immediately upon publication. In this model, the costs of publication are typically covered by Article Processing Charges (APCs), which are paid by authors, their institutions, or funders.

Another model is Green Open Access, which allows authors to deposit a version of their published work (often a preprint or postprint) in an institutional or subject repository, making it freely accessible without cost. This version may have an embargo period, depending on the publisher's policy. Hybrid Open Access refers to subscription journals that offer OA options for individual articles if the APC is paid. Diamond or Platinum Open Access represents journals that do not charge either authors or readers, relying instead on institutional support or public funding.

Each of these models has its strengths and challenges. Gold OA offers immediate access but may exclude researchers from underfunded institutions due to high APCs. Green OA is more inclusive but may delay access. Hybrid OA has been criticized for "double-dipping," where publishers receive both subscription fees and APCs. Diamond OA aligns best with the principles of equity and inclusivity but often struggles with financial sustainability. These diverse models reflect the complexity of transitioning from traditional to open publishing and highlight the importance of institutional policies and funding mechanisms that support equitable Open Access.

7.2.3 Role of Licensing

Licensing is a fundamental aspect of Open Access, as it defines how published works can be used, reused, and redistributed. Unlike traditional publishing, where all rights are usually retained by publishers, OA emphasizes more flexible licensing arrangements that promote wider dissemination and use of research. The most widely used licensing framework in OA is provided by Creative Commons (CC). These licenses offer a standardized way for authors to grant permissions while protecting their rights. The most liberal of these licenses is CC BY (Attribution), which allows users to distribute, remix, adapt, and build upon the work, even for commercial purposes, provided proper credit is given to the author. Other variants, such as CC

BY-SA (ShareAlike), CC BY-ND (NoDerivatives), and CC BY-NC (NonCommercial), impose additional restrictions to protect the author's intent and control over their work. Creative Commons licenses are essential in ensuring that the ethos of Open Access is not compromised. They provide clarity about what users can and cannot do with the content, reducing legal uncertainties and fostering confidence among users and authors alike. Importantly, they allow authors to retain ownership of their work while encouraging responsible reuse. The use of appropriate licenses helps maximize the impact of research by enabling broader dissemination, educational use, translation, and the creation of derivative works, all of which are critical in advancing knowledge and addressing global challenges.

7.2.4 Institutional and Governmental Support

The success of the Open Access movement depends significantly on the support and commitment of academic institutions, funding bodies, and governments. Many universities have established institutional repositories and adopted OA mandates that require faculty members to deposit their research outputs.

These policies aim to preserve institutional knowledge and ensure public access to scholarly work. Similarly, funding agencies worldwide are increasingly mandating that the research they support be published in OA formats. Organizations such as the Wellcome Trust, the Bill and Melinda Gates Foundation, and the European Commission have been pioneers in this regard. The Plan S initiative, led by cOAlition S, exemplifies a strong commitment to Open Access by requiring that all publicly funded research be published in compliant OA journals or platforms.

Governments also play a crucial role in shaping OA policy and infrastructure. National-level initiatives to support OA publishing, develop digital repositories, and establish legal frameworks for copyright reform are essential in creating an enabling environment. In countries like India, South Africa, and Brazil, government-supported repositories and publishing platforms have emerged to promote indigenous research and enhance access. However, disparities remain, and continued investment is needed to build robust OA ecosystems, particularly in developing regions.

7.2.5 Challenges in Implementing Open Access

Despite its growing popularity, Open Access faces several challenges. One of the primary concerns is the financial model that supports OA publishing. The reliance on APCs has raised questions about affordability and inclusivity, particularly for early-career researchers, scholars from low-income institutions, and researchers in developing countries. Another challenge is the resistance from established commercial publishers, who view OA as a threat to their profit-driven models. These publishers often impose restrictive policies, long embargoes, and high APCs that undermine the principles of Open Access. Additionally, there are concerns about the quality of OA journals, with the proliferation of predatory journals that exploit the OA model without providing rigorous peer review or editorial oversight.

There is also a lack of awareness and understanding among researchers about Open Access and licensing options. Many scholars are unsure about their rights, the implications of different licenses, or the best practices for self-archiving and repository use. Institutional capacity building, training, and advocacy are therefore essential components of a successful OA strategy. Academic libraries, in particular, play a vital role in educating researchers, supporting OA publishing, and managing repositories.

7.3 DIGITAL JOURNALS AND ONLINE PLATFORMS

Digital journals and online platforms have fundamentally transformed academic and professional publishing, offering unprecedented access to knowledge and fostering global collaboration. By leveraging digital technologies, these platforms have enhanced the speed, accessibility, and interactivity of scholarly communication, benefiting researchers, practitioners, and the public alike.

However, challenges such as predatory publishing, digital preservation, and inequitable access must be addressed to ensure the sustainability and inclusivity of this ecosystem. As new technologies like AI and blockchain emerge, they present opportunities to further innovate and improve the integrity of digital publishing. The ongoing evolution of digital journals and online platforms will undoubtedly continue to shape the future of research dissemination, reinforcing their vital role in the advancement of knowledge across all fields.

The future of digital journals and online platforms is likely to be shaped by ongoing technological advancements and shifting scholarly communication practices. Blockchain technology, for instance, holds promise for ensuring the authenticity and traceability of published research, potentially combating issues like paper mills and citation manipulation. Augmented and virtual reality could transform how readers interact with journal content, enabling immersive experiences for data visualization or virtual lab simulations. There is also growing interest in decentralized publishing models, where researchers have greater control over their work outside traditional journal structures. Furthermore, as interdisciplinary research becomes more prevalent, digital platforms will need to adapt to support cross-disciplinary collaboration and integration. The continued evolution of these platforms will play a critical role in meeting the changing needs of the global research community.

7.3.1 Key Features and Advantages

Digital journals offer a range of features that enhance the research experience beyond what print journals could provide. One of the most notable advantages is the ability to incorporate multimedia elements, such as videos, interactive graphs, and hyperlinked references, which enrich the presentation and understanding of complex data. Advanced search capabilities, powered by indexing tools and keyword tagging, allow users to quickly locate relevant articles, saving time and improving efficiency. Additionally, digital journals often include metrics such as citation counts, download statistics, and altmetrics, providing authors and readers with insights into the impact and reach of published work. The instantaneous publication process also ensures that research findings are shared promptly, keeping pace with the rapid evolution of many fields. These features collectively contribute to a more dynamic and interactive scholarly communication ecosystem.

7.3.2 Role of Online Platforms in Hosting Digital Journals

Online platforms serve as the backbone of digital journal publishing, providing the infrastructure needed to host, manage, and distribute scholarly content. Platforms like JSTOR, ScienceDirect, and PubMed Central aggregate thousands of journals, offering centralized access to a vast array of research. These platforms often include tools for peer review, editorial management, and digital preservation, streamlining the publishing process for journal editors and publishers. Many platforms also integrate social sharing and annotation tools, enabling readers to engage with content in new ways, such as by highlighting text or sharing articles on social media. Furthermore, subscription-based and open-access platforms coexist, catering to different funding models and audience needs. The scalability and flexibility of these platforms have made them indispensable in modern academic publishing.

7.3.3 Open Access and Its Impact on Digital Journals

The open-access movement has profoundly influenced the landscape of digital journals, challenging traditional subscription-based models and advocating for free, unrestricted access to research. Open-access journals, funded through article processing charges (APCs) or institutional support, eliminate paywalls, ensuring that knowledge is available to anyone with an internet connection.

This model has been particularly transformative for researchers in low-income countries, who previously faced significant barriers to accessing premium scholarly content. Initiatives like Plan S, which mandates open-access publishing for publicly funded research, have further propelled this shift. However, the open-access model is not without controversy, as concerns about the quality of predatory journals and the financial burden of APCs on authors persist. Despite these challenges, open access continues to gain momentum, reshaping the economics and ethics of academic publishing.

7.3.4 Peer Review and Quality Assurance in Digital Publishing

Peer review remains the cornerstone of quality assurance in digital journals, ensuring that published research meets rigorous academic standards. Digital platforms have modernized this process by introducing automated workflows, double-blind review systems, and transparent review protocols. Some journals have adopted innovative approaches, such as open peer review, where reviewer comments and author responses are published alongside the article, enhancing accountability and transparency. Post-publication peer review, facilitated by platforms like PubPeer, allows the academic community to continue evaluating and discussing research after it has been published. These advancements have strengthened the integrity of digital journals, though they also raise questions about the potential for bias in reviewer selection and the increasing workload on academics tasked with peer review duties.

7.3.5 Challenges Facing Digital Journals and Online Platforms

Despite their many advantages, digital journals and online platforms face several challenges that threaten their sustainability and credibility. The proliferation of predatory journals, which exploit the open-access model by charging fees without providing proper peer review or editorial oversight, has undermined trust in digital publishing. Digital preservation is another concern, as technological obsolescence and data corruption risks jeopardize long-term access to scholarly content.

Additionally, the dominance of a few major publishing platforms has led to monopolistic practices, with high subscription fees and restrictive licensing agreements straining library budgets. There is also the issue of digital divide, where disparities in internet access and technological infrastructure limit the ability of some researchers to fully participate in the digital scholarly ecosystem. Addressing these challenges requires coordinated efforts from publishers, institutions, and policymakers.

7.3.6 Integration of Artificial Intelligence in Digital Journals

Artificial intelligence (AI) is increasingly being integrated into digital journals and online platforms, offering new possibilities for enhancing research discovery, peer review, and content personalization. AI-powered tools can assist in manuscript screening, detecting plagiarism, and even suggesting potential reviewers based on their publication history. Machine learning algorithms are also being used to recommend relevant articles to readers, improving the serendipity of research discovery. Some platforms employ natural language processing to generate summaries or highlight key findings within articles, saving researchers time. However, the use of AI in scholarly publishing raises ethical questions, such as the potential for algorithmic bias and the need for transparency in AI-driven decisions. As AI technology evolves, its role in digital journals is expected to expand, presenting both opportunities and challenges for the academic community.

7.4 MULTIMEDIA AND TRANSMEDIA STORYTELLING

Multimedia and transmedia storytelling in Digital Humanities represent a dynamic and innovative approach to exploring and interpreting cultural heritage. These methods leverage digital tools and technologies to create immersive, interactive, and engaging narratives that transcend traditional boundaries of media and storytelling. Multimedia storytelling involves the integration of various media forms, such as text, images, audio, and video, to create a rich and layered narrative experience. Transmedia storytelling extends this concept by distributing narrative content across multiple platforms and media channels, allowing audiences to engage with the story in diverse and interconnected ways. Together, these approaches offer new opportunities for scholars, educators, and the public to explore and understand complex historical, cultural, and literary themes.

Multimedia and transmedia storytelling in DH are characterized by interactivity, multimedia richness, and narrative complexity, as well as multi-platform distribution, interconnected narratives, and audience engagement. These approaches have a wide range of applications, from academic research to public education and cultural heritage preservation. Technology plays a crucial role in multimedia and transmedia storytelling in DH, providing the tools and resources needed to create, disseminate, and preserve narratives. Digital tools and technologies, such as VR, AR, and interactive multimedia platforms, enable creators to develop immersive and interactive narratives that cater to different learning styles and preferences.

Despite their potential, multimedia and transmedia storytelling in DH face several challenges, including the need for digital literacy, the availability and quality of digital tools and resources, and ethical and methodological challenges. To address these challenges, creators must provide ongoing training and support in digital literacy, invest in high-quality digital tools and resources, and adhere to ethical guidelines and best practices. The future of multimedia and transmedia storytelling in DH lies in the integration of AI and ML, the development of immersive and interactive narrative experiences, and the creation of collaborative and participatory narrative experiences that engage a wider range of stakeholders in the creation and dissemination of narratives. By addressing the challenges and exploring new directions, creators can ensure that multimedia and transmedia storytelling in DH are effective, inclusive, and ethically sound, providing new opportunities for research, learning, and growth. The principles of multimedia and transmedia storytelling in DH, with their dynamic and interactive narrative experiences, will continue to influence the development of the humanities, ensuring that the narrative process is engaging, inclusive, and relevant to a wider audience. Through the use of digital tools and methodologies, creators can develop a more comprehensive and nuanced understanding of narratives, providing new insights and perspectives on the themes, motifs, and stylistic features that shape our cultural heritage.

As digital technologies continue to evolve, multimedia and transmedia storytelling in Digital Humanities are poised to play an increasingly important role in the field. One of the key future directions in multimedia and transmedia storytelling in DH is the integration of artificial intelligence (AI) and machine learning (ML) to enhance the accuracy and sophistication of narratives.

AI and ML can be used to analyze large and complex datasets, identify patterns and anomalies, and generate insights that would be difficult or impossible to achieve through traditional methods. For example, an AI-driven multimedia narrative might use machine learning algorithms to model the evolution of a particular narrative style, providing new insights into the factors that contributed to its development and influence. Additionally, AI and ML can be used to enhance the delivery of content, providing users with adaptive and personalized narrative experiences.

Another future direction in multimedia and transmedia storytelling in DH is the development of immersive and interactive narrative experiences that engage users in new and innovative ways. Virtual reality (VR) and augmented reality (AR) technologies can be used to create immersive and interactive narrative experiences that allow users to explore narratives in a more engaging and experiential way. For example, a VR-based multimedia narrative might allow users to walk through a virtual representation of a historical site, interacting with virtual artifacts and characters. Similarly, an AR-based transmedia narrative might overlay digital information onto the real world, allowing users to explore and interact with narratives in their immediate environment. This approach can help to enhance user engagement, motivation, and learning outcomes, as it provides a more immersive and interactive narrative experience.

The future of multimedia and transmedia storytelling in DH also lies in the development of collaborative and participatory narrative experiences that engage a wider range of stakeholders in the creation and dissemination of narratives. Collaborative narrative experiences can bring together scholars, institutions, and communities to co-create and co-interpret narratives, providing a more inclusive and democratic approach to the humanities. For example, a collaborative multimedia narrative might involve scholars, institutions, and community members working together to analyze the cultural significance of a historical event, providing new insights and perspectives on the event. Participatory narrative experiences can also be used to engage the public in the creation and dissemination of narratives, providing opportunities for learning, reflection, and action.

7.4.1 Characteristics of Multimedia Storytelling

Multimedia storytelling in Digital Humanities is characterized by several key features, including interactivity, multimedia richness, and narrative complexity. Interactivity is a fundamental aspect of multimedia storytelling, as it allows users to engage with the narrative in a dynamic and personalized way. Interactive elements, such as hyperlinks, quizzes, and simulations, enable users to explore different aspects of the story, make choices, and experience the consequences of their actions. For example, an interactive multimedia narrative about a historical event might allow users to explore different perspectives, make decisions, and observe the outcomes of their choices. This interactive approach not only enhances the user experience but also fosters a deeper understanding and engagement with the narrative.

Multimedia richness is another key feature of multimedia storytelling, as it incorporates a variety of media forms to create a rich and layered narrative experience. Multimedia storytelling often includes text, images, audio, and video, each contributing to the overall narrative in unique ways. For example, a multimedia narrative about a literary work might include images of the original manuscript, audio recordings of the text, and video animations of the narrative structure. This multimedia approach caters to different learning styles and preferences, making the narrative more accessible and engaging to a wider audience. Additionally, multimedia richness enhances the narrative's emotional and sensory impact, providing users with a more immersive and memorable experience.

Narrative complexity is also a crucial feature of multimedia storytelling, as it involves the creation of intricate and layered narratives that explore multiple themes, perspectives, and dimensions. Multimedia storytelling often incorporates non-linear narratives, branching storylines, and multiple points of view, allowing users to explore the narrative in depth and from different angles. For example, a multimedia narrative about a historical period might include multiple perspectives, such as those of different social groups, cultural contexts, and historical events. This narrative complexity provides users with a more comprehensive and nuanced understanding of the subject matter, as well as a more engaging and thought-provoking experience.

7.4.2 Characteristics of Transmedia Storytelling

Transmedia storytelling in Digital Humanities is characterized by several key features, including multi-platform distribution, interconnected narratives, and audience engagement. Multi-platform distribution is a fundamental aspect of transmedia storytelling, as it involves the dissemination of narrative content across multiple platforms and media channels. Transmedia storytelling often includes websites, social media, mobile apps, and physical installations, each contributing to the overall narrative in unique ways. For example, a transmedia narrative about a cultural event might include a website with background information, a social media campaign with user-generated content, and a mobile app with interactive features. This multi-platform approach allows users to engage with the narrative in diverse and interconnected ways, providing a more comprehensive and immersive experience.

Interconnected narratives are another key feature of transmedia storytelling, as they involve the creation of narratives that are distributed across multiple platforms and media channels but are interconnected and complementary. Transmedia storytelling often includes narrative fragments, clues, and puzzles that are spread across different platforms, encouraging users to explore and connect the different pieces of the story. For example, a transmedia narrative about a historical mystery might include clues and puzzles that are hidden across different platforms, such as a website, a social media campaign, and a mobile app. This interconnected approach not only enhances the user experience but also fosters a deeper understanding and engagement with the narrative.

Audience engagement is also a crucial feature of transmedia storytelling, as it involves the active involvement of users in the creation, exploration, and interpretation of the narrative. Transmedia storytelling often includes participatory and collaborative elements, such as user-generated content, crowdsourcing, and social media interactions, which allow users to contribute to the narrative and engage with other users. For example, a transmedia narrative about a cultural event might include a social media campaign that encourages users to share their own stories, experiences, and perspectives. This participatory approach not only enhances the user experience but also fosters a sense of community and belonging, as users work together towards a common goal.

7.4.3 Applications of Multimedia and Transmedia Storytelling

Multimedia and transmedia storytelling in Digital Humanities have a wide range of applications, from academic research to public education and cultural heritage preservation. In academic research, multimedia and transmedia storytelling are used to explore and analyze complex narratives, providing scholars with new insights and perspectives on historical, cultural, and literary themes. For example, a multimedia narrative about a historical event might include interactive timelines, maps, and simulations, providing scholars with a more comprehensive and nuanced understanding of the event. Similarly, a transmedia narrative about a cultural practice might include narrative fragments, clues, and puzzles that are spread across different platforms, encouraging scholars to explore and connect the different pieces of the story. In public education, multimedia and transmedia storytelling are used to create interactive and immersive learning experiences that engage students and the public in the exploration and interpretation of narratives. For example, a multimedia narrative about a literary work might include images, audio recordings, and video animations, providing students with a more engaging and accessible learning experience. Similarly, a transmedia narrative about a historical period might include narrative fragments, clues, and puzzles that are spread across different platforms, encouraging students to explore and connect the different pieces of the story. This interactive and immersive approach not only enhances the learning experience but also fosters a deeper understanding and engagement with the narrative.

In cultural heritage preservation, multimedia and transmedia storytelling are used to document, preserve, and disseminate cultural narratives, providing new insights and perspectives on cultural heritage. For example, a multimedia narrative about a cultural event might include images, audio recordings, and video animations, providing a more comprehensive and engaging record of the event. Similarly, a transmedia narrative about a cultural practice might include narrative fragments, clues, and puzzles that are spread across different platforms, encouraging users to explore and connect the different pieces of the story. This approach not only preserves and disseminates cultural narratives but also fosters a deeper understanding and appreciation of cultural heritage.

7.4.4 Role of Technology in Multimedia and Transmedia Storytelling

Technology plays a crucial role in multimedia and transmedia storytelling in Digital Humanities, providing the tools and resources needed to create, disseminate, and preserve narratives. Digital tools and technologies, such as virtual reality (VR), augmented reality (AR), and interactive multimedia platforms, enable creators to develop immersive and interactive narratives that cater to different learning styles and preferences. For example, VR tools can be used to create virtual environments, allowing users to explore historical sites, cultural artifacts, and scientific phenomena in a more engaging and experiential way. Similarly, AR tools can be used to overlay digital information onto the real world, allowing users to explore and interact with narratives in their immediate environment.

Interactive multimedia platforms are also important in multimedia and transmedia storytelling, as they provide a flexible and dynamic way to create and disseminate narratives. Interactive multimedia platforms often include features such as hyperlinks, quizzes, and simulations, which allow users to explore different aspects of the story, make choices, and experience the consequences of their actions. For example, an interactive multimedia platform might include a simulation of a historical event, allowing users to explore different perspectives, make decisions, and observe the outcomes of their choices. This interactive approach not only enhances the user experience but also fosters a deeper understanding and engagement with the narrative.

Social media and mobile technologies are also crucial in transmedia storytelling, as they provide a way to distribute narrative content across multiple platforms and media channels. Social media and mobile technologies often include features such as user-generated content, crowdsourcing, and social media interactions, which allow users to contribute to the narrative and engage with other users. For example, a transmedia narrative might include a social media campaign that encourages users to share their own stories, experiences, and perspectives. This participatory approach not only enhances the user experience but also fosters a sense of community and belonging, as users work together towards a common goal.

7.4.5 Benefits of Multimedia and Transmedia Storytelling

Multimedia and transmedia storytelling in Digital Humanities offer numerous benefits, both for scholars and for the broader field of the humanities. One of the primary benefits is the enhancement of narrative engagement and immersion, as multimedia and transmedia storytelling provide users with a more dynamic, interactive, and personalized way to explore and engage with narratives.

For example, an interactive multimedia narrative might include hyperlinks, quizzes, and simulations, allowing users to explore different aspects of the story, make choices, and experience the consequences of their actions. Similarly, a transmedia narrative might include narrative fragments, clues, and puzzles that are spread across different platforms, encouraging users to explore and connect the different pieces of the story. This enhancement of narrative engagement and immersion can lead to a more comprehensive and nuanced understanding of the narrative, as well as to a more engaging and thought-provoking experience.

Another benefit of multimedia and transmedia storytelling in DH is the enhancement of narrative accessibility and inclusivity, as these approaches provide users with a more flexible, dynamic, and personalized way to explore and engage with narratives. For example, a multimedia narrative might include text, images, audio, and video, catering to different learning styles and preferences. Similarly, a transmedia narrative might include narrative fragments, clues, and puzzles that are spread across different platforms, allowing users to explore and connect the different pieces of the story in diverse and interconnected ways. This enhancement of narrative accessibility and inclusivity can lead to a more comprehensive and nuanced understanding of the narrative, as well as to a more engaging and inclusive experience. Multimedia and transmedia storytelling in

DH also foster a sense of community and belonging, as they provide users with a more engaging, interactive, and collaborative way to explore and engage with narratives. This collaborative and participatory approach not only enhances the user experience but also fosters a sense of community and belonging, as users work together towards a common goal. For example, a transmedia narrative might include a social media campaign that encourages users to share their own stories, experiences, and perspectives. This sense of community and belonging is important for the success of the narrative, as it provides users with the support and encouragement needed to achieve the narrative's goals and objectives.

7.4.6 Challenges

Despite their potential, multimedia and transmedia storytelling in Digital Humanities face several challenges that can limit their effectiveness and impact. One of the primary challenges is the need for digital literacy, which refers to the ability to use digital tools and technologies effectively and responsibly. Digital literacy is essential for both creators and users, as it enables them to navigate the digital landscape, evaluate information, and communicate effectively. To address this challenge, educational institutions must provide ongoing training and support in digital literacy, ensuring that all creators and users have the skills and knowledge needed to succeed in the digital age. Additionally, creators must integrate digital literacy into the narrative, providing users with opportunities to develop and apply digital skills in meaningful and relevant contexts.

Another challenge in multimedia and transmedia storytelling in DH is the availability and quality of digital tools and resources. Digital tools and resources can be expensive, and their quality can vary widely, which can affect the outcomes of multimedia and transmedia narratives. To address this challenge, educational institutions must invest in high-quality digital tools and resources, ensuring that creators and users have access to the tools and resources needed to succeed in the digital age. Additionally, creators must be aware of the potential biases and limitations of digital tools and resources, ensuring that they are used in a responsible and ethical manner.

Multimedia and transmedia storytelling in DH also face ethical and methodological challenges, particularly in relation to the interpretation and representation of narratives. Multimedia and transmedia narratives can be subject to bias and interpretation, which can affect the outcomes of the narrative and the insights they provide. For example, a multimedia narrative might be influenced by the creator's own biases and interpretations, leading to a skewed or incomplete representation of the narrative. To address these challenges, creators must use a range of ethical and methodological guidelines, including transparency, peer review, and interdisciplinary collaboration, to ensure the accuracy and reliability of multimedia and transmedia narratives.

7.4.7 Ethical Considerations

Ethical considerations are crucial in the development and use of multimedia and transmedia storytelling in Digital Humanities, as they involve the interpretation and representation of narratives. One of the primary ethical considerations is the potential for bias and misrepresentation in multimedia and transmedia narratives.

These narratives can be influenced by the creator's own biases and interpretations, leading to a skewed or incomplete representation of the narrative. To address this challenge, creators must use a range of ethical guidelines, including transparency, peer review, and interdisciplinary collaboration, to ensure the accuracy and reliability of multimedia and transmedia narratives. For example, creators might use peer review to evaluate the assumptions and methods used in a multimedia or transmedia narrative, ensuring that the results are based on sound evidence and rigorous analysis.

Another ethical consideration in multimedia and transmedia storytelling in DH is the potential for misuse or misinterpretation of the narrative. Multimedia and transmedia narratives can be used to support a wide range of interpretations and narratives, some of which may be inaccurate or misleading. To address this challenge, creators must use a range of ethical guidelines, including transparency, accountability, and public engagement, to ensure that the results of multimedia and transmedia narratives are interpreted and used responsibly. For example, creators might use public engagement to share the results of a multimedia or transmedia narrative with a wider audience, providing context and interpretation to ensure that the results are understood and used appropriately.

Multimedia and transmedia storytelling in DH also raise ethical considerations related to the representation of marginalized or vulnerable groups. Multimedia and transmedia narratives can inadvertently perpetuate stereotypes or misrepresent the experiences of marginalized groups, leading to harm or injustice. To address this challenge, creators must use a range of ethical guidelines, including inclusivity, representation, and cultural sensitivity, to ensure that multimedia and transmedia narratives are respectful and accurate in their representation of diverse groups. For example, creators might use inclusive data collection and analysis techniques to ensure that the voices and experiences of marginalized groups are represented in the narrative.

7.5 PODCASTS, BLOGS, AND PUBLIC-FACING SCHOLARSHIP

Podcasts, blogs, and other forms of public-facing scholarship are transforming the ways in which academic knowledge is created, shared, and used. These platforms offer scholars a unique opportunity to reach beyond the ivory tower, connect with diverse audiences, and contribute meaningfully to public life. While challenges remain in terms of institutional recognition, digital literacy, and ethical engagement, the potential benefits are profound. By embracing these new forms of communication, academia can become more accessible, accountable, and responsive to the needs of society. In doing so, it affirms the enduring value of scholarship as a public good and strengthens the role of knowledge in shaping a more informed and just world.

Rise of Podcasts in Scholarly Communication

Podcasts have become a powerful tool for sharing academic knowledge in an engaging and conversational format. Unlike traditional academic publishing, which often relies on complex jargon and formal presentation, podcasts offer a more personal and accessible means of communication. Scholars can use this medium to explain their research, discuss pressing issues in their field, or interview other experts and stakeholders. This audio format allows for a level of spontaneity and intimacy that written scholarship often lacks. The portability of podcasts, which can be consumed while commuting, exercising, or performing daily tasks, also contributes to their growing popularity among diverse audiences.

Academic podcasts serve multiple functions. They are used as teaching tools, providing supplementary material for students; they act as outreach platforms, helping scholars share their insights with non-specialist audiences; and they create spaces for interdisciplinary dialogue. For example, podcasts such as "The History of Philosophy Without Any Gaps" or "The Dig" have successfully bridged the gap between academia and the public, demonstrating how complex ideas can be communicated clearly and compellingly. These podcasts often attract large audiences, proving that there is a public appetite for in-depth, thoughtful analysis outside traditional academic circles.

Blogs as a Medium for Scholarly Expression

Blogs have long served as a digital outlet for personal expression, but their value as a form of public-facing scholarship is now widely recognized. Academic blogs offer a flexible, immediate, and informal way to present research findings, reflections, and commentary. Unlike peer-reviewed journal articles, blog posts are not subject to long publication cycles, making them ideal for responding to current events or emerging developments within a field. This timeliness allows scholars to participate actively in public conversations, offering informed perspectives that can counter misinformation or broaden understanding.

The tone and format of blogs also encourage a more relatable and humanized portrayal of academic work. Scholars can use blogs to share their research journey, discuss methodological challenges, or reflect on the societal implications of their work. Such transparency helps demystify academic research and makes it more relatable to the general public. Additionally, blogs often foster dialogue through comments and social media sharing, creating a more interactive and participatory mode of knowledge exchange. Academic blogging has also played a crucial role in building communities, especially in niche or emerging fields, where traditional publication venues may be limited or inaccessible.

Public-Facing Scholarship and Its Broader Impact

Public-facing scholarship encompasses all efforts by academics to engage wider audiences beyond their disciplinary peers. This includes not only podcasts and blogs but also public lectures, op-eds, social media engagement, open-access publications, and participation in community events. The goal of public-facing scholarship is to make academic research relevant and accessible to those outside the academy, including policymakers, educators, activists, and the general public. It represents a commitment to the idea that knowledge should serve society and that scholars have a responsibility to contribute to the public good.

One of the key benefits of public-facing scholarship is its potential to amplify the societal impact of academic research. When scholars communicate their findings in accessible formats, they can inform policy decisions, shape public opinion, and contribute to social change. This is particularly important in fields such as public health, climate science, education, and social justice, where evidence-based insights are critical for informed decision-making. By participating in public discourse, scholars can challenge dominant narratives, highlight marginalized perspectives, and promote a more nuanced understanding of complex issues.

Challenges and Critiques of Public-Facing Scholarship

Despite its growing significance, public-facing scholarship is not without challenges. One major concern is the lack of institutional recognition and reward. In many academic settings, traditional metrics such as peer-reviewed publications, citations, and grant funding continue to dominate evaluation and promotion criteria. As a result, scholars who invest time and effort in podcasts, blogs, or public engagement activities may find that their contributions are undervalued or overlooked. This can create a disincentive for academics, particularly early-career researchers, to engage in public scholarship despite their interest and commitment.

Another challenge relates to the tension between accessibility and academic rigor. Critics argue that in simplifying complex ideas for a general audience, there is a risk of oversimplification or loss of nuance. While this concern is valid, it underestimates the intelligence of public audiences and the skill of scholars in translating complex ideas without compromising their integrity. Moreover, public-facing scholarship does not replace traditional research outputs but rather complements them, offering a different mode of engagement that broadens the impact of academic work. There are also concerns about exposure and vulnerability, especially in highly politicized or controversial fields. Scholars who speak publicly about issues such as race, gender, or climate change may face online harassment, personal attacks, or professional repercussions. Institutions must provide support and protection for scholars engaged in public discourse, recognizing both the value and the risks of such work.

Role of Digital Literacy and Training

As podcasts and blogs become integral to scholarly communication, the need for digital literacy and training becomes more pressing. Many academics are unfamiliar with the technical, editorial, and promotional aspects of podcasting or blogging. Skills such as scripting, audio editing, web design, search engine optimization, and social media strategy are often outside the traditional training of scholars. To bridge this gap, universities and research institutions must offer support through workshops, media training programs, and dedicated communication teams.

Digital scholarship centers, academic libraries, and interdisciplinary hubs are playing a crucial role in this area. They provide platforms, resources, and mentorship for scholars interested in developing public-facing projects. Such support not only enhances the quality and reach of individual initiatives but also fosters a culture of openness and collaboration within academia. Encouragingly, many graduate programs are beginning to include public scholarship components, signaling a shift toward more inclusive and outward-looking models of scholarly engagement.

Ethics and Accountability in Public Scholarship

As with any form of scholarly communication, public-facing scholarship must adhere to ethical standards. This includes ensuring accuracy, acknowledging sources, respecting intellectual property, and being transparent about the limitations of one's expertise. In the age of misinformation and digital manipulation, the credibility of scholarly voices is more important than ever. Scholars must balance the freedom of informal platforms with a commitment to evidence-based communication and responsible engagement.

Accountability also involves reflecting on the audiences and communities served by public scholarship. It is not enough to speak; scholars must also listen, engage respectfully, and remain open to feedback and dialogue. This reciprocal approach can deepen trust, enrich research, and ensure that public scholarship is truly inclusive and socially responsive.

CHAPTER 8

Ethics, Inclusion, and Critical DH

8.1 ETHICS OF DATA USE AND REPRESENTATION

Ethics in Digital Humanities is a dynamic and evolving field that goes beyond compliance to embrace reflection, responsibility, and respect. As the field continues to grow and intersect with diverse forms of data, cultures, and technologies, ethical considerations must remain central to every stage of research. From data collection and consent to representation and preservation, DH scholars must approach their work with a deep sense of accountability to the subjects they study, the audiences they reach, and the communities they serve. By embedding ethical principles into the very fabric of digital scholarship, the Digital Humanities can fulfill its promise as an inclusive, thoughtful, and socially engaged mode of knowledge production.

In Digital Humanities, data can take various forms, including digitized texts, images, sound recordings, metadata, geospatial information, and user-generated content. These data sets are often drawn from archives, libraries, cultural heritage institutions, or digital platforms. What distinguishes DH from other data-intensive fields is its close engagement with cultural, historical, and social contexts. Unlike purely quantitative fields, DH data is often qualitative, interpretive, and context-dependent. Therefore, ethical considerations around data use must go beyond privacy and consent to include issues of cultural sensitivity, historical accountability, and interpretive fairness.

Scholars must recognize that data is not neutral. How data is selected, classified, digitized, and curated reflects underlying assumptions and power dynamics. These decisions can either reinforce existing biases or challenge them, depending on the ethical awareness of the researcher. In DH, where data often involves marginalized communities or contested histories, the stakes of ethical representation are especially high.

8.1.1 Informed Consent and Privacy in Data Collection

One of the most pressing ethical issues in DH research is the question of consent, particularly when working with living individuals or recent historical subjects. Projects that incorporate interviews, social media content, or oral histories must navigate the boundaries of privacy and public interest. Even when data is publicly available, such as tweets or blog posts, ethical researchers must consider whether using this data respects the rights and expectations of the individuals involved. The principle of informed consent should guide data collection practices, especially when the research involves vulnerable groups or sensitive topics.

Privacy concerns are also relevant when digitizing personal archives, letters, or diaries. Although these materials may be part of public collections, they often contain intimate or sensitive information. Researchers must weigh the historical value of such data against the potential for harm or misinterpretation. This is particularly important when representing individuals who are no longer alive and cannot speak for themselves. Ethical data use requires a deep respect for the dignity and complexity of historical subjects.

8.1.2 Representation, Bias, and Inclusivity

The representation of data in Digital Humanities projects plays a crucial role in shaping public understanding of history, culture, and identity. Visualizations, databases, and digital exhibits are not just neutral containers of information; they are interpretive acts that can either illuminate or obscure the stories they aim to tell. Scholars must be aware of the biases that may be embedded in their data sets, as well as the tools and algorithms they use to analyze them.

Bias can emerge in many forms—through incomplete archives, Eurocentric taxonomies, gendered language, or racial stereotypes. When DH projects fail to acknowledge or address these biases, they risk perpetuating systemic inequalities and misrepresenting marginalized groups. Ethical representation requires scholars to critically examine their sources, include diverse voices, and design their projects with an awareness of how power and exclusion operate in cultural narratives.

Inclusivity in data representation also involves making DH projects accessible to a wide range of audiences. This includes using clear language, providing multilingual options, and designing platforms that are navigable for people with disabilities. Ethical representation is not only about what is shown, but also about who is included and how audiences are invited to engage with the material.

8.1.3 Transparency and Accountability in Methodology

Ethical data use in DH demands transparency in how data is collected, processed, and interpreted. Researchers must clearly document their sources, methods, and assumptions to allow others to understand, replicate, or challenge their findings. This is particularly important in computational projects that rely on algorithms, machine learning, or data mining, where results can be opaque or difficult to interpret. Transparency also fosters accountability. When scholars make their methods and decisions visible, they invite critical dialogue and ethical scrutiny.

This openness is essential for building trust, both within the academic community and with the public. It also allows for collaborative approaches to ethics, where researchers, participants, and users can work together to address concerns and improve practices.

Documentation and metadata are key tools in achieving transparency. By providing detailed information about data provenance, digitization processes, and interpretive frameworks, researchers ensure that their work can be evaluated in its proper context. This not only enhances the credibility of DH projects but also contributes to the broader goal of ethical knowledge production.

8.1.4 Cultural Sensitivity and Community Engagement

Digital Humanities projects often involve data that pertains to specific communities, particularly Indigenous, diasporic, or historically marginalized groups. In such cases, ethical considerations extend beyond academic norms to include cultural protocols, community values, and historical responsibilities. Researchers must engage with these communities not merely as subjects but as partners in the research process.

This involves seeking permission, consulting with community members, and ensuring that the project serves their interests as well as academic goals. Ethical representation may require modifying research questions, altering presentation formats, or even refraining from publishing certain materials. The principle of "nothing about us without us" is particularly relevant in DH, where digital tools can either amplify or appropriate community voices.

Cultural sensitivity also involves respecting traditional knowledge systems and intellectual property rights. In many Indigenous contexts, knowledge is not meant to be freely shared or digitized without consent. DH scholars must be aware of these norms and avoid imposing Western notions of openness or data sharing inappropriately. Ethics in DH must be adaptable and responsive to the cultural contexts in which data is situated.

8.1.5 Sustainability and Long-Term Responsibility

The ethics of data use also encompass long-term considerations about preservation, access, and sustainability. Digital Humanities projects often produce data sets, platforms, and tools that outlive their initial funding cycles. Researchers have an ethical responsibility to consider the future of their projects: Who will maintain the data? Will it remain accessible to the public? How will updates, corrections, or reinterpretations be handled? Neglecting these questions can result in digital decay, where once-promising projects become inaccessible or obsolete. This undermines not only scholarly integrity but also the trust of participants and users who engaged with the project in good faith. Ethical DH practice requires a commitment to stewardship, including archiving data responsibly, planning for platform longevity, and ensuring that future users can understand and build upon the work. Sustainability also involves economic and institutional support. Scholars must advocate for funding models and infrastructure that prioritize ethical data use and preservation. This may include collaborating with libraries, archives, or community organizations to ensure that DH projects remain viable and accountable over time.

8.2 ALGORITHMIC BIAS AND HUMANITIES RESEARCH

The problem of algorithmic bias in humanities research presents both a significant challenge and an important opportunity for the field. By confronting these issues directly, digital humanities scholars can develop more rigorous and ethically responsible approaches to computational methods. This requires moving beyond simplistic notions of technological solutionism and instead cultivating a deep awareness of how tools shape knowledge production.

The humanities' traditional strengths in critical analysis, historical contextualization, and ethical reflection position the field uniquely to lead in developing bias-aware computational research practices. As the digital transformation of scholarship continues, maintaining this critical perspective will be essential for ensuring that computational methods enhance rather than undermine the humanistic values of inclusivity, diversity, and nuanced understanding that lie at the heart of meaningful research.

As digital humanities continues to evolve, researchers are exploring innovative approaches to conducting bias-aware computational research. One promising direction involves developing alternative machine learning models that explicitly incorporate humanistic values such as ambiguity and multiple interpretations. Another area of exploration focuses on creating more inclusive datasets through community-engaged digitization projects that center marginalized voices. Some scholars are working on visualization techniques that make algorithmic bias visible and interpretable to humanists without technical backgrounds. The development of open-source, customizable tools that allow researchers to interrogate and adjust their algorithms represents another important frontier. These emerging approaches suggest a future where computational methods can be harnessed for humanities research without sacrificing the field's commitment to critical thinking and ethical scholarship.

8.3 DECOLONIZING DIGITAL HUMANITIES

Decolonizing Digital Humanities is a critical and urgent imperative, aiming to challenge and transform the existing power dynamics in the field. This process involves a critical examination of the assumptions, biases, and methodologies that underpin DH, as well as the development of new approaches that prioritize diversity, equity, and cultural sensitivity. Decolonizing DH requires a deep and sustained engagement with the ways in which colonial legacies and power dynamics shape the field, as well as with the ways in which these legacies and dynamics can be challenged and transformed. This process involves a willingness to question and challenge the existing power dynamics in DH, as well as to develop and implement new approaches that prioritize the voices and experiences of marginalized communities.

Despite its potential, decolonizing DH faces several challenges, including the need for a critical and reflexive approach to the assumptions, biases, and methodologies that underpin the field, the need for inclusive and collaborative approaches that center the voices and experiences of marginalized communities, and institutional and structural challenges. To address these challenges, scholars must engage in a deep and sustained critical and reflexive approach to the assumptions, biases, and methodologies that underpin the field, as well as to develop and implement inclusive and collaborative approaches that center the voices and experiences of marginalized communities. Additionally, scholars must engage in a deep and sustained institutional and structural approach to the ways in which the field is funded, supported, and recognized, ensuring that the voices and experiences of marginalized communities are prioritized and represented.

Ethical considerations are crucial in the development and implementation of decolonizing DH, involving the potential for bias and misrepresentation in the digital representations of cultural heritage, the potential for misuse or misinterpretation of the digital representations of cultural heritage, and the representation of marginalized or vulnerable groups. To address these ethical considerations, scholars must engage in a deep and sustained ethical approach to the development and implementation of decolonizing DH, ensuring that the voices and experiences of marginalized communities are prioritized and represented.

The future of decolonizing DH lies in the integration of critical and reflexive approaches to the assumptions, biases, and methodologies that underpin the field, the development and implementation of inclusive and collaborative approaches that center the voices and experiences of marginalized communities, and the development and implementation of digital projects that prioritize diversity, equity, and cultural sensitivity. By addressing the challenges and exploring new directions, scholars can ensure that decolonizing DH is effective, inclusive, and ethically sound, providing new opportunities for research, learning, and growth. The principles of decolonizing DH, with their dynamic and inclusive approaches, will continue to influence the development of the humanities, ensuring that the field is engaging, inclusive, and relevant to a wider audience. Through the use of digital tools and methodologies, scholars can create a more comprehensive and nuanced understanding of cultural heritage, providing new insights and perspectives on the themes, motifs, and stylistic features that shape our cultural heritage.

As the field of Digital Humanities continues to evolve, decolonizing DH is poised to play an increasingly important role in challenging and transforming the existing power dynamics in the field. One of the key future directions in decolonizing DH is the integration of critical and reflexive approaches to the assumptions, biases, and methodologies that underpin the field. This critical and reflexive approach involves a deep and sustained engagement with the ways in which colonial legacies and power dynamics shape the field, as well as with the ways in which these legacies and dynamics can be challenged and transformed. This approach involves a willingness to question and challenge the existing power dynamics in DH, as well as to develop and implement new approaches that prioritize diversity, equity, and cultural sensitivity.

Another future direction in decolonizing DH is the development and implementation of inclusive and collaborative approaches that center the voices and experiences of marginalized communities. This inclusive and collaborative approach involves a deep and sustained engagement with the ways in which marginalized communities have been marginalized or silenced in the field, as well as with the ways in which these communities can be prioritized and represented. This approach involves a willingness to engage with marginalized communities in the development and implementation of digital projects, as well as to prioritize the voices and experiences of these communities in the field. Additionally, this approach involves a willingness to challenge and transform the existing power dynamics in DH, ensuring that the voices and experiences of marginalized communities are prioritized and represented.

The future of decolonizing DH also lies in the development and implementation of digital projects that prioritize diversity, equity, and cultural sensitivity. This practical work involves engaging with digital tools and technologies that prioritize inclusivity and accessibility, as well as with digital platforms and networks that prioritize collaboration and community engagement. For example, scholars might develop digital projects that prioritize the voices and experiences of marginalized communities, using digital tools and technologies that prioritize inclusivity and accessibility. Additionally, scholars might develop digital platforms and networks that prioritize collaboration and community engagement, ensuring that the voices and experiences of marginalized communities are prioritized and represented.

Several case studies illustrate the potential and challenges of decolonizing Digital Humanities. One notable example is the "Decolonizing the Museum" project, which aims to challenge and transform the ways in which museums represent and interpret cultural heritage. This project involves a critical examination of the assumptions, biases, and methodologies that underpin museum practices, as well as the development of new approaches that prioritize diversity, equity, and cultural sensitivity. For example, the project might involve collaborating with marginalized communities to co-create and co-curate digital exhibitions that prioritize the voices and experiences of these communities. This collaborative and participatory approach not only challenges and transforms the existing power dynamics in museum practices but also fosters a more inclusive and democratic approach to the representation and interpretation of cultural heritage.

Another case study is the "Digital Indigenous Storytelling" project, which aims to prioritize and represent the voices and experiences of Indigenous communities in digital storytelling. This project involves a critical examination of the assumptions, biases, and methodologies that underpin digital storytelling practices, as well as the development of new approaches that prioritize diversity, equity, and cultural sensitivity. For example, the project might involve collaborating with Indigenous communities to co-create and co-curate digital stories that prioritize the voices and experiences of these communities. This collaborative and participatory approach not only challenges and transforms the existing power dynamics in digital storytelling but also fosters a more inclusive and democratic approach to the representation and interpretation of Indigenous voices and experiences.

A third case study is the "Decolonizing the Archive" project, which aims to challenge and transform the ways in which archives represent and interpret cultural heritage. This project involves a critical examination of the assumptions, biases, and methodologies that underpin archival practices, as well as the development of new approaches that prioritize diversity, equity, and cultural sensitivity. For example, the project might involve collaborating with marginalized communities to co-create and co-curate digital archives that prioritize the voices and experiences of these communities. This collaborative and participatory approach not only challenges and transforms the existing power dynamics in archival practices but also fosters a more inclusive and democratic approach to the representation and interpretation of cultural heritage.

8.4 ACCESSIBILITY AND INCLUSIVE DESIGN

Accessibility and inclusive design are fundamental principles in Digital Humanities, ensuring that digital tools, resources, and experiences are accessible and usable by all individuals, regardless of their abilities, backgrounds, or circumstances. Accessibility in DH involves the design and development of digital tools, resources, and experiences that can be used by people with disabilities, while inclusive design involves creating digital tools, resources, and experiences that are accessible, usable, and relevant to a diverse range of users. Together, accessibility and inclusive design promote equity, diversity, and inclusion in DH, ensuring that digital tools, resources, and experiences are accessible and usable by all individuals.

Accessibility and inclusive design in DH involve a multifaceted approach that encompasses technical, methodological, and ethical dimensions. Technically, accessibility and inclusive design in DH involve the use of digital tools and technologies that are designed and developed to be accessible, usable, and relevant to a diverse range of users. Methodologically, accessibility and inclusive design in DH involve the use of inclusive and participatory research methods that prioritize the voices and experiences of a diverse range of users. Ethically, accessibility and inclusive design in DH involve a commitment to promoting equity, diversity, and inclusion in the field.

Despite their potential, accessibility and inclusive design in DH face several challenges, including the need for a critical and reflexive approach to the assumptions, biases, and methodologies that underpin the field, the need for inclusive and participatory approaches that center the voices and experiences of a diverse range of users, and technical and methodological challenges. To address these challenges, designers must engage in a deep and sustained critical and reflexive approach to the assumptions, biases, and methodologies that underpin the field, as well as to develop and implement inclusive and participatory approaches that center the voices and experiences of a diverse range of users. Additionally, designers must engage in a deep and sustained technical and methodological approach to the design, development, and evaluation of digital tools, resources, and experiences.

Ethical considerations are crucial in the development and implementation of accessibility and inclusive design in DH, involving the potential for bias and misrepresentation in the design, development, and evaluation of digital tools, resources, and experiences, the potential for misuse or misinterpretation of the results, and the representation of marginalized or vulnerable groups. To address these ethical considerations, designers must engage in a deep and sustained ethical approach to the development and implementation of accessibility and inclusive design in DH, ensuring that the voices and experiences of a diverse range of users are prioritized and represented.

The future of accessibility and inclusive design in DH lies in the integration of AI and ML, the development of immersive and interactive experiences, and the creation of collaborative and participatory experiences that engage a wider range of stakeholders in the design, development, and evaluation of digital tools, resources, and experiences. By addressing the challenges and exploring new directions, designers can ensure that accessibility and inclusive design in DH are effective, inclusive, and ethically sound, providing new opportunities for research, learning, and growth. The principles of accessibility and inclusive design in DH, with their dynamic and inclusive approaches, will continue to influence the development of the humanities, ensuring that the field is engaging, inclusive, and relevant to a wider audience. Through the use of digital tools and methodologies, designers can create a more comprehensive and nuanced understanding of digital tools, resources, and experiences, providing new insights and perspectives on the themes, motifs, and stylistic features that shape our cultural heritage.

8.5 FEMINIST AND QUEER DIGITAL HUMANITIES

Feminist and Queer Digital Humanities challenge us to think differently about the digital world and our place within it. They remind us that technologies are not neutral tools but cultural artifacts embedded with values and assumptions. Through critical engagement, creative intervention, and ethical practice, these approaches work to create digital spaces that are inclusive, just, and transformative. As the Digital Humanities continue to evolve, the insights and methodologies of feminist and queer scholarship will remain essential for shaping a field that is as socially conscious as it is intellectually innovative.

Feminist and Queer DH are not merely subfields within the broader DH landscape; they represent transformative approaches that question the very foundations of digital scholarship. They push the field to consider whose knowledge matters, how technologies shape power, and what ethical responsibilities scholars hold. By insisting on inclusivity, critical reflection, and community engagement, these approaches expand the possibilities of what Digital Humanities can be.

They also highlight the importance of intersectionality—the understanding that gender and sexuality intersect with race, class, ability, and other axes of identity. This framework allows for a more nuanced and comprehensive analysis of digital cultures and systems. Feminist and Queer DH thus contribute not only to the diversification of the field but to its deepening and enrichment.

CHAPTER 9

Infrastructures and Institutions

9.1 DH CENTERS AND LABS

DH centers and labs are vital engines of innovation, collaboration, and engagement within the Digital Humanities. They provide the infrastructure, expertise, and community necessary to support transformative scholarship that bridges disciplines and reaches beyond the academy. As the field continues to grow and diversify, these centers will remain essential in shaping its direction and ensuring that digital tools are used thoughtfully, ethically, and creatively. In fostering both critical inquiry and technological experimentation, DH centers uphold the core mission of the humanities: to understand, interpret, and enrich the human experience in all its complexity. As the Digital Humanities continue to evolve, DH centers and labs are likely to play an even more influential role in shaping the future of the field. Emerging areas such as artificial intelligence, machine learning, immersive media, and critical infrastructure studies offer new opportunities for innovation and reflection. DH centers are well positioned to lead explorations into these frontiers, provided they continue to cultivate critical awareness alongside technical expertise.

There is also a growing emphasis on sustainability, both in terms of digital preservation and institutional continuity. Centers must think strategically about how to maintain and grow their programs in an environment of shifting budgets and academic priorities. Building strong relationships with libraries, securing endowments, and developing open-access resources are some of the ways DH centers can enhance their resilience and impact. Moreover, the global expansion of DH calls for greater collaboration across regions and cultures. DH centers can contribute to this effort by supporting multilingual projects, facilitating international exchanges, and engaging with global digital infrastructures. In doing so, they help ensure that the Digital Humanities reflect a truly global and inclusive vision.

9.2 LIBRARIES, MUSEUMS, AND ARCHIVES AS DH PARTNERS

Libraries, museums, and archives have emerged as essential collaborators in the growing field of digital humanities, providing not only source materials but also technological expertise and institutional support. These cultural memory organizations serve as natural partners for digital humanities projects due to their dual roles as custodians of vast collections and innovators in digital access. As digital humanities methodologies increasingly emphasize large-scale data analysis, visualization, and computational approaches to cultural materials, these institutions have adapted their traditional preservation and access missions to include digital curation and scholarly collaboration. Their involvement ranges from digitizing fragile manuscripts for textual analysis projects to creating linked open data platforms that connect artifacts across collections. This partnership represents a fundamental reimagining of how cultural heritage institutions can contribute to academic research in the digital age.

As digital humanities continues to evolve, libraries, museums, and archives are positioning themselves as central hubs for digital scholarship on campus and in the community. Many institutions are creating digital scholarship centers that bring together faculty, students, librarians, and technologists to collaborate on projects. Some are developing new staff roles—such as digital humanities librarians, computational archivists, or museum data scientists—that bridge traditional expertise with digital methods.

Forward-looking institutions are experimenting with approaches like artificial intelligence for enhancing collection access, virtual reality for immersive research environments, and blockchain for tracking provenance in digital scholarship. These developments suggest a future where cultural institutions serve not just as repositories of knowledge but as active laboratories for digital humanities innovation, where collections become dynamic datasets that can be continually reinterpreted through new computational lenses while maintaining their cultural and historical integrity.

9.3 DH CONSORTIA AND PROFESSIONAL NETWORKS

9.3.1 ADHO

The Alliance of Digital Humanities Organizations (ADHO) is a global umbrella organization that fosters and supports digital humanities (DH) research, teaching, and practice. It unites several regional consortia and professional networks such as EADH (Europe), ACH (USA), CSDH/SCHN (Canada), JADH (Japan), and aaDH (Australasia). These consortia promote collaboration, interdisciplinary scholarship, and community building across linguistically and culturally diverse contexts. ADHO facilitates international conferences, promotes standards and best practices, and supports open-access initiatives. Its professional networks provide platforms for knowledge exchange, mentorship, and advocacy, advancing DH as an inclusive and innovative field of academic and cultural inquiry. ADHO's professional networks play a crucial role in shaping the landscape of digital humanities by enabling scholars, technologists, librarians, and students to collaborate on diverse digital projects. Through its member organizations, ADHO promotes scholarly communication via journals like Digital Scholarship in the Humanities and open-access forums. It encourages inclusivity through special interest groups (SIGs) focusing on multilingualism, digital pedagogy, and global perspectives. Annual DH conferences organized by ADHO serve as key events for presenting cutting-edge research and fostering partnerships. The consortia model empowers regional representation while maintaining a unified global vision, making ADHO a dynamic hub for innovation in the digital humanities.

9.3.2 HASTAC

HASTAC stands as a transformative force within Digital Humanities and beyond, fostering a culture of critical engagement, interdisciplinary collaboration, and social responsibility. Its contributions to digital pedagogy, open scholarship, and inclusive research have reshaped how we think about the role of technology in academic and public life. Through its scholars, projects, and global network, HASTAC continues to demonstrate that the digital can and should be used in service of equity, creativity, and collective well-being. As both a community and a movement, HASTAC invites all those who care about the future of education, technology, and the humanities to join in its mission.

As digital technologies continue to transform higher education, research, and public life, the role of organizations like HASTAC becomes ever more important. The challenges of misinformation, algorithmic bias, digital surveillance, and inequitable access to technology require sustained, interdisciplinary, and ethically grounded responses. HASTAC is uniquely positioned to address these challenges, thanks to its broad network, flexible structure, and deeply rooted values.

Moving forward, HASTAC is likely to continue expanding its reach, deepening its impact, and fostering new generations of scholars who are equipped to navigate and shape the digital future. Its emphasis on collaboration, openness, and critical inquiry ensures that it will remain a vital space for innovation and reflection in an ever-changing digital landscape.

9.3.3 DARIAH

DARIAH has established itself as a vital enabler of digital humanities research across Europe, creating connections between scholars, institutions, and resources that transcend traditional academic boundaries. By providing shared infrastructure, fostering communities of practice, and advocating for the needs of humanities researchers in the digital age, DARIAH has significantly advanced the scale and sophistication of digital scholarship in Europe. The organization's distributed model offers a compelling example of how to balance national particularities with transnational cooperation in humanities research. As digital methods become increasingly central to humanities scholarship, DARIAH's role in ensuring these developments remain grounded in scholarly rigor, ethical practice, and collaborative spirit will only grow in importance. The infrastructure's continued evolution will play a determining role in shaping the future of humanities research in Europe's digital research landscape.

Despite its successes, DARIAH faces ongoing challenges that require strategic attention. The linguistic and cultural diversity of Europe presents both a strength and a complexity for developing truly pan-European services and standards. Differences in national research funding cycles and priorities can create coordination challenges for the infrastructure's multinational operations. Technological developments in artificial intelligence and advanced data science present both opportunities and demands for continuous adaptation of services and expertise. Looking ahead, DARIAH is focusing on deeper integration with other research infrastructures, expanded support for interdisciplinary research at the intersection of humanities and sciences, and enhanced services for working with increasingly complex and large-scale digital cultural datasets. The infrastructure's ability to navigate these challenges while maintaining its core mission will determine its continued relevance in the evolving landscape of digital humanities research.

9.3.4 CLARIN

CLARIN (Common Language Resources and Technology Infrastructure) is a vital initiative in the field of Digital Humanities (DH) that aims to create a sustainable, integrated infrastructure for language resources and tools across Europe and beyond. The primary goal of CLARIN is to facilitate access to digital language data, tools, and services that support research in linguistics, history, literature, and other humanities disciplines. By establishing a federated network of repositories and providing standardized access protocols, CLARIN enables scholars to share, discover, and utilize a wide array of digital resources seamlessly. This infrastructure is especially significant because it addresses the fragmentation often seen in digital language data, which can be stored in disparate formats, locations, and with varying levels of accessibility.

Through its comprehensive approach, CLARIN promotes interoperability, ensuring that different datasets and tools can work together efficiently, thereby fostering innovation and collaborative research in DH. The infrastructure also offers a range of services, including data curation, metadata management, and user support, which are essential for maintaining the quality and usability of digital resources. Moreover, CLARIN's emphasis on open access and community-driven development encourages scholars to contribute their data and tools, enriching the overall ecosystem and promoting a culture of sharing and transparency. The initiative is supported by a network of national consortia, each responsible for developing and maintaining local repositories, which are interconnected through common standards and protocols, facilitating cross-border and interdisciplinary research. CLARIN also provides training and workshops to help researchers and students acquire the skills needed to effectively utilize digital language resources, thus lowering the barrier to entry in digital humanities research. As the digital landscape continues to evolve, CLARIN remains adaptable by incorporating new technologies such as linked data, semantic web, and artificial intelligence, ensuring that the infrastructure remains relevant and capable of supporting cutting-edge research.

9.4 DIGITAL HUMANITIES IN THE GLOBAL SOUTH

Digital Humanities in the Global South represent a powerful and innovative approach to exploring and interpreting cultural heritage. By leveraging the power of digital tools and methodologies, scholars can uncover patterns, themes, and insights that might not be immediately apparent through traditional close reading. Digital Humanities in the Global South enable researchers to explore vast corpora of cultural heritage efficiently, identifying key themes, motifs, and stylistic features. This method can also help in comparing and contrasting different works, authors, or genres, providing a more comprehensive view of cultural heritage and its significance.

The evolution of Digital Humanities in the Global South has been driven by advancements in computational power, data availability, and digital technologies. From traditional exegetical methods to sophisticated machine learning and AI-driven models, Digital Humanities in the Global South have become more nuanced and context-aware, allowing scholars to delve deeper into the complexities of cultural heritage. The integration of digital corpora and repositories has made it possible for scholars to conduct large-scale Digital Humanities analyses, exploring patterns and trends across entire cultural periods or genres.

Despite its potential, Digital Humanities in the Global South face several challenges, including the digital divide, the need for digital literacy, and ethical and methodological considerations. To address these challenges, scholars must ensure equitable access to digital tools and resources, provide ongoing training and support in digital literacy, and adhere to ethical guidelines and best practices. The future of Digital Humanities in the Global South lies in the integration of AI and ML, the development of immersive and interactive Digital Humanities experiences, and the creation of collaborative and participatory Digital Humanities experiences that engage a wider range of stakeholders in the exploration and interpretation of cultural heritage.

As digital technologies continue to evolve, Digital Humanities in the Global South will play an increasingly important role in the study and interpretation of cultural heritage. By addressing the challenges and exploring new directions, scholars can ensure that Digital Humanities in the Global South are accurate, reliable, and ethically sound, providing new opportunities for research, learning, and growth. The principles of Digital Humanities in the Global South, with their dynamic and interactive representations of cultural heritage, will continue to influence the development of the humanities, ensuring that the study of cultural heritage is engaging, inclusive, and relevant to a wider audience. Through the use of digital tools and methodologies, scholars can create a more comprehensive and nuanced understanding of cultural heritage, providing new insights and perspectives on the themes, motifs, and stylistic features that shape our cultural heritage.

9.5 POLICY AND INSTITUTIONAL SUPPORT FOR DH

Policy and institutional support are foundational to the future of Digital Humanities. Without thoughtful planning, sustained investment, and inclusive governance, even the most innovative DH projects risk being undervalued or unsustainable. Institutions must recognize that DH is not merely a trend or a set of tools, but a vital mode of scholarly inquiry that reflects the changing nature of knowledge production in the digital age. By developing robust policies, building flexible infrastructures, and fostering interdisciplinary collaboration, institutions can ensure that DH continues to grow, evolve, and contribute meaningfully to research, education, and public life. One of the first steps in developing meaningful institutional support for DH is the formal recognition of its scholarly value. This means acknowledging DH as a legitimate domain of research and teaching, not merely a set of technical skills or support services. In many institutions, this recognition has led to the creation of DH centers, labs, and dedicated faculty positions. However, for DH to thrive, such recognition must be embedded within the broader policies that govern hiring, promotion, tenure, and curriculum design. Institutions must create mechanisms to evaluate digital projects with the same rigor and respect afforded to monographs and journal articles. This involves developing peer review standards for digital scholarship and ensuring that hiring and tenure committees understand how to assess collaborative, multimodal, or experimental work.

CHAPTER 10

Future Directions in Digital Humanities

10.1 EMERGING TECHNOLOGIES IN DH

10.1.1 VR

The integration of VR in DH represents a significant shift in the way scholars engage with cultural heritage. By providing immersive experiences, preservation solutions, educational tools, and new forms of scholarship, VR has the potential to revolutionize our understanding of the past and its cultural artifacts. While there are challenges and limitations to consider, the benefits of VR in DH are undeniable, making it an exciting area of research that will continue to evolve in the years to come. As VR continues to evolve, we can expect to see even more innovative applications in DH. Future research will focus on developing more sophisticated tools for creating and analyzing VR experiences, as well as addressing the challenges and limitations outlined above. Scholars will also need to consider the long-term preservation and sustainability of VR projects, ensuring that they remain accessible and usable over time. Finally, as VR becomes increasingly mainstream, we can expect to see more interdisciplinary collaborations between humanities scholars and technologists, leading to new forms of scholarship and creative expression.

10.1.2 AR

Augmented Reality (AR) is a transformative technology in Digital Humanities, offering immersive and interactive experiences that enhance the exploration and interpretation of cultural heritage. AR overlays digital information onto the real world, allowing users to interact with and experience digital content in their immediate environment.

This technology provides new opportunities for scholars, educators, and the public to engage with historical, cultural, and literary themes in innovative and engaging ways. The integration of AR in Digital Humanities has been driven by the increasing availability of advanced digital tools and technologies, the growing recognition of the importance of immersive and interactive learning experiences, and the desire to create more engaging and inclusive educational environments. AR in Digital Humanities has a wide range of applications, from educational tools to cultural heritage preservation and public engagement. These technologies enhance the exploration and interpretation of cultural heritage, providing users with immersive and interactive experiences that foster a deeper understanding and engagement with the cultural heritage. Technology plays a crucial role in the development and implementation of AR in DH, providing the tools and resources needed to create immersive and interactive experiences. Advanced digital tools and technologies, such as high-resolution displays, motion tracking, and haptic feedback, enable the creation of highly immersive and interactive AR experiences.

Despite their potential, AR in Digital Humanities face several challenges, including the need for technical expertise and resources, the need for inclusive and accessible design, and ethical and methodological challenges. To address these challenges, designers must engage in a deep and sustained technical and methodological approach to the development and implementation of AR experiences, as well as to develop and implement inclusive and accessible design approaches that prioritize the voices and experiences of a diverse range of users. Additionally, designers must engage in a deep and sustained ethical approach to the development and implementation of AR experiences, ensuring that the voices and experiences of a diverse range of users are prioritized and represented.

Ethical considerations are crucial in the development and implementation of AR in Digital Humanities, involving the potential for bias and misrepresentation in AR experiences, the potential for misuse or misinterpretation of the results, and the representation of marginalized or vulnerable groups. To address these ethical considerations, designers must engage in a deep and sustained ethical approach to the development and implementation of AR in DH, ensuring that the voices and experiences of a diverse range of users are prioritized and represented.

The future of AR in DH lies in the integration of AI and ML, the development of immersive and interactive experiences, and the creation of collaborative and participatory experiences that engage a wider range of stakeholders in the exploration and interpretation of cultural heritage. By addressing the challenges and exploring new directions, designers can ensure that AR in DH are effective, inclusive, and ethically sound, providing new opportunities for research, learning, and growth.

The principles of AR in DH, with their dynamic and interactive experiences, will continue to influence the development of the humanities, ensuring that the exploration and interpretation of cultural heritage are engaging, inclusive, and relevant to a wider audience. Through the use of digital tools and methodologies, designers can create a more comprehensive and nuanced understanding of cultural heritage, providing new insights and perspectives on the themes, motifs, and stylistic features that shape our cultural heritage.

10.1.3 XR

Extended Reality represents a frontier of exploration and transformation in the Digital Humanities. By enabling immersive, spatial, and interactive experiences, XR redefines how humanists research, teach, and share knowledge. Its applications span historical reconstruction, literary analysis, education, public engagement, and more, offering unprecedented opportunities to deepen understanding and foster empathy. However, realizing the full potential of XR in DH requires critical reflection, ethical responsibility, and sustained institutional support. As the field continues to evolve, XR will play an increasingly central role in shaping a digital humanities that is innovative, inclusive, and attuned to the complexities of human experience.

The future of XR in DH promises continued innovation, particularly with the integration of artificial intelligence, real-time data visualization, and interactive storytelling. As XR technologies become more affordable and accessible, their adoption in DH will likely expand across educational levels, institutional contexts, and geographical regions. The development of web-based XR platforms and mobile AR applications will further lower the barriers to entry, allowing more scholars and students to engage with immersive humanities content. At the same time, ongoing research into usability, narrative design, and ethical frameworks will shape the evolution of XR as a scholarly practice.

10.1.4 Blockchain

Blockchain technology presents digital humanities with both transformative opportunities and significant challenges that require careful scholarly consideration. While not a panacea for all of the field's technological needs, blockchain offers specific solutions to problems of verification, preservation, and scholarly credit that have long troubled digital scholarship. Its adoption must be guided by humanistic values—prioritizing accessibility, inclusivity, and ethical responsibility over uncritical techno-optimism.

As digital humanists experiment with blockchain applications, they have an opportunity to shape the technology's development in ways that serve scholarly rather than purely commercial interests. The coming years will likely see blockchain move from speculative possibility to practical tool in certain DH domains, even as its limitations and risks become clearer.

This evolving relationship between blockchain and digital humanities promises to yield important insights about how emerging technologies can best serve the study of human culture and history in the digital age. As blockchain technology matures, digital humanities stands to benefit from several emerging developments. Interoperability between different blockchain networks could enable more comprehensive scholarly ecosystems where research data, publications, and cultural artifacts are connected across platforms. The integration of blockchain with other emerging technologies like the Semantic Web and artificial intelligence may create powerful new tools for knowledge representation and discovery. Decentralized autonomous organizations (DAOs) built on blockchain principles could facilitate new models for collaborative research funding and governance in digital humanities projects. Perhaps most significantly, as blockchain platforms become more energy-efficient and accessible, they may enable broader participation in digital scholarship from institutions and communities currently excluded by technological or financial barriers. These developments suggest that blockchain's role in digital humanities will likely expand and diversify in coming years.

10.2 THE ROLE OF ARTIFICIAL INTELLIGENCE AND LARGE LANGUAGE MODELS

Artificial Intelligence (AI) has become a transformative force across numerous sectors, fundamentally changing how tasks are performed and how decisions are made. At the forefront of AI advancements are large language models (LLMs), which are sophisticated algorithms trained on vast amounts of text data. These models have demonstrated remarkable capabilities in understanding, generating, and translating human language, thereby playing a critical role in various applications.

In the realm of technology, AI-powered chatbots and virtual assistants have become commonplace, providing instant customer service and support while reducing the need for human intervention. These systems rely heavily on LLMs to interpret user queries and generate coherent, contextually appropriate responses, enhancing user experience and operational efficiency. In the field of healthcare, AI and LLMs assist in diagnostics, medical research, and personalized treatment plans by analyzing extensive medical literature and patient data, ultimately improving patient outcomes.

The legal industry benefits from AI-driven document analysis and contract review, where LLMs can quickly sift through large volumes of text to identify relevant information, saving time and reducing errors. Similarly, in education, AI models are used to develop personalized learning experiences, adapt content to individual student needs, and automate administrative tasks, thereby making education more accessible and tailored. Large language models are also central to advancements in translation services, enabling real-time, high-quality translations that facilitate cross-cultural communication, commerce, and diplomacy. Their ability to process and generate human-like text has profound implications for content creation, journalism, and entertainment, where AI assists in drafting articles, scripts, or creative writing. However, despite these benefits, there are significant challenges associated with AI and LLMs, including concerns over bias, misinformation, and ethical considerations. These models can inadvertently perpetuate stereotypes or produce misleading information if not carefully monitored and regulated. As such, responsible development and deployment are crucial to harness their potential while mitigating risks. Looking ahead, the role of AI and large language models is poised to expand further, integrating with other emerging technologies like robotics, augmented reality, and the Internet of Things.

This integration promises more intelligent, autonomous systems capable of complex reasoning and decision-making, which could profoundly impact industries and everyday life. Nonetheless, ongoing research, ethical oversight, and public discourse are essential to ensure that the deployment of AI and LLMs benefits society as a whole, promoting innovation while safeguarding human rights and societal values.

10.3 BIG DATA, SMALL DATA, AND THICK DATA IN HUMANITIES

Big data, small data, and thick data in Digital Humanities offer unique opportunities and challenges for scholars in the humanities, enabling them to explore and interpret cultural heritage in diverse and innovative ways. Big data involves the analysis of large and complex datasets, providing scholars with new insights into the patterns, themes, and structures that shape cultural and historical phenomena.

Small data involves the analysis of detailed case studies and qualitative data, providing scholars with rich and nuanced insights into the cultural and social dynamics that shape human societies. Thick data emphasizes the qualitative and contextual aspects of data, providing scholars with rich and nuanced insights into the cultural and social practices that shape human societies.

The integration of big data, small data, and thick data in Digital Humanities has been driven by the increasing availability of digital tools and technologies, the growing recognition of the importance of data-driven research, and the desire to create more engaging and inclusive learning experiences. Digital tools and technologies, such as text mining, data visualization, and machine learning, enable scholars to analyze and interpret large and complex datasets, uncovering patterns, themes, and insights that might not be immediately apparent through traditional methods.

The growing recognition of the importance of data-driven research has also driven the development of big data, small data, and thick data in DH, as scholars seek to leverage data to enhance their research and teaching practices. Additionally, the desire to create more engaging and inclusive learning experiences has led to the development of big data, small data, and thick data in DH, which prioritize the active involvement of users in the exploration and interpretation of cultural heritage. Despite their potential, big data, small data, and thick data in Digital Humanities face several challenges, including the need for technical expertise and resources, the need for inclusive and accessible design, and ethical and methodological challenges. To address these challenges, researchers must engage in a deep and sustained technical and methodological approach to the development and implementation of big data, small data, and thick data projects, as well as to develop and implement inclusive and accessible design approaches that prioritize the voices and experiences of a diverse range of users.

Additionally, researchers must engage in a deep and sustained ethical approach to the development and implementation of big data, small data, and thick data projects, ensuring that the voices and experiences of a diverse range of users are prioritized and represented.

Ethical considerations are crucial in the development and implementation of big data, small data, and thick data in Digital Humanities, involving the potential for bias and misrepresentation in big data, small data, and thick data projects, the potential for misuse or misinterpretation of the results, and the representation of marginalized or vulnerable groups. To address these ethical considerations, researchers must engage in a deep and sustained ethical approach to the development and implementation of big data, small data, and thick data in DH, ensuring that the voices and experiences of a diverse range of users are prioritized and represented.

The future of big data, small data, and thick data in DH lies in the integration of AI and ML, the development of immersive and interactive experiences, and the creation of collaborative and participatory experiences that engage a wider range of stakeholders in the exploration and interpretation of cultural heritage. By addressing the challenges and exploring new directions, researchers can ensure that big data, small data, and thick data in DH are effective, inclusive, and ethically sound, providing new opportunities for research, learning, and growth.

The principles of big data, small data, and thick data in DH, with their dynamic and interactive experiences, will continue to influence the development of the humanities, ensuring that the exploration and interpretation of cultural heritage are engaging, inclusive, and relevant to a wider audience. Through the use of digital tools and methodologies, researchers can create a more comprehensive and nuanced understanding of cultural heritage, providing new insights and perspectives on the themes, motifs, and stylistic features that shape our cultural heritage.

10.4 THE POST-DIGITAL TURN AND CRITICAL INFRASTRUCTURE STUDIES

The post-digital turn and Critical Infrastructure Studies together offer a powerful framework for rethinking the foundations and futures of Digital Humanities. They move DH beyond a focus on tools and methods to a deeper engagement with the cultural, political, and material conditions of digital scholarship. By critically examining the infrastructures that support and shape DH, scholars are better equipped to navigate the ethical, environmental, and institutional challenges of the digital age.

This approach calls for a DH that is not only technologically innovative but also critically informed, socially responsible, and committed to building inclusive and sustainable digital futures. The post-digital turn also encourages engagement with public infrastructures and community-based digital initiatives. In a world increasingly dominated by corporate platforms and proprietary technologies, DH scholars have a role to play in advocating for open, public, and community-controlled digital spaces.

This includes supporting open-source software, public data repositories, and participatory archiving projects. By aligning DH with broader movements for digital justice, access, and community empowerment, scholars can help build infrastructures that serve the public good and resist privatization and surveillance. Community-centered approaches to infrastructure challenge the dominance of top-down, institutional models and prioritize local knowledge, user agency, and collaborative governance.

10.5 REIMAGINING SCHOLARSHIP IN A DIGITAL CULTURE

The emergence of digital culture has fundamentally altered the landscape of academic scholarship, necessitating a comprehensive reimagining of research methodologies, publication formats, and knowledge dissemination practices. Digital humanities sits at the forefront of this transformation, challenging traditional epistemologies while creating new possibilities for humanistic inquiry. Where scholarship once privileged the solitary scholar working with printed texts in physical archives, contemporary research increasingly involves collaborative teams analyzing digitized collections with computational tools.

This shift extends beyond mere technological adoption to question foundational assumptions about authorship, peer review, evidence, and argumentation. The digital turn has revealed how deeply our scholarly practices were shaped by the limitations of print culture while demonstrating how digital environments enable alternative modes of knowledge production that better reflect the interconnected nature of humanistic study.

Digital humanities has dramatically expanded the forms and channels through which scholarly knowledge circulates, breaking free from the constraints of traditional monograph and journal article formats. Multimodal digital publications now incorporate interactive visualizations, embedded datasets, and networked annotations that create more nuanced and accessible representations of complex research. Platforms like Scalar and Omeka enable scholars to construct non-linear arguments that mirror the associative nature of humanistic thought rather than forcing research into predetermined print structures. These new formats challenge conventional notions of academic rigor while offering richer ways to present evidence and engage audiences. The digital environment also facilitates more immediate scholarly conversation through preprint servers, academic blogging, and social media engagement, creating faster feedback loops between research production and community response. This expansion of communicative possibilities requires new evaluative frameworks that recognize diverse forms of scholarly contribution beyond traditional publication metrics.

CHAPTER 11

Case Studies and Exemplary Projects

11.1 MAPPING THE REPUBLIC OF LETTERS

The concept of mapping the Republic of Letters refers to the scholarly endeavor of visualizing, analyzing, and understanding the networks of correspondence, ideas, and intellectual exchange among writers, thinkers, and scholars across different periods and regions. This approach aims to illuminate the interconnectedness of historical figures and their influence on the development of knowledge and culture. One prominent case study in this field is the mapping of correspondence networks among Enlightenment thinkers, where digital tools and data visualization techniques help scholars trace the flow of ideas, identify key nodes, and reveal previously unnoticed connections.

These projects often involve extensive digitization efforts, where letters, manuscripts, and publications are systematically collected and linked to create intricate maps that demonstrate the spread of Enlightenment ideals across Europe and beyond. An exemplary project in this area is the "Digital Atlas of the Republic of Letters," which employs geospatial visualization to showcase the geographic distribution of intellectual exchanges, revealing how ideas traveled along trade routes, diplomatic channels, and social circles. Such projects provide valuable insights into the social and cultural geography of intellectual history, emphasizing the importance of place and network in shaping scholarly discourse.

Another significant case study involves the mapping of correspondence networks within the scientific community of the 17th and 18th centuries, where the exchanges among figures like Newton, Leibniz, and others are visualized to understand the collaborative nature of scientific discovery. These visualizations often highlight the role of central figures who acted as hubs of communication, fostering innovation and dissemination of knowledge. Beyond the Enlightenment and scientific networks, mapping projects have also been instrumental in exploring literary circles, political movements, and philosophical debates, demonstrating the versatility of digital mapping tools in humanities research. These projects often combine textual analysis, geospatial data, and social network analysis to produce dynamic, interactive maps that serve both scholarly research and public engagement. The benefits of such mapping initiatives are manifold; they not only enhance our understanding of historical networks but also facilitate interdisciplinary collaboration, allowing historians, digital humanists, and data scientists to work together. Despite their many advantages, these projects face challenges related to data completeness, accuracy, and interpretation, requiring careful curation and critical analysis. As technology advances, future mapping efforts are likely to incorporate more sophisticated visualizations, real-time data integration, and immersive experiences, broadening our understanding of the complex web of intellectual history.

11.2 THE ROSSETTI ARCHIVE

The Rossetti Archive is a pioneering digital humanities project that provides scholars, students, and the general public with access to a comprehensive collection of primary and secondary materials related to Dante Gabriel Rossetti's life, art, and literary works. The archive leverages digital technologies to preserve, disseminate, and analyze Rossetti's extensive body of work, offering new insights and perspectives on his contributions to the Pre-Raphaelite movement and Victorian culture. The Rossetti Archive includes a wide range of materials, such as manuscripts, letters, paintings, drawings, and photographs, as well as scholarly essays, biographies, and critical analyses. The archive's digital tools and technologies, such as search and browse functions, image galleries, and interactive timelines, enhance the user experience and facilitate research and learning.

The Rossetti Archive has had a significant impact on the field of digital humanities, as well as on the study of Dante Gabriel Rossetti and the Pre-Raphaelite movement. The archive's comprehensive collection of primary and secondary materials, as well as its innovative use of digital tools and technologies, have provided scholars, students, and the general public with new insights and perspectives on Rossetti's life, art, and literary works. The Rossetti Archive has also set a precedent for future digital humanities projects, demonstrating the potential of digital technologies in preserving, disseminating, and analyzing cultural heritage.

Despite its potential, the Rossetti Archive faces several challenges and limitations, including the need for ongoing maintenance and updates, the need for inclusive and accessible design, and ethical and methodological challenges. To address these challenges, the Rossetti Archive must invest in ongoing maintenance and updates, as well as in the development and innovation of its digital tools and technologies. Additionally, the Rossetti Archive must engage in a deep and sustained inclusive and accessible design approach, ensuring that its digital tools and technologies are accessible, usable, and respectful of diverse cultural and linguistic backgrounds. Furthermore, the Rossetti Archive must use a range of ethical and methodological guidelines, including transparency, peer review, and interdisciplinary collaboration, to ensure the accuracy and reliability of its digital tools and technologies. Ethical considerations are crucial in the development and implementation of the Rossetti Archive, involving the potential for bias and misrepresentation in the archive's digital tools and technologies, the potential for misuse or misinterpretation of the results, and the representation of marginalized or vulnerable groups.

To address these ethical considerations, the Rossetti Archive must engage in a deep and sustained ethical approach to the development and implementation of its digital tools and technologies, ensuring that the voices and experiences of a diverse range of users are prioritized and represented. The future of the Rossetti Archive lies in the integration of AI and ML, the development of immersive and interactive digital experiences, and the creation of collaborative and participatory digital experiences that engage a wider range of stakeholders in the exploration and interpretation of Rossetti's life, art, and literary works.

By addressing the challenges and exploring new directions, the Rossetti Archive can ensure that its digital tools and technologies are effective, inclusive, and ethically sound, providing new opportunities for research, learning, and growth. The principles of the Rossetti Archive, with their dynamic and interactive digital experiences, will continue to influence the development of the humanities, ensuring that the exploration and interpretation of cultural heritage are engaging, inclusive, and relevant to a wider audience. Through the use of digital tools and methodologies, the Rossetti Archive can create a more comprehensive and nuanced understanding of Rossetti's life, art, and literary works, providing new insights and perspectives on the themes, motifs, and stylistic features that shape our cultural heritage.

11.2.1 Rossetti Archive: Case Studies and Exemplary Projects

The Rossetti Archive has been the basis for numerous case studies and exemplary projects, which demonstrate the potential of digital humanities in preserving, disseminating, and analyzing cultural heritage. One notable case study is the "Rossetti's Manuscripts" project, which focuses on the digitization and analysis of Rossetti's manuscripts. This project involved the digitization of Rossetti's manuscripts, as well as the development of digital tools and techniques for analyzing and interpreting the manuscripts. The project's findings revealed new insights into Rossetti's writing and revision processes, as well as his collaborations with other artists and writers. Additionally, the project's digital tools and techniques have been used in other digital humanities projects, demonstrating the potential of digital technologies in preserving and analyzing cultural heritage. Another exemplary project based on the Rossetti Archive is the "Rossetti's Letters" project, which focuses on the digitization and analysis of Rossetti's correspondence. This project involved the digitization of Rossetti's letters, as well as the development of digital tools and techniques for analyzing and interpreting the letters. The project's findings revealed new insights into Rossetti's personal life, relationships, and artistic practices, as well as the social and cultural contexts that shaped his life and career. Additionally, the project's digital tools and techniques have been used in other digital humanities projects, demonstrating the potential of digital technologies in preserving and analyzing cultural heritage.

A third exemplary project based on the Rossetti Archive is the "Rossetti's Artwork" project, which focuses on the digitization and analysis of Rossetti's paintings and drawings. This project involved the digitization of Rossetti's artwork, as well as the development of digital tools and techniques for analyzing and interpreting the artwork. The project's findings revealed new insights into Rossetti's artistic style and contributions to the Pre-Raphaelite movement, as well as the historical and cultural contexts that shaped his artistic practices. Additionally, the project's digital tools and techniques have been used in other digital humanities projects, demonstrating the potential of digital technologies in preserving and analyzing cultural heritage.

11.3 THE SLAVE VOYAGES PROJECT

The Slave Voyages Project is a landmark digital humanities initiative that transforms historical data into accessible, meaningful, and impactful scholarship. Through its detailed databases, interactive visualizations, and biographical records, it provides a comprehensive view of the transatlantic and intra-American slave trades. Its collaborative and open-access ethos promotes global scholarly engagement and public education. By foregrounding the human cost of slavery while employing the tools of digital scholarship, the project exemplifies how Digital Humanities can contribute to historical understanding, memory work, and social justice. As it continues to evolve, the Slave Voyages Project will remain a vital resource for interrogating the past and informing the future.

11.3.1 Trans-Atlantic Slave Trade Database

At the heart of the Slave Voyages Project is the Trans-Atlantic Slave Trade Database, which includes detailed information on more than 36,000 transatlantic slave voyages. Each entry provides data such as the names of ships, departure and arrival ports, dates, national affiliation, and the number of enslaved Africans embarked and disembarked. This information allows users to trace the movements of slave ships across the Atlantic and analyze patterns in the slave trade over time. The data is drawn from a wide range of archival sources including ship logs, port records, and tax registers, all of which have been meticulously cross-verified. The database is not only a powerful research tool but also a platform for asking complex historical questions about mortality, resistance, and economic networks within the context of the slave trade.

11.3.2 Visualizations and Mapping Tools

One of the most striking features of the Slave Voyages Project is its use of interactive visualizations and mapping technologies. Through animated maps and dynamic timelines, users can observe the ebb and flow of the transatlantic slave trade across centuries. These visualizations help to convey the sheer magnitude of the trade and highlight regional patterns, such as the concentration of slave shipments from West Africa to the Caribbean and Brazil. By turning numerical data into visual narratives, the project enhances both comprehension and emotional impact. This visual approach invites users to see history in motion, making abstract numbers more tangible and immediate. Such tools are particularly effective in educational settings, where they support experiential learning and critical engagement with historical evidence.

11.3.3 The Intra-American Slave Trade Database

In addition to its focus on transatlantic routes, the project also includes the Intra-American Slave Trade Database, which documents the movement of enslaved people between colonies and countries within the Americas. This component broadens the scope of the project by showing how slavery was not limited to the initial crossing from Africa but continued in the form of secondary trades among the Americas. It provides insights into how enslaved Africans were redistributed among plantations, mines, and urban centers in regions such as the Caribbean, Brazil, and North America. By highlighting the intra-regional dimensions of slavery, the project challenges narrow interpretations and underscores the complexity and interconnectedness of colonial slave economies.

11.3.4 People of the Atlantic Slave Trade and Biographical Data

Another recent and innovative addition to the Slave Voyages Project is the "People of the Atlantic Slave Trade" section, which seeks to humanize the trade by collecting biographical information about individual enslaved Africans. This aspect of the project includes data on names, ethnic backgrounds, ages, and experiences derived from ship logs, court records, and missionary reports. By focusing on individuals rather than just aggregate data, this section restores a sense of identity and humanity to those who were dehumanized by the slave system. It also allows users to engage with the personal stories and lived experiences of enslaved people, thereby transforming abstract statistics into compelling narratives of survival, resilience, and resistance.

11.3.5 Collaborative Nature and Global Contributions

The success and richness of the Slave Voyages Project are largely due to its collaborative and transnational character. Historians, archivists, digital humanists, and software developers from across the globe have contributed to the research, design, and maintenance of the platform. Institutions in Africa, Europe, Latin America, and North America have provided source material and contextual expertise, making the project a truly global endeavor. This collaborative model reflects the ethics of shared scholarship and reinforces the idea that understanding the legacy of slavery requires international cooperation. The project's open-access policy ensures that its findings are available to researchers, educators, and descendants of enslaved people, thereby supporting both academic inquiry and social justice initiatives.

11.4 EUROPEANS AND OTHER LARGE-SCALE CULTURAL PORTALS

Europeana stands as the flagship initiative in Europe's ambitious project to create unified access to the continent's cultural heritage through digital means. Established in 2008 with funding from the European Commission, this massive aggregation platform has grown to connect over 50 million digitized items from thousands of cultural institutions across all EU member states. The portal represents more than just a technical achievement in data interoperability; it embodies a cultural and political vision of European identity constructed through shared access to artistic works, historical documents, and artifacts.

Unlike traditional digitization projects focused on single institutions or collections, Europeana operates as a meta-platform that preserves the contextual richness of locally-held materials while making them discoverable within a pan-European framework. Its development has required unprecedented cooperation between national libraries, museums, and archives alongside technical experts in metadata standards, semantic web technologies, and user experience design.

11.4.1 Comparative Case Study: The Digital Public Library of America

The Digital Public Library of America (DPLA) represents the most direct counterpart to Europeana in North America, founded in 2013 with support from American philanthropic organizations and federal agencies. While sharing Europeana's fundamental mission of cultural democratization through digital access, DPLA exhibits distinct architectural and philosophical approaches shaped by its national context.

Its hub model federates content through regional service providers rather than direct institutional connections, reflecting the decentralized nature of American cultural heritage stewardship. DPLA places stronger emphasis on rights clearance and reuse, with all metadata dedicated to the public domain and clear indicators of object usage rights. The platform has pioneered innovative ebook lending programs and tools for historical geographic exploration that differ from Europeana's more exhibition-driven approach. Comparing these two mega-portals reveals how similar technological goals manifest differently based on cultural policies, funding landscapes, and institutional traditions in their respective regions.

11.4.2 National Implementations: France's Gallica and Germany's Deutsche Digitale Bibliothek

At the national level, France's Gallica and Germany's Deutsche Digitale Bibliothek (DDB) exemplify how large-scale cultural portals adapt to specific linguistic and heritage contexts while connecting to broader European frameworks. Gallica, operated by the Bibliothèque nationale de France, stands out for its comprehensive digitization of French printed heritage, including sophisticated OCR for historical typefaces and handwritten materials. Its thematic collections on French revolutions, colonial history, and literary movements demonstrate deep contextualization missing from more generalized portals.

The DDB emphasizes Germany's federal structure, serving as a national aggregator that respects the autonomy of Germany's sixteen Bundesländer in cultural matters. Both portals function as crucial national nodes in the Europeana network while maintaining distinct identities tailored to their domestic user bases, illustrating the balance between local relevance and international connectivity in digital cultural infrastructure.

11.5 LOCAL DH PROJECTS AND COMMUNITY-ENGAGED SCHOLARSHIP

Local Digital Humanities (DH) projects and community-engaged scholarship exemplify the transformative potential of digital tools in fostering collaboration between academic institutions and local communities. These initiatives focus on preserving regional histories, cultural practices, and social issues through digital platforms that are accessible and meaningful to community members. One prominent case study is the digitization of local archives, where community members, historians, and students work together to collect, organize, and share photographs, documents, and oral histories that reflect the unique stories of a specific area.

Such projects often incorporate crowdsourcing elements, allowing residents to contribute their personal histories, thereby democratizing the process of historical preservation. An exemplary project is a digital archive dedicated to indigenous cultural heritage, which empowers communities to control how their histories and traditions are represented and accessed, fostering a sense of ownership and pride. Additionally, projects utilizing digital mapping to document neighborhood changes, social movements, or local environmental issues serve as powerful tools for community advocacy and education, offering visual narratives that resonate with residents. Community engagement is central to these endeavors, often involving workshops, public events, and collaborative decision-making processes to ensure that the digital outputs reflect community priorities and lived experiences. These projects not only contribute to scholarly research but also promote social cohesion and civic participation by amplifying marginalized voices and addressing local concerns. Despite challenges such as digital divides, resource limitations, and ensuring equitable participation, these initiatives demonstrate the significant impact of integrating digital humanities with community activism. Looking ahead, the evolution of local DH projects is likely to incorporate new media, interactive elements, and more inclusive practices, further strengthening the link between academic scholarship and community empowerment.

CHAPTER

Appendices 12

12.1 GLOSSARY OF DIGITAL HUMANITIES TERMS

- **Accessibility:** The design and development of digital tools, resources, and experiences that can be used by people with disabilities, including those with visual, auditory, motor, and cognitive impairments. Accessibility in DH ensures that digital tools, resources, and experiences are accessible and usable by all individuals, promoting equity, diversity, and inclusion.
- **AI (Artificial Intelligence):** The simulation of human intelligence processes by machines, particularly computer systems. AI in DH involves the use of machine learning algorithms and other AI techniques to analyze large and complex datasets, identify patterns and anomalies, and generate insights that would be difficult or impossible to achieve through traditional methods.
- **Annotation:** The process of adding explanatory notes or comments to a text or artifact. Annotation in DH involves the use of digital tools to add metadata, tags, and other information to digital texts, images, and artifacts, providing context, analysis, and interpretation.
- **AR (Augmented Reality):** A technology that overlays digital information onto the real world, allowing users to interact with and experience digital content in their immediate environment. AR in DH provides new opportunities for scholars, educators, and the public to engage with historical, cultural, and literary themes in innovative and engaging ways.
- **Big Data:** Large and complex datasets that require advanced computational techniques to analyze and interpret. Big data in DH involves the use of digital tools and technologies to analyze and interpret large and complex datasets, uncovering patterns, themes, and insights that might not be immediately apparent through traditional methods.

- **Blog:** A regularly updated website or web page, typically one run by an individual or small group, that is written in an informal or conversational style. Blogs in DH provide a platform for scholars, educators, and the public to share research findings, methodologies, and best practices, as well as to engage in discussions and collaborations.
- **Book History:** The study of the material and cultural history of books, including their production, distribution, and reception. Book history in DH involves the use of digital tools and technologies to analyze and interpret the material and cultural history of books, providing new insights and perspectives on the development of literature and culture.
- **Collaboration:** The process of working together with others to achieve a common goal. Collaboration in DH involves working with other scholars, institutions, and communities to share resources, expertise, and knowledge, fostering a more inclusive and democratic approach to the humanities.
- **Crowdsourcing:** The practice of obtaining information or input into a task or project by enlisting the services of a large number of people, either paid or unpaid, typically via the internet. Crowdsourcing in DH involves engaging the public and other stakeholders in the research process, providing them with opportunities to contribute to the project's goals, methods, and findings.
- **Cultural Heritage:** The full range of tangible and intangible assets of a society that are inherited from past generations, maintained in the present, and bestowed for the benefit of future generations. Cultural heritage in DH involves the use of digital tools and technologies to preserve, disseminate, and analyze cultural heritage, providing new insights and perspectives on the development of culture and society.
- **Data Mining:** The process of extracting patterns and knowledge from large and complex datasets. Data mining in DH involves the use of digital tools and technologies to analyze and interpret large and complex datasets, uncovering patterns, themes, and insights that might not be immediately apparent through traditional methods.
- **Data Visualization:** The graphical representation of information and data. Data visualization in DH involves the use of digital tools and technologies to represent and explore complex data sets, enabling scholars to identify patterns, trends, and relationships within the data.

- **Decolonization:** The process of challenging and transforming the existing power dynamics in the field of Digital Humanities, promoting inclusivity, diversity, and cultural sensitivity. Decolonization in DH involves a critical examination of the assumptions, biases, and methodologies that underpin the field, as well as the development of new approaches that prioritize the voices and experiences of marginalized communities.
- **E-Learning:** The use of digital technologies to facilitate learning and teaching. E-learning in DH involves the use of digital tools and technologies to create interactive and immersive learning experiences, providing scholars, educators, and the public with new opportunities for research, learning, and growth.
- **Ethnography:** The study of people and cultures. Ethnography in DH involves the use of digital tools and technologies to analyze and interpret cultural and social phenomena, providing new insights and perspectives on the development of culture and society.
- **Exhibit:** A public display of objects or information, typically in a museum or gallery. Exhibits in DH involve the use of digital tools and technologies to create interactive and immersive displays, providing scholars, educators, and the public with new opportunities for research, learning, and engagement.
- **Facsimile:** An exact copy or reproduction of an original document or artifact. Facsimiles in DH involve the use of digital tools and technologies to create high-quality, accurate, and accessible reproductions of original texts and artifacts, providing scholars, educators, and the public with new opportunities for research, learning, and engagement.
- **Feedback:** Information about reactions to a product, a person's performance of a task, etc. which is used as a basis for improvement. Feedback in DH involves the use of digital tools and technologies to collect, analyze, and interpret feedback from users, providing scholars, educators, and the public with new opportunities for research, learning, and engagement.
- **Geographic Information System (GIS):** A system designed to capture, store, manipulate, analyze, manage, and present spatial or geographic data. GIS in DH involves the use of digital tools and technologies to map and analyze cultural and historical data, providing new insights and perspectives on the development of culture and society.

- **Glossary**: An alphabetical list of terms or words found in or relating to a specific subject, text, or dialect, with explanations. A glossary in DH provides definitions and explanations of key terms and concepts in the field, offering a comprehensive overview of the field and its applications.
- **Haptic Feedback**: The use of the sense of touch in a user interface design to provide information to end users. Haptic feedback in DH provides users with tactile feedback, enhancing their immersion and engagement with the digital content.
- **Heritage**: The full range of tangible and intangible assets of a society that are inherited from past generations, maintained in the present, and bestowed for the benefit of future generations. Heritage in DH involves the use of digital tools and technologies to preserve, disseminate, and analyze cultural heritage, providing new insights and perspectives on the development of culture and society.
- **Image Gallery**: A collection of images, typically displayed in a digital format. Image galleries in DH provide users with access to high-resolution images of cultural and historical artifacts, providing new opportunities for research, learning, and engagement.
- **Inclusive Design**: The design of products, environments, programs, and services to be accessible to and usable by as many people as possible, regardless of age, ability, or situation. Inclusive design in DH involves the creation of digital tools, resources, and experiences that are accessible, usable, and relevant to a diverse range of users.
- **Interactive Timeline**: A digital tool that provides users with a visual and chronological overview of historical events, cultural phenomena, or literary works. Interactive timelines in DH allow users to explore the chronological development of historical events, cultural phenomena, or literary works, providing new insights and perspectives on the development of culture and society.
- **Journal**: A scholarly publication that contains articles, research papers, and other content related to a specific field or discipline. Journals in DH provide a platform for scholars, educators, and the public to share research findings, methodologies, and best practices, as well as to engage in discussions and collaborations.
- **Knowledge Graph**: A knowledge base that uses a graph structure with entities, attributes, and relationships. Knowledge graphs in DH provide a structured and interconnected representation of knowledge, enabling

scholars to explore and analyze complex data sets, uncovering patterns, themes, and insights that might not be immediately apparent through traditional methods.

- **Learning Management System (LMS):** A software application for the administration, documentation, tracking, reporting, and delivery of educational courses, training programs, or learning and development programs. LMS in DH provides a centralized hub for course materials, assessments, and communication, enabling educators to organize and deliver content more effectively.
- **Linked Data:** A set of best practices for publishing and connecting structured data on the web. Linked data in DH involves the use of digital tools and technologies to connect and integrate data from different sources, providing new opportunities for research, learning, and engagement.
- **Literary Criticism:** The study, evaluation, and interpretation of literature. Literary criticism in DH involves the use of digital tools and technologies to analyze and interpret literary texts, providing new insights and perspectives on the development of literature and culture.
- **Machine Learning (ML):** A subset of artificial intelligence that involves the use of algorithms and statistical models to enable computers to improve their performance on a specific task with experience over time. Machine learning in DH involves the use of machine learning algorithms to analyze large and complex datasets, identify patterns and anomalies, and generate insights that would be difficult or impossible to achieve through traditional methods.
- **Metadata:** Data that provides information about other data. Metadata in DH provides context, analysis, and interpretation for digital texts, images, and artifacts, enabling scholars to explore and analyze cultural and historical data in new and innovative ways.
- **Multimedia:** The use of multiple forms of media, such as text, images, audio, and video, to create a rich and layered narrative experience. Multimedia in DH involves the integration of various media forms to create a rich and layered narrative experience, providing scholars, educators, and the public with new opportunities for research, learning, and engagement.
- **Natural Language Processing (NLP):** A subfield of artificial intelligence that focuses on the interaction between computers and humans through natural language. NLP in DH involves the use of computational

techniques to analyze and interpret human language, providing new insights and perspectives on the development of language and culture.

- **Network Analysis:** The process of identifying and analyzing the relationships and connections within a network. Network analysis in DH involves the use of digital tools and technologies to analyze and interpret the relationships and connections within cultural and historical data, providing new insights and perspectives on the development of culture and society.
- **Open Access:** The practice of providing online access to scholarly research and literature free of charge and without most copyright and licensing restrictions. Open access in DH provides scholars, educators, and the public with free and unrestricted access to scholarly research and literature, promoting the dissemination and sharing of knowledge.
- **Oral History:** The collection and study of historical information using audio recordings of people's memories, experiences, and perspectives. Oral history in DH involves the use of digital tools and technologies to collect, analyze, and interpret oral histories, providing new insights and perspectives on the development of culture and society.
- **Participatory Action Research (PAR):** A research approach that involves the active participation of the community in the research process. PAR in DH involves engaging the public and other stakeholders in the research process, providing them with opportunities to contribute to the project's goals, methods, and findings.
- **Peer Review:** The evaluation of work by others of similar competence to the producers of the work. Peer review in DH involves the evaluation of research findings, methodologies, and best practices by other scholars in the field, ensuring the accuracy, reliability, and validity of the research.
- **Preservation:** The process of maintaining and protecting cultural and historical artifacts, documents, and sites for future generations. Preservation in DH involves the use of digital tools and technologies to preserve and protect cultural and historical artifacts, documents, and sites, providing new opportunities for research, learning, and engagement.
- **Qualitative Analysis:** The process of analyzing and interpreting data that is not numerical or statistical in nature. Qualitative analysis in DH involves the use of qualitative data, such as interviews, focus groups, and case studies, to analyze and interpret cultural and social phenomena, providing new insights and perspectives on the development of culture and society.

- **Quantitative Analysis**: The process of analyzing and interpreting data that is numerical or statistical in nature. Quantitative analysis in DH involves the use of quantitative data, such as surveys, statistical analysis, and performance metrics, to analyze and interpret cultural and historical data, providing new insights and perspectives on the development of culture and society.
- **Reconstruction**: The process of recreating or restoring an original artifact, document, or site using digital tools and technologies. Reconstruction in DH involves the use of digital tools and technologies to recreate or restore original artifacts, documents, and sites, providing new opportunities for research, learning, and engagement.
- **Repository**: A digital archive or database that stores and provides access to digital texts, images, and artifacts. Repositories in DH provide scholars, educators, and the public with access to a wide range of digital texts, images, and artifacts, providing new opportunities for research, learning, and engagement.
- **Research Data Management (RDM)**: The process of managing and preserving research data throughout its lifecycle. RDM in DH involves the use of digital tools and technologies to manage and preserve research data, ensuring its accuracy, reliability, and accessibility.
- **Scholarly Communication**: The process of sharing and disseminating research findings, methodologies, and best practices within the academic community. Scholarly communication in DH involves the use of digital tools and technologies to share and disseminate research findings, methodologies, and best practices, promoting the dissemination and sharing of knowledge.
- **Search and Browse**: A digital tool that allows users to search and browse digital texts, images, and artifacts using various criteria, such as keywords, dates, and authors. Search and browse in DH enables users to quickly and easily locate specific materials or topics within a digital archive or database, as well as to explore the archive's content in a systematic and organized way.
- **Small Data**: Smaller, more manageable datasets that can be analyzed using traditional methods. Small data in DH involves the use of digital tools and technologies to analyze and interpret smaller, more manageable datasets, providing new insights and perspectives on the development of culture and society.

- **Social Media:** Websites and applications that enable users to create and share content or to participate in social networking. Social media in DH provides a platform for scholars, educators, and the public to share research findings, methodologies, and best practices, as well as to engage in discussions and collaborations.
- **Storytelling:** The process of sharing and interpreting stories, experiences, and perspectives. Storytelling in DH involves the use of digital tools and technologies to create and share stories, experiences, and perspectives, providing new opportunities for research, learning, and engagement.
- **Tagging:** The process of adding keywords or labels to a digital text, image, or artifact. Tagging in DH provides context, analysis, and interpretation for digital texts, images, and artifacts, enabling scholars to explore and analyze cultural and historical data in new and innovative ways.
- **Text Mining:** The process of extracting patterns and knowledge from large and complex datasets of textual data. Text mining in DH involves the use of digital tools and technologies to analyze and interpret large and complex datasets of textual data, uncovering patterns, themes, and insights that might not be immediately apparent through traditional methods.
- **Thick Data:** Data that emphasizes the qualitative and contextual aspects of data, providing rich and nuanced insights into cultural and social phenomena. Thick data in DH involves the use of qualitative and contextual data to analyze and interpret cultural and social phenomena, providing new insights and perspectives on the development of culture and society.
- **Transcription:** The process of converting spoken language into written text. Transcription in DH involves the use of digital tools and technologies to convert spoken language into written text, providing new opportunities for research, learning, and engagement.
- **User Experience (UX):** The overall experience of a person using a product such as a website or computer application, especially in terms of how easy or pleasing it is to use. UX in DH involves the design and development of digital tools, resources, and experiences that are accessible, usable, and engaging for users.
- **Virtual Reality (VR):** A technology that creates a simulated environment, allowing users to interact with and experience digital content in a fully immersive and interactive way. VR in DH provides new

opportunities for scholars, educators, and the public to engage with historical, cultural, and literary themes in innovative and engaging ways.

- **Visualization:** The graphical representation of information and data. Visualization in DH involves the use of digital tools and technologies to represent and explore complex data sets, enabling scholars to identify patterns, trends, and relationships within the data.
- **Webinar:** A seminar or presentation conducted over the internet. Webinars in DH provide a platform for scholars, educators, and the public to share research findings, methodologies, and best practices, as well as to engage in discussions and collaborations.
- **Workflow:** A sequence of industrial, administrative, or other processes through which a piece of work passes from initiation to completion. Workflow in DH involves the use of digital tools and technologies to manage and organize the sequence of processes involved in a project, ensuring its successful completion.
- **XML (eXtensible Markup Language):** A markup language that defines a set of rules for encoding documents in a format that is both human-readable and machine-readable. XML in DH provides a structured and standardized format for encoding and sharing digital texts, images, and artifacts, enabling scholars to explore and analyze cultural and historical data in new and innovative ways.
- **Youth Engagement:** The process of involving and engaging young people in research, learning, and engagement. Youth engagement in DH involves the use of digital tools and technologies to involve and engage young people in research, learning, and engagement, providing new opportunities for research, learning, and growth.
- **Zoom:** A video conferencing platform that allows users to conduct virtual meetings, webinars, and online courses. Zoom in DH provides a platform for scholars, educators, and the public to share research findings, methodologies, and best practices, as well as to engage in discussions and collaborations.

12.2 LIST OF KEY TOOLS AND PLATFORMS

12.2.1 Text Analysis and Mining Tools

- **Voyant Tools:** A web-based text analysis and visualization platform that allows users to analyze and visualize textual data. Voyant Tools provides a range of tools for text analysis, including word frequency, keyword in context, and trend analysis, enabling scholars to explore and interpret textual data in new and innovative ways.

- **TAPoR:** A web-based text analysis and visualization platform that allows users to analyze and visualize textual data. TAPoR provides a range of tools for text analysis, including word frequency, keyword in context, and trend analysis, enabling scholars to explore and interpret textual data in new and innovative ways.
- **AntConc**: A free, open-source text analysis tool that allows users to analyze and visualize textual data. AntConc provides a range of tools for text analysis, including word frequency, keyword in context, and collocation analysis, enabling scholars to explore and interpret textual data in new and innovative ways.
- **MALLET**: A Java-based toolkit for statistical natural language processing, document classification, and information extraction. MALLET provides a range of tools for text analysis, including topic modeling, document classification, and information extraction, enabling scholars to explore and interpret textual data in new and innovative ways.
- **RapidMiner**: A data science platform that provides a range of tools for data analysis, visualization, and machine learning. RapidMiner provides a range of tools for text analysis, including text mining, natural language processing, and machine learning, enabling scholars to explore and interpret textual data in new and innovative ways.

12.2.2 Data Visualization Tools

- **Tableau:** A data visualization tool that allows users to create interactive and shareable dashboards. Tableau provides a range of tools for data visualization, including charts, graphs, and maps, enabling scholars to explore and interpret data in new and innovative ways.
- **D3.js**: A JavaScript library for producing dynamic, interactive data visualizations in web browsers. D3.js provides a range of tools for data visualization, including charts, graphs, and maps, enabling scholars to explore and interpret data in new and innovative ways.
- **Gephi**: An open-source network analysis and visualization software package. Gephi provides a range of tools for network analysis and visualization, including graphs, charts, and maps, enabling scholars to explore and interpret network data in new and innovative ways.
- **RAWGraphs**: An open-source data visualization tool that allows users to create customizable and interactive visualizations. RAWGraphs

provides a range of tools for data visualization, including charts, graphs, and maps, enabling scholars to explore and interpret data in new and innovative ways.

- **Plotly:** A graphing library that makes interactive, publication-quality graphs online. Plotly provides a range of tools for data visualization, including charts, graphs, and maps, enabling scholars to explore and interpret data in new and innovative ways.

12.2.3 Geographic Information Systems (GIS)

- **ArcGIS:** A geographic information system (GIS) for working with maps and geographic information. ArcGIS provides a range of tools for GIS, including mapping, spatial analysis, and data management, enabling scholars to explore and interpret geographic data in new and innovative ways.
- **QGIS:** A free and open-source geographic information system (GIS) that allows users to create, edit, visualize, analyze, and publish geospatial information. QGIS provides a range of tools for GIS, including mapping, spatial analysis, and data management, enabling scholars to explore and interpret geographic data in new and innovative ways.
- **Google Earth Engine:** A cloud-based platform for planetary-scale geospatial analysis. Google Earth Engine provides a range of tools for GIS, including mapping, spatial analysis, and data management, enabling scholars to explore and interpret geographic data in new and innovative ways.
- **Carto:** A web-based mapping and data visualization platform that allows users to create, share, and analyze maps and geographic data. Carto provides a range of tools for GIS, including mapping, spatial analysis, and data management, enabling scholars to explore and interpret geographic data in new and innovative ways.
- **Mapbox:** A web-based mapping and data visualization platform that allows users to create, share, and analyze maps and geographic data. Mapbox provides a range of tools for GIS, including mapping, spatial analysis, and data management, enabling scholars to explore and interpret geographic data in new and innovative ways.

12.2.4 Digital Archives and Repositories

- **Omeka:** A free, flexible, and open-source web publishing platform for the display of library, museum, archives, and scholarly collections and exhibitions. Omeka provides a range of tools for digital archives and repositories, including metadata management, digital exhibits, and data visualization, enabling scholars to explore and interpret cultural heritage in new and innovative ways.

- **Dspace**: An open-source repository software package typically used for creating open access repositories for scholarly and/or published digital content. Dspace provides a range of tools for digital archives and repositories, including metadata management, digital preservation, and data visualization, enabling scholars to explore and interpret cultural heritage in new and innovative ways.
- **Fedora**: An open-source repository software platform for the management and dissemination of digital content. Fedora provides a range of tools for digital archives and repositories, including metadata management, digital preservation, and data visualization, enabling scholars to explore and interpret cultural heritage in new and innovative ways.
- **ContentDM**: A web-based digital asset management system that allows users to create, manage, and share digital collections. ContentDM provides a range of tools for digital archives and repositories, including metadata management, digital preservation, and data visualization, enabling scholars to explore and interpret cultural heritage in new and innovative ways.
- **Islandora**: An open-source software framework designed to help institutions and organizations manage and share digital collections. Islandora provides a range of tools for digital archives and repositories, including metadata management, digital preservation, and data visualization, enabling scholars to explore and interpret cultural heritage in new and innovative ways.

12.2.5 Virtual and Augmented Reality Tools

- **Unity**: A cross-platform game engine used to create 2D, 3D, VR, and AR experiences. Unity provides a range of tools for virtual and augmented reality, including 3D modeling, animation, and interactive design, enabling scholars to create immersive and interactive experiences.
- **Unreal Engine**: A real-time 3D creation tool that provides world-class graphics, simulation, and other core engine technology to developers and creators. Unreal Engine provides a range of tools for virtual and augmented reality, including 3D modeling, animation, and interactive design, enabling scholars to create immersive and interactive experiences.

- **ARKit:** A framework that allows you to easily create augmented reality experiences for iOS devices. ARKit provides a range of tools for augmented reality, including 3D modeling, animation, and interactive design, enabling scholars to create immersive and interactive experiences.
- **ARCore:** A platform for building augmented reality experiences. ARCore provides a range of tools for augmented reality, including 3D modeling, animation, and interactive design, enabling scholars to create immersive and interactive experiences.
- **SketchUp:** A 3D modeling software that allows users to create, edit, and share 3D models. SketchUp provides a range of tools for 3D modeling, including 3D modeling, animation, and interactive design, enabling scholars to create immersive and interactive experiences.

12.2.6 Machine Learning and AI Tools

- **TensorFlow:** An open-source platform for machine learning. TensorFlow provides a range of tools for machine learning, including data analysis, model training, and deployment, enabling scholars to explore and interpret data in new and innovative ways.
- **PyTorch:** An open-source machine learning library based on the Torch library, used for applications such as natural language processing. PyTorch provides a range of tools for machine learning, including data analysis, model training, and deployment, enabling scholars to explore and interpret data in new and innovative ways.
- **Scikit-learn:** A Python library for machine learning built on NumPy, SciPy, and matplotlib. Scikit-learn provides a range of tools for machine learning, including data analysis, model training, and deployment, enabling scholars to explore and interpret data in new and innovative ways.
- **Weka:** A collection of machine learning algorithms for data mining tasks. Weka provides a range of tools for machine learning, including data analysis, model training, and deployment, enabling scholars to explore and interpret data in new and innovative ways.
- **RapidMiner:** A data science platform that provides a range of tools for data analysis, visualization, and machine learning. RapidMiner provides a range of tools for machine learning, including data analysis, model training, and deployment, enabling scholars to explore and interpret data in new and innovative ways.

12.2.7 Social Media and Collaboration Platforms

- **Twitter:** A social media platform that allows users to share short messages, images, and videos. Twitter provides a range of tools for social media and collaboration, including messaging, sharing, and networking, enabling scholars to share research findings, methodologies, and best practices.
- **Facebook:** A social media platform that allows users to share messages, images, and videos, as well as to join groups and participate in discussions. Facebook provides a range of tools for social media and collaboration, including messaging, sharing, and networking, enabling scholars to share research findings, methodologies, and best practices.
- **LinkedIn:** A social media platform that allows users to connect with other professionals, share research findings, and participate in discussions. LinkedIn provides a range of tools for social media and collaboration, including messaging, sharing, and networking, enabling scholars to share research findings, methodologies, and best practices.
- **Slack:** A messaging app for teams that allows users to communicate, collaborate, and share files. Slack provides a range of tools for social media and collaboration, including messaging, sharing, and networking, enabling scholars to share research findings, methodologies, and best practices.
- **Microsoft Teams:** A unified communication and collaboration platform that combines chat, video conferencing, file storage, and application integration. Microsoft Teams provides a range of tools for social media and collaboration, including messaging, sharing, and networking, enabling scholars to share research findings, methodologies, and best practices.

12.2.8 Learning Management Systems (LMS)

- **Moodle:** A learning management system (LMS) that allows educators to create personalized learning environments. Moodle provides a range of tools for LMS, including course management, assessment, and communication, enabling educators to organize and deliver content more effectively.
- **Blackboard:** A learning management system (LMS) that allows educators to create personalized learning environments. Blackboard provides a range of tools for LMS, including course management, assessment, and communication, enabling educators to organize and deliver content more effectively.

- **Canvas:** A learning management system (LMS) that allows educators to create personalized learning environments. Canvas provides a range of tools for LMS, including course management, assessment, and communication, enabling educators to organize and deliver content more effectively.
- **Sakai:** A learning management system (LMS) that allows educators to create personalized learning environments. Sakai provides a range of tools for LMS, including course management, assessment, and communication, enabling educators to organize and deliver content more effectively.
- **D2L (Desire2Learn):** A learning management system (LMS) that allows educators to create personalized learning environments. D2L provides a range of tools for LMS, including course management, assessment, and communication, enabling educators to organize and deliver content more effectively.

12.2.9 Digital Storytelling and Multimedia Tools

- **Adobe Premiere Pro:** A video editing software that allows users to create and edit professional-quality videos. Adobe Premiere Pro provides a range of tools for digital storytelling and multimedia, including video editing, animation, and special effects, enabling scholars to create immersive and interactive experiences.
- **Final Cut Pro:** A professional non-linear video editing software application that runs on macOS. Final Cut Pro provides a range of tools for digital storytelling and multimedia, including video editing, animation, and special effects, enabling scholars to create immersive and interactive experiences.
- **Adobe After Effects:** A digital visual effects, motion graphics, and compositing application developed by Adobe Systems. Adobe After Effects provides a range of tools for digital storytelling and multimedia, including video editing, animation, and special effects, enabling scholars to create immersive and interactive experiences.
- **Adobe Audition:** A digital audio workstation from Adobe Systems. Adobe Audition provides a range of tools for digital storytelling and multimedia, including audio editing, mixing, and mastering, enabling scholars to create immersive and interactive experiences.
- **Audacity:** A free, open-source, cross-platform audio software for multi-track recording and editing. Audacity provides a range of tools for digital storytelling and multimedia, including audio editing, mixing,

and mastering, enabling scholars to create immersive and interactive experiences.

12.3 GRANT AGENCIES AND FUNDING OPPORTUNITIES

12.3.1 National Endowment for the Humanities (NEH)

The National Endowment for the Humanities (NEH) is an independent federal agency in the United States that supports research and education in the humanities. The NEH offers a variety of grant programs that support projects in the Digital Humanities, including research and development, digital preservation, and public engagement. Some of the key grant programs offered by the NEH include:

- **Digital Humanities Start-Up Grants:** These grants support the planning and development of innovative digital projects in the humanities. The grants provide funding for the initial stages of a project, including research, prototyping, and pilot testing. The goal of these grants is to support the development of new and innovative digital projects that have the potential to advance the field of Digital Humanities.
- **Digital Humanities Advancement Grants:** These grants support the implementation and completion of digital projects in the humanities. The grants provide funding for the final stages of a project, including development, testing, and dissemination. The goal of these grants is to support the completion and dissemination of digital projects that have the potential to advance the field of Digital Humanities.
- **Digital Humanities Implementation Grants:** These grants support the implementation and completion of digital projects in the humanities. The grants provide funding for the final stages of a project, including development, testing, and dissemination. The goal of these grants is to support the completion and dissemination of digital projects that have the potential to advance the field of Digital Humanities.
- **Digital Humanities Preservation and Access Grants:** These grants support the preservation and access of digital humanities projects. The grants provide funding for the preservation, migration, and access of digital projects, ensuring their long-term sustainability and accessibility. The goal of these grants is to support the preservation and access of digital projects that have the potential to advance the field of Digital Humanities.

12.3.2 Andrew W. Mellon Foundation

The Andrew W. Mellon Foundation is a private foundation that supports higher education and the arts. The foundation offers a variety of grant programs that support projects in the Digital Humanities, including research, digital preservation, and public engagement. Some of the key grant programs offered by the Andrew W. Mellon Foundation include:

- **Digital Humanities Research Grants:** These grants support research projects in the Digital Humanities, including the development of new methodologies, tools, and approaches. The grants provide funding for research, development, and dissemination, enabling scholars to explore and interpret cultural heritage in new and innovative ways.
- **Digital Humanities Preservation Grants:** These grants support the preservation and access of digital humanities projects. The grants provide funding for the preservation, migration, and access of digital projects, ensuring their long-term sustainability and accessibility. The goal of these grants is to support the preservation and access of digital projects that have the potential to advance the field of Digital Humanities.
- **Digital Humanities Public Engagement Grants:** These grants support public engagement and outreach activities in the Digital Humanities. The grants provide funding for the development and implementation of public engagement and outreach activities, enabling scholars to share their research findings, methodologies, and best practices with a wider audience.

12.3.3 Institute of Museum and Library Services (IMLS)

The Institute of Museum and Library Services (IMLS) is an independent federal agency in the United States that supports museums, libraries, and archives. The IMLS offers a variety of grant programs that support projects in the Digital Humanities, including digital preservation, access, and public engagement. Some of the key grant programs offered by the IMLS include:

- **National Digital Platforms:** This grant program supports the development and implementation of national digital platforms that provide access to cultural heritage collections. The grants provide funding for the development, implementation, and dissemination of digital platforms, enabling museums, libraries, and archives to share their collections with a wider audience.
- **National Leadership Grants for Libraries:** This grant program supports projects that address challenges faced by the library and archives fields and advance the role of libraries and archives in society. The grants provide funding for the development, implementation, and

dissemination of projects that have the potential to advance the field of Digital Humanities.

- **National Leadership Grants for Museums:** This grant program supports projects that address challenges faced by the museum field and advance the role of museums in society. The grants provide funding for the development, implementation, and dissemination of projects that have the potential to advance the field of Digital Humanities.

12.3.4 National Science Foundation (NSF)

The National Science Foundation (NSF) is an independent federal agency in the United States that supports research and education in science and engineering. The NSF offers a variety of grant programs that support projects in the Digital Humanities, including research, digital preservation, and public engagement. Some of the key grant programs offered by the NSF include:

- **Documenting Endangered Languages:** This grant program supports projects that document and preserve endangered languages. The grants provide funding for the development, implementation, and dissemination of projects that have the potential to advance the field of Digital Humanities.
- **Documenting the Built Environment:** This grant program supports projects that document and preserve the built environment. The grants provide funding for the development, implementation, and dissemination of projects that have the potential to advance the field of Digital Humanities.

12.3.5 European Research Council (ERC)

The European Research Council (ERC) is a European Union body that supports frontier research in Europe. The ERC offers a variety of grant programs that support projects in the Digital Humanities, including research, digital preservation, and public engagement. Some of the key grant programs offered by the ERC include:

- **Starting Grants:** These grants support early-career researchers in conducting frontier research. The grants provide funding for research, development, and dissemination, enabling scholars to explore and interpret cultural heritage in new and innovative ways.
- **Consolidator Grants:** These grants support researchers who have already established a research team and have a track record of research achievements. The grants provide funding for research, development, and dissemination, enabling scholars to advance their research and contribute to the field of Digital Humanities.

- **Advanced Grants**: These grants support researchers who have a track record of significant research achievements. The grants provide funding for research, development, and dissemination, enabling scholars to advance their research and contribute to the field of Digital Humanities.

12.3.6 Social Sciences and Humanities Research Council (SSHRC)

The Social Sciences and Humanities Research Council (SSHRC) is a Canadian federal research funding agency that promotes and supports research and research training in the social sciences and humanities. The SSHRC offers a variety of grant programs that support projects in the Digital Humanities, including research, digital preservation, and public engagement. Some of the key grant programs offered by the SSHRC include:

- **Insight Grants:** These grants support research projects that address social, cultural, economic, and technological issues of relevance to Canadians. The grants provide funding for research, development, and dissemination, enabling scholars to explore and interpret cultural heritage in new and innovative ways.
- **Connection Grants**: These grants support events and activities that engage Canadians in the discussion and sharing of research results. The grants provide funding for the development and implementation of public engagement and outreach activities, enabling scholars to share their research findings, methodologies, and best practices with a wider audience.
- **Partnership Grants:** These grants support formal partnerships between academic researchers, partner organizations, and communities. The grants provide funding for the development, implementation, and dissemination of projects that have the potential to advance the field of Digital Humanities.

12.3.7 British Academy

The British Academy is the UK's national academy for the humanities and social sciences. The British Academy offers a variety of grant programs that support projects in the Digital Humanities, including research, digital preservation, and public engagement. Some of the key grant programs offered by the British Academy include:

- **Mid-Career Fellowships**: These fellowships support mid-career researchers in conducting research in the humanities and social sciences. The fellowships provide funding for research, development, and dissemination, enabling scholars to explore and interpret cultural heritage in new and innovative ways.

- **Postdoctoral Fellowships**: These fellowships support early-career researchers in conducting research in the humanities and social sciences. The fellowships provide funding for research, development, and dissemination, enabling scholars to advance their research and contribute to the field of Digital Humanities.
- **Global Challenges Research Fund**: This fund supports research that addresses global challenges, including those related to the Digital Humanities. The fund provides funding for research, development, and dissemination, enabling scholars to explore and interpret cultural heritage in new and innovative ways.

12.3.8 Australian Research Council (ARC)

The Australian Research Council (ARC) is an Australian Government agency that provides funding for research and research training. The ARC offers a variety of grant programs that support projects in the Digital Humanities, including research, digital preservation, and public engagement. Some of the key grant programs offered by the ARC include:

- **Discovery Projects**: These projects support research that advances knowledge and addresses key challenges facing Australia. The projects provide funding for research, development, and dissemination, enabling scholars to explore and interpret cultural heritage in new and innovative ways.
- **Linkage Projects**: These projects support collaborative research between universities and other organizations. The projects provide funding for the development, implementation, and dissemination of projects that have the potential to advance the field of Digital Humanities.
- **Future Fellowships**: These fellowships support early- to mid-career researchers in conducting research in the humanities and social sciences. The fellowships provide funding for research, development, and dissemination, enabling scholars to explore and interpret cultural heritage in new and innovative ways.

12.4 RECOMMENDED READINGS AND ONLINE RESOURCES

12.4.1 Foundational Texts in Digital Humanities

- **Berry, David M. "Understanding Digital Humanities." Palgrave Macmillan, 2014:** This book provides a comprehensive introduction to the field of Digital Humanities, exploring its history, theories, and methodologies. Berry discusses the key concepts and debates in the field, as well as the tools and technologies used in Digital Humanities. The book also includes case studies and examples, providing practical insights into the application of Digital Humanities.

- **Kirschenbaum, Matthew G. "What Is Digital Humanities and What's It Doing in a Place Like This?" A Companion to Digital Humanities. Wiley-Blackwell, 2016:** This chapter provides an overview of the field of Digital Humanities, exploring its history, theories, and methodologies. Kirschenbaum discusses the key concepts and debates in the field, as well as the tools and technologies used in Digital Humanities. The chapter also includes case studies and examples, providing practical insights into the application of Digital Humanities.
- **Rockwell, Geoffrey, and Andrew F. Stauffer. "The Digital Humanities and the Digital Modern." PMLA 128.2 (2013): 485-504:** This article explores the intersection of Digital Humanities and modernism, discussing the ways in which digital tools and technologies can be used to analyze and interpret modernist literature. The authors discuss the key concepts and debates in the field, as well as the tools and technologies used in Digital Humanities. The article also includes case studies and examples, providing practical insights into the application of Digital Humanities.
- **Presner, Todd. "Digital Humanities 2.0: A Report on Knowledge." In Debates in the Digital Humanities, edited by Matthew K. Gold, 2012:** This report provides an overview of the field of Digital Humanities, exploring its history, theories, and methodologies. Presner discusses the key concepts and debates in the field, as well as the tools and technologies used in Digital Humanities. The report also includes case studies and examples, providing practical insights into the application of Digital Humanities.

12.4.2 Key Journals in Digital Humanities

- **Journal of Digital Humanities (JDH):** The Journal of Digital Humanities is an open-access, peer-reviewed journal that publishes research and scholarship in the field of Digital Humanities. The journal covers a wide range of topics, including text analysis, data visualization, digital archives, and public engagement. The journal also includes case studies and examples, providing practical insights into the application of Digital Humanities.
- **Digital Humanities Quarterly (DHQ):** Digital Humanities Quarterly is an open-access, peer-reviewed journal that publishes research and

scholarship in the field of Digital Humanities. The journal covers a wide range of topics, including digital preservation, digital storytelling, and digital mapping. The journal also includes case studies and examples, providing practical insights into the application of Digital Humanities.

- **International Journal of Digital Humanities (IJDH):** The International Journal of Digital Humanities is an open-access, peer-reviewed journal that publishes research and scholarship in the field of Digital Humanities. The journal covers a wide range of topics, including digital text analysis, digital archives, and digital storytelling. The journal also includes case studies and examples, providing practical insights into the application of Digital Humanities.

12.4.3 Online Resources and Digital Archives

- **Digital Humanities Now (DHNow):** Digital Humanities Now is an online resource that provides news, reviews, and commentary on the field of Digital Humanities. The website includes articles, blog posts, and multimedia content, providing a comprehensive overview of the field and its applications. The website also includes a directory of Digital Humanities projects and initiatives, providing practical insights into the application of Digital Humanities.
- **The Rossetti Archive:** The Rossetti Archive is an online resource that provides access to a comprehensive collection of primary and secondary materials related to the life and works of Dante Gabriel Rossetti. The archive includes a wide range of materials, such as manuscripts, letters, paintings, drawings, and photographs, as well as scholarly essays, biographies, and critical analyses. The archive also includes digital tools and features, such as search and browse functions, image galleries, and interactive timelines.
- **The Walt Whitman Archive:** The Walt Whitman Archive is an online resource that provides access to a comprehensive collection of primary and secondary materials related to the life and works of Walt Whitman. The archive includes a wide range of materials, such as manuscripts, letters, and photographs, as well as scholarly essays, biographies, and critical analyses. The archive also includes digital tools and features, such as search and browse functions, image galleries, and interactive timelines.

12.4.4 Digital Tools and Technologies

- **Voyant Tools:** Voyant Tools is a web-based text analysis and visualization platform that allows users to analyze and visualize textual data. Voyant Tools provides a range of tools for text analysis, including word frequency, keyword in context, and trend analysis, enabling scholars to explore and interpret textual data in new and innovative ways.

- **TAPoR (Text Analysis Portal for Research):** TAPoR is a web-based text analysis and visualization platform that allows users to analyze and visualize textual data. TAPoR provides a range of tools for text analysis, including word frequency, keyword in context, and trend analysis, enabling scholars to explore and interpret textual data in new and innovative ways.
- **AntConc:** AntConc is a free, open-source text analysis tool that allows users to analyze and visualize textual data. AntConc provides a range of tools for text analysis, including word frequency, keyword in context, and collocation analysis, enabling scholars to explore and interpret textual data in new and innovative ways.
- **MALLET (Machine Learning for Language Toolkit):** MALLET is a Java-based toolkit for statistical natural language processing, document classification, and information extraction. MALLET provides a range of tools for text analysis, including topic modeling, document classification, and information extraction, enabling scholars to explore and interpret textual data in new and innovative ways.

12.4.5 Online Courses and Tutorials

- **Coursera: Digital Humanities:** Coursera offers a range of online courses in Digital Humanities, covering topics such as text analysis, data visualization, digital archives, and public engagement. The courses are taught by leading scholars in the field and include video lectures, readings, and assignments. The courses also provide practical insights into the application of Digital Humanities, including case studies and examples.
- **edX: Digital Humanities:** edX offers a range of online courses in Digital Humanities, covering topics such as digital preservation, digital storytelling, and digital mapping. The courses are taught by leading scholars in the field and include video lectures, readings, and assignments. The courses also provide practical insights into the application of Digital Humanities, including case studies and examples.
- **FutureLearn: Digital Humanities:** FutureLearn offers a range of online courses in Digital Humanities, covering topics such as digital text analysis, digital archives, and digital storytelling. The courses are taught

by leading scholars in the field and include video lectures, readings, and assignments. The courses also provide practical insights into the application of Digital Humanities, including case studies and examples.

12.4.6 Professional Organizations and Networks

- **Alliance of Digital Humanities Organizations (ADHO):** The Alliance of Digital Humanities Organizations (ADHO) is an international organization that promotes the development and application of Digital Humanities. ADHO provides a range of resources and services, including conferences, workshops, and publications, as well as a directory of Digital Humanities projects and initiatives. ADHO also provides networking and collaboration opportunities, enabling scholars to connect and collaborate with others in the field.
- **European Association for Digital Humanities (EADH):** The European Association for Digital Humanities (EADH) is an organization that promotes the development and application of Digital Humanities in Europe. EADH provides a range of resources and services, including conferences, workshops, and publications, as well as a directory of Digital Humanities projects and initiatives. EADH also provides networking and collaboration opportunities, enabling scholars to connect and collaborate with others in the field.
- **Society for Digital Humanities (SDH):** The Society for Digital Humanities (SDH) is an organization that promotes the development and application of Digital Humanities. SDH provides a range of resources and services, including conferences, workshops, and publications, as well as a directory of Digital Humanities projects and initiatives. SDH also provides networking and collaboration opportunities, enabling scholars to connect and collaborate with others in the field.

References

A Companion to Digital Humanities: Edited by Susan Schreibman, Ray Siemens, John Unsworth, 2004

A Companion to Digital Literary Studies: Edited by Susan Schreibman, Ray Siemens, 2008

A New Companion to Digital Humanities: Edited by Susan Schreibman, Ray Siemens, John Unsworth, 2016

Between Humanities and the Digital: Edited by Patrik Svensson, David Theo Goldberg, 2015

Big Digital Humanities: Imagining a Meeting Place for the Humanities and the Digital: Patrik Svensson, 2016

Critical Digital Humanities: The Search for a Methodology: James E. Dobson, 2019

Debates in the Digital Humanities: Edited by Matthew K. Gold, 2012

Defining Digital Humanities: A Reader: Edited by Melissa Terras, Julianne Nyhan, Edward Vanhoutte, 2013

Digital History: A Guide to Gathering, Preserving, and Presenting the Past on the Web: Daniel J. Cohen, Roy Rosenzweig, 2006

Digital Humanities and Architecture: Edited by Anetta Kepczynska-Walczak, Szymon Ruszczewski, 2022

Digital Humanities and Art History: Edited by Murtha Baca, Anne Helmreich, 2021

Digital Humanities and Digital Media: Conversations on Politics, Culture, Aesthetics and Literacy: Roberto Simanowski, 2016

Digital Humanities and Film Studies: Edited by Adelheid Heftberger, 2022

Digital Humanities and Laboratories: Edited by Urszula Pawlicka-Deger, Christopher Thomson, 2023

Digital Humanities and Latin American Studies: Edited by Hector Fernandez L'Hoeste, Juan Carlos Rodriguez, 2021

Digital Humanities and Libraries and Archives in Religious Studies: Edited by Clifford B. Anderson, 2019

Digital Humanities and Material Religion: Edited by Emily Suzanne Clark, Rachel McBride Lindsey, 2022

Digital Humanities and Musicology: Edited by Joseph Auner, 2021

Digital Humanities and New Ways of Teaching: Edited by Anna Wing-bo Tso, 2019

Digital Humanities and Research Methods in Religious Studies: Edited by Christopher D. Cantwell, Hussein Rashid, 2021

Digital Humanities and Shakespeare: Edited by Brett D. Hirsch, 2021

Digital Humanities and the Lost Drama of Early Modern England: Matthew Steggle, 2015

Digital Humanities and the Study of African Literature: Edited by Daria Tunca, 2023

Digital Humanities and the Study of Classical Antiquity: Edited by Gabriel Bodard, Matteo Romanello, 2022

Digital Humanities and the Study of Colonialism: Edited by Roopika Risam, 2022

Digital Humanities and the Study of Comics: Edited by Ernesto Priego, 2022

Digital Humanities and the Study of Gender and Sexuality: Edited by Isabel Davis, Emma Parker, 2021

Digital Humanities and the Study of Indigenous Languages: Edited by Hartmut Haberland, Bent Preisler, 2023

Digital Humanities and the Study of Medieval Literature: Edited by Orietta Da Rold, Elaine Treharne, 2020

Digital Humanities and the Study of Migration: Edited by Domenico Fiormonte, Sukanta Chaudhuri, 2022

Digital Humanities and the Study of Modernism: Edited by James O'Sullivan, 2022

Digital Humanities and the Study of Religion: Edited by Tim Hutchings, Joanne McKenzie, 2020

Digital Humanities and the Study of Theater: Edited by Sarah Bay-Cheng, 2023

Digital Humanities in Biblical, Early Jewish and Early Christian Studies: Edited by Claire Clivaz, Andrew Gregory, 2014

Digital Humanities in Practice: Edited by Claire Warwick, Melissa Terras, Julianne Nyhan, 2012

Digital Humanities Pedagogy: Practices, Principles and Politics: Edited by Brett D. Hirsch, 2012

Digital Humanities: Current Perspective, Practices, and Research: Bryan Carter, 2013

Digital Humanities: Knowledge and Critique in a Digital Age: David M. Berry, Anders Fagerjord, 2017

Digital Methods: Richard Rogers, 2013

Digital Scholarly Editing: Theories and Practices: Edited by Matthew James Driscoll, Elena Pierazzo, 2016

Digital_Humanities: Anne Burdick, Johanna Drucker, Peter Lunenfeld, Todd Presner, Jeffrey Schnapp, 2012

Doing Digital Humanities: Practice, Training, Research: Edited by Constance Crompton, Richard J. Lane, Ray Siemens, 2016

Hacking the Academy: New Approaches to Scholarship and Teaching from Digital Humanities: Edited by Daniel J. Cohen, Tom Scheinfeldt, 2013

Humanities Computing: Willard McCarty, 2005

Teaching the Digital Humanities: Edited by Christopher J. Young, Shannon Marie Robinson, 2022

The Digital Humanist: A Critical Inquiry: Domenico Fiormonte, Teresa Numerico, Francesca Tomasi, 2015

The Emergence of the Digital Humanities x: Steven E. Jones, 2015

The Shape of Data in Digital Humanities: Modeling Texts and Text-based Resources: Julia Flanders, Fotis Jannidis, 2018

Understanding Digital Humanities: Edited by David M. Berry, 2012

Index

A

Access

1, 2, 3, 5, 6, 7, 9, 12, 13, 14, 15, 18, 19, 21, 22, 23, 25, 26, 27, 34, 40, 62, 63, 64, 74, 78, 87, 89, 90, 91, 97, 98, 100, 103, 111, 112, 118, 130, 141, 151, 153, 161, 163, 164, 167, 168, 169, 170, 171, 172, 174, 178, 183, 188, 189, 192, 193, 194, 197, 198, 200, 201, 202, 212, 213, 214, 220, 222, 223, 224, 225, 226, 227, 234, 237, 241, 249, 250, 251, 252, 253, 261, 264, 266, 268, 274, 276, 277, 281, 286, 287, 291, 292

Algorithms

6, 30, 32, 43, 45, 56, 59, 77, 80, 89, 90, 93, 95, 102, 104, 105, 106, 111, 118, 119, 120, 123, 124, 125, 146, 158, 165, 166, 179, 181, 186, 200, 206, 216, 227, 229, 240, 242, 258, 271, 275, 283

Annotation

14, 36, 50, 55, 58, 113, 127, 144, 148, 156, 157, 171, 173, 215, 217, 218, 219, 220, 226

Archives

1, 3, 4, 5, 10, 11, 12, 13, 15, 18, 21, 22, 23, 26, 34, 62, 63, 64, 67, 77, 87, 97, 98, 99, 100, 102, 103, 118, 137, 167, 168, 173, 188, 197, 239, 240, 242, 245, 249, 250, 261, 268, 269, 281, 282, 287, 291, 292, 293

Artificial Intelligence

3, 5, 11, 14, 78, 87, 92, 111, 115, 119, 124, 125, 144, 158, 165, 166, 179, 186, 191, 199, 206, 216, 222, 229, 249, 250, 252, 253, 257, 258, 275

Augmented Reality

5, 11, 87, 90, 92, 93, 120, 150, 152, 155, 158, 162, 166, 176, 179, 181, 186, 200, 207, 216, 219, 229, 232, 259, 282, 283

B

Born-Digital

20, 26, 33

C

Citation

5, 7, 63, 78, 79, 80, 81, 82, 140, 225, 226

Clouds

116

Collaboration

2, 6, 9, 23, 35, 175, 189, 198, 199, 200, 202, 203, 204, 272, 283

Collaboration Platforms

283

Communication

7, 26, 27, 30, 32, 39, 40, 41, 42, 62, 65, 73, 75, 125, 141, 162, 167, 199, 203, 215, 219, 220, 225, 226, 236, 238, 251, 258, 263, 275, 277, 284, 285

Computational Analysis

35, 116, 117

Computational Linguistics

2, 51

Computational Methods

4, 12, 89, 97, 99, 113, 115, 117, 144, 148, 213, 242

Corpus

30, 31, 45, 112, 116, 117, 141, 142, 143, 144, 154, 175, 176, 188, 208, 219

Crowdsourcing

198, 201, 272

D

Databases

3, 17, 25, 27, 37, 76, 78, 80, 82, 97, 102, 136, 168, 217, 240, 266

Data Curation

34, 190, 191, 192, 193, 194, 252

Data Management

68, 91, 192, 212, 281

Data Mining

272

Data Modeling

35

Data Visualization

5, 6, 9, 10, 94, 108, 113, 131, 146, 147, 148, 152, 154, 155, 156, 157, 164, 175, 176, 187, 188, 190, 208, 215, 218, 219, 225, 257, 259, 263, 280, 281, 282, 291, 293

DH Projects

173, 188, 269

Digital Access

23, 250, 268

Digital Archives

62, 98, 281, 292

Digital Art

125

Digital Editions

215, 217, 218, 219, 220, 221

Digital History

97, 295

Digital Library

4, 154

Digital Literacy

2, 3, 6, 9, 40, 42, 121, 125, 161, 163, 164, 167, 168, 169, 173, 174, 176, 177, 178, 215, 220, 228, 234, 236, 238, 253

Digital Mapping

9, 13, 168, 263, 269, 291, 293

Digital Media

5, 8, 26, 27, 28, 167, 168

Digital Narratives

93

Digital Preservation

5, 15, 19, 20, 25, 64, 99, 137, 193, 195, 196, 198, 212, 225, 226, 249, 282, 286, 287, 288, 289, 290, 291, 293

Digital Projects

5, 10, 12, 34, 173, 243, 244, 251, 254, 286, 287

Digital Publishing

7, 9, 225, 227

Digital Storytelling

245

Digitization Efforts

12, 13, 263

Disciplinary Recognition

1

E

Encoding

2, 4, 9, 36, 37, 38, 44, 118, 120, 279

Ethics

1, 14, 97, 99, 119, 120, 121, 122, 124, 125, 167, 169, 191, 195, 199, 226, 241, 268

F

Fair Use

27

Feminist

247

G

Gamification

180, 181

Geographical Information Systems

83

Geospatial Analysis

281

Global DH

14

H

Haptic Feedback

274

Humanities

1, 2, 3, 4, 5, 6, 7, 8, 9, 10, 11, 12, 13, 14, 29, 30, 31, 32, 33, 34, 36, 37, 38, 65, 66, 75, 87, 88, 89, 91, 97, 161, 166, 167, 168, 169, 170, 171, 172, 173, 185, 198, 199, 200, 201, 202, 203, 204, 205, 206, 207, 208, 209, 210, 211, 213, 215, 216, 217, 218, 219, 220, 221, 228, 229, 230, 231, 232, 233, 234, 235, 239, 240, 241, 242, 244, 245, 247, 249, 250, 251, 252, 253, 254, 255, 256, 257, 259, 260, 266, 269, 271, 272, 285, 286, 287, 288, 289, 290, 291, 292, 293, 294, 295, 296, 297

Humanities Computing

297

Hypertext Theory

4

I

Inclusive Design

245, 274

Infrastructure

3, 13, 63, 73, 169, 181, 191, 193, 197, 211, 222, 224, 226, 227, 242, 249, 251, 252, 253, 261, 269

Interactive Timeline

274

Interdisciplinary Research
32, 225, 252, 253

K

Knowledge Graph
274

L

Linked Data
275

Literary Criticism
275

M

Machine Learning
44, 87, 275, 283, 293

Markup Language
37, 139, 279

Metadata
9, 10, 20, 22, 23, 24, 25, 26, 33, 34, 35, 37, 62, 63, 64, 97, 100, 102, 116, 118, 131, 140, 144, 156, 191, 192, 193, 195, 197, 239, 241, 252, 268, 271, 281, 282

Modelling
44

Multilingualism
251

Multimodal
170, 254

N

Natural Language Processing
5, 43, 275

Network Analysis
2, 30, 31, 34, 74, 99, 263, 280

Network Analysis
74, 275

New Media
270

O

OCR
18, 20, 90, 98, 269

Open Access
222, 223, 224, 225, 226, 276

Open Data
38, 78, 191, 222, 250

Open Source
58

Oral History
276

P

Participatory Action Research
276

Pedagogy
93, 169, 172, 251

Peer Review
32, 109, 113, 114, 120, 132, 133, 148, 149, 157, 158, 178, 189, 204, 210, 214, 221, 222, 225, 226, 227, 234, 235, 254, 261, 264

Peer Review
227, 276

Preservation
2, 5, 12, 13, 15, 18, 19, 20, 23, 25,

26, 35, 38, 62, 63, 64, 84, 86, 91, 97, 98, 99, 105, 107, 112, 117, 118, 128, 129, 130, 131, 137, 152, 155, 156, 176, 188, 191, 192, 193, 194, 195, 196, 197, 198, 201,

Programming

10, 88, 121, 140, 182

Q

Qualitative Analysis

276

Quantitative Analysis

32, 144

R

Repository

277

Research Data Management

277

Resource Description Framework

37

S

Scalability

188, 226

Scholarly Communication

7, 26, 27, 62, 167, 215, 219, 220, 225, 226, 238, 251

Scholarly Communication

236, 277

Scholarly Editing

297

Semantic Web

36, 253, 268

Small Data

259, 277

Social Media

277, 283

Sustainability

35, 188, 194, 196, 197, 198, 205, 206, 207, 209, 210, 211, 212, 213, 223, 225, 227, 241, 249, 255, 286, 287

T

Text Analysis

5, 51, 99, 118, 144, 145, 146, 147, 148, 149, 279, 280, 291, 292, 293

Text Encoding Initiative

2, 4, 36

Text Mining

9, 30, 99, 110, 112, 113, 114, 146, 278

Text Mining

110, 111, 278

Transcription

14, 91, 100, 113, 144, 148, 156, 157, 197, 202

V

Visualization

30, 74, 104, 116, 272, 278, 280

W

Webinar

279

Workflow

279

www.ingramcontent.com/pod-product-compliance
Lightning Source LLC
LaVergne TN
LVHW081938200926
848484LV00009B/2464